CAREFUL VILLAGE AND OTHER *KHASHAG* FROM TIBET

Careful Village and Other *Khashag* from Tibet

The Amdo Comedies of Menla Jyab

Menla Jyab
With translation and introduction by
Timothy Thurston and Tsering Samdrup

https://www.openbookpublishers.com

©2025 Menla Jyab
(author)
©2025 Timothy Thurston and Tsering Samdrup
(translation and notes)

This work is licensed under the Creative Commons Attribution-NonCommercial 4.0 International (CC BY-NC 4.0). This license allows you to share, copy, distribute and transmit the text; to adapt the text for non-commercial purposes of the text providing attribution is made to the authors (but not in any way that suggests that they endorse you or your use of the work). Attribution should include the following information:

Menla Jyab, *Careful Village and Other Khashag from Tibet. The Amdo Comedies of Menla Jyab*. Translation and notes to the text by Timothy Thurston and Tsering Samdrup. Cambridge, UK: Open Book Publishers, 2025, https://doi.org/10.11647/OBP.0452

Further details about CC BY-NC licenses are available at
https://creativecommons.org/licenses/by-nc/4.0/

All external links were active at the time of publication unless otherwise stated and have been archived via the Internet Archive Wayback Machine at
https://archive.org/web

Digital material and resources associated with this volume are available at
https://doi.org/10.11647/OBP.0452#resources

World Oral Literature Series, vol. 13
ISSN Print: 2050-7933 | ISSN Digital: 2054-362X
ISBN Paperback: 978-1-80511-525-0
ISBN Hardback: 978-1-80511-526-7
ISBN Digital (PDF): 978-1-80511-527-4
ISBN HTML: 978-1-80511-529-8
ISBN Digital ebook (epub): 978-1-80511-528-1

DOI: 10.11647/OBP.0452

Cover image: Labtse Festival, photo by Tsemdo (CAIDUO), CC BY, ID number: labtse250629. Cover design: Jeevanjot Kaur Nagpal

For Tsomo and Yangsi, who watched me dedicate too many days to this project, TT

For Sonam Wangmo, whose support has been invaluable throughout this journey, TS

Table of Contents

Statement about Romanization and Languages ... ix

Acknowledgements ... xvii

Foreword
Mark Turin ... xix

Translators' Introduction: Contextualizing Amdo Tibetan Comedy in Post-Mao China
Timothy Thurston and Tsering Samdrup ... 1

1. The Artist སྒྱུ་རྩལ་པ། ... 47
2. Boasting ལབ་རྒྱག་པ། ... 59
3. The Dream རྨི་ལམ། ... 83
4. All-good Menla སྨན་བླ་ཀུན་བཟང་། ... 109
5. Elders' Conversations བོ་ལོན་ཚོའི་ཁ་བརྡ། ... 133
6. Please, Dear Leader དཔོན་པོ་མཐྲིན། ... 153
7. The Telephone ཁ་པར། ... 177
8. Careful Village's Grassland Dispute སེམས་ཆུང་སྡེ་བའི་ས་རྩོད། ... 193
9. Careful Village's Bride སེམས་ཆུང་སྡེ་བའི་མནའ་མ། ... 223
10. Careful Village's Wedding སེམས་ཆུང་སྡེ་བའི་སྟོན་མོ། ... 241
11. Careful Village's Thief སེམས་ཆུང་སྡེ་བའི་རྐུན་མ། ... 271

Index ... 299

Statement about Romanization and Languages

This book focuses on a series of popular comedic dialogues originally performed in the Amdo dialect of Tibetan, spoken in the Northeastern part of the Tibetan Plateau. The performances mix highly localized (and sometimes earthy) expressive practices, with oral traditions and eloquent turns of phrase, all sprinkled liberally with literary and honorific registers of Tibetan. Some performances present ungrammatical speech, and others insert Chinese language words and phrases within otherwise Tibetan speech. This has presented some difficulties for how we render non-Tibetan terms in Tibetan transcription, as well as how we have approached translation and transliteration. This note introduces some of the conventions we have used throughout this book.

Presentation of Amdo Dialect

The Tibetan versions are based on transcriptions made from recordings of the performances, rather than original scripts. Some readers may be aware that Menla Jyab (the comedian whose work is translated in this volume) recently published his collected works (Sman bla skyabs 2024), including a volume containing the eleven scripts presented here. Menla Jyab is aware of this project and has given permission for us to translate and publish these texts. He did not, however, provide us with his scripts when we began the project. As a result, we have chosen to transcribe the texts directly from the recordings we have accessed online. Our transcriptions differ from Menla Jyab's recent publication primarily in terms of presentation and spelling of oral Amdo Tibetan (Sman bla skyabs 2024). Menla rendered many of the colloquial terms and grammatical syllables into literary Tibetan, aligning them with standard written forms, and often used his own distinctive spellings for certain colloquial expressions and words rarely seen in literary texts. In contrast, we transcribed them as they were spoken during the performances, aiming to reflect how an Amdo speaker would hear and write them.

We have tried to render the Tibetan of the Amdo dialect as we hear it. This is likely to be a controversial choice in Tibetan (and Tibetological) circles, where writing often follows strict conventions of spelling, grammar, and lexicon, and many Tibetans tend to resist attempts to write oral forms of Tibetan. In Amdo, attempts to write in "vernacular" (ཕལ་སྐད།) date back at least to the seventeenth-century songs of realization (མགུར་གླུ།) by Shar Kalden Gyamtso (ཤར་སྐལ་ལྡན་རྒྱ་མཚོ། see Mog chung phur kho 2010). In these songs he sometimes used words like *re ma* (རེ་མ།) meaning "quickly," which are specific to the oral registers of Tibetan. More recently, many Amdo Tibetan authors of modern literature have written some words and particles of Amdo Tibetan speech in the dialogues of their characters, including, perhaps most famously, Dondrup Gyal (དོན་གྲུབ་རྒྱལ།) who is sometimes credited as one of the founders of modern Tibetan literature. Despite these fleeting attempts, writing in vernacular remains much closer to the literary Tibetan ideal than a true writing in dialect.

Suzuki and Zou (2024, p. 7), writing from the perspective of language preservation research, argue that it is important to present language as it is spoken. In an attempt to make language documentation materials more available to Tibetan communities, they have attempted to write oral folktales in Tibetan using literary Tibetan orthography as much as possible, but writing grammatical words and particles as pronounced. This stems from a novel sort of intervention in Tibetan language, built on collaborations between foreign and local scholars and based in a particular set of sociolinguistic discourses about entextualizing language and communication for documentation purposes.

Our project and its approach parallel that of Suzuki and Zou (though we were unaware of it until a reviewer brought it to our attention) in many ways. We are a collaboration of Tibetan and non-Tibetan scholars, working from a sociolinguistic perspective to study the languages and cultures of Amdo. Our solution, however, differs significantly from theirs. Because the

texts that we translate here emphasize and foreground verbal art and play—
including rhyme, assonance, punning, and more—that only make sense in
the Amdo dialect, our treatment thus privileges spelling conventions based
in oral Amdo pronunciations. This practice is not without precedent, but is
done in dialogue with (though not always in agreement with) the spelling
practices employed by Amdo's authors and intellectuals.

Tibetan authors and intellectuals are also not in agreement about how
best to render Amdo dialect in Tibetan script. For example, for the verb
"to do," often written as བྱེད།, author Don grub rgyal writes *ye* (ཡེ།) in his
1980 comedy script "Studying Tibetan" (བོད་ཡིག་སློབ་པ།), while the *Amdo
Oral Dictionary* (ཨ་མདོའི་ཁ་སྐད་ཚིག་མཛོད།) uses *yed* (ཡེད།) ('Brug rgyal mkhar
2007). In other instances, our choices were more straightforward. With
the verb "to go," for example, most sources agree on *jyo* (འགྱོ།) instead of
the literary *dro* (འགྲོ།). Pronouns provide another point of disagreement.
Amdo Tibetans rarely use *khyed* or *khyed rang* for the second singular
pronoun (and when they do it is often because they are attempting to
speak more formally or interact with someone who might be from another
region). Instead, Amdo Tibetans usually say something that sounds to
English speakers like *cho* (/cʰo/ in the International Phonetic Alphabet).
Authors often write this either as ཁྱོ། or ཁྱོད།. With the agentive, it is often
pronounced *chee* and may be written as ཁྱོས།, and the genitive is written as
ཁྱོའི།, which Menla Jyab pronounced like *choo*. Even though each of these
terms have standard literary Tibetan spellings, literary spellings obscure
the way Tibetans in Amdo speak and understand their dialect.[1]

Lacking consensus, we have done what makes the most sense to
us based on our understandings of the region and its languages. We
do not follow the spellings used by any single author or textbook, but
we consistently use conventions that Amdo Tibetan readers should
understand when they hear it read aloud, and that are consistent with
Tibetan understandings of their written and spoken language. Some
spellings are relatively stable. One example is when authors write *myi*
(མྱི།) to express the colloquial Amdo version of the word for "person,"
often written in literary Tibetan as *mi* (མི།). Even though this makes the

---

1   Amdo dialect textbooks also provide interesting models for spelling Amdo
    Tibetan. See, for example, Dpal ldan bkra shis 2016, and Sung and Lha byams
    rgyal 2005.

Tibetan texts a little confusing for Tibetan readers less familiar with the Amdo dialect, we consider this approach an essential component of understanding the texts on their own terms and as originally performed. The following is a partial list comparing literary Tibetan terms with the spellings we have chosen for oral Amdo.

Literary Tibetan	Our Amdo Transcription	Translation
འགྲོ།	འགྲོ།	to go (present)
བྱེད།	ཡེད།	do (present)
བྱས།	ཡས།	do (past)
མི།	ཻྨི།	person/people
ཁྱོད།	ཁོ། ཁོ་དེ།	you
ཁྱོད་ཀྱི།	ཁོའི།	you + genitive marker
སླ།	སྐླ།	easy
མིག	ཻྨིག	eye
ཞིག ཅིག	བཞིག	indefinite article
རེད་ཙག ང་ཚོ། རེད་ཚང་།	རེད་ཀ། རི་ཚོ།	we
ཚོ།	ཚོ།	plural marker
ཟེར།	བཟེ།	quotative marker
འགྲན།	འགུན།	comparable
བྱིས་པ།	ཉ་ཡས།	children
ཁྱོད་ཀྱིས།	ཁོས།	you + ergative marker
ཁོ་ཚོ།	ཁིར་ཚོ།	they
ཅི་ལ་ཡིན།	ཅེ་ཡིན།	no
ཅི་འདྲ།	ཅེ་མོ།	how
ཐེ།	ཐེ།	crying

ཐེག	ཁུག	to be able to lift
དེ་འད།	དི་ར	that much
དེ།	དི།	that
དགོས།	དགོ	to need/have to
བུད་མེད།	ཨ་ཡེ	women/wife

This table may begin to make some of the features of Amdo Tibetan available to readers of Tibetan, but we have also preserved Amdo grammatical and pragmatic features, many of which differ significantly from literary Tibetan. Additionally, for many interjections, aspect and tense markers, and even some terminologies, there are no equivalents in literary Tibetan. In these instances, we are again guided by some of the options presented by Tibetan authors. Examples include the particle *no* (ནོ།) used to create relative clauses, as well as the particle *ni* (ནི།) used in the formation of past aspect verb phrases. Beyond these, there are several words, interjections, and phrases specific to Amdo Tibetan speech like the noun *laha* (ལ་ཧ།) referring to a particular breed of sheep, *tsaya* (ཚ་ཡ།) meaning "good" or "impressive," as well as the phrase *dokwo*, meaning "the so-called" or "that thing which is," and which we have seen rendered as བདག་པོ as well as བདག་གོ and བདོག་གོ. Many of these have no commonly accepted standard spelling even within Amdo, and we have used our judgement with how to render it in text. The Introduction also describes many other features of the language used in performance in hopes of making these texts legible and comprehensible, without obscuring their embeddedness in the language practices of a particular place (Amdo) and time (the 1980s and 1990s).

Presentation of Chinese Words

Additionally, in performances in which Mandarin words are used, Tibetan transliteration of Chinese terms and phrases follows Tsering Samdrup's ear and approximation of the sounds. We had considered using the system in the Chinese-Tibetan Dictionary (汉藏字典), but decided that since the pronunciations are based on the Lhasa dialect of Tibetan, these spellings would obstruct the Tibetan reader's ability to approach the text on Amdo Tibetan terms. We also include the Chinese character in parentheses at the first usage in both the Tibetan and in the English translation. In the English translations, we mark the Mandarin word in bold, and include the *pinyin* before the character. The following excerpt from "Boasting" may provide an example.

A: [scoffing] Heh, you really **don't understand** (*bu liaojie* 不了解) my **uncle's temper** (*piqi* 脾气). When he's in a bad **mood** (*xinqing* 心情), he comes, breaks all the **furniture** (*jiaju* 家具) in the home, and then leaves. Do you think it is okay to borrow from him?   ཀ ཧེ། ཁྱོས་རེད་ཀའི་ཇོའུ་ཇེའུ་舅舅གི་ཕིས་ཆིས་脾气རེད། ཕོམས་པོའུ་ལེའོ་ཇེ་不了解། ཞིན་ཆིན་心情མེ་ཧུ་དས་བ་ཚོ། ཡོང་དས་ཁྱིམ་གི་ཙ་ཇོའུ་家具ཚོ་རེ་རྡོག་བཏང་དས་བྱུད་འགྲོ་གི་ར། དེ་ཧུ་ར་བཞིག་སྦྱེ་ཉན་རྒྱུ་ཨེ་རེད།

B: [sighing] Huh, right. Right. It's a lot of **trouble** (*mafan* 麻烦) for a small **matter** (*shiqing* 事情). Yeah?   ཁ། ཧུ། རེད། རེད། ཧེ་ཆེན་事情ཆུང་དུང་མ་ཧྥན་麻烦མང་གི་ཡིན་ན།

Additionally, in some instances, the Chinese used places the predicate at the end of a phrase, in accordance with Tibetan (rather than Standard Mandarin) grammatical rules. In these cases, we have added an asterisk (*) in front of the Chinese characters in the Tibetan transcription (for example, *交道打), while using the structure of the Mandarin Chinese in the translation (打交道). In doing so, we aim to preserve readability while also letting readers recognize the language play in the original.

Presentation of Tibetan and Chinese Terms Transliterated in the English

Given that this is a translation, we have generally tried to keep transliterations of Tibetan words to a minimum. Nevertheless, transliteration of Tibetan terms has occasionally been unavoidable (particularly in the Introduction) and this translation presents yet another complication. There are several ways to transliterate Tibetan, none of them particularly suited for the Amdo dialect, and we have attempted an English transliteration based roughly on our own pronunciation of the words. Systems like the Extended Wylie Transliteration System are based on the Tibetan writing system. While this could ensure intelligibility for people who read Tibetan, the unwieldy consonant clusters it renders are not exactly ideal for non-specialist readers. Nor does it seem especially suitable for such a thoroughly colloquial set of texts meant to be understood and read in Amdo Tibetan terms. We find other transliteration systems based solely on the Lhasa dialect (most widely studied and taught outside of China) similarly unsuitable.

As such, we have chosen to transliterate most Tibetan terms in the Introduction and in translations in a way that approximates Amdo Tibetan pronunciation. The one major exception is for names of public figures (authors, etc.) who may be best known by a transliteration in another system. For example, the name of author Dondrup Gyal might be pronounced as Dondrupjya in Amdo dialect, but we maintain the former spelling to ensure legibility for readers. In the Introduction, we accompany most transliterations with Tibetan script in parentheses. Within the comedies, transliterations are relatively few in the text and are limited primarily to names and interjections. For example, the names of the performers and characters like Menla Jyab, Phagmo, Phurwa, and Jyamtso, as well as common Amdo Tibetan interjections like *aro, olé, ashirego,* and *ayoshe* (for more, see the Introduction), and the interjection *wei* which may be from either Chinese (at the beginning of a sentence) or Tibetan (at the end of a sentence). Where necessary, we complement these with Tibetan script in parentheses to avoid potential misunderstandings.

Finally, though we have endeavoured to maintain uniformity throughout the text, some of these translations have been completed, edited, and re-organized over the course of several years. As such, some regrettable inconsistencies may remain and fault for this remains entirely our own.

Acknowledgements

The translators are grateful, in the first instance, to Menla Jyab for graciously allowing us to work on these transcripts. For Tim, these texts basically provided his primary source for studying the Amdo dialect of Tibetan, and very little of what has happened over the past fifteen years would have been possible without him/them.

We are grateful to our families for years of support as we have worked on this and other projects, sometimes apart from those we love. Tim Thurston is especially grateful to Tsomo and Yangsi who have patiently waited for him (for too long) to finish working with these comedies. Tsering Samdrup is extremely thankful for the unwavering support and encouragement provided by Sonam Wangmo throughout the many months of working on this project.

At the same time, we also wish to acknowledge and express our thanks to several people who have helped to make this publication possible. At the University of Leeds, we are grateful to project mentor Professor Thea Pitman, for offering guidance about this at different stages of the process. Tim also wishes to thank Ohio State's Mark Bender who—both with his words and his examples—has always encouraged translation and deep engagement with languages and cultures as a valuable component of the academic project. We are also grateful to the editors of Open Books Publishers and especially to Mark Turin, in his role as editor of the World Oral Literature Series, for his enthusiastic support of the project and willingness to work with bilingual publication. We are grateful for the comments of the peer reviewers whose work has improved our final publication.

We also wish to acknowledge the support of UKRI. A Future Leaders Fellowship has made this collaboration possible. We are grateful for grant funding from UKRI (administered through the University of Leeds Library) to support open access publication.

Finally, some English-only versions of two performances have previously been published elsewhere. An early translation of "Careful Village's Grassland Dispute" was published in full in *CHINOPERL: Journal of Chinese Oral and Performance Literature* (Thurston, 2013), and a translation of "The Dream" has previously appeared in volume 2 of *Yeshe: A Journal of Tibetan Arts Literature and Humanities* (Tsering Samdrup, 2022). Our thanks go to the reviewers of these journals for their constructive comments, as well as to the editors who have allowed us to republish these translations here.

Foreword

Mark Turin

In 2012, through a dynamic and collaborative partnership with Open Book Publishers, we launched the World Oral Literature Series to promote and preserve endangered and underrepresented forms of verbal art. Since then, the series has grown to include a wide range of unique texts that illuminate the diversity and creativity of spoken expression across the world. Each title in the series has presented new insights into what it means to speak, perform, remember, and create culture through language. It is with great pleasure and deep admiration that I welcome this new volume—*Careful Village and Other Khashag from Tibet: The Amdo Comedies of Menla Jyab*—into the growing collection of works that make up the World Oral Literature Series.

This volume is remarkable at many levels. First, it brings together a selection of comedic dialogues originally composed and performed in the Amdo dialect of Tibetan by the legendary artist Menla Jyab, and it makes these performances available to global readers for the first time through a richly annotated, bilingual edition. The work of translation and contextualization has been undertaken with extraordinary care by Timothy Thurston and Tsering Samdrup, two scholars whose combined linguistic fluency, cultural sensitivity, and ethnographic insights make them ideal stewards of this important material.

The genre at the heart of this book—*khashag*—may be unfamiliar to some readers. These fast-paced, witty dialogues are a cornerstone of modern Tibetan oral performance, blending satire, verbal artistry, parody, and pointed social commentary. While sometimes likened to Han Chinese *xiangsheng* (crosstalk), *khashag* is in fact a distinctively Tibetan form, rooted in local speech genres, performance traditions, and cultural concerns. These performances reflect and refract contemporary life in Amdo, offering humorous yet incisive critiques of everything from marriage customs to administrative corruption. The texts are deeply embedded in Tibetan oral culture and yet engage fluidly with new media technologies, circulating online and on air, through radio broadcasts, cassette tapes, CDs, and now digital platforms.

And yet, for all their popularity among Tibetan audiences, these comedies have been largely overlooked in the scholarly literature on Tibet. In a field that has often prioritized classical texts, religious literature, and literary modernism, the colloquial, performative, and humorous dimensions of Tibetan cultural expression remained marginalized. This volume challenges that oversight head-on. It elevates *khashag* not only as a vital genre of Tibetan verbal art but also as a valuable source of historical, linguistic, and sociopolitical commentary. By rendering these scripts into English—and, crucially, by presenting the Tibetan original alongside for comparative analysis—the translators invite us to take *khashag* seriously as art and artifact.

The care with which this volume has been assembled is evident in every detail. The translators have transcribed the performances as they were spoken, preserving the distinctiveness of the Amdo dialect rather than smoothing and softening it into literary Tibetan. They have annotated the texts with linguistic and cultural notes that enhance accessibility without flattening the complexity of the source material. And they have introduced the volume with a deeply informed and engaging discussion of Menla Jyab's life, the history of the *khashag* genre, and the sociolinguistic environment in which these texts were created and are circulated.

Timothy Thurston and Tsering Samdrup have been collaborators for many years. Their partnership—marked by mutual respect, shared purpose, and an abiding commitment to community-engaged scholarship—shines through on every page. This is not translation from a distance. It is a form of sociocultural immersion and co-creation, and a manifestation of care. It is also, I believe, an exemplar of what collaborative scholarship in the twenty-first century can and should be.

That this work should focus on comedy is significant. In an era when Tibetan communities—like so many others—are navigating dramatic political, social, ecological, and technological transformations and challenges, humour becomes a vital mode of survival and critique. The comedies in this volume do not shy away from difficult topics. To the contrary, they speak of generational tensions, shifting gender roles, state intrusion, and changing pastoral economies. But they do so with wit, warmth, and a profound sense of the absurd. They invite laughter not to trivialize, but to illuminate and endure, restore and reclaim.

It is also worth noting that *Careful Village and Other Khashag from Tibet* arrives at a moment when orality and performance are enjoying renewed attention across disciplines. Scholars in anthropology, linguistics, literary studies, and performance studies are increasingly recognizing that spoken genres carry knowledge, memory, and social commentary in forms that are no less sophisticated than the written word. In this regard, the *khashag* comedies of Menla Jyab stand alongside other great oral traditions of the world: Nigerian *stand-up* satire, Indigenous Australian songlines, or Icelandic rímur poetry. They call out to be shared and celebrated, and uplifted through careful scholarly attention.

In the face of the erosion of minority languages, challenges to the established multilingual order (such as Donald Trump's executive order designating English as the sole official language of the United States on 1 March, 2025) and the flattening effects of algorithmic culture, works like *Careful Village and Other Khashag from Tibet* matter profoundly. They remind us that local speech communities are not passive victims of change but active producers of meaning. They show us how orality adapts, resists, and thrives, even under adverse conditions. And they encourage us to listen—really listen—to voices that might otherwise be dismissed as marginal or merely satirical.

This volume, like others in our fast-growing series, affirms our belief that oral genres are vital to cultural continuity and creative innovation and our commitment to their dissemination. This compelling text demonstrates that even within settings of profound constraint—censorship, surveillance, marginalization—humour can be a form of critique and community. And it confirms what many Tibetan listeners have known for decades: that Menla Jyab, affectionately known as "Uncle Menla", is not just a comedian, but a cultural visionary and documenter of the social fabric of Tibet.

As readers, we are indeed fortunate to now have these comedies available in this contemporary and thoughtful edition. And we are fortunate, too, to have translators and scholars who are willing to do the slow, painstaking work of listening, interpreting, and amplifying Tibetan voices. I commend this volume to you with enthusiasm and gratitude.

Dr Mark Turin
Series Editor, World Oral Literature Series
Vancouver, Canada
July 2025

Translators' Introduction: Contextualizing Amdo Tibetan Comedy in Post-Mao China

Timothy Thurston and Tsering Samdrup

Two long-haired men stand across from each other on a stage. One is slight and always keeps his right hand tucked inside a pocket or the long sleeve of his robe to hide a childhood injury. He is Menla Jyab. The other, Phagmo Drashi, is slightly taller with a stronger build. They interact as friends, sometimes telling stories about fantastic experiences, sometimes imitating the language and behaviours of different types of people one might meet when travelling among Tibetan communities: pious elders, local government officials, and even foreign travellers. Throughout their conversation, they rhyme, pun, intentionally misconstrue each other's speech, and parody oral traditions in a contest of rhetorical skill, each trying to get one over on the other. Watching and listening to them, an audience hangs on every word, laughing and applauding at particularly humorous imitations or uniquely eloquent turns of phrase. In the future, a potential audience of thousands more do the same in rapt attention as they huddle around radio and cassette tape players across the Tibetan Plateau. Some still listen and appreciate these comedies at their leisure on CDs and smart phones.

This is a brief description of a *khashag* (ཁ་བཤགས།): the genre featured in this volume. Between the early 1980s and 2015, *khashag* and their successor genre *garchung* (གར་ཆུང་།) were arguably some of the most popular and widely known cultural texts on the Tibetan Plateau. Look at recent publications and news coverage of modern Tibetan culture and one could be forgiven for being unaware of these comedies. Indeed, dominant trends in Tibetan studies leave the impression that literature and film are the most popular and noteworthy forms of cultural production in Tibetan communities. This is not so much an inaccurate portrayal of major trends of Tibetan cultural production as an incomplete one. Authors and film directors have indeed shaped the Tibetan intellectual and cultural world and remain important figures in Tibetan society even (in some cases) after their passing. But to focus attention too exclusively on these media is to miss important trends within Tibetan society. Literature circulates within a fairly small circle in a society where illiteracy rates remained over 40% throughout the 1980s and 1990s when the comedies below were written and initially performed (Fischer 2009, p. 16). Film, meanwhile, is a relatively new introduction to the Tibetan cultural scene. But comedy, music, and traditional practices have been a central part of Tibetan everyday experience for decades (at least), and they have reached and shaped the experiences of many Tibetans both inside the People's Republic of China (PRC) and in the international diaspora community. As such, they are essential to our understanding of contemporary Tibetan life.

The comedies translated in this volume are deeply embedded in the language practices and lived experiences of communities in the northeastern part of the Tibetan Plateau that Tibetans call Amdo (see below), but they also play with, exaggerate, reimagine, and subvert lived experiences in nuanced ways that have gone on to shape the Tibetan world. For example, friends may use well-known lines from famous comedies to win a point in a conversation, and people both in Amdo and in the international exile community may call a companion "Zalejyal" if he marries or dates foreign women, as that character does in "Careful Village's Bride" (Chapter 9 of this volume). As such, we view *khashag* as valuable texts that act as both mirror and as prism: reflecting the issues facing Tibetan society at the time of their writing, and refracting them with exaggeration and distortion so as to render these issues both humorous and visible for broader contemplation. Reaching audiences through emerging mass media, meanwhile, has circumvented issues of limited literacy on the one hand, and the spatial and temporal immediacy of live performance on the other.

Despite the popularity and importance of these texts, their linguistic and cultural complexity (particularly their use of local dialect, slang, and reference to local policies and fashion trends) provide significant obstacles to scholars, and precious few of these texts have been made available in English. Indeed, to date just two pieces have been translated into English (Thurston 2013 and Tsering Samdrup 2023). This volume seeks to fill some of this gap by providing the first ever bilingual edition of eleven such *khashag* from the genre's premier star: Menla Jyab (སྨན་བླ་སྐྱབས།). Selected from Menla Jyab's broader corpus and translated with his consent,[1] the texts are arranged chronologically, including his earliest comedy, "The Artist," and some of his final *khashag*, the four performances about a so-called "Careful Village," as well as a selection of several others. We have selected these eleven texts for their readability, for what they can tell us about both the *khashag* genre and the prevailing cultural trends of Amdo in the 1980s and 1990s.

Our contention in translating these scripts and transcripts is that they provide valuable ways of understanding Tibetan life at a moment of intense social and cultural changes, when Tibetans were considering what the future of Tibetan culture looks like after the upheavals of the Maoist period. In publishing them bilingually with Tibetan and English in parallel, we argue that there is both an ethical obligation to present these comedies in their original language of composition and performance, and an intellectual value to this exercise as well: this helps to recognize Tibetan conventions of verbal art and eloquence, and the interplay of these conventions

---

1   In his collected works, Menla Jyab publishes a total of twenty-six *khashag* scripts (see Sman bla skyabs 2024).

can provide insights into oral and written Tibetan. To students of the Amdo Tibetan dialect, meanwhile, the highly colloquial idioms will likely provide insights into regional expressive practices beyond the sort of material frequently taught in textbooks. However, understanding these temporally and culturally unique comedies requires first understanding how Tibetans in Amdo apprehend their language, history, and contemporary experience within the PRC. This introduction attempts to provide some of this necessary background to help situate these comedies within the linguistic, cultural, and political contexts that have made them both humorous and deeply meaningful to Tibetan audiences.

Amdo: A (Comically) Brief Introduction

Amdo, sometimes called "Dohmal" (མདོ་སྨད།), is one of the three major ethnolinguistic sub-regions of the Tibetan cultural area.[2] It makes up portions of the contemporary Chinese administrative areas of Qinghai,[3] Kanlho (གན་ལྷོ།, Ch. Gannan 甘南) Tibetan Autonomous Prefecture in southern Gansu Province, and the northern part of Ngawa (རྔ་བ།, Ch. Aba 阿坝) Tibetan and Qiang Autonomous Prefecture in Sichuan. It covers a space approximately the size of contemporary France that is home to roughly 7.5 million people. Of these, estimates of the number of Amdo dialect speakers ranges from 800,000 on the low end (Tournadre and Suzuki 2023, p. 529) to as many as 1.8 million (Reynolds 2012, p. 19). Within this region, the areas where Tibetans comprise the greatest percentage of the population are, in many cases, higher altitude and less densely populated pastoral regions. Lower altitude agricultural regions are, by contrast, more diverse, with Tibetan communities and villages often living in close proximity to if not intermingled with other ethnic groups including people now recognized as Han (汉) Chinese, Hui (回), Salar (撒拉尔), and Tu (土).

---

2 Some people would write this as Domé, but we have used Dohmal to approximate how speakers of the Amdo dialect would pronounce this term.

3 With the exception of Yushu (ཡུལ་ཤུལ།, Ch. Yushu 玉树) Tibetan Autonomous Prefecture, which is part of the region Tibetans call Kham ཁམས།.

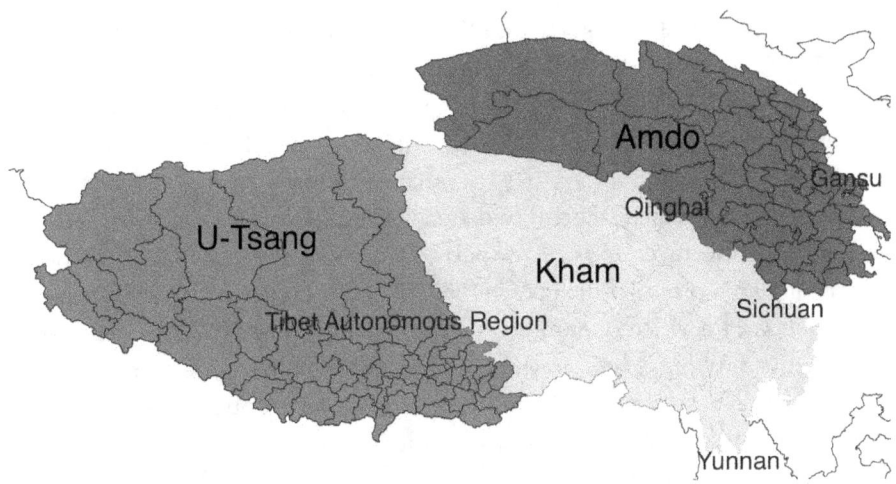

Fig. 1. A map roughly delineating the three cholkha: three regions of Tibet. Map created by Timothy Thurston.

Amdo Tibetan speech bears many hallmarks of Tibetic languages more generally, including features of egophoricity, ergativity, and evidentiality (Tribur 2019). Unlike U-Tsang and Kham, however, Amdo's dialects also tend to be atonal and marked with complex consonant clusters that generally follow Tibetan spellings. Many grammatical and lexical features of Amdo Tibetan are also distinctive compared to other Tibetic languages due in no small part to Amdo's long history of interaction with other groups. Linguists sometimes use Amdo Sprachbund to discuss the linguistic relationships between the several languages on the easternmost edge of the Tibetan Plateau, of which Amdo Tibetan is a dominant language influencing and sometimes influenced by other non-Tibetic, even non-Sino-Tibetan, languages in the region (Sandman and Simon 2016, see also Janhunen 2004 and 2005).

There is also diversity in each region around specific pronunciations, regional terminologies, and colloquialisms. Indeed, the languages spoken in Amdo are popularly divided into "pastoral" (འབྲོག་སྐད།) and "farming" (རོང་སྐད།) versions. Linguists in China further create an etic distinction between northern and southern varieties of each. Amdo Tibetan linguist Chamtshang Padma Lhundrup uses the term "innovative pastoral dialect" (འབྲོག་སྐད་འཕེལ་མ།) to describe the northern pastoral dialect spoken in Tsolho (མཚོ་ལྷོ, Ch. Hainan 海南), Malho (རྨ་ལྷོ,

Ch. Huangnan 黄南), Tsoshang (མཚོ་བྱང་།, Ch. Haibei 海北), and Tsonub (མཚོ་ནུབ།, Ch. Haixi 海西) Prefectures, and Machen (རྨ་ཆེན།, Ch. Maqin 玛沁) County in Golok (མགོ་ལོག, Ch. Guoluo 果洛), as well as parts of Kanlho Prefecture in Gansu Province. He contrasts this with "archaic pastoral dialect" (འབྲོག་སྐད་རྙིང་མ།) spoken in most of Golok Prefecture in Qinghai Province, Machu and Luchu Counties in Gansu Province's Kanlho Prefecture, as well as parts of Ngawa Prefecture and some pastoralists areas of Karmdze (དཀར་མཛེས།, Ch. Ganzi 甘孜) Prefecture in Sichuan Province (Cham thsang pad+ma lhun grub 2009).[4] Despite this diversity, speakers from Amdo can generally understand each other regardless of where in Amdo they are from, though the dialect is unintelligible to Tibetans from Kham and U-Tsang.

Amdo maintains a strong Tibetan identity in spite of these linguistic distinctions. Many Tibetan communities in Amdo tell narratives tracing their origins to Central Tibet (Roche 2011, p. 92; Sangs rgyas rin chen 2010, p. 3; Brag dgon pa dkon mchog bstan pa rab rgyas 1982 [1865], pp. 16–17). Strong monastic centres like Kumbum (སྐུ་འབུམ།, Ch. Taersi 塔尔寺) and Labrang (བླ་བྲང་།, Ch. Labuleng 拉卜楞) monasteries (to name only two) also speak to Amdo's ongoing religious connections to the rest of the Tibetan cultural world, while oral traditions like *tamhwé* (གཏམ་དཔེ།) "proverb," *natam* (གནའ་གཏམ།) "folktales," and *shépa* (བཤད་པ།) "speech-making" traditions demonstrate strong continuities within the Tibetan world both in terms of the poetic and linguistic conventions and their content (see, for example, Thurston 2012 and 2019 and Bendi Tso et al. 2023). The region's unique traditions, meanwhile, speak also to considerable exchange with neighbouring groups. For example, the Chinese deities Erlang shen (二郎神, རི་ལང་།) and Wenchang (文昌, ཡུལ་སྐྱེ།) are venerated in both the *Luroo* (ཀླུ་རོལ།) harvest festival in the villages of Rebgong (རེབ་གོང་།, Ch. Tongren 同仁) County and the Drugpe lhatsé (དྲུག་པའི་ལྷ་རྩེད།) festival which draws Han, Hui, and Tibetan devotees to Trika (ཁྲི་ཀ, Ch. Guide 贵德) County.[5] Folksong traditions in Amdo also exemplify this complex history of interethnic communication. For example, Tibetans in the part of northeastern Amdo called Huaree

---

4 It should be noted, however, that Karmdze's pastoralist communities identify as Khampas rather than as Amdowas.

5 See, for example, Buffetrille 2002 for more on this phenomenon in Trika.

(དཔའ་རིས།) sing Chinese language Hua'er folksongs alongside singers of other ethnicities, while members of nearby groups may learn Tibetan language for religious purposes, or for certain song traditions (see Li and Roche 2017). The presence of Tibetan-speaking Muslim communities and Tibetan-speaking Mongolians in Henan (སོ་སྐྱོ།, Ch. Henan 河南) County also suggests histories of interethnic interaction with Hui, Salar, and Mongolian peoples. This location at the physical and cultural borders of Tibetan space has helped to make the regions simultaneously conservative (it is, for example, home to several large Gelukpa sect monasteries, and the heart of the Tibetan language purism movement), and a site of tremendous intercultural interaction that has spurred linguistic and cultural innovation.

The region is also notable for its important role in Tibet's cultural, religious and political history. Amdo's ethnic diversity, and its location on the cultural frontiers between Han-dominated lowland regions and the rest of the Tibetan Plateau, perhaps helped to make the region and its leaders important intermediaries between the Chinese and Tibetan worlds. Tuttle (2005), for example, recognizes that many religious figures from the region—including both ethnically Tibetan *lamas* and Tibetan Buddhist *lamas* from the region's other ethnicities—played an important role in representing Tibet and its interests to imperial and republican era Chinese leaders. This continues into the present, with some of Tibet's most significant religious and cultural figures hailing from the region, including the 10th Panchen Lama (1938–89) from contemporary Xunhua Salar Autonomous County, and the 14th Dalai Lama (b.1935) from what is now called Ping'an County.

Since at least the beginning of the twentieth century, Amdo has also been the centre for a remarkable boom in secular cultural production. Gendun Chophel (དགེ་འདུན་ཆོས་འཕེལ།, 1903–51), often considered one of the founders of modern Tibetan Literature, hails from Rebgong. Amdo's prominence in Tibetan cultural production has continued into the post-Mao period. A low degree of Tibetan language education continued throughout the Cultural Revolution, and when policies relaxed, a number of Tibetan language institutions opened in the early years of the post-Mao era, supported also by a cohort of clerics who took up key positions in universities and government (see Willock 2021). These developments ensured that Amdo's educated youth were well-placed to take advantage of the opportunities for cultural production. Indeed, many of Tibet's most famous writers of modern literature and (more recently) filmmakers call Amdo home (Thurston 2017). Authors like Dondrup Gyal (དོན་གྲུབ་རྒྱལ།, 1953–85), often credited as one of the founders of modern Tibetan literature, Takbum Gyal (སྟག་འབུམ་རྒྱལ།, b.1966), and Tsering Dondrup (ཚེ་རིང་དོན་གྲུབ, b.1961)—all from Amdo—continue to stand as prominent authors of modern Tibetophone literature. Filmmakers Pema Tsedan (པདྨ་ཚེ་བརྟན།, 1969–2023) and Zonthar Gyal (བཟོད་ཐར་རྒྱལ།, b.1974) also come from Amdo. Intellectual Shokdung (ཞོགས་དུང་།, b.1963), whose iconoclastic writings have made him a controversial figure in Tibetan communities, also calls Amdo home. Menla Jyab (b.1963), the author of the comedies translated in this volume, rose to prominence in dialogue with many of these luminaries.

Since the region's incorporation into the People's Republic of China in the 1950s, Amdo Tibetan communities have experienced incredible amounts of social change (as have almost all communities on the Tibetan Plateau and around the PRC). Collectivization in the 1960s and 1970s, followed by privatization in the 1980s, all reshaped the fabric of Amdo Tibetan life through material and political interventions in the structures of communities and management of traditional resources. In the twenty-first century, a campaign to "Open the West" (Ch. *xibu da kaifa* 西部大开发) and efforts to protect the health of the grassland ecosystem have seen efforts to settle pastoralists in newly built homes and apartment buildings on the edges of Tibet's growing urban communities (Ptackova 2020). Improving economic conditions in the post-Mao era have also seen a variety of new technologies enter the region, including media technologies like radio, television, and most recently mobile phones, computers, smart devices, etc. Not limited to media, mass automobile ownership, as well as new technologies for farming and pastoral management, have all changed everyday practices in the region. The technological and social developments of this period also coincide with the emergence of new forms of expressive cultural production, including a highly popular (but little studied) form of comic dialogue: *khashag*.

About *Khashag*

The comic scripts translated in this volume belong to a genre of performance that Tibetans in Amdo call *khashag*. They are fast-paced comic conversations (or, more rarely, monologues) that may be performed by anywhere between one and five or six people. They are usually scripted and performers either memorize them or read directly from the script. Although some of these comedies have appeared in print form (Sman bla skyabs 1985 and 2024, Phur ba 1993) in the 1980s and 1990s, these circulated primarily among Amdo Tibetan communities in the People's Republic of China in local stage performances, radio broadcasts, and audio cassettes.[6] More recently, audiences and fans have also been able to listen to favourite performances online, both on platforms in China and on international platforms like YouTube.

The origins of *khashag* are a matter of some debate. One Tibetan language advocate, for example, argues that they are of natively Tibetan origin, dating back to the nineteenth-century instructional text "Gonpo Dorje's Tea Prayer" (མགོན་པོ་རྡོ་རྗེའི་ཇ་མཆོད།) written as a dialogue between a master and his disciple (see Mog chung phur kho 2013). Despite this argument, most comedians believe that they are performing Tibetan versions of the Han Chinese *xiangsheng* (相声) tradition. In the years after the 1949 establishment of the PRC, *xiangsheng* "crosstalk"—which also trace their origins to the eighteenth century—gained patronage from key figures of the Chinese political and literary world, including Mao Zedong and Lao She respectively (see Cai and Dunn 2020). With their support, *xiangsheng* were introduced across the country as a way of teaching the new policies and terminologies of the nascent PRC to people, including Tibetan communities.

Lhasa-based comedian Suoci (素次) describes the arrival of comedic dialogues in central Tibet prior to the Cultural Revolution as follows.

> The Eastern Lhasa Propaganda Team's primary performer and director was Luosang duojie [Blo bzang rdo rje]. People all loved to call him Zang mu jiawu [Bzang mo rgyal po], which is the name of a role in the Tibetan opera Zhuo wa zang mu ['Gro ba bzang mo]. He was a teacher:

---

6   A smaller audience of Amdo-speaking Tibetans living in exile also exists.

he studied at the Central Nationalities Institute and later also became a teacher there. Making use of the Tibetan language's rich layers of meaning and the performance principles of traditional Tibetan Xie kai ba [བཞད་གད་པ།; "comedy"], he went on to study and make use of the artistic characteristics of crosstalks from Inner China. He began by translating the famous crosstalk performer Hou Baolin's [1917–93] crosstalk: "Drunk," adding into this crosstalk a few phenomena found in contemporary Tibetan life (Suoci 2003, pp. 14–15, cited in Thurston 2013, p. 158).

He then goes on to describe how new composition of Tibetan-language "crosstalk" comedic dialogues did not begin until after the end of the Cultural Revolution. Amdo's comedians generally agree with this history that places the origins of *khashag* with state-sponsored troupes performing Tibetan translations of government-approved Chinese language comedies during the Maoist period. By the 1980s at least, artists had begun to write Tibetan language comedies that aimed to reflect Tibetan materials and issues, as evidenced by Dondrup Gyal's script "Studying Tibetan" (བོད་ཡིག་སློབ་པ།, see Don grub rgyal 1997 [1980] and Thurston 2025).

Xiangsheng and Amdo Tibetan *khashag* undoubtedly share many formal properties in the present. They are short, scripted performances, generally twenty minutes in length or shorter. *Khashag* are generally "spoken" (བཤད།) on a stage by two or more "speaking partners." The performers (frequently male) toss the conversation back and forth in a fast-paced encounter in which they may tell stories, sing songs, banter, imitate others, and break into traditional verbal art like wedding speeches. They may play with traditional forms or certain kinds of social events, coin new terms, and make reference to recent policies and events. Many performances begin and end with a reference to the act of writing, preparing, or performing a *khashag*, which Moser (1990) notes is common also in Han *xiangsheng* performances. In this volume, the entirety of "The Artist" (Chapter 1), for example, centres on the qualities a performer must possess; "Elders' Conversations" (Chapter 5) begins with an extended discussion of the qualities of a good *khashag* performer, and "Careful Village's Grassland Dispute" (Chapter 8) begins with Menla Jyab saying that he had gone to the village in hopes of finding material for a *khashag* script.

In addition to self-reflexivity as a framing technique, many performances also either engage in conversational storytelling or suggest a situation and then proceed to act it out. "Menla Kunzang" and the final four scripts of this volume about "Careful Village" stand out as notable examples of conversational storytelling, with one speaker telling a story while his partner asks questions, responds to the different statements, or provides other prompts to push the story forward. By contrast, "The Artist," "Elders' Conversations," and "The Telephone" (Chapter 7) all feature sections in which the two speakers describe a situation and then temporarily act out the speech of different sorts of characters. What these all share is a tendency to use quoted speech. Voicing the speech of a variety of Tibetans puts the performers' vocal talents on display and allows the speakers to characterize the thoughts and behaviours of people from a variety of Tibetan backgrounds: young and old, male and female, nomads and farmers, and even (more rarely) deities and great figures from Tibetan history (as in "The Dream," Chapter 3). Many of these features are also common to Chinese *xiangsheng*. Also, like Chinese-language *xiangsheng*, Tibetan *khashag* from Amdo seem to have greater leeway to engage in social critique than many other forms of cultural production. Although it must be done carefully, the comic scripts contain many veiled references to the ineffectiveness and corruption of officials, the misbehaviour of monks, and more, all discussed in greater detail below.

Despite these formal similarities, however, *khashag* from Amdo are also uniquely Tibetan. Performers entertain audiences by drawing on a range of uniquely Tibetan expressive practices including the extensive use of double negatives, oaths and curses (Thurston 2018), honorifics and humilifics (Tsering Samdrup and Suzuki 2019), the creative re-working of traditional forms like wedding speeches and *tamhwé* "proverbs," and more. Their social critique, meanwhile, takes aim at issues facing communities across the Tibetan plateau. In many cases, these critiques link to or mirror the Chinese government's own political goals, like promoting the elements of the government's marriage law or discussing the values of state education and an ambivalence to religion and tradition.

This should be unsurprising given the genre's tight links to government sponsorship. Lacking professional comedians, most of Amdo's comic dialogues were written and performed by people employed by government troupes and/or those able to get on state broadcast channels, including performers like Phurwa (ཕུར་བ།), Gomé Dorje Rinchen (སྒོ་མེ་རྡོ་རྗེ་རིན་ཆེན།), Phuntshogjyal (ཕུན་ཚོགས་རྒྱལ།), Kangtsa Sherab (ཀང་ཚའི་ཤེས་རབ།), Golok Dabhe (མགོ་ལོག་ཟླ་བྷེ།), and the late Jamyang Lodro (འཇམ་དབྱངས་བློ་གྲོས།).⁷ Performance also took place overwhelmingly on state-sponsored stages (schools, broadcast stations, etc.) and there was little record of any privately sponsored performance before 2014.⁸ Such *khashag* scripts intended for performance in state-controlled media are also subject to government censorship and approval.⁹ But even state censorship does not completely stop comedians from embedding critiques of government in their comedies. Although direct critique of central government policy is out of the question, performers use the complexity and pace of their performance to articulate critiques that subtly resist government discourses by obliquely poking fun at the behaviour of government officials, and by modelling uniquely Tibetan approaches to modern life through implications that certain Tibetan attitudes and practices are backward and others are more appropriately modern. Few, if any, performers, were able to do this as successfully as "Uncle Menla."

---

7   In U-Tsang, The *Xizang* television station airs performances called *dgod bro'i gtam gleng* (དགོད་བྲོའི་གཏམ་གླེང་།) which appear very similar to Amdo *khashag* and which subtitles also translate with the Chinese *xiangsheng*. We have not completed research to compare the two, nor have we found any research to this effect. Doing so is beyond the scope of the current project, but we would welcome studies that look into this form and/or compare the two.

8   We have seen and heard of some more private performances. Students sometimes perform comedies at school events, and I have heard anecdotally that some people would perform in village. However, in these cases, people re-performed familiar favourites rather than creating new ones for these occasions. The first private comedy-only show took place in Chungmchu County (ཁྱུང་མཆུ།, Ch. 红原 *Hongyuan*) County in 2014 with sponsorship from two local businessmen.

9   In addition to official media, we have also heard anecdotally that Menla Jyab performed at schools in the 1980s and 1990s, and that local communities staged comedic performances during Losar (Tibetan New Year) gatherings. We have also seen students at schools and universities reproduce favorite comedic performances on school stages. However, these performances are infrequent, and less likely to have been the way enjoyed these comedies. Local performances, meanwhile, also frequently reproduce performances already approved for and aired on State media.

Uncle Menla

Menla Jyab was born in 1963 in a pastoralist community of Sumdo Township, Mangra (Ch. Guinan 贵南) County, Qinghai Province. Growing up during the Cultural Revolution (1966–76, Ch. *wenhua da geming* 文化大革命 རིག་གནས་གསར་བརྗེ་ཆེན་པོ།) and reaching adulthood in the early years of the post-1978 period of "reform and opening up" (Ch. *gaige kaifang* 改革开放 བཅོས་བསྒྱུར་སྒོ་འབྱེད།) undoubtedly influenced Menla Jyab. According to his own narrative, he initially attended schools in a tent on the grassland before eventually matriculating to the famous Tsolho Nationalities Normal School (Ch. 海南州民族师范学校 མཚོ་ལྷོ་མི་རིགས་དགེ་འོས་སློབ་གྲྭ།), in the early years after the Cultural Revolution. At the age of seventeen, he received a job first in a song and dance troupe, before later moving to a dubbing office in Ziling which was his official affiliation for the remainder of his career. In 1985, at the age of twenty-two, he published his first *khashag* script, "The Artist" (སྒྱུ་རྩལ་པ།, see Thurston 2018). Between 1992 and 1994, he attended a training program in Shanghai Theatre Academy (Ch. 上海戏剧学院), during which he wrote many other comedic dialogues.

Shooting to fame on the back of writing and performing these *khashag* dialogues, Menla Jyab travelled across Amdo, performing in schools and theatres and on the Amdo Tibetan broadcasting station's radio broadcasts. For his later performances, Tibetans also purchased audio cassettes and listened to them at their leisure. But Menla Jyab's career and influence is not limited to *khashag*. He spent many years working in the dubbing office of Qinghai Ethnic Language Film and Television Dubbing Centre (Ch. 青海民族语影视译制中心 མཚོ་སྔོན་མི་རིགས་སྐད་བརྒྱུད་འཕྲིན་བསྒྱུར་སྐྲུན་བྱེ་གནས།), and is also famous as a poet, lyricist, and essayist.

The popularity of these comedic dialogues reached its peak in the mid-1990s, before tapering off in the early 2000s. Now very few comedians perform comedic dialogues. As television ownership grew on the Tibetan plateau, he also began performing a more visual and physical form of sketch comedy called *garchung* or *shadgar* (བཞད་གར།). Despite the different performance style, audiences initially called both sketches and dialogues by the single name of *khashag* perhaps due to the continuity of the performers, or the similar subject matter. But comedians insist on using these other terms in recognition of the different skills these performances require. Where *khashag* focus on the performer's verbal skills, *garchung* take advantage of the affordances provided by the visual medium of television to require that a performer entertain not simply through their rhetorical skills, but also through posture, movement, as well as the use of stage space, props, and set design.

Menla Jyab made a seamless transition to these *garchung* and has become, if anything, more famous as a result. So familiar is he in many Amdo Tibetan communities that people often refer to him simply and affectionately as "Uncle Menla" (ཨ་ཁུ་སྨན་བླ།), a term of respect used not only for relatives but for any older male. It is not an exaggeration to say that at one point, Menla Jyab was probably among the most recognizable names and faces in Amdo. Phagmo Drashi—Menla Jyab's frequent partner in the *khashag* performances translated in this book—chose not to continue performing the more visual sketch comedies with Menla Jyab, pursuing other intellectual projects in the twenty-first century instead.[10]

Menla Jyab is also a controversial figure in some circles. His work brings him close to the Chinese state and his performances sometimes promote policy directions specific to society in the 1980s and 1990s. Additionally, he has, at times, participated in lively debates about the place of Tibetan traditions in modern life that are now dormant in the Amdo intellectual community (more on this below). These stances have led some like Lobsang Yongdan—who goes by the internet handle of "Donkey Herder" (བོང་རྫི།)—to accuse him and others like him of being mouthpieces for Communist party ideology. Despite this, Menla Jyab remained a popular public figure in Amdo for nearly three decades

---

10 Most notably, Phagmo Drashi founded and edited the now defunct "New Youth" (ན་གཞོན་གསར་བ།) website, featuring news, literature, and essays from other intellectuals.

(1985 to 2015), due in no small part to his incredible capacity to combine social critique with humorous language play.[11]

The Language of Menla Jyab

Menla Jyab's language in performance largely conforms to the "innovative pastoral speech" spoken in his home region, with heavy influences from literary forms that index his status as an urban intellectual. However, as a creative comedian (and the author of these dialogues), Menla Jyab employs unique methods of dealing with language. Menla Jyab is especially famous for using a wide range of Amdo Tibetan expressive practices to keep audiences on their toes from the opening lines of performances to the final moments of the dialogues. He overemphasizes specific language practices (for example, swearing oaths and cursing at a rate that far exceeds everyday speech). He makes extensive use of assonance, alliteration, and double negatives, all of which are common in Amdo speech. He uses a number of sayings and proverbs that take "black words" (ཚིག་ནག) of everyday speech, and raises them to a more artistic level (sometimes called *gtam* གཏམ). He also invents new instances of traditional language forms, as with his novel oath "Picasso" in "Careful Village's Grassland Dispute" (for more, see Thurston 2013 and 2018). Additionally, as an intellectual voicing written texts, his speech does include some intentional and unintentional hypercorrections and literary Tibetan terms and phrases. He sometimes also uses certain words from other dialects of Tibetan for comedic purposes:

---

11 While Menla Jyab's popularity in Amdo is without doubt, and the popular uptake of the name Zalejya (see Chapter 9) suggests that there is some audience in the Tibetan diaspora community, there is less data available to suggest how widely these texts were consumed in Kham or U-Tsang. Anecdotal evidence suggests that the audience for his comedies was limited, though the new publication of his collected works (Sman bla skyabs 2024) may present these texts to a broader audience.

A: (in normal voice) So then I also sincerely explained, "If I were a *lama*, then my monastery would be a distillery, my monks would not have perfected the study of the "perfection of wisdom" sutra, **and they would have attained perfection only in smoking cigarettes.** If there is a *lama* like this, let alone in the next life, would the government[12] even accept him?"

ད་དས་ར་སེམས་གཏིང་ནས་འགྲེལ་བཤད་བརྒྱབ་བརྒྱབ་ན། ད་བླ་མ་བཟིག་ཡིན་དུས། དའི་དགོན་པ་དེ་ཆང་བཅགས་ས་བཟིག་ཡིན། དའི་གྲྭ་བ་ཚོ་ཡར་ཕྱིན་སྦྱངས་ནས་ཕ་རོལ་ཏུ་ཕྱིན་སོང་ནི་མིན། **ཐ་མག་འཐེན་ནས་མཐར་ཕྱིན་སོང་ནི་ཡིན།** དེ་མོ་བླ་མ་བཟིག་ཡོད་དུས་ད་ཕྱི་མ་མ་དགོ་གོང་མ་ཚང་གིས་ར་ཁས་ལེན་ནས།

This brief excerpt illustrates some of these principles. For example, the use of the word *tha mag* "cigarette" is used primarily in Lhasa dialect. Menla Jyab, however, can employ it to create alliteration with the bolded phrase, which repeats the aspirated alveolar stop *tha*. The lines about the perfection of wisdom and the smoking of cigarettes, meanwhile, use similar grammar (only with the first negated) to create a particular rhythm and parallelism in delivery, and to invert a famous set of Buddhist teachings to make a novel joke. The effect with the audience is instant, and they laugh and clap heartily in response to this line.

This is just one example. Without going into further detail about the phonological or syntactic features of Amdo (discussed briefly in the note on romanization and transcription), the remainder of this section demonstrates how Menla Jyab uses this tremendous range of Tibetan expressive features for comedic purposes. These include the use of revolutionary-influenced neologisms, metaphors, *tamhwé* "proverbs" and "formulaic" idioms, Amdo-specific interjections and fillers, honorifics and humilifics, oaths and cursing, and code-switching. These are just a few of the noteworthy features of Amdo language used in Menla Jyab's performances. Although few of these features have received attention in linguistic studies of Amdo,[13] all of them appear in the performances below and therefore bear some comment.

---

12 The Tibetan term *gongma tshang* (གོང་མ་ཚང་།) is traditionally a way of referring to emperors and their officials. Here, however, it is used to refer to the government as it is sometimes used today.

13 Exceptions may include Tsering Samdrup and Suzuki 2020 on humilifics; Thurston 2018, Tournadre 2003, Kalsang Yeshe 2008, Haller 2004, Tsering Shakya 1994 and

Interjections, Fillers, and Discourse Markers

To understand the intricacies of Menla Jyab's language in his performances, it is important for us first to understand some special features of the language. Some of the most conspicuous and pervasive features are the Amdo-specific interjections and fillers that are used throughout the dialogues. The list that follows is representative rather than exhaustive. Examples include:

- *O* (ཨོ།) is a response particle.
- *Olé* (ཨོ་ལེ།) is used to express confirmation or agreement with someone's statement.
- *Eh, eh* (ཨེ་ཨེ།) is an interjection used for interrupting someone.
- *Aro* (ཨ་རོ།) is used when speaking with someone of equal or lower social status. At the beginning of a sentence it tries to get attention from the listener. At the end of a sentence, it calls for attention to the preceding information.
- *Yaya* (ཡ་ཡ།) is used to confirm the previous sentence from the other speaker.
- *Ashirégo* (ཨ་ཕི་རེ་གོ།) expresses the meaning of regrets and remorse.
- *Ahawo* (ཨ་ཧུ་བོ།) is used to express regret and remorse.
- *Ahawonahawo* (ཨ་ཧུ་བོ་ན་ཧུ་བོ།), similar to *Ahawo*, expresses regret and remorse.
- *Wei* (ཝེ།) is a telephone greeting borrowed from the Chinese that is widely used in Tibetan nowadays.
- *Alahohoye* (ཨ་ལ་ཧོ་ཧོ་ཡེ།) is often used by women when disparaging or laughing at someone.[14]

Dak Lhagyal 2019 on neologisms and code-switching; and Pirie 2009 and Sørenson and Erhard 2013a and 2013b on proverbs.

14 It can also be used as an opener or a reply during public verbal arguments at a wedding between the entourage accompanying the bride and groom to the wedding with the women from the side of the host family. These verbal arguments are exchanged over the issue of presenting a gift known as "bridal cloth" (བག་རས།)

- "Karmically wicked one" (ལས་དན་པོ/མོ) is used when speaking to someone close to the speaker. The usage is sometimes similar to "you poor thing" in English, but other times it is reflexive, expressing the speaker's own misfortune rather than that of the listener. Some speakers even use it as a verbal tic.
- *Heh* (ཧེ།) and *ha* (ཧ།) are interjections used for expressing disgust or a dismissive attitude towards a statement or a situation.
- "How pitiful" (སྙིང་མ་རྗེ།) is a phrase expressing the speaker's strong sympathy towards something or someone.
- *Ona* (ནོ་ན།) is a discourse marker for inquiring the reasons for the preceding statement.
- *Sha dena shade* (བྱ་དེ་ན། བྱ་དེ།), literally, "that action;" this phrase expresses extreme surprise or astonishment about a situation.
- *Un* (ཨུན།) is used when someone is surprised, or sometimes for affirmation.

These interjections are highly context-dependent, and the same interjection can sometimes mean different things when spoken in a different way.

Pro-drop and Delayed Subject

An additional characteristic of Menla Jyab's language is the extensive use of "pro-drop" sentences, in which pronouns are either omitted or spoken at the end of the sentence. Historically, Tibetan sentences place pronouns at the beginning of the sentence, but both Menla Jyab and Phagmo Drashi tend to re-assert the subject or pronoun at the end of a sentence. This seems to be an emerging practice in Amdo. Here are two examples:

| What can you gain from studying negative things? ("Boasting") | དན་པ་ཞིབ་འཇུག་ཡས་ན་གྲུབ་འབྲས་ཅི་བཞིག་ ཐོབ་ནི་རེད། ཁྱོ། |

---

by the bride's entourage and "water scarf" (ཆུ་དར།) by the groom's entourage to women of the host family at a wedding.

As well as

| Whether I say it or not, she's on full display, their bride. ("Careful Village's Bride") | བཤད་ན་མ་བཤད་ན། བཤམ་མས་བཞག་ཡོད་ཀྱི་སྟེ་གི་མནའ་མ་ད། |

In both instances, the speaker re-asserts the subject of the sentence by adding the subject at the end (bolded in the Tibetan). While omitting subjects and pronouns is common to many Asian languages (including Tibetan), this re-assertion of the subject or pronoun at the end of a sentence is probably a new phenomenon in Amdo. From anecdotal data, it seems that educated people with a high degree of proficiency in other languages—particularly Chinese (Mandarin Chinese is known for being a pro-drop language)—are more likely to produce such utterances.

Oaths and Cursing

Oath-taking is common for Amdo pastoralists both in formal and informal settings. Someone may swear an oath to prove their innocence to an accusation (an accusation of stealing, for example), while individuals or villages may also swear oaths to end a conflict or to agree to collaborate. Additionally, two or more people may form a brotherhood through the swearing of oaths (called a *nachal* མནའ་བཅད།, in which the term refers both to the act of becoming sworn brothers, and the status itself). Informally, people are also accustomed to swearing oaths in their speech to emphasize the truthfulness of what has been said or just as a habit. Oaths in Amdo primarily fall into two categories: religious and consanguineous. Religious oaths appearing in Menla Jyab's *khashag* include:

- By the Great Mother (ཡུམ།) is a common Tibetan name used for the *Prajñāpāramitā* "the Perfection of Wisdom" sutra (used in multiple performances)
- By Kumbum [monastery] (སྐུ་འབུམ།) ("The Dream")
- By Shachong [monastery] (བྱ་ཁྱུང་།) ("The Dream")
- By the Kanjur (བཀའ་འགྱུར།) ("The Dream")
- By the Tenjur (བསྟན་འགྱུར།) ("The Dream")
- By all the pure virtues (དཀར་པོ་དགེ་བ།) ("The Dream")

- By the one and only Mani (མ་ཎི་ཁེར་གོ།) ("The Dream")
- By the twelve volumes of *yum* (ཡུམ་དུམ་པ་བཅུ་གཉིས།) ("The Dream")
- By all the scriptures that have been written and chanted (བྲིས་པ་བཏོན་པ།) ("The Dream")
- By the three jewels (དགོན་མཆོག་གསུམ།) ("Careful Village's Thief")

Consanguineous oaths in Menla Jyab's *khashag* include:
- By the flesh of my parents (ཕ་མ་གཉིས་ཀའི་ཤ།) ("Careful Village's Thief")
- By the flesh of father (ཨ་རྒྱའི་ཤ།) ("Careful Village's Grassland Dispute")
- By the flesh of mother (ཨ་མའི་ཤ།) ("Careful Village's Bride")
- By the flesh of [my] son (ཞི་ལིའི་ཤ།) ("Careful Village's Wedding")
- By the blood of [my] children (ན་ཡས་ཚོའི་ཁྲག) ("Careful Village's Thief")
- By all the ancestors (སྐྱི་རིང་སྐྱི་རྒྱུད།) ("Careful Village's Thief")

Menla Jyab's use of oaths in performances generally represents how people use them in their daily lives. More than merely imitating everyday pastoralist expressive practices, Menla Jyab also uses oaths to formulate particular social critiques. For example, in "The Dream" (Chapter 3) oath swearing is one of the practices used to exemplify and criticize Tibetan language practices. In the "Careful Village" series, oaths are sworn almost exclusively by villagers, with the lone exception of innovative oath "Picasso," swearing by the name of famous artist Pablo Picasso. In doing so, Menla Jyab links oath swearing to rural pastoralists and not to modern intellectuals.

Menla Jyab also uses a number of cursing phrases common in Amdo Tibetan speech, especially when imitating the speech of others. All of these cursing phrases are marked with the future tense marker རྒྱུ། followed by nominalisers ནོ or གོ. This suggests that the target of the curse is "one who should" do the action or one to whom the action "should happen." For example:

- "The one who should not have bright future" (བུ་ལམ་མ་མི་འགྲོ་རྒྱུ་འོ།) ("Careful Village's Grassland Dispute")
- "The one who should have a bright future" (བུ་ལམ་མ་འགྲོ་རྒྱུ་འོ།) plays on the previous curse; this sudden change in the middle of the sentence might be the speaker's attempt to make the curse less severe by eliminating the negation to make it a wish rather than a curse. ("Careful Village's Grassland Dispute")
- "The one who should embarrass oneself [in public]" (ཤུག་ག་སྟོན་རྒྱུ་འོ།) ("Careful Village's Thief")
- "The one who should have died in an untimely fashion" (བླ་བསད་གོ) ("All-good Menla")[15]
- "The one who just does not die" (འཆི་མེད་གོ) conveys the speaker's wish that someone die ("Careful Village's Bride")
- "The one who should grow wings on [their back]" (གཤོག་སྟོ་སླེབ་རྒྱུ་བདོག་གོ) ("Careful Village's Thief")
- Literally, one whose face should be turned back (དོ་རྟོགས་རྒྱུ་འོ།); we translate this curse (sometimes pluralized as དོ་རྟོགས་རྒྱུ་ཚ་འོ།) loosely in the following performances to capture the meaning in the specific context. ("All-good Menla," "Telephone," "Careful Village's Grassland Dispute," and "Careful Village's Bride")

Metaphors

Metaphors or figurative ways of speaking are common both in the literary and in Amdo Tibetan spoken language. Menla Jyab, who is well-versed in both traditional and modern literature of Tibetan, uses traditional metaphors both with literary and spoken origins. For example, the phrase "becoming like an empty sack" (ཁུག་སྟོང་གི་ལོག་ཐལ།) in the "The Artist" (Chapter 1)—a metaphor of an empty sack for someone who is very thin—is commonly used in spoken Amdo. Similarly, "to poke

---

15 This term can also be used to refer to someone who has already died. In these cases, the phrase is not a curse but is used to avoid breaking the taboo against saying the name of the deceased.

somebody with needs and awls" in ཁབ་གཙག་འབིག་གཙག་བཟིག་ཡོད ("Boasting") originates completely from the spoken words of Amdo pastoralists and refers to verbally ridiculing or critiquing others. These oral metaphors are traditional, in that they are commonly used in pastoralist communities, and therefore recognizable to audiences.

Other metaphors come more from the literary register. For example, in "The Artist," Menla Jyab uses the term *pho nya* (ཕོ་ཉ།), meaning "messenger," which is limited primarily to the written register. These more literary metaphors often deploy the literary register in novel ways, often with hilarious consequences. For example, in "Boasting" (Chapter 2), Menla Jyab refers to Tibet as "an ocean of song and dance" (གླུ་གར་གྱི་རྒྱ་མཚོ།). In the literary tradition, calling something "an ocean" suggests tremendous breadth and depth. But using this metaphor to describe Tibet's varied song and dance traditions is a novel application. Later in the same performance, Menla Jyab describes Tibetan regions as "a Pureland of research" (ཞིབ་འཇུག་གི་ཞིང་ཁམས།). This phrase, which was very likely coined by Menla Jyab himself, uses the religious metaphor of the "Pureland" to again describe the potential value and benefits to be gained from conducting research in the area. In still other instances, he uses entirely traditional metaphors in new contexts. For example, in "The Artist" (Chapter 1), Menla Jyab uses the honorific phrase "go to the Pureland" (ཞིང་ད་ཕེབས།), which usually refers to *lamas* who have passed away, to describe how a landlord's lackey might threaten to kill a poor person in order to extort payments from him. These metaphors are part of why audiences find Menla Jyab's performances so engaging, though we have not always translated them literally in the texts that follow. Some examples of metaphors in these performances include:

- "The messenger of old age" (ལོ་གི་ཕོ་ཉ།), which is more literary than colloquial since ཕོ་ཉ། "messenger" is not exactly a spoken word. ("The Artist")

- "The ocean of songs and dance" (གླུ་གར་གྱི་རྒྱ་མཚོ།) is to say that a group of people or a region is known for having many types of music and dance. ("Boasting")

- "A Pureland of research" (ཞིབ་འཇུག་གི་ཞིང་ཁམས།) is a phrase very likely coined by Menla Jyab himself, with its literary Tibetan nature. ("Boasting")

- "Becoming like an empty sack" (ཁུག་སྟོང་གི་ལོག་ཐལ།); the *empty sack* is a metaphor used in spoken Amdo for someone who is very thin. ("The Artist")
- "Too thin to the point it becomes hard" (སྐམ་ནས་སྒྱོང་སོང་།) is a way of saying that someone is becoming extremely thin in Amdo. ("The Artist")
- "To poke someone with needles and awls" (ཁབ་གཅིག་འབིག་གཅིག་བཟིག་ཡོད།) originates entirely from the spoken words of Amdo pastoralists, with a meaning verbally ridiculing or critiquing others. ("Boasting")
- "Explodes one's heart" (སྙིང་གད།) describes someone who is extremely frightened. ("The Artist")
- "Head got damaged" (མགོ་ཉོག་ཐལ།) describes being discombobulated. ("The Dream")
- "Dropped like a shooting star" (སྐར་མདའ་ལྟུང་ལྟུང་།) is a metaphor for a speedy movement. ("All-good Menla")
- "To close one's eyes" (མིག་བཙུམ།) means to die. ("Elder's Conversations")
- "To cook porridge" (ཐུ་རུ་བསྐོལ།) means talking nonsense. ("All-good Menla")
- "Nine mountain passes away" (ཕ་རིའི་ལ་དགུ།) refers to something that is highly unlikely to be done, or an impossible task. ("Elders' Conversations")
- "Something that has been dead for a long time/ something from way, way back" (གནའ་བཟིག་གི་གནའ་ཕྱི་རུལ་བ།). ("Boasting") is a phrase to describe something from the distant past—something that is no longer useful or relevant.
- "To go to the Pureland" (ཞིང་ང་ཕེབས།) is an honorific phrase usually used for *lamas* who have passed away. ("The Artist")
- "A valley-full of something" (ལུང་བ་གང་།) suggests that there is a large amount of something. ("Careful Village's Grassland Disputes," "The Dream")

- "A wheel of gossip" (མཁའ་གི་འཁོར་ལོ།) describes a person who constantly gossips about other people. The turning of the wheel spreads the gossip, similar to how the spinning of prayer wheels spreads the merits of the scriptures inside. ("Boasting")
- "Setting sun on top of the mountain" (ལ་ཁའི་ཉི་མ།) is an expression used for describing someone as being old and past their prime. ("Careful Village's Grassland Dispute")
- "Making an ugly scene" (སྒྲིག་བཟེད།) is usually used for someone who did something that is unfavourable to oneself. ("Careful Village's Bride")
- "Until eyes had holes" (མིག་ཕུ་རགས་གོ) describes someone who is desperately hoping for something to happen or waiting for someone to come. ("Careful Village's Thief")
- "Destiny" (བོད་པའི་ཁ་ཡིག), literally "the words on one's forehead," describes a predestined situation. ("Careful Village's Bride")
- "Thumb-index finger-span length body" (རང་ལུས་མཛོ་གང་།) is probably Menla's purposeful humorous play on the common Amdo expression of one's "arm-span length body" རང་ལུས་ འདོམ་གང་།, likely suggesting that he is describing a very short person in the performance. ("The Artist")
- "Make someone faint" (དབང་བོར་བཏང་།) suggests that a person's good performance has impressed someone. The phrase is, sometimes, used like the English expression "killed it." ("The Artist")
- "A little box of bullshits, a bag of lies" (ལབ་གི་སྒམ་ཆུང་། གཡོག་གི་ རྒྱལ་བ།); the first part is probably coined by Menla Jyab himself with the term "little box" (སྒམ་ཆུང་།) adding some literary flavour, but the second part is a common expression in Amdo for describing someone as a vicious liar. ("Boasting")
- Literally, "dog-speech" (ཁྱི་གཏམ།) is a figurative phrase for false or nonsensical utterances. ("The Artist," "Please, Dear Leader," "The Dream")

- "Wild yaks walking single file" (འབྲོང་གཉརྀ།) figuratively describes someone having lice on their head. ("Boasting")

Tamhwé (གཏམ་དཔེ།)

Tamhwé, literally meaning "exemplary speech" and often translated simply as "proverbs," are used to emphasize a speaker's point and eloquently insert poetic language into everyday speech. For example, in "Careful Village's Grassland Dispute," the village leader states:

The disputes of men are like boulders that do not break,	ཕོ་གྱོད་པ་བོང་ཤིགས་རྒྱུ་མེད།།
The disputes of women are like juniper that doesn't rot.	མོ་གྱོད་ཤུག་པ་རུལ་རྒྱུ་མེད།།

This *tamhwé* is commonly used during conflict mediation sessions when the speaker wishes to describe a conflict as severe and needing to be resolved, lest it escalate into a long-term feud.

As with metaphors, Menla Jyab sometimes uses proverbs in unconventional ways, by changing the context and words of existing proverbs, sometimes even coming up with new proverb-like phrases to confuse people and to make them laugh. For example,

[Why don't I], the forest crow become a garuda and grassland skunk a tiger?	ནགས་རྒྱ་རྫོང་ཁྱི་ཏུ་བྱུང་གི་ལོག་གས་ཐང་སྲུང་ དགར་ཉིའུ་ལོ་སྟག་གི། [མི་ལོག་ག་ཆེད་རེ།]

In this example, Menla Jyab phrases an existing proverb as a rhetorical question. The proverb is generally used to disparage someone who acts more important than they are. But in "The Artist," Menla Jyab uses it for himself, saying that he will make himself seem more important.

Other proverbs from throughout this volume include:

- "If I tell you to run to the paths of the dead, you will. If I tell you to hit your father's head, you will" (རྒྱགས་ཟེར་ན་གཤིན་རྗེའི་ འཕྲང་། རྒྱོབ་ཟེར་ན་ཨ་བའི་མགོ). This is usually used to describe someone who is obedient to their superiors, and it is used this way in "Careful Village's Grassland Dispute." However, in "Boasting," he changes the *tamhwé* slightly, to read: If you tell me to run to the paths of the dead, I would. If you tell me to hit my father's head, I would (རྒྱགས་ཟེར་ན་ང་གཤིན་རྗེའི་འཕྲང་ང་རྒྱུག་ག ཀྱོབ་ཟེར་ན་ངས་ཨ་ཕའི་མགོར་རྒྱག་ག). Whereas the original uses the common practice of ellipsis, Menla Jyab makes his meaning more explicit in the second version by adding the verbs to each clause.

- "People these days, and the colour of yellow amber" (དེང་སང་ནངས་གའི་མི། སྤོས་ཤུར་སེར་པོའི་མདོག) compares people to yellow amber. Amber can change colour over time as it oxidizes, and people are changing these days as well. ("Elders' Conversations")

- "Though he wouldn't be able to race horses alone, he would be able to go be a bandit with the other men" (རྟ་འདོ་བའི་གོང་ནས་ཁེར་རྒྱགས་མིན་རུང་། ཕ་ཨ་ཁུའི་རྗག་གི་དཔུང་ལ་མི་ཉན་ནས). This *tamhwé* describes the expectations people have for a man when he comes of age, usually between fifteen to eighteen: to be able to accompany adult male members of his community and become involved in banditry. ("Elders' Conversations")

- "A man shouldn't be called old at thirty" (ཕོ་ལོ་སུམ་ཅུར་ཉས་ཟྱེད་མེད) is half of a *tamhwé*. The second half is a misogynistic clause, "a woman shouldn't be called young at thirty" (མོ་ལོ་སུམ་ཅུར་གཞོན་ཟྱེད་མེད). In the performance, which is exclusively about three male characters, Menla Jyab uses only the first half to obsequiously praise the addressee, who is a leader at thirty-three. ("Please, Dear Leader")

- "Our fathers' bones are gold, and our mothers' bones are conch" (ཕ་བཟང་རུས་པ་གསེར་ཡིན། མ་བཟང་རུས་པ་དུང་ཡིན). *Rus pa*, or "bone," here refers to family lineage. In Tibetan matchmaking, great attention is paid to family lineage with concerns about a lineage's "purity" (specifically with reference to histories of body odour, leprosy, etc.). This *tamhwé* suggests that the speaker is from a good lineage. ("Careful Village's Bride")

- "The axe that destroys what's without and the hatchet that destroys what's within" (ཕྱི་བཤིག་གི་སྟ་རེ་ར། ནང་བཤིག་གི་སྟེའུ). ("Boasting")

- "[I've] seen the other side of the mountain and learned that the wild yak's head was bare" (རྟ་ཕྱུག་ཡག་ཕར་ནང་རིག་སོང་ནས། འབྲོང་མགོ་རྟོ་ཡིན་ནོ་ཞེས་སོང་ནས།). This *tamhwé* suggests that the appearance of a situation does not match reality. ("All-good Menla")

- "Making plans like chess on a square board, having discussions that are circular like a drum" (ཁོག་རྩིས་གྲུ་བཞི་འགྱིག་འདྲ་འདུ། གྲོས་ཁ་གོར་མོ་རྔ་འདུ་འདུ།) first compares complex discussion to playing a chess game, which requires planning and strategizing. The second part refers to how people sit in a circle for such discussions. ("Careful Village's Wedding")

- "When I open my mouth, I talk about the origins of the universe. When I shut my eyes, I know the creation and destruction of the universe" (ཁ་བཤིག་གདང་ན་སྲིད་པའི་ཆགས་རབས་བཤད་ལ། སྨིག་བཤིག་བཙུམས་ན་སྲིད་པའི་ཆགས་འཇིག་མཁྱེན་ནོ།). This *tamhwé* is a boastful statement in which the speaker claims to possess knowledge of the formation of the universe and the ability to prophesize its future, specifically when and how the world will eventually end. ("Boasting")

- "When I am unhappy, I bind the sun and moon under oath. When I am angry, I topple Shinjé Chojya from his throne" (དས་ཁམས་མ་དགས་ན་ཉི་ཟླ་དམ་མ་འདོགས་ག ཐུགས་ཁྲོས་བཏང་ན་གཤིན་རྗེའི་ཁྲི་ལས་འཕབ་བ།). Again, this *tamhwé* is a boastful statement in which the speaker claims that when they are angry, they possess the supernatural power to subdue even the sun and moon in the sky and to dethrone Shinjé Chojya, the Lord of the Dead. ("Boasting")

This list is representative rather than exhaustive, but with these selected explanations, we hope that readers will be able to make better sense of other *tamhwé* appearing in the performances that follow.

Khahwé (ཁ་དཔེ།)

In Amdo, *khahwé* are often different from *tamhwé*, based on the context, though the two terms can sometimes be used interchangeably. Unlike *tamhwé*, which are usually known by many across regions, *khahwé* are locally known expressions that may derive from popular narratives. The examples here do not have related narratives.

- "Came as the groom and left as a bandit" (མག་པར་བསྔད་ནས་རྐུ་པ་བཅོས།) is a common expression used by Amdo Tibetans for deceiving someone by pretending to be someone else to enter the community and then rob it. The phrase, which rhymes *mag pa* and *jag pa*, is similar to the English expression "wolf in sheep's clothing." ("Careful Village's Grassland Disputes")

- "There is a certain order for birth, but not for death" (སྐྱེས་པ་སྟ་གཤིན་ཡོད་རུང་འཆི་བ་སྟ་གཤིན་མེད།) recognizes the unpredictability of someone's death and is used especially for a young person's untimely death. ("Careful Village's Thief")

- "From now on, everything is great" (དེང་ཕྱིན་ཡིན། དེའི་རྒྱུན་ཡིན།) is a stock phrase people use when they agree to resolve a problem. ("Careful Village's Bride")

- "Things can't be hidden from the *lama* or from the next rebirth" (བླ་མར་གསང་ང་བླ་མར་གསང་།) means that the speaker will be completely truthful without hiding anything, since the *lama* and the next life will reveal the truth anyway. ("Careful Village's Thief")

Formulaic Epithets

Formulaic epithets are one of the poetic features that distinguish oral literature from plain everyday language. These are usually stable, trisyllabic noun phrases that help the artist fulfil the metrical requirements of seven- and eight-syllabled lines common in Amdo oral literature. The three syllables may follow a number of grammatical patterns. Some, for example, use a noun-adjective structure, as in *sa dogmo* (ས་དོག་མོ།), which is used to describe the earth. Others use an adjective-noun structure, as with *shang khushuk* (བྱང་ཁུ་བྱུག) "northern cuckoo." Still others combine two nouns like *dudtsi chang* (བདུད་རྩི་ཆང་།) which literally combines the words "nectar/ambrosia" and *chang* (a type of liquor) to create a three-syllable epithet for liquor.

Traditionally, these formulaic epithets may be linked to certain genres of secular oratory and singing traditions (see, for example, Thurston

2012 and 2019). Some epithets are specific to individual genres, while others are common across multiple genres. "Southern turquoise dragon" (ལྷོ་གཡུ་འབྲུག) and "northern cuckoo" (བྱང་ཁུ་བྱུག), for example, are common in a variety of versified traditions including *tamhwé*, speeches, and folksongs (དམངས་གླུ།). The list below includes some of the other formulaic epithets used throughout Menla Jyab's performances. Translations may be different in the texts presented in this volume to take context into account:

- Horse (རྟ་འདོ་བ།) ("Careful Village's Wedding")
- Mule (སྲུག་ཆུང་དྲེལ།) ("Careful Village's Wedding")
- Donkey (བོང་སྒྱུ་མི།) ("Careful Village's Wedding")
- China (སྲྀད་རྒྱ་ནག) ("Careful Village's Wedding," "Careful Village's Thief")
- Uncles (ཕ་ཨ་ཁུ།) ("Careful Village's Wedding") referring to men of an older generation
- Aunts (མ་སྲུ་མོ།) ("Careful Village's Wedding") referring to women of an older generation
- Ngari (སྟོད་མངའ་རིས།) ("Careful Village's Wedding")
- U-Tsang (བར་དབུས་གཙང་།) ("Careful Village's Wedding")
- Dokham (སྨད་མདོ་ཁམས།) ("Careful Village's Wedding")
- Tibet (སྒྱུ་རྒྱལ་བོད།) ("Careful Village's Wedding")
- Silk and lambskin robes (གོས་ཚ་རུ།) ("Careful Village's Wedding")
- Enemy (དགྲ་ནག་པོ།) ("Careful Village's Wedding")
- India (སྟོད་རྒྱ་གར།) ("Careful Village's Thief")

Honorifics and Humilifics

Honorifics and humilifics are another intriguing component of Menla Jyab's performances, for how they both help to create realistic dialogue and support his cultural critique. Tibetan speakers in Amdo use the honorific register less frequently than speakers of Lhasa dialects. In Amdo, the register is often reserved for religious figures, honoured guests at weddings, and sometimes for leaders. This practice is reflected also in Menla Jyab's comedies. When characters believe that are speaking to a religious figure or an important leader, they will suddenly switch to honorific. By way of example, in "Please, Dear Leader" (Chapter 6), Menla Jyab initially treats a person coldly until he learns that that speaker works in the government, at which point he switches to honorifics:

"What thou sayest was not wrong."   དེ་ར་**ཆེད་གིས་གསུངས**་ནོ་ནོར་མེད་གི

In this sentence, the second person pronoun and the verb "to speak" (both in bold) are honorifics. Given how infrequently honorifics are used in Amdo, the exaggerated use of honorifics for officials in this instance pokes fun at people who place officials on a par with religious leaders.

Additionally, some of Menla Jyab's comedies also make use of "humilifics," which are morphological constructions that speakers use to refer to themselves and their belongings in a negative or belittling fashion. For example, in "The Dream," Menla Jyab uses several humilifics in quick succession དེད་ཁའི་སྦྲ་རིག་ནང་ང་འགྱོ་ཇ་དན་བཞིག་འཐུང་ཁ་ཡིན། "Let's go inside our tent and drink some tea." In this example, Menla Jyab appends words for "torn" (རིག), "evil" (དན), and "mouth" (ཁ) to the nouns "tent," "tea," and the verb "drink" respectively to transform them into humilifics. Amdo pastoralists also may use "humilifics" as a way to lower their status while speaking with others (see Tsering Samdrup and Suzuki 2019, pp. 247–53).

When Menla Jyab uses honorifics and humilifics, he often does so to make specific points about the characters he voices and about Tibetan language practices in Amdo. In "The Dream" (Chapter 3), for example, he uses humilifics alongside cursing and what he calls "filthy speech" to criticize these language practices. In the "Careful Village" series, the villagers use honorifics when speaking to Menla Jyab, which is simultaneously appropriate given that they believe him to be a *lama*, while also indexing their misplaced faith.

Ways of Speaking/Imitating Different People

Menla Jyab often voices the speech of people with different social roles and regional accents in his performances which leads to the presentation of various ways of speaking, from elderly pastoralist men (a common character for him) and women to civil servants and principals. In most instance, this involves changing his pitch (higher for a female speaker), or adding some forceful laughs (for the village leader) in the "Careful Village" series. In some cases, this also involves making intentional grammatical mistakes. For instance, in "The Telephone" (Chapter 7), he portrays a cadre making a phone call:

A: **Your hometown is Jentsa.**	ཀ ཁྱོ་གི་ཕ་ཡུལ་གཅན་ཚ་རེད།
B: Wouldn't I know that?	ཁ དེ་ཡིན་ནོ་ངས་མི་ཤེས་ནི་ཨེ་རེད།
A: *Wei*! I'm also from Jentsa. **Would you know?**	ཀ ཝེ། ང་ར་གཅན་ཚ་གི་རེད། ཁྱོ་གི་ཤེས་རྒྱུ་ཨེ་རེད།
B: I don't, but tell me and I would. Who are you?	ཁ ཤེས་རྒྱུ་མ་རེད་ད། ཁྱོས་བཤད་ད་ཤེས་རྒྱུ་རེད། ཁྱོ་སུ་ཡིན།
A: Ah, **I is a cadre... Is a cadre from Jentsa.**	ཀ ཨ། ང་ལས་བྱེད་པ་རེད། གཅན་ཚ་གི་ལས་བྱེད་པ་རེད།
B: As if there aren't any cadres from Jentsa! Wei, do you have something to say to me?	ཁ གཅན་ཚ་ན་ལས་བྱེད་པ་ཅི་ར་མེད་གི་ནས། ཝེ། ང་བཤད་རྒྱུ་བཟིག་ཡོད་ལ།

Here the cadre does not speak Tibetan fluently. In addition to the cadre's humorous lack of fluency, Menla Jyab's performance also highlights the cadre's condescending tone and emphasis on the importance of his civil servant job.

Similarly, in "Careful Village's Bride," a foreign woman's linguistic incompetence is highlighted through her misuse of evidential markers:

I **goed** and I will **returns**.	ང་བྱུད་ཐལ། ཕྱིར་ར་ཡོང་རྒྱུ་རེད།

The auxiliaries *thal* and *red* are both more appropriate for the third person. A grammatical sentence would instead use the egophoric auxiliaries *song* and *yin* (ང་བྱུད་སོང་། ཕྱིར་ར་ཡོང་རྒྱུ་ཡིན།). The woman's mistakes are a source of great amusement for Tibetan audiences, and have made this into one of the most commonly quoted lines from Menla's body of comedic work.

Loanwords

In the twenty-first century, communities in Amdo have taken part in a widespread purism movement, discouraging the mixing of Tibetan and Chinese, focusing particularly on the use of loanwords (See Thurston 2018c, Tsering Samdrup and Hiroyuki Suzuki 2022, Lhagyal Dak 2019). When Menla Jyab performed these *khashags* in the 1980s and 90s, this purism movement had not yet begun. At that time, Menla Jyab was among the first group of intellectuals critiquing the excessive use of Chinese loanwords in the speech of Tibetans as exemplified by characters in "The Telephone" (Chapter 7) and "Boasting" (Chapter 2).

Importantly, at this time Menla Jyab was not against all loanwords. In many of his performances he uses loanwords as natural parts of language. Throughout the sketches he uses loanwords for new technologies and objects, like "car" (ཆེ།车), "billiards" (བེ་ཆེག 台球), and "motorcycle" མོ་ཏོ། (摩托). Instead of critiquing the entire practice, Menla Jyab's critique focuses on the excessive use of loanwords. In these instances, he and Phagmo Drashi frequently make this explicit with direct comments on the practice, as in "Boasting," where Menla Jyab and Phagmo Drashi role-play two characters who use excessive Chinese loanwords (too many to list here) in their speech and, as Menla comments, "gradually it became Chinese."

Additionally, Menla Jyab also occasionally uses English loanwords in the speech of his characters. One female character in "The Telephone" uses, "Okay" and "Byebye," which is followed by a comment from Phagmo Drashi that "although she says 'ok' with her mouth, she has no *ka* and *kha* in her chest," with *ka* and *kha* being the first two consonants of the Tibetan syllabary, and standing in for the entirety of the Tibetan language. Across the entire corpus, then, the critique against excessive use of loanwords is clear.

Revolutionary-influenced Neologisms

After the establishment of the People's Republic of China in 1949, and in the wake of Amdo's incorporation into the new country in the 1950s, many new terms were introduced to the Tibetan language to communicate the new government policies and ideologies. As a performer on state-sponsored media in post-Mao China, Menla Jyab cannot avoid using some politically tinged neologisms in his work.[16] In some cases, this is likely a product of the times in which he was writing and performing them. For example, throughout the performances, he references Cultural Revolution-era slogans and reform era policies. Earlier performances also sometimes use the word "comrade" (བློ་མཐུན།), translating the Chinese word *tongzhi* 同志) to address others. Before long, the term disappears from Menla's comedies, mirroring how the term ceases to be used in China more generally. Sometimes he uses loanwords that have become an inextricable part of Tibetan language in China. For example, the Chinese *Shuji* 书记 "party secretary" ("The Telephone") is quite common among Tibetan speakers, and it would be impossible to create dialogues on certain topics without using it.[17] Finally, some neologisms are entirely of Menla Jyab's own creation. Examples of the neologisms in Menla Jyab's include:

- Film (གློག་བརྙན། 电影) ("The Elders' Conversations")
- Comrade (བློ་མཐུན། 同志) ("The Artist")
- Processing factory (ལས་སྟོན་བཟོ་གྲྭ། 加工厂) used as metaphor for brain ("The Elders' Conversations")
- Import Company (ནང་འདྲེན་ཀུང་སི། 进口公司) ("The Elders' Conversations")
- Export Company (ཕྱིར་གཏོང་ཀུང་སི། 出口公司) ("The Elders' Conversations")
- Culture and arts gala (རིག་རྩལ་དགོང་ཚོགས། 文艺晚会) ("Please, Dear Leader")
- Serve the People (མི་དམངས་ལ་ཞབས་འདེགས་ཞུ། 为人民服务) ("Please, Dear Leader")
- Colluding of dogs and wolves (ཁྱི་སྤྱང་དན་འབྲེལ། 狼狈为奸) ("Careful Village's Thief")

---

16   A neologism here means a term with a recent origin, especially the ones that came into the Tibetan language after the establishment of the People's Republic of China in 1949.

17   Though some written works use the literary Tibetan translation དྲུང་ཆེ།, it has never won favour among writers in Amdo, let alone the broader population.

- United as one (སློབས་ཤུགས་གཅིག་སྒྲིལ| 团结一心) ("Careful Village's Thief")

- Work more, get paid more; work less, get paid less; work no more, not get paid (མང་ལས་མང་ཐོབ་ཡས། ཉུང་ལས་ཉུང་ཐོབ། མ་ལས་ན་ཅི་མི་ཐོབ། 多劳多得, 少老少得, 不老不得) a propaganda phrase from the era of People's Commune (人民公社时期 1958 to 1984) in China (Careful Village's Thief)

- Capitalism (མ་ཆུ་རིང་ལུགས| 资本主义) ("Careful Village's Thief")

- Proletariat (འབྱོར་མེད་གྲལ་རིམ| 无产阶级) ("Careful Village's Thief")

- Manual labourers (ལུས་ཤུགས་ངལ་རྩོལ་པ| 体力劳动者) ("Careful Village's Thief")

- Mental worker/intellectuals (བློ་ཤུགས་ངལ་རྩོལ་པ| 脑力劳动者) ("Careful Village's Thief")

Sarcastic Toponyms and Names

Menla Jyab often subtly points to social problems he sees facing Tibetan communities in Amdo with creative but sarcastic names for the characters and communities in his performances.

For instance:

- "Careful Village" (སེམས་ཆུང་སྡེ་བ།), the name is used in the series of performances, probably one of his most famous pieces. The message in this title is that Tibetans are timid or too careful when dealing with their surroundings and that that is a source of many of the problems that Tibetans are facing.

- "Old-Brain Village" (བློ་རྙིང་སྡེ་བ།) ("Elders' Conversations"), Menla Jyab uses this name probably to criticise the conservative stands people may take.

- "Headless-Tailless Village" (མགོ་མེད་གཞུག་རུམ་སྡེ་བ།) ("The Dream"), suggesting that it is a disorderly and leaderless village.

- "Tell-Everything Village" (མི་བཤད་དགུ་བཤད་སྡེ་བ།) ("The Dream"), this suggests that the villagers talk behind each other's backs and that gossip travels fast in this village.
- "Primitive Village" (ཡ་ཐོག་སྡེ་བ།) ("The Dream") suggests the community's backwardness.
- "Black-Nose Black-Tongue Village" (སྣ་ནག་ལྕེ་ནག་སྡེ་བ།) ("The Dream") suggests inauspiciousness.

In addition to such sarcastic placenames, Menla Jyab sometimes comes up with creative names for fictional characters.

- "Uncle complaint mouth" (ཨ་ཁུ་སྲུག་སྨྲེ་ཁ།)
- "Fake" (ར་རྫུན་མ།): in "Careful Village's Thief," this is the name of a *lama*. But the name is composed of the components used to spell the word "fake."
- Granny Lugujyi (ཨ་ཡེ་ལུ་གུ་སྐྱིད།)
- Zalejya (ཟ་ལེ་རྒྱལ།)

Reading Uncle Menla's Cultural Critique

Menla Jyab's language play and ability to voice believable characters alone, however, is not enough to account for his tremendous popularity and staying power. Instead, Tibetan fans of Menla Jyab's comedies praise his work primarily because each performance engages in a form of cultural critique targeting a range of "social ills." Menla Jyab's expansive and biting critique is evident across the translations in this volume.

The volume opens with "The Artist," Menla Jyab's first *khashag* script. In this comedy, Menla Jyab references the ways that an artist must learn to perform. Probably relying on his own experience dubbing popular television and radio shows into Tibetan, he references a number of different character types that would be recognizable to audiences at the time. For example, he imitates the laughter of a hero who has just subdued his enemy, and the laughter of the enemy begging for his life. He imitates the laughter of revolutionary enemies like a landlord and his lackey discussing how to oppress the masses, and more. Later in the performance he also sings songs that play on revolutionary lyrics. A tremendous display of his talent at voicing different types of characters and their speech styles, this comedy announces Menla Jyab's presence in the world of Tibetan cultural production.

The second performance, "Boasting" begins with the intriguing premise that there is value in researching negative things about Tibetan society, even the practice of competitive "boasting" (ཁབ་རྒྱག་པ།). Such boasting is not normally considered worthy of academic study, but Menla asks the audience to consider it form a different perspective. He proceeds to compete with his partner with increasingly outlandish boasts. Menla Jyab and Phagmo Drashi sometimes make claims about their own academic prowess and sometimes denigrate their partner's bad habits or imitate their hygiene habits. In the end, they move from boasting to the language practices in their villages. This final point is ultimately the target of Menla Jyab's satirical critique, as the performers mix Chinese and Tibetan and ultimately leave the audience feeling that they should not mix language in this fashion. This remains a key theme throughout Menla Jyab's career.

Language practices again take centre stage in the next comedy, "The Dream," in which Menla Jyab imagines how the great kings and ministers of Tibet's past might respond if they saw Tibetan society today. Through putative conversations with the minister Gar Tongtsen (མགར་སྟོང་བཙན།) and others, Menla Jyab concludes that they would not be impressed, particularly with the language practices of many Tibetans. Later, he comes to understand their point when he visits several villages where people swear, curse, or denigrate their own belongings using humilific language. These are then taken to illustrate the assertions of the luminaries from Tibet's history: the Tibetan people and the Tibetan language are not as great as they once were, and things must change.

In "All-good Menla," Menla Jyab continues with his unique brand of highly imaginative and fantastic storytelling, with a narrative in which—after a fight with his wife—he first ascended to the heavens and then into hell, and even took a trip to America. It all begins with Menla Jyab insisting that he be called "Menla Kunzang," which literally means "the all-good Menla" after his wife derisively called him this while quarrelling. The patently ridiculous story stretches the audience's suspension of disbelief near to breaking, in a fashion that would seem more similar to the American tall tale than to any traditionally Tibetan form of expression.[18] At the same

---

18   For more on the American tall tale genre, see Mullen 1978, pp. 130–48.

time, no matter how far he pushes the boundaries, Menla Jyab's work is also simultaneously deeply embedded in Tibetan cosmologies and everyday experience as demonstrated through references to everything ranging from intimate partner violence common in Tibetan communities (Rajan 2018), to fashions of the day, and to Shinjé Chojya (གཤིན་རྗེ་ཆོས་རྒྱལ): the Lord of Death in Tibetan Buddhist cosmologies.

This deep attention to the details and the changes experienced in Tibetan life is equally evident in the next script, "Elders' Conversations." Beginning with a long statement about how a *khashag* performer must be a skilled observer of the human condition, the performers then put this to the test by acting out the how elders converse with their peers and with members of the younger generation. In doing so, he illustrates the massive changes rocking Tibetan society in post-Mao Amdo, particularly in terms of changing generational attitudes and social relations.

The sixth contribution in the volume, "Please, Dear Leader," is a three-person *khashag* performed with his usual partner Phagmo Drashi and the well-known emcee, Phurwa. Menla Jyab initially treats the two other speakers with contempt until he learns that they are leaders, upon which he turns obsequious and fawning to the point where he lets them call him names. Here, rather than telling stories or placing a specific traditional language practice on display, Menla satirizes the behaviour of officials, but more importantly the treatment officials often receive from ordinary people.

Next, "The Telephone" uses the eponymous technology to show how new technologies are shaping Tibetan language and culture in new ways. In the 1980s and 1990s, telephones were still relatively new to Tibetan communities and many villages might have only one landline for the entire village. As a result, many Tibetans were, at the time, unaccustomed to using telephones. Again, acting out the dialogues of different types of people—patients in hospital, officials, and young women trying to call off work—the rupture created by the telephone provided a tremendous opportunity to creatively imagine and model language practices in the modern moment.

The volume closes with four comedies from the celebrated "Careful Village" series, in which the comedian describes his travels to a fictional pastoral community that believes him to be a holy man. He accepts their mistake and then takes it upon himself to help the village solve their problems. In the first performance, he assigns each villager a "karmic enemy" (འདུལ་སྐལ།)—a person that someone is destined to defeat—to suggest that each villager may only fight one specific target. By "coincidence," each villager is a close relative to the "karmic enemy" selected for them. Grassland wars were common in Amdo at this time (see, for example, Yeh 2003), but in helping the villagers to realize their kinship ties as Tibetans, he urges them to rethink the fight. At the same time, in relying on him, a fake *lama*, to solve the problem, he satirizes the village's misplaced faith. In place of religion, he proposes education.

In "Careful Village's Bride," a stubborn young man's desire to marry a foreign woman causes an uproar in the village. The villagers describe how the young man Zalejyal and the foreign woman initially meet over a language exchange and then describe the woman's brazen behaviour—public displays of affection and directly describing her affections for the man. They can't understand why no Tibetan woman is good enough. Again, their trusted "lama," Menla Jyab, helps them resolve the issue by siding with the boy and his family in a strong defence of free choice marriage.

In "Careful Village's Wedding," Menla Jyab orates a wedding speech. Although superficially similar to a traditional wedding speech, Menla Jyab has added a number of changes to its content in order to modernize it, in the name of intelligibility and closeness to real life. In the process, he discusses modern technologies, the behaviour of monks and officials, and the quality of Tibetan education (among many other topics).

"Careful Village's Thief" is the final performance of the series and of this volume. In this performance, the village again asks the comedian's help, this time to fend off a rash of thievery besetting the village. The village had previously asked another "*lama*" named Ra dzu na ma for help, but his religious remedy had been both expensive and ineffective. Menla Jyab, however, does his best to help by convincing most of the villagers to confess their own prior misdeeds (some hilarious for how minor they are and how embarrassed the villagers seem). In the end, the audience learns that the previous *lama*, whose name literally spells out the Tibetan word for "fake" (*rdzun ma* རྫུན་མ།), had stolen money from the village (and presumably others) and had been arrested.

Reading across these performances, one may notice that pastoralists and religious clerics are regular targets of Menla's satirical critique at this time. Menla Jyab's portrayal of intergenerational encounters between pastoralists and educated young intellectuals put tradition, religion, and language practices on display and on trial. Education (modern and secular education, that is) and free-choice marriage are favourite topics as well. In this way, Menla Jyab's satirical critiques generally promote a modernity based in a pointed critique of many traditional attitudes, behaviors, and beliefs (Thurston 2018). This work generally aligns with the approaches of the "New Thought" (བསམ་བློ་གསར་པ།) movement—a movement with which Menla Jyab and speaking partner Phagmo Drashi were both aligned in the late 1990s and early 2000s—that were beginning to spread in Amdo's intellectual circles around this time (see Hartley 2002, Wu Qi 2012, and Peacock 2020). Many of these social critiques—including free choice marriage, technological advancement, secular education, and a mistrust of religion—also parallel discourses of modernity promoted by the State.

Nevertheless, there are also important places in which Menla Jyab's critique distinguishes his own voice from the State's, particularly in the realm of language practice. The reference to Tibetan kings and ministers in "The Dream" (Chapter 3) for example, harkens back to key figures within the Tibetan historical imagination to understand perceived Tibetan backwardness in the present. Other performances, like "Boasting," focus on a specific linguistic practice, but use this to point the finger both at some forms of Tibetan oral tradition, but more importantly (towards the end) to changing Tibetan verbal practices in the present, specifically the tendency to mix Tibetan and Chinese languages. Similarly, "The Telephone" also critiques the language practices of Tibetans as they navigate modern life. Focusing on the linguistic breaks brought on by the arrival of new technologies, he pokes fun at both urban Tibetans and pastoralists, specifically around their language practices. Doing so, through the medium of Tibetan, moreover, creates a more complicated critique based on ensuring space for Tibetan language in the present and for the future, but also in promoting specific language practices while satirizing others (including certain traditional expressive practices).[19] Taken together, the *khashag* scripts and translations presented in this volume model a new, and uniquely Tibetan, way of being modern in contemporary China based especially in new language practices whilst also poking fun at the ignorance and anti-modern behaviours of certain segments of Tibetan society (Thurston 2018). This introduction

---

19 For the purposes of space, we have abbreviated this discussion of Menla Jyab's complex and dynamic social criticism. For a fuller discussion of this critique and these ideas, see Thurston 2018 and Thurston 2025.

has highlighted some of the key issues, but it should be noted that each performance is filled with intricate discussions that poke fun at still other practices in ways far more nuanced than this short introduction can adequately introduce. We encourage readers to seek these critiques further as they engage with this volume.

About the Translations

We understand that a translation of a comedic text should ideally be humorous in the target language as well as the source language. And yet, as described above, Menla Jyab's humour rests in no small part on his unparalleled ability to create dialogues that are both realistic and ridiculous. He creates and voices a variety of different male and female characters that people might recognize from their own communities and places them in situations that seem to be exaggerated versions of situations people might face in their own lives. In reacting to these situations, Menla's characters deploy the range of expressive practices in Tibetan language: sometimes playing with words, sometimes parodying traditional expressive forms, sometimes making up his own unique phrases, and sometimes applying traditional forms in new contexts.

Foreign readers are not Menla's target audience, and it is difficult to convey in text the hilarity of hearing Menla Jyab imitating different types of speech. Similarly, English readers will likely have difficulty replicating the novelty of what were, to Tibetan communities at the time, unfamiliar situations like using a telephone or meeting an American. We have, however, done our best. We narrow or widen the gap with the original at different moments in ways that we believe best represent the aesthetic qualities of the texts and the unique talents of their performers. In some situations, we have even tried to replicate alliteration and assonance used throughout. When honorifics are used, we have employed archaic English language to indicate this change. For example, Amdo's formal second person pronoun ཁྱེད་ཀ is translated as "thee" or "thou," and the honorific form of the verb "to speak" (གསུང་) is translated as "speakest" or a related archaic form. In some cases, characters speak ungrammatically—either inappropriately using honorifics, or using the wrong evidential markers—and we have indicated these with disfluencies in the English translation as well as footnotes (where we deem it necessary). We have also added stage notes in parentheses to indicate the different characters Menla is voicing on a turn-by-turn basis.

Where stuck, however, we believe that conveying the content and the linguistic nuance of the performances takes priority over English-language humour and have therefore opted in most situations to prioritize these. Where we feel that the language is particularly noteworthy or engages heavily with Tibetan and Chinese concepts with which readers may be unfamiliar, we have provided annotations in the form of footnotes at the bottom of the pages to clarify. We hope that together these create a highly approachable and engaging text.

References

Bendi Tso, Marnyi Gyatso, Naljor Tsering, Mark Turin, and Members of the Choné Tibetan Community. 2023. *Shépa: The Tibetan Oral Tradition in Choné*. Cambridge: Open Book Publishers. https://doi.org/10.11647/OBP.0312

Brag dgon pa dkon mchog bstan pa rab rgyas བྲག་དགོན་པ་དགོན་མཆོག་བསྟན་པ་རབ་རྒྱས།. 1982 [1865]. *Deb ther rgya mtsho* དེབ་ཐེར་རྒྱ་མཚོ། [The Oceanic Book]. Lan gru: kan su'u mi rigs dpe skrun khang [Lanzhou: Gansu Minzu Press].

'Brug rgyal mkhar འབྲུག་རྒྱལ་མཁར།, ed. 2007. *A mdo'i kha skad tshig mdzod* ཨ་མདོའི་ཁ་སྐད་ཚིག་མཛོད། [Amdo Dialect Dictionary]. Lanzhou: Kan su'i mi rigs dpe skrun khang [Lanzhou: Gansu Minzu Press].

Buffetrille, Katia. 2002. "Qui est Khri ka'i yul lha? Dieu tibétain du terroir, dieu chinois de la littérature ou de la guerre? Un problème d'identité divine en A mdo." In *Territory and Identity in Tibet and the Himalayas*, Edited by K. Buffetrille and H. Diemberger, pp. 135–58. Leiden: Brill.

Cai, Shenshen, and Emily Dunn. 2020. *Xiangsheng and the Emergence of Guo Degang in Contemporary China*. Singapore: Palgrave MacMillan. https://doi.org/10.1007/978-981-15-8116-8

Cham tshang pad+ma lhun grub ཆམ་ཚང་པདྨ་ལྷུན་གྲུབ།. 2009. *Amdo'i yul skad kyi sgra gdangs la dpyad pa* ཨ་མདོའི་ཡུལ་སྐད་ཀྱི་སྒྲ་གདངས་ལ་དཔྱད་པ། [Study of the Sound of Amdo Dialect]. Zi ling : mtsho sngon mi rigs dpe skrun khang [Xining: Qinghai Minzu Press].

Chos bstan rgyal. 2014. "Following the Herds: Rhythms of Pastoral Life in A mdo." *Asian Highlands Perspectives* 32: 1–212.

Dak Lhagyal. 2019. "'Linguistic Authority' in State-Society Interaction: Cultural Politics of Tibetan Education in China." *Discourse: Studies in the Cultural Politics of Education* 42(3): 353–67. https://doi.org/10.1080/01596306.2019.1648239

Dge bshes chos grags དགེ་བཤེས་ཆོས་གྲགས། 1957. *Dge bhes chos kyi grags pas brtsams pa'i brda dag ming tshig gsal ba bzhugs so* དགེ་བཤེས་ཆོས་ཀྱི་གྲགས་པས་བརྩམས་པའི་བརྡ་དག་མིང་ཚིག་གསལ་བ་བཞུགས་སོ།། [Correct Spellings of Terminologies by Geshe Chokyi Dakpa]. Pe cing: Mi rigs dpe skrun khang [Beijing: Minzu Press]

Dondrup, Donyol, and Charlene Makley. 2017. "'The Body Hair that Grows on the Head': Menla-kyap's 'View on Hair and Hairstyles' (2009)." *Ateliers d'anthropologie: Revue éditée par Laboratoire d'ethnologie et de sociologie comparative* 45. https://doi.org/10.4000/ateliers.10550

Don grub rgyal དོན་གྲུབ་རྒྱལ། 1997 [1980]. "Bod yig slob pa" བོད་ཡིག་སློབ་པ། [Studying Tibetan]. In *Dpal Don grub rgyal gyi gsung 'bum* དཔལ་དོན་གྲུབ་རྒྱལ་གྱི་གསུང་འབུམ། [The Collected Works of Don grub rgyal], Vol. 6, pp. 43–55. Pe cing: Mi rigs dpe skrun khang [Beijing: Minzu Press].

Dpal ldan bkra shis. 2013. "Amdo Tibetan Language: An Introduction to Normative Oral Amdo Form, Meaning, Use." *Asian Highlands Perspectives* 43.

Fischer, Andrew M. 2009. "Educating for Exclusion in Western China: Structural and Institutional Dimensions of Conflict in the Tibetan Areas of Qinghai and Tibet." *CRISE Working Paper* 69. https://repub.eur.nl/pub/17871/Fischer%20CRISE%202009%20wp69.pdf

Green, R. Jeffrey. 2012. "Amdo Tibetan Media Intelligibility." *SIL Electronic Report 2012-019*. https://www.sil.org/system/files/reapdata/25/97/22/259722280941218282774161946325503321089/silesr2012_019.pdf

Haller, Felix. 2004. *Dialekt und Erzählungen von Themchen. Sprachwissenschaftliche Beschreibung eines Nomadendialektes aus Nord-Amdo* (Beiträge zur tibetischen Erzählforschung, herausgegeben von Dieter Schuh 14). Bonn: VGH Wissenschaftsverlag.

Hartley, Lauran R. 1999. "Themes of Tradition and Change in Modern Tibetan Literature." *Lungta* 12: 29–44.

—. 2002. "'Inventing Modernity' in A mdo: Views on the Role of Traditional Culture in a Developing Society." In *Amdo Tibetans in Transition: Society and Culture in the Post-Mao Era*, edited by Toni Huber, pp. 1–25. Leiden: Brill.

Janhunen, Juha. 2004. "On the Hierarchy of Structural Convergence in the Amdo Sprachbund." In *The Typology of Argument Structure and Grammatical Relations*, edited by Bernard Comrie, Pirkko Suihkonen, and Valery Solovyev, pp. 72–74. Helsinki: John Benjamins.

--. 2005. "The Role of the Turkic Languages in the Amdo Sprachbund." In *Turks and Non-Turks: Studies on the History of Linguistic and Cultural Contacts*, edited by Marzanna Pomorska and Ewa Siemieniec-Gołaś, pp. 113–22 (Studia Turcologica Cracoviensia 10). Krakow: Archeobooks.

Kalsang Yeshe. 2008. "A Preliminary Note on Chinese Codeswitching in Modern Lhasa Tibetan." In *Tibetan Modernities: Notes from the Field on Cultural and Social Change*, edited by Robert Barnett and Ronald Schwartz, pp. 213–48. Leiden: Brill.

Lama Jabb. 2015. *Oral and Literary Continuities in Tibetan: The Inescapable Nation*. Lanham, MD: Rowman and Littlefield.

Li Dechun (李德春, Limusishiden) and Gerald Roche. 2017. *Long Narrative Songs from the Mongghul of Northeast Tibet*. Cambridge: Open Books Publishers. https://doi.org/10.11647/OBP.0124

Mog chung phur kho མོག་ཆུང་ཕུར་ཁོ།. 2010. *Pha mas bdag la 'di skad gsungs—A mdo'i mkhas dbang dang a mdo'i phal skad* ཕ་མས་བདག་ལ་འདི་སྐད་གསུངས། ཨ་མདོའི་མཁས་དབང་དང་ཨ་མདོའི་ཕལ་སྐད། [My Parents Spoke to me Thus: Amdo's intellectuals and Vernacular Amdo]. pe cing: mi rigs dpe skrung khang [Beijing: Minzu Press].

--. 2013. "Bod kyi kha shags kyi phyi mo—phal skad brtsams chos 'Ja mchod' la rob tsam dpyad pa" བོད་ཀྱི་ཁ་ཤགས་ཀྱི་ཕྱི་མོ་—ཕལ་སྐད་བརྩམས་ཆོས་ཇ་མཆོད་ལ་རོབ་ཙམ་དཔྱད་པ། [The First Tibetan Comedic Dialogue—A Brief Examination of the Vernacular Work *The Tea Libation*]. In *Kha shags thos pa dga' skyed* ཁ་ཤགས་ཐོས་པ་དགའ་སྐྱེད། [Comedic Dialogues Produce Joyful Learning], edited by Mang tshogs sgyu rtsal rtsom sgrig khang, pp. 186–222. Zi ling: Mtsho sngon mi rigs dpe skrun khang [Xining: Qinghai Minzu Press].

Mullen, Patrick B. 1978. *I Heard the Old Fishermen Say: Folklore of the Texas Gulf Coast*. Logan, UT: Utah State University Press.

Peacock, Christopher. 2020. "Intersecting Nations, Diverging Discourses: The Fraught Encounter of Chinese and Tibetan Literatures in the Modern Era." Ph.D. Thesis: Columbia University.

Phur ba ཕུར་བ།. 1993. *A mdo'i kha shags* ཨ་མདོའི་ཁ་ཤགས། [Amdo *Khashag*]. Zi ling: Mtsho sngon mi rigs dpe skrun khang [Xining: Qinghai Minzu Press].

Pirie, Fernanda. 2009. "The Horse with Two Saddles: Tamxhwe in Modern Golok." *Asian Highlands Perspectives* 1: 205–27.

Ptackova, Jarmila. 2019. Traditionalization as a Response to State-induced Development in Rural Tibetan areas of Qinghai, PRC. *Central Asian Survey* 38(3): 417–31.

--. 2020. *Exile from the Grasslands: Tibetan Herders and Chinese Development Projects*. Seattle, WA: University of Wahington Press. https://doi.org/10.1515/9780295748207

Rajan, Hamsa. 2018. "When Wife-beating is not Necessarily Abuse: A Feminist and Cross-Cultural Analysis of the Concept of Abuse as Expressed by Tibetan Survivors of Domestic Violence." *Violence against Women* 24(1): 3–27.

Reynolds, Jermay J. 2012. "Language Variation and Change in an Amdo Tibetan Village: Gender, Education and Resistance." Ph.D. Thesis: Georgetown University.

Roche, Gerald. 2011. "Nadun: Ritual and Dynamics of Cultural Diversity in Northwest China's Hehuang Region." Ph.D. Thesis: Griffith University.

Sangs rgyas rin chen. 2010. *Mdo smad g.yon ru'i lo rgyus bden don gtam gyi rang sgra zhes bya ba bzhugs so* མདོ་སྨད་གཡོན་རུའི་ལོ་རྒྱུས་བདེན་དོན་གཏམ་གྱི་རང་སྒྲ་ཞེས་བྱ་བ་བཞུགས་སོ༎ [True Spontaneous Sound of Narrative: A History of Yonru in Domé]. Lan gru: kan su'u mi rigs dpe skrun khang [Lanzhou: Gansu Minzu Press].

Sandman, Erika, and Camille Simon. 2016. "Tibetan as a Model Language in the Amdo Sprachbund: Evidence from Salar and Wutun." *Journal of South Asian Languages and Linguistics* 3(1): 85–122.

Shakya, Tsering W. 1994. "Politicisation and the Tibetan language." In *Resistance and Reform in Tibet*, edited by R. Barnett and S. Akiner, pp. 157–65. Bloomington, IN: Indiana University Press.

Sman bla skyabs སྨན་བླ་སྐྱབས། 1985. "Sgyu rtsal pa" སྒྱུ་རྩལ་པ། [The Artist]. *Mtsho sngon mang tshogs sgyu rtsal* མཚོ་སྔོན་མང་ཚོགས་སྒྱུ་རྩལ། [Tsongon Folk Art] 1: 70–75.

--. 2023. "The Dream." Trans. Tsering Samdrup. *Yeshe* 3. https://yeshe.org/the-dream/

--. 2024. *Sman bla skyabs kyi bris rtsom gces btus deb phreng kha shgs 'dam sgrug ma* སྨན་བླ་སྐྱབས་ཀྱི་བྲིས་རྩོམ་གཅེས་བཏུས་དེབ་ཕྲེང་། ཁ་ཤགས་འདམ་སྒྲུག་མ། [Collected Writings of Sman bla skyabs Series, Selected Crosstalk]. Lan gru: kan su'u mi rigs dpe skrun khang [Lanzhou: Gansu Minzu Press].

Sørenson, Per K., and Franz Xaver Erhard. 2013a. "An Inquiry into the Nature of Tibetan Proverbs." *Proverbium* 30: 281–309.

---. 2013b. "Tibetan Proverbial Literature: Semantics and Metaphoricity in Context." In *Nepalica-Tibetica Festgabe for Christoph Cüppers*, edited by Franz-Karl Ehrhard and Petra Maurer, pp. 237–52. Andiast: International Institute for Tibetan and Buddhist Studies GmbH.

Sung, Kuo-ming, and Lha byams rgyal. 2005. *Colloquial Amdo Tibetan: A complete Guide of Adult English Speakers*. Beijing: National Press for Tibetan Studies.

Suoci 索次. 2003. Lun Zangyu xiangsheng de lishi he xianzhuang 论藏语相声的历史和现状 [On the History and Current State of Tibetan Language *Xiangsheng*]. *Xizang yishu yanjiu* 西藏艺术研究 [Tibet Arts Research] 2003(3): 12–24.

Suzuki, Hiroyuki, and Yuxia Zou (G.yu 'brug mtsho). 2024. Writing Oral Varieties with the Tibetan Script. A Case Study on Coné Tibetan. Études Mongoles et Sibériennes, Tibétains et Centrasiatiques 55. https://doi.org/10.4000/126ly

Thurston, Timothy. 2012. "An Introduction to Tibetan Sa bstod Speeches in A mdo." *Asian Ethnology* 71(1): 49–73.

---. 2013. "Careful Village's Grassland Dispute: An A mdo Dialect Tibetan Crosstalk Performance by Sman bla skyabs." *CHINOPERL: Journal of Chinese Oral and Performing Literature* 32(2): 156–81. https://doi.org/10.1353/cop.2013.0002

---. 2017. "On Artistic and Cultural Generations in Northeastern Tibet." *Asian Ethnicity* 19(2): 143–62. https://doi.org/10.1080/14631369.2017.1386542

---. 2018a. "A Korean, An Australian, a Nomad, and a Martial Artist Meet on the Tibetan Plateau: Encounters with Foreigners in a Tibetan Comedy from Amdo." *Journal of Folklore Research* 55(3): 1–24. https://doi.org/10.2979/jfolkrese.55.3.01

---. 2018b. "A Careful Village: Comedy and Linguistic Modernity in China's Tibet, ca. 1996." *Journal of Asian Studies* 77(2): 453–74. https://doi.org/10.1017/s0021911817001383

---. 2018c. "The Purist Campaign as Metadiscursive Regime in China's Tibet." *Inner Asia* 20(2): 199–218. https://doi.org/10.1163/22105018-12340107

--. 2019. "An Examination of the Poetics of Tibetan Secular Oratory: An Amdo Tibetan Wedding Speech." *Oral Tradition* 33(1): 23–50.

--. 2025. *Satirical Tibet: The Politics of Humor in Contemporary Amdo*. Seattle, WA: University of Washington Press.

Tournadre, Nicolas. 2003. "The Dynamics of Tibetan-Chinese Bilingualism: The Current Situation and Future Prospects." *China* Perspectives 45. https://doi.org/10.4000/chinaperspectives.231

Tournadre, Nicolas, and Hiroyuki Suzuki. 2023. *The Tibetic Languages: An Introduction to the Family of Languages Derived from Old Tibetan* (Linguistic Diversity 2). Villejuif: LACITO-Publications,

Tribur, Zoe. 2019. "Verbal Morphology of Amdo." Ph.D. Thesis: University of Oregon.

Tsering Samdrup and Hiroyuki Suzuki. 2019. "Humilifics in mabzhi Pastoralist Speech of Amdo Tibetan." *Linguistics of the Tibeto-Burman Area* 42(2): 222–59. https://doi.org/10.1075/ltba.17008.sam

--. 2022. "Politeness strategies, language standardization, and language purism in Amdo Tibetan." In *Language Standardization and Language Variation in Multilingual Contexts: Asian Perspectives*, edited by Nicola McLelland and Hui Zhao, pp. 223–40. Bristol: Multilingual Matters.

Tsering, Rahel. 2016. "Labtse Construction and Differentiation in Rural Amdo." *Revue d'Etudes Tibétaines* 37: 451–68.

Weiner, Benno. 2020. *The Chinese Revolution on the Tibetan Frontier*. Ithaca, NY: Cornell University Press.

Willock, Nicole R. 2021. *Lineages of the Literary: Tibetan Buddhist Polymaths of Socialist China*. New York: Columbia University Press.

Wu, Qi. 2013. "Tradition and Modernity: Cultural Continuum and Transition among Tibetans in Amdo." Ph.D. Thesis: University of Helsinki.

Yeh, Emily T. 2003. "Tibetan Range Wars: Spatial Politics and Authority on the Grasslands," *Development and Change* 34(3): 499–523. https://doi.org/10.1111/1467-7660.00316

1. The Artist སྒྱུ་རྩལ་པ།[1]

A: *Aro*, Jyamtso! What is up with the wrinkles of your forehead reaching the top of your pate?

ཀ ཨ། ཨ་རོ་རྒྱ་མཚོ། ཁྱོའི་ཐོད་པའི་མདུད་པ་
སྤྱད་པའི་དཀྱིལ་ལ་སླེབ་ཐལ་ནོ་ཅི་མ་ཞུན་
ནས།

B: Oh, why wouldn't I? That is called being trapped by aging wrinkles following the arrival of the messenger of old age, *aro*. But looking at you, you are becoming like an empty sack. Is your wife not feeding you or are you worried you won't be able to feed your dependents?

ཁ ཨོ། དེ་ད་ལོ་གི་ཕོ་ཉ་སློན་ནས་རྒས་གི་གཉེར་
མས་བཟུང་ནས་བཟེ་ནོ་དེ་རེད་ཨ་རོ། ང་ཚོ་
ཁག་སྒྱུ། ཁྱོ་ན་ཁྲི་བལྟས་བལྟས་རིག་རིག་ག་
ཁུག་སྟོང་གི་ལོག་ཐལ་ནོ། བུད་མེད་གིས་ཅིག་
མ་བྱུད་ནི་རེད་ལ་བཟའ་ཕྱུག་གི་ཁ་མ་སོས་
སེམས་སྡུག་ཡོད་གོ་ནས།

A: [scoffing] Ha, I am not you. Even though I am thin, I have thrown my thumb-length body into the culture and arts.[2]

ཀ ཧ། ང་ཅང་ཁྱོ་མ་ར། ང་བཙོ་སྐམ་མས་གྱང་
བོང་ན་ར་རྒྱལ་ཁབ་ར་མི་རིགས། རིག་གནས་
ར་སྒྱུ་རྩལ་གི་དོན་ན་ར་ལུས་མཐེ་གང་བོ་
བཙོ་གཡུག་བཏང་བོའི་ཀྱེན་རེད།

---

1 In this performance, A is performed by Menla Jyab, B (identified in the script as "Jyamtso") is voiced by Phagmo Drashi.

2 This is probably a play on the common expression "body of one's arm-length" (རང་ལུས་འདོམ་གང་བོ). Here Menla Jyab takes it to an extreme to indicate that he is small in stature.

B: [interrupting] Hey! Hey! Let me ask you: If you've become like empty intestines for the sake of culture and arts, then you must be good at culture and arts, right?

A: Oh, though I am not a performing artist, when I buck I have more than enough strength to knock you out.

B: You're pathetic. Do not rush to boast. Well then, perform something for me here.

A: Oh, if I relax my body, and put lyrics into a tune, it is usually easy for me to sing songs and perform dances. But *ashirego*, I am a bit busy today.

B: [agreeing] *Yaya*, if you are truly busy, then I will not ask you about difficult things like art and culture, performance and performance styles, the many types of characters to voice, and theory. But I have one or two questions. You will answer my questions, right?

A: Ah, ask away.

B: *Ya*, Well then, when performing plays and films, or any other kind of playful thing, it is common to laugh like *ha ha ho ho*, ... ok then, do a laugh!

1. The Artist

A: [scoffing] Ha, there are many types of laughter. You tell me what sort of person is having what sort of conversation in what sort of situation, and I'll do a laugh for each.

ཀ། ཧ། དགོད་རྒྱུའི་བཟེ་སྣ་ཁ་མང་ནི་རེད། ཁྱོད་ང་སྐབས་ཚེ་མོ་བཞིག་གི་གནས་ཚུལ་འོག་ནས་མི་ཆེ་མོ་བཞིག་གིས་སྐད་ཆ་བཤད་གོ་ནས་དེའི་རྣམ་པ་སྟོན་དུ་ད། ངས་ཁྱི་གཅིག་གཅིག་གཞིས་གཞིས་ཡེད་ལ་དགོད།

B: *Ha*, that's fine. Let me tell you, if a brave young man caught a cowardly enemy after tracking him down, how would he laugh?

ཁ། ཧ། དེ་ཚོགས་གི་ངས་ཁྱི་བཤད། དཔའ་རྩལ་ཅན་གི་གསར་བོད་བཞིག་གིས་སྙིང་མེད་ཅན་གི་དགྲ་བོ་བཞིག་བདའ་ཡས་འཛིན་གོ་རྒྱུ་བཞིག་ག ་དེ་ཆེ་ཡས་དགོད་རྒྱུ་རེད།

A: Oh, for that: "Hahaha, Jyamtso, my archenemy, I will take your head and make it my chamberpot!"

ཀ། ཨོ། དེ་ད་ད་ད་ད། དགྲ་ཆེན་རྒྱ་མཚོ། ངས་ཁྱོད་ཀྱི་མགོ་བླངས་ནས་ཆབ་ཏོ་ཡེད་རྒྱ་ཟེར་གོ

B: What....what did you say to me?

ཁ། ཁྱོས་...་ཁྱོས་ང་ཆེ་བཟེ།

A: I was telling you how I'd laugh. *Ya*, you ask.

ཀ། ངས་ཁྱི་དགོད་སྟོབས་བཤད་གོ་ནས་གོ ཡ་དུ་ཁྱི་དགོས་དྲིས།

B: What about when this enemy pleads for forgiveness?

ཁ། ཨོ་དེ་ན་དགྲ་དན་དེས་ཕྱིར་ར་ཞུ་བ་ཡེད་གོ རྒྱུ་ན།

A: H-hero, please spare my life once. Hehe, don't kill me...hehe, I will give you whatever you want. He would say like this.

ཀ། དཔའ་...་དཔའ་བོ། ཚེ་ཐར་ར་ཅིག་སྟོངས། ཧེ་ཧེ་...ཁྱོས་ང་མ་གསོད་ར་...ཧེ་ཧེ་ཁྱི་ཆེ་བཞིག་དགོ་ན་ངས་ཁྱི་དེ་སྟེར་ཡ། དེ་ཟེར་རྒྱུ་རེད།

B: What about when a person shares an exciting secret with someone?

ཁ། མི་བཞིག་གིས་ཅིག་ག་དགའ་གཏམ་གསང་གཏམ་ཡས་བཤད་གོ་རྒྱུ་ན།

A: For that: "*Aro*, Jyamtso! It's said that no one knew we stole a chicken, I have also heard that...... hehe."

ཀ། ཨོ་དེ་ད། ཨ་རོ་རྒྱ་མཚོ་བཟེ་ཡ། ཉུ་གཉིས་ཀྱས་བྱ་བོ་བཞིག་བརྐུས་ནོ་དེ་ཅང་གི་ར་མ་ཤེས་བཞིག་ཟེར་གི་གོ་ནོ་ཡིན་ན་ད་རུང་བཟོ་ཧེ་ཧེ།

B: You lie! When did I steal a chicken?

ཁ། ཁྱིའི་ཕྱི་གཏམ་ད། ངས་ནམ་བཞིག་ག་བྱ་བོ་བཞིག་བརྐུས་ནས།

A: Heh, I was just telling how one would laugh.

ཀ། ཧེ། ངས་ཁྱི་དགོད་སྟོབས་བཤད་གོ་ནས་བཟེ་ན།

B: [scoffing] Ha, then what if you have understood something?

ཁ། དུ། ཨོ་ན་དོན་དག་བཟིག་གི་ཏུ་གོ་སོང་ཅུ་ན།

A: Oh. One would say, "hehe, Jyamtso, you are such a thief after all. Ya, well, well!"

ག ཨོ། དེ་དེ། རྒྱ་མཚོ་ཁྱོད་དེ་མོ་རྐུན་འཕྲུས་བཟིག་རེད་བཟེ་ར། ཡ། དག་གི་དག་གི་དེ་ཟེར་རྒྱུ་རེད།།

B: If someone saw something funny?

ཁ། སྐྱི་བཟིག་གིས་དགོད་སྒྲུད་ཀྱི་དངོས་པོ་བཟིག་རིག་བཏང་ཅུ་ན།

A: "Hahahaha, aro, Jyamtso! Get over here quick, those two marmots fighting over there are really funny. Come quickly. Hahahaha." That's what they would say.

ག ཧ་ཧ་ཧ་ཧ་ཧ། ཨ་རོ་རྒྱ་མཚོ་བཟེ་ཡ། ཁྱོ་རེམ་མ་འདིར་ཤོག་ར། ཕར་ཀའི་ཕྱི་བ་གཉིས་ཀས་དུང་རེས་ཡེད་གོ་ནོ་བསོ་གི་རེ། རེམ་མ་ཤོག་ར། ཨོ། ཧ་ཧ་ཧ་ཧ། དེ་ཟེར་རྒྱུ་རེད།

B: Then what about when a landlord's lackey tries to give the landlord a suggestion?

ཁ། ཡ། ཨོ་ན་ཞིང་བདག་གི་རྒྱགས་ཁྱི་བཟིག་གིས་ཞིང་བདག་ག་ཐབས་བཟིག་ཞུ་དགོ་ཅུ་ན།

A: "En, hehe, my lord, hehe, this time when we are collecting taxes..." Then he would whisper something in the master's ear.

ག ཨུན་དེ་དེ་... སྐུ་རོ། དེ་དེ།...། དུ་ཐེངས་འདྲུ་བོགས་བསྡུ་གོ་དུས།...། ཟེར་ཞོར་ར་ད་ཞིང་བདག་གི་ན་གི་ནང་ད་ཁ་རོག་ག་བཏད་རྒྱུ་རེད།

B: And if the landlord was very pleased with the suggestion?

ཁ། ཞིང་བདག་ཁོ་ག་ཐབས་དེར་འཧད་ལས་གཞིས་གི་དགའ་བཏང་ཅུ་ན།

A: He would say, "Enen, hehe, haha, impressive, Heh, impressive."

ག ཨུན་ཨུན་... དེ་དེ་... ཧ་ཧ་ཧ་ཧ་... ངར་བ་རེད། ཧི། ངར་བ་རེད། དེ་ཟེར་རྒྱུ་རེད།

B: Ya, that's correct. And what if that lackey looted and plundered, and did all sorts of terrible things to a guttersnipe, and the guttersnipe became desperate?

ཁ། ཡ། དེ་རེད་དེ་རེད། ཡང་རྒྱགས་ཁྱི་དེ་སོང་ངས་དབུལ་པོ་བཟིག་གི་ལག་ནས་འཕྲོག་རྒྱུ་འཕྲོག་གས་བཅོམ་རྒྱུའི་བཅོམ་མས་འགྲོ་འགྲོ་བཟིག་བཅོམ་བཏང་ངས་དབུལ་པོ་དི་ཨུ་ཐུག་སོང་ཅུ་ན།

1. The Artist

A: For that, he would say, "hehehe! You man-eating beast! Kill me, kill me, kill me.... hehe" and come at the lackey.

ཀ དེད། ཧུ་ཧུ་ཧུ་......ཤི་ཤ་གསོན་པོར་ཟ་བོ་གཞེད་མ་ཁྱི། ཁྱོས་ང་སོད། ང་སོད། ང་སོད། ཧུ་ཧུ་ བཟེད་བློག་གཡོར་རྒྱུ་རེད།

B: And then the lackey?

ཁ དེས་ན་རྒྱགས་ཕྲི་དེས།

A: Uh, the lackey would point to those behind him with guns on their shoulders, "Hehe, hit me, if you want to die.[3] Hehe, hit me, hehe!" That's what he'll say.

ཀ ཨེ། རྒྱགས་ཕྲི་དེས་ཁོ་གའི་དཔུང་གི་བོའུ་ཁུར་རིག་ག་བསྟན་ནས། ཧེ་ཧེ། ཁྱོ་དགེ་ཞིང་ང་ཡེབས་ན་འདོད་ན་རྒྱོབ་ཡ་ཧེ་ཧེ་རྒྱོབ་མོ་ཧེ་ཧེ། དེ་ཟེར་རྒྱུ་རེད།

B: Well then, how would a comrade laugh while watching a play in the theatre and seeing one hilarious action after another?

ཁ ཨེ། འོ་ན་གྲོ་མཐུན་བཟིག་གིས་ཁྲོམ་གར་ཁང་ནས་ཅེད་མོ་བལྟ་གོ་དུས་དགོད་སྒྲད་གི་འཛུབ་སྟངས་གཅིག་འཕོར་གཅིག་བྱུད་བཏང་ན་དེ་ཅི་ཡས་དགོད་རྒྱུ་རེད།

A: For that, they would say, "hahaha..." and would laugh until they cried.

ཀ དེད། ཧ་ཧ་ཧ་......བཟེད་ད་ཤིག་རྒྱུ་ཡོང་རགས་གོ་ད་དགོད་རྒྱུ་རེད་ཡ།

B: If they get exhausted from all the laughing?

ཁ བགད་བགད་ལས་ཅད་བཏང་ན།

A: They would say "hahaha... Ayoshe!"

ཀ ཧ་ཧ་ཧ་......ཨ་ཡོ། དེ་ཟེར་རྒྱུ་རེད།

B: Well then, if a drunkard is laughing to himself while stumbling along?

ཁ ཡིན་ན། ཆང་འཐུང་བཟིག་གིས་ཁེར་དགོད་ཡས་འབྱུར་རེ་འབྲོར་རེ་འགྲོ་གོ་རྒྱུ་ན།

A: I'm not drunk, hehe, I'm not drunk, hehe... I'll fight you. I'll fight... urk [retching sound]!

ཀ ང་བཟི་མེད། ཧེ་ཧེ། ང་བཟི་མེད་ཨ། ཧེ། ངས་རྡུང་རེས་ཡིན་ལ་......རྡུང་རེས་ཡེ་......ཨལུ།

B: [dismissively] Heh, that's enough.

ཁ ཧེ། ད་ཆོག་གི

---

3   The lackey literally says "if you want to go to a Pureland," suggesting he will die and reincarnate.

A: What's up?

ཀ   ཡ་ཅི་རེད།

B: Well then, what if someone needs to quickly change a word when they realize they've misspoken.

ཁ   དོ་ན་ཁྱི་བཟིག་གིས་སྟོན་ན་བཤད་ནོ་འཆུག་སོང་ནོ་ཤེས་ཡས་རེས་མ་ཚིག་དེ་བསྒྱུར་དགོ་རྒྱུ་ན།

A: This person would say "A ha ha! I was kidding just now. My wife…" and then he would change topics.

ཀ   ཨ་ཧ་ཧ། ད་གི་དེ་བཟོ་ངས་ཁྱོ་ཞད་དངེད་ནི་ར། དེད་གི་ཨ་ཡེ་གིས་ཟེར་ནོར་ར་ད་དོན་དག་གཞན་པ་བཟིག་གི་ཐོག་ག་སྐྱིད་རྒྱུ་རེད།

B: Oh, that's it! That's it! Aro, speaking of that, how do women laugh?

ཁ   ཨོ་དེ་རེད་དེ་རེད། ཨ་རོ་དེ་བཟེ་ན་ཨ་ཡེ་བཟོ་ཚེ་བཟིག་ཡས་དགོད་ནི་རེད།

A: Uh, tell me what they do when laughing, and I'll tell you.

ཀ   ཨ། ཚེ་བཟིག་ལས་གོ་དུས། ཁྱིས་དགོད་ར་ད་ངས་ཁྱོ་བཤད་རོ།

B: If two women were tickling each other.

ཁ   ཨ་ཡེ་གཉིས་གི་འཛིན་རེས་ཡེད་གོ་རྒྱུ་ན།

A: Alahohoye! Heh, that's enough, that's enough. Heh, that's enough. Un, un.

ཀ   ཨ་ལ་ཧོ་ཧོ་ཡེ། ཧེ་…ད་ཚོག་གི་ད་ཚོག་གི་ཧེ་…ད་ཚོག་གི་ད་…ཨུན་ཨུན།

B: Aro, what was wrong with her?

ཁ   ཨ་རོ། དེར་ཚེ་བཟིག་མ་ཐུན་ཐལ།

A: Oh, she was saying she was in pain.

ཀ   ཨོ། སྦེ་གིས་ཨ་ཡོ་བཚོས་བཏང་ཐལ་ཟེར་གོ་ནི་མིན་ནས།

B: Oh, she wants to cry then. Today if your wife and children were here, they would fear that you have a heart problem and have heart attacks.

ཁ   ཨོ། ད་དེ་འདེབས་ན་འདོད་གོ་ནི་རེད་ལ། དེ་རིང་ཁྱོའི་བུད་མྱེད་ར་ཕྱིས་པ་ཚོ་ཡོད་རྒྱུ་ན་ཁྱོ་སྙིང་ནད་བྱུང་བཏང་བཟིག་འདོད་ལས་སྙིང་གད་རྒྱ་རེད་ཡ།

A: If they fear, it's probably because they were amazed that I had such acting skill.

ཀ   སྙིང་འགད་གོ་དུས་ད་འབབ་སྟོན་གི་རྩལ་ཡོད་རྒྱོའི་མང་སོང་ངས་ཡ་མཚར་སོང་ནི་ཡིན་རྒྱོའི་རེད།

1. The Artist

B: Well, I don't know if you have skills, but it's certain that you are unhinged.

A: You don't know. Appearing unhinged is the inherent characteristic of an artist.

B: Oh, that's possible. What artist can't lift a satchel?[4]

A: Though I'm not a pundit of performing arts, when compared with you why wouldn't I, a crow of the forest become a *garuda*, and a skunk on the grassland become a tiger.[5]

B: *Yayaya*. I'm not arguing with you. Let's say that you are an artist. I still have a question for you: since you're an artist, aren't you fluent with folk music, modern music, and dancing?

A: Of course I am.

B: Well then, you'll sing, right?

---

4   This appears to be playing on the similar pronunciations of the first syllable in the words "artist" (སྒྱུ་རྩལ་པ།) pronounced *jyutselpa* and "sack" (སྒྱེ་མོ།) pronounced *jyemo* and translated here as "satchel").

5   This plays on a sort of proverbial phrase, comparing the speaker first to the less auspicious animals "crow" and "skunk," and then to greater animals in the same category (bird and mammal respectively) of *garuda* and tiger. Thus the speaker becomes great in comparison to his partner. Traditionally, it is used to sarcastically scold someone who tries to make themselves seem more important around inferiors.

A: *Aha*,[6] both the turquoise dragon of the south and I, and the northern cuckoo too, who told you that we three keep silent?

ཀ ཨ་ཧ། བྲོ་གཡུ་འབྲུག་ར་དེད་གཉིས་ཀ བྱང་ཁུ་བྱུག་ར་དེད་གསུམ་པོ་ཁ་རོག་ག་འདུག་གི་བཟེ་བྱི་སུས་བཤད་གི

B: Ok, ok! Enough, enough. Then sing a song.

ཁ ཡ་ཡ། ད་ཆོག་གི་ཆོག་གི་ དོ་ན་ཁྱོས་གླུ་དབྱངས་བཞིག་ལོངས་ར།

A: Singing songs is easy. You listen and I'll sing for you. [clearing throat] *Un, un.*
   I am not giving you breakfast,
   I am not giving you lunch,
   I am not giving you dinner
   without having food and drink.
   you starve to death!
It's your fault. *Soyalaso*.[7] It's all your fault.

ཀ གླུ་དབྱངས་ལེན་རྒྱུ་ལོ་བཟོ་སྟབ་ནི་རེད། ཁྱོས་ཉོན་ར་ངས་ཁྱོ་ལེན། ཤུན་ཤུན།
   ཞོགས་ཇ་སྤྲད་རྒྱུ་མིན་ཡ།
   གུང་ཇ་སྤྲད་རྒྱུ་མིན་ཡ།
   དགོང་ཇ་སྤྲད་རྒྱུ་མིན།
   ཟ་རྒྱུ་འཐུང་རྒྱུ་མེད་ལ།
   ལྟོགས་གས་ཤི་འགྲོ་ན་ར།
   ཁྱེད་རང་རང་གི་སྐྱུག་གྱོང་རེད། སོ་ཡ་ལ་སོ། ཁྱེད་རང་གི་སྐྱུག་གྱོང་རེད།

B: [scoffing] Heh! What was that? I've never heard a "song" like that before!

ཁ ཧེ། ཁྱོའི་དེ་བཟོ་ཆེ་བཞིག་ཡིན་ནས། ངས་དེ་མོ་གླུ་དབྱངས་བཞིག་ཟོ་གོ་ར་མ་མྱོང་གོ

A: [dismissively] *Aha*! Not only don't you know how to sing, you also don't know how to listen. Ok, I'll sing you another. Listen.

ཀ ཨ་ཧ། ཁྱོས་ད་ལེན་ད་ཆེ་ཤེས་ར་ཉན་ར་མི་ཤེས་གི་ཡ། ཡ་ཡ། ངས་ཁྱོ་གཞན་པ་བཞིག་ལེན། ཁྱོས་ཉོན་གོ

B: Ok.

ཁ ཡ།

A: If I kill Jyamtso it must be tonight.[8]

ཀ རྒྱ་མཚོ་གསོད་ན་དེ་དགོང་ལ་བསྟུན་དགོ

---

6   *Aha* is used here to make a strong assertion, meaning something along the lines of, "of course."

7   *Soyalaso* is a commonly used set of vocables in Tibetan songs. It is also frequently used to index Tibetanness in Chinese language songs.

8   This plays with the lyrics of a Revolutionary song, "Sailing the Seas Depends on the Helmsman" (རྒྱ་མཚོར་བསྐྱོད་ན་དེད་དཔོན་ལ་བསྟེན་དགོ ས།), where the character's name Jyamtso literally translates as "seas."

B: Ok! Enough. enough. Don't you have anything else to tell and sing about beyond me dying and killing me?

|ཁ ཡད་ཚོག་གི་ཚོག་གི་ཁྱོད་ད་ཉེ་རྒྱུ་བཟིག་རང་གསོད་རྒྱུ་བཟིག་མེན་ན་ད་བཤད་རྒྱུ་བཟིག་ར་ལེན་རྒྱུ་བཟིག་མེད་ནི་ཨེ་རེད།

A: You have a lot to say. Whatever, I will sing one more song.
I am a soldier, fully armed.
If the enemy approaches, I'll dislocate his cheek.[9]

|ག ཁྱོ་འདིར་བཤད་རྒྱུ་བཟིག་མང་གི་ར་གོ་ཡ་ད་ཆེ་བཟིག་ཡིན་ན་ཡིན་གི་རྐྱགས། དས་ཁྱོ་ད་དྲུང་གཅིག་ཡིན་ན་བདུད། ང་ནི་དམག་བཟིག་ཡིན། དག་ཆས་སྤྲས་ནས་ཡོད། ཕྱི་དག་ཙིབ་བ་བཏུད་ན་འགུམ་པ་སྒྲོ་ཡས་རྟོགས།

B: [interrupting] Ok, enough. I don't know what that was. How about you sing me something easy to understand in everyday life instead.

|ག ཡ། ད་རེད་རེད། ཁྱོའི་དི་བཟོ་ཆེ་བཟིག་ཡིན་ནི་ན་ར་མི་ཤེས་གི། དེར་བསྱས་ན་ཁྱོས་ང་འཚོ་བའི་ནང་གི་གོ་བདེ་ནི་བཟིག་ལོངས་ད་ཐོངས།

A: Tell me what kind of song you'd like.

|ག ཁྱོ་སྒྱུ་ཆེ་མོ་བཟིག་དགོ་ནི་བཟེ་ཨོ།

B: Uh, you'd know how to sing a lullaby, right?

|ཁ ཨི། ན་ཡས་བསྐྱལ་གོ་དུས་གི་སྒྱུ་ཁྱོས་ལེན་ཤེས་ནི་རེད་ལ།

A: Oh, the song to make children stop crying and sleep, that one?

|ག ཨོ། ན་ཡས་དུས་བཏང་ན་དུ་ཁ་སྣངས་ནས་གཉིད་ལ་འགྱག་སྱུད་གོ་དི་ཡིན།

B: *Olé olé*, I mean that.

|ཁ ཨོ་ལེ་ཨོ་ལེ། དི་བཟེ་ནས།

---

9 Again, he is playing with a revolutionary song, very likely this one: https://baike.baidu.com/item/%E6%88%91%E6%98%AF%E4%B8%80%E4%B8%AA%E5%85%B5/4644
https://baike.baidu.com/item/%E5%A4%A7%E6%B5%B7%E8%88%AA%E8%A1%8C%E9%9D%A0%E8%88%B5%E6%89%8B/4423362

A: Oh, when children cry, you can sing like this and then they will fall asleep.
> Ah Ah! Don't cry, dear, go to sleep.
> Go to sleep and I'll give you a horse.
> And I'll give you a saddle atop the horse.
> And I'll give you reins covered with silk
> Baby, don't cry, go to sleep
> When the daughter-in-law comes, I'll give you a conch shell[10]
> Give you a conch shell with silk decorations
> When the merchant comes, I'll give you a *mdzo*.[11]
> Give you a *mdzo* with a load on its back.
> Baby, protected by heaven
> Don't cry and sleep quickly
> Oh, baby, don't cry and sleep!
> I'll butcher a mottled billy goat and give it to you.
> And give you its kidneys rolled in fat
> Catch stars in sky and give them to you
> Pluck flowers on the ground and give them to you
> If you still cry, then I'll punch you
> I'll twist your neck if you cry more
> This karma of mine![12] You still want to cry? Cry more, cry more……

---

10 *Wagma* བག་མ་ usually is used for a bride but may also be used by parents-in-law to refer to their daughter-in-law. This seems to be sung from the perspective of a child's grandparents, saying that when the child's mother comes, she will give these things to the child.
11 A yak-cow hybrid.
12 This is a common way of sighing and complaining in Amdo.

B: [as if in pain] Ow! My head can't take that much hitting, *aro*.

ཁ༽ ཨ། དེ་ར་བཤིག་བཟོ་ད་དབེ་བཟོའི་མགོ་གི་ར་མི་བ་གི་གོ། ཨ་རོ།

A: [as if suddenly realizing] Oh, but you are not the child.

ཀ༽ ཨོ་ཁྱོ་ཞ་ཡས་ཡིན་ནི་མ་རེད་ལོ།

A and B: Ha ha ha

ཀ༽ ཁ༽ ཧ་ཧ་ཧ།

2. Boasting ལབ་རྒྱག་པ།[1]

A: Since this snowy land of Tibet is not only an ocean of songs and dance, but also a Pureland of research, if you live here you should research both the positive and the negative things. And in particular, we must research about the negative things.

ཀ བོད་གངས་ཅན་གྱི་ཡུལ་འདི། གླུ་གར་གྱི་རྒྱ་མཚོ་བཞིག་ཡིན་ནས་མི་ཚད། དུད་ཞིབ་འཇུག་གི་ཞིང་ཁམས་བཞིག་ཡིན་བོའི་སྐབས་གྱི་ཡུལ་འདི་ནས་བསྡད་ན་བཟང་ངན་གཉིས་ཀ་ཞིབ་འཇུག་ཡེད་དགོ་ནི་རེད། དེའི་ནང་ནས་ར་ངན་པ་གི་སྐོར་ར་ཞིབ་འཇུག་ཡེད་དགོ་ནི་རེད་ཡ།

B: I haven't heard that before, *aro*.

ཁ གོ་ར་མ་མྱོང་། ཨ་རོ།

A: There are many benefits to researching negative things.

ཀ ངན་པར་ཞིབ་འཇུག་ཡས་ན་ཕན་པ་མང་ནི་རེད།

B: I don't buy it.

ཁ ཆར་མི་འགྲོ་གི

A: You can gain a lot from studying negative things.

ཀ ངན་པ་ཞིབ་འཇུག་ཡས་ན་གྱུབ་འབྲས་ཐོབ་ནི་རེད།

B: What can you gain from studying negative things?

ཁ ངན་པ་ཞིབ་འཇུག་ཡས་གྱུབ་འབྲས་ཅི་བཞིག་ཐོབ་ནི་རེད་ཁོ།

A: That is, when we truthfully tell the negative behaviours, even a fool's brain can turn on.

ཀ དེ་ད། ངན་པའི་སྤྱོད་པ་བདེན་པ་ཡས་གཅིག་བརྗོད་ན་ད། བླེན་པ་གི་ཀླད་པ་ར་འཁོར་རྒྱུ་བཞིག་ཡོད་ནི་རེད་ཡ།

---

[1] In the recordings, A is performed by Menla Jyab.

B: Oh, now I understand. You are going to make fun of the ones who lie and boast.

A: *Olé*, it goes without saying. My goal is to poke boasters and liars with needles and awls, and to make people who are guilty of it jump at every word I say.

B: Okay, that's right. That's right. Well then, I agree to boasting and lying.

A: Okay, if you agree then let's begin.

B: Huh? Wh..who should begin?

A: You should start.

B: Really? Shall we boast first or lie first?

A: It's one and the same. Boast and we will be lying anyways.

B: That's right. That's right. Um, I will boast then.

A: Do it, do it!

B: Um, I, um, I......

A: Well, be quick!

B: Umm, I-, I'm not boasting, boy, but I......

2. Boasting

A: What do you mean "not boasting"? I told you to boast!

ཀ། ལབ་བརྒྱབ་ནི་མིན་བདོག་གོ་ཁྱོ་ལབ་རྒྱུང་བཞེ་ནི་ཡ།

B: Uh. [with self-reproach] Heh. I have never boasted before, so I don't know how to boast.

ཁ། ཨ། ཧེ། ད་དས་ལ་བརྒྱབ་མ་མྱོང་ནི་ཁོའུ་གི་དས་ལབ་ཆེ་ཡས་རྒྱག་དགོ་ནི་མི་ཤེས་ཨོ།

A: Boast! Boast! Don't be polite. I know you are excellent at boasting.

ཀ། ལབ་རྒྱོབས། ལབ་རྒྱོབས། ད་ཁྱོས་རྟ་མ་ཡེད་དོ་ཁྱོ་ལབ་བརྒྱབ་བས་བྱད་ལས་བསྡད་ཡོད་ནོ་དས་ཤེས་ནི་རེད།

B: Yep, that's true, but I'm no match for you. You are famous for boasting.

ཁ། ཡུན། དི་བདེན་ད། ཁྱོ་འགྱུན་ནི་མ་རེད་ཡ། ཁྱོ་ལབ་བརྒྱབ་བས་གྱིང་ང་གྱགས་གས་བསྡད་ཡོད་ནོ་རེད་མོ།

A: How can I compete with you? You are a box of boasts, and a bag of lies.

ཀ། ང་ཁྱོ་ཆེ་འགྱུན་བཞེ་ར། ཁྱོ་སྟེ་ལབ་གི་སྒམ་ཆུད། གསོབ་གི་རྒྱལ་བ་རེད་མོ།

B: I can't compete with you. You are one who was scolded by people up there and cursed by people down there.

ཁ། ང་ཁྱོ་འགྱུན་ནི་མ་རེད། ཁྱོ་སྟེ་ཡར་གི་ཤྲིགས་ཤོ། མར་གི་དམོད་ཤོའི་རེད།

A: Even so, how could I compete with you? You are a rumour mill, and a driver of feuds.

ཀ། དི་ཡིན་རུང་ད། ང་ཁྱོ་ཆེ་འགྱུན་བཞེ་ར། ཁྱོ་སྟེ་མཁན་གི་འཁོར་ལོ། ཁྱོད་གི་སྤ་འདྲེན་རེད་མོ།

B: I can't compete with you, you are an axe that destroys what's without and a hatchet that destroys what's within.[2]

ཁ། ང་ཁྱོ་མི་འགྱུན་ན། ཁྱོ་ཕྱི་བཤིག་གི་སྟ་རེ་ར། ནང་བཤིག་གི་སྟེའུ་རེད་མོ།

A: I can't compete with you. You are an evil spirit to your village, and a disaster-causing demon to your family.

ཀ། ང་ཁྱོ་འགྱུན་ནི་མ་རེད་ཡ། ཁྱོ་སྟེ་སྡེ་བ་གི་གདོན་འདྲེ་ར། ཁྱིམ་ཚང་གི་འཕྱུང་འདྲེ་རེད།

---

2   "Without" means "external to the community," and "within" refers to one's family and the community.

B: Even so, I'm still no match for you, *aro*! You are a burden to the country and a yoke on the people.

ཁ། དེ་ཡིན་ན་ར། ང་ཁྱོ་མི་འགྱུན་གྱི་ཨ་རོ། ཁྱོ་སླ་རྒྱལ་ཁབ་གྱི་ཁུར་རོ་ར། མི་དམངས་གྱི་གདོས་རོ་རེད་མོ།

A: How can I compete with you? You are your family's leader, and a hero to your mother.[3]

ག ང་ཁྱོ་ཆེ་འགྱུན་བཟེ་ར། ཁྱོ་སླ་ཁྱིམ་ཚང་གི་དཔོན་པོ་ར། ཨ་མའི་མགོ་གི་དཔའ་པོ་རེད་ཡ།

B: [dismissively] Hehe. I'm not competing with you, *aro*. You are the only one with learning, you even know how to write your own name! You do!

ཁ། ཧེ། ཧེ། ང་ཁྱོ་མི་འགྱུན་གྱི་ཨ་རོ། ཁྱོ་སླ་ཡོན་ཏན་ཅན་ཁེར་མོ་རེད་མོ། རང་གི་མིང་ར་འབྲི་ཤེས་གི་མོ་ཁྱོས།

A: How can I compete with you? As far as letters you completely... you've got the Tibetan alphabet down pat.

ག ང་ཁྱོ་ཆེ་འགྱུན་བཟེ་ར། ཡི་གེ་བཤད་ན་ད་བབ་གི་ཁྱོ་སླ་ཀ་ཁ་སུམ་ཅུ་བོ་ཐོགས་རྒྱ་མེད་ནོ།

B: I can't compete with you. You write and write and add extras to the thirty letters.

ཁ། ང་ཁྱོ་མི་འགྱུན་གྱི་ཁྱོ་སླ་བྲིས་གི་བྲིས་གི་ཀ་ཁ་སུམ་ཅུ་བོ་བཟོ་ལྷག་ག་བྱུད་འཛོག་ནོ།

A: Huh! How can I compete with you though. When you write the letter *ka* (ཀ) you write it with four legs![4]

ག ཇུ། ང་ཁྱོ་ཆེ་འགྱུན་བཟེ་ར། ཁྱོས་ཀ་བྲིས་ན་ཀང་བ་བཞི་བཟོ་ཡོད་ནོ།

B: I'm not competing with you, *aro*! When you write Tibetan, you don't even need a *tseg* (་)![5]

ཁ། ང་ཁྱོ་མི་འགྱུན་གྱི་ཨ་རོ། ཁྱོས་སླ་བོད་ཡིག་བྲིས་ན་ཚེག་མི་དགོ་མོ།

---

3   This is probably a sarcastic statement suggesting that "B" abuses his family.
4   The syllable *ka* has three vertical lines. Adding a fourth suggests that the speaker's writing is poor.
5   This is the dot that separates syllables. The implication is that he cannot even write multisyllable words.

2. Boasting

A: How can I compete with you? You can cut the leg off of *da* (ད) and put it under *tha* (ཐ).[6]

ཀ ང་ཁྱོད་ཆེ་འགྲན་བཟེ་ན། ཁྱོས་སྟེ་ད་གི་སུག་རྟ་
བཅད་ལམ་ཐ་གི་ཞབས་ལ་འཐེན་ན་ཆོག་གོ

B: I am not competing with you, *aro*! You can write *zha* (ཞ) backwards.

ཁ ང་ཁྱོ་མི་འགྲན་གི་ཨ་རོ། ཁྱོས་ཞ་གི་ཁ་ཕྱིར་ར་
བསྐོར་རས་བྲིས་ན་ཆོག་གོ།

A: How can I compete with you? You can turn *nya* (ཉ) on its end and make it lie down.[7]

ཀ ང་ཁྱོད་ཆེ་འགྲན་བཟེ་ར། ཁྱོས་སྟེ་ཉ་གི་ཁ་ཕྱུར་
ར་བསྐོར་རས་ཉལ་གི་བཞག་ན་ཆོག་གོ།

B: Hehe, *ala*, I can't compete with you, *aro*. You know that two plus one is three.

ཁ ཧེ། ཧེ། ཨ་ལ། ང་ཁྱོ་མི་འགྲན་གི་ཨ་རོ། ཁྱོས་
སྟེ་གཅིག་གི་ཁ་གཉིས་བསྣན་ན་གསུམ་ཡིན་
ནོ་ཤེས་གི་མོ།

A: How can I compete with you? You know that one take away zero is zero!

ཀ ང་ཁྱོད་ཆེ་འགྲན་བཟེ་ར། ཁྱོས་སྟེ་གཅིག་གི་ཁ་
ནས་སྟོག་འཐེན་ན་སྟོག་ཡིན་ནོ་ཤེས་གི་མོ།

B: I'm no match for you. You know zero times zero makes two!

ཁ ང་ཁྱོ་མི་འགྲན་གི་ཁྱོས་སྟེ་སྟོག་སྟོག་ག་བསྒྱུར་
ན་གཉིས་ཡིན་ནོ་ཤེས་གི་མོ།

A: How can I compete with you? You know that five divided by two is four.

ཀ ང་ཁྱོད་ཆེ་འགྲན་བཟེ་ར། ཁྱོས་སྟེ་ལྔ་གཉིས་ལ་
བགོས་ན་བཞི་ཐེམ་ནོ་ཤེས་གི་མོ།

B: I'm no match for you, you are the bravest one out there.

ཁ ང་ཁྱོ་མི་འགྲན་གི་ཁྱོ་སྟེ་དཔའ་བོ་ཡོད་ལ་མེད་
ལ་བོ་རེད།

A: Haha, if we're discussing bravery, how can I compete with you? You are the one who drops his gun when you see an enemy.

ཀ ཧ། ཧ། དཔའ་སྦྱོལ་བཤད་ན་ད། ང་ཁྱོད་ཆེ་འགྲན་
བཟེ་ར། ཁྱོ་སྟེ་དགྲ་རིག་ན་བོའུ་ཧུད་འཇོག་ནོ་
རེད་མོ།

---

6   The Tibetan *da* (ད) has a long line trailing down the right of side of the glyph. *Tha* (ཐ), the syllable that immediately precedes it in the Tibetan syllabary, by contrast does has no such "leg." The speaker is thus suggesting his partner's illiteracy by being unable even to write these two basic glyphs correctly.

7   Here the speaker plays on the similar pronunciations of the consonant *nya* (ཉ) and the verb *nyal* (ཉལ) "to lie down" or "to sleep."

B: I'm also not brave like you, *aro*! You are the one who cries for his mommy when he sees a nanny [goat].

|ང་ར་ཁྱོད་འདྲ་བཟིག་མི་དཔའ་གི་ཨ་རོ། ཁྱི་སྤྲེ་ར་མ་རིག་ན་ཨ་མ་འབོད་ནོ་རེད་མོ།

A: How can I compete with you? You are the one who brings your pops when you go for a poo.

ག ང་ཁྱི་ཆེ་འགྱུན་བཟེ་ན། ཁྱི་སྤྲེ་སྐྱུག་པ་གཏོང་སར་ཨ་པ་འཁྲིད་ནོ་རེད་མོ།

B: Huh? I can't compete with you. You know where your dad keeps his tobacco bag and where your mother keeps her money.[8]

|ཨེ། ང་ཁྱི་མི་འགྱུན་གི་ཁྱིས་སྤྲེ་ཨ་པའི་དུད་ཁུག་སྡུད་ས་བོ་ར། ཨ་མའི་སྒོར་མོ་སྡུད་ས་བོ་མི་འཁྲུག་ནོ།

A: I can't compete with you *aro*. You cannot be stopped by the walls and locks of your neighbors.

ག ང་ཁྱི་ཆེ་འགྱུན་བཟེ་ན། ཁྱི་སྤྲེ་ཁྱིམ་མཚེས་གི་གྱང་ར་སྒོ་ཁ་གི་ཟུ་གིས་ར་མི་ཐོག་ནོ།

B: I'm no match for you, *aro*. You see the money in someone's pocket before you even see their face.

|ང་ཁྱི་མི་འགྱུན་གི་ཨ་རོ། ཁྱིས་སྤྲེ་ཉི་གི་དོ་མ་རིག་གོང་ང་། རྫས་གི་སློང་མོ་རིག་བསྡད་ཡོད་མོ།

A: How can I compete with you? Your hands arrive before your body does.[9]

ག ང་ཁྱི་ཆེ་འགྱུན་བཟེ་ར། ཁྱི་སྤྲེ་སྒྲིའི་ལུས་མ་སློན་གོང་ང་ཡིན་ན། ལག་པ་སློན་ནས་བསྡད་ཡོད་ནོ།

B: Uh, I can't compete with you; you are the most beautiful person.

|ཨེ། ང་ཁྱི་མི་འགྱུན་གི་ཁྱི་སྤྲེ་ཡག་པ་བོ་ཤེར་མོ་རེད་མོ།

A: How can I compete with you? You are the cleanest person.

ག ང་ཁྱི་ཆེ་འགྱུན་བཟེ་ར། ཁྱི་སྤྲེ་གཙང་མ་བོ་རེད་མོ།

B: I can't compete with you; you are the one who wears a flower-patterned shirt.

|ང་ཁྱི་མི་འགྱུན་གི་ཁྱི་སྤྲེ་སྟོད་ཅེ་མེ་ཏོག་ཅན་པོ་གོན་ནོ་རེད་མོ།

---

8   This suggests that "A" steals from his parents.
9   Suggesting that "B" is always asking for or stealing money.

2. Boasting

A: How can I compete with you? You are the one who wears bell-bottoms.

B: I can't compete with you; you are the one who wears flat caps.[10]

A: How can I compete with you? You are one who wears pointy red shoes.[11]

B: I can't compete with you, *aro*; you are the owner of stinky feet and companion with the smell of alcohol.

A: How can I compete with you? You are sworn-brothers with pigs and bedfellows with lice.

B: [with husky laughter] Hehe. I can't compete with you. When you're at home, you're a fool, and when you go out, you're a bandit.

A: How can I compete with you? From the outside, you look like a foreign woman, and on the inside, you are a goat of your own country.[12]

B: I can't compete with you. You, uh, you... Wait. Wait. You and I. What were you saying about me, that from the outside I look like a foreign woman and from the inside I am a local goat?

ཀ ང་ཁྱོད་ཆེ་འགྱུན་བཟེ་ན། ཁྱོ་སྟེ་ཀང་སྨམ་དུང་ཅེན་ཁ་གོན་ནོ་རེད་མོ།

ཁ ང་ཁྱོ་མི་འགྱུན་གི་ཁྱོས་སྟེ་ཞུ་སྨ་འབུར་གོན་ནས་བསྟུད་ཡོད་ནོ།

ཀ ང་ཁྱོད་ཆེ་འགྱུན་བཟེ་ན། ཁྱོ་སྟེ་ལྷམ་དམར་མདུང་གོན་ནོ་རེད་མོ།

ཁ ང་ཁྱོ་མི་འགྱུན་གི་ཨ་རོ། ཁྱོ་སྟེ་ཀང་རུལ་གི་བདག་པོ་ར། ཆང་ཏི་གི་འགྲོ་རོགས་རེད་མོ།

ཀ ང་ཁྱོད་ཆེ་འགྱུན་བཟེ་ར། ཁྱོ་སྟེ་ཕག་གི་མནའ་བཅད་ར། ཤིག་གི་ཉལ་རོགས་རེད་མོ།

ཁ ཧུ། ཧུ། ང་ཁྱོ་མི་འགྱུན་ན། ཁྱོ་སྟེ་ཡུལ་ན་བསྡད་ཡོད་དུས་སྒྱུག་དུ་ར། ཕྱང་ད་བུད་བདང་ན་རྐུ་པ་རེད་མོ།

ཀ ང་ཁྱོད་ཆེ་འགྱུན་བཟེ་ན། ཁྱོ་སྟེ་ཕྱི་ནས་བལྟས་ན་ཕྱི་རྒྱལ་གི་འགྱལ་མོ་ར། ནང་ནས་བལྟས་ན་རང་རྒྱལ་གི་ར་མ་རེད་མོ།

ཁ ང་ཁྱོ་མི་འགྱུན་ན། ཁྱོ་སྟེ། ཨེ། ཁྱོ། ཁྱོ་སྡོད། སྡོད། ཁྱོས་ད་ད། ཁྱོ་སྟེ་ཕྱི་ནས་བལྟས་ན་ཕྱི་རྒྱལ་གི་འགྱལ་མོ་ར། ནང་ནས་བལྟས་ན་རང་རྒྱལ་གི་ར་མ་བཟེ་ནོ། དེ་ཁྱོས་ང་ཆེ་བཟེ་ནས།

---

10   This style of hat, like a Yorkshire flat cap, was fashionable in Amdo in the 1980s and 1990s.
11   These hats and shoes were popular with Tibetans at this time. The pointy red shoes with heels were worn by both men and women at this time.
12   Meaning that the person only appears modern.

A: Oh, I will tell you. That is, in the past, you looked like it when you wore the hat tilted, dangling a cigarette from your mouth, swaggering, boasting, lying, tricking, robbing, drinking, and stealing.

B: Um, that's... That's a dead issue.

A: Hehe. That's right. That's right. We were boasting and forgot to lie.

B: We wouldn't forget. Now boast on. Now lie on.

A: Who's first?

B: Let's start with you this time.

A: Start with me?

B: Uh-huh.

A: Ok. What's difficult about boasting and lying? When I open my mouth, I talk about the origins of the universe. When I shut my eyes, I know the creation and destruction of the universe. Do you think it would be difficult for me to boast and lie?

B: [dismissively] Huh, you're nothing special compared to me.

A: Ah?

2. Boasting

B: When I am unhappy, I bind the sun and moon under oath. When I am angry, I topple Yama from his throne.

ཁ ངས་ཁམས་མ་དངས་ན། ཉི་ཟླ་དམ་མ་འདོགས་ག ཁགས་ཁོས་བཏང་ན་གཤིན་རྗེ་ཁྲི་ལས་འཕབ་བ།

A: It's as if you're not human.

ག ཁྱོ་སྨྱི་བཟིག་མིན་ས་ཡོད་ག

B: If you boast, you have to do it like that.

ཁ ལབ་རྒྱག་ན་དེ་ཡས་རྒྱག་དགོ་ནི་རེད།

A: Yep! Boast like that yourself!

ག ཡ། ཡ། རང་གི་དེ་ཡས་ལབ་སྐྱོན།

B: *Olé*. If you tell me run to the paths of the death, I would. If you tell me to hit my father's head, I would.[13]

ཁ ཨོ་ལེ། ང་རྒྱགས་ཟེར་ན་གཤིན་རྗེའི་འཕྲང་ང་རྒྱག་ག རྐྱོབ་ཟེར་ན་ངས་ཨ་པའི་མགོ་ར་རྒྱག་ག

A: *Aro, aro*! There's no boast like that. *Wei*!

ག ཨ་རོ། ཨ་རོ། དེ་མོ་ལབ་བཟིག་ར་ཡོད་ནི་ཨེ་རེད། སེ།

B: If there isn't, I'll boast again: there's no one so learned as me.

ཁ དེ་མོ་བཟིག་མེད་ན། ངས་འོར་གི་ལབ་རྒྱག་ང་འདུ་འདུའི་ཡོན་ཏན་ཅན་བཟིག་མེད།

A: How so?

ག ཅི་མོ་ཡིན།

B: I'm fluent in the *Sum*, *Htag*, and *Dag*.[14]

ཁ ང་སུམ་རྟགས་དག་གསུམ་པོ་ཐོགས་རྒྱུ་མེད།

A: You can't compete with me!

ག ང་མི་འགྲན་གོ

B: Yeah?

ཁ ཡ།

A: I am not only fluent in them, I am fluent in poetry, history, and debate.

ག ང་དེ་གསུམ་པོ་དུ་ཆེ་ཐོགས་ར། སྙན་དག་ལོ་རྒྱུས་བསྡུས་གྲྭ་གསུམ་པོ་ཐོགས་རྒྱུ་མེད།

---

13 This plays with a well-known *tamhwé* and suggests that the speaker is obedient.
14 This refers to three major grammatical treatises for the Tibetan language: the *sumchupa* (སུམ་ཅུ་པ), the *htagjug* (རྟགས་འཇུག) and the *dagyig* (དག་ཡིག). These three are often said together.

B: Right. I am fluent in the five greater and lesser sciences.[15] Between us, I'm better.

ཁ། ཨོ་ཡ། ང་རིག་གནས་ཆེ་བ་ལྔ་ར། ཆུང་ང་ལྔ་ ཕོགས་རྒྱུ་མེད། ཉུ་གཉིས་གའི་ང་དར་གི

A: I'm better! Not only am I perfect at all of Tibetan culture, but I have also mastered Chinese script.

ཀ། ང་དར་གི ང་བོད་གི་རིག་གནས་ཡོད་ཚད་པོ་ བྱང་ནས་མི་ཚད། རྒྱ་ཡིག་གཱ་ར་ཕོགས་རྒྱུ་མེད།

B: Maybe so, but I'm stronger. Not only do I have perfect Chinese, I've mastered foreign scripts, too.

ཁ། དེ་ཡིན་ན་ར། ང་དར་གི ང་རྒྱ་ཡིག་གཱ་བྱང་ ནས་མི་ཚད། ཕྱི་ཡིག་གཱ་ར་ཕོགས་རྒྱུ་མེད།

A: I am stronger. I, uh, what country's script do you know?

ཀ། ང་དར་གི ད། ཨེ། ཁྱོད་རྒྱལ་ཁབ་གང་གི་ཡི་ གེ་ཤེས།

B: I know Indian script.

ཁ། ངས་རྒྱ་གར་གི་ཡི་གེ་ཤེས།

A: You can't compete with me. I know Burma's script. Ya, you torma-like one![16]

ཀ། ཁྱོང་མི་འགྲན་གི ངས་འབར་མ་རྒྱལ་ཁབ་ གི་ཡི་གེ་ཤེས་ཡ། ཡ། ཨ་གཏོར་མ་བཟིག་འདུ་ འདུ་བོ།

B: Hey, you can't compete with me! I know French script. Ah! Lutor like one.[17]

ཁ། ང་མི་འགྲན་གི་ཨ་རོ། ངས་ཕྲ་རན་སི་གི་ཡི་གེ་ ཤེས་ཡ། ཨ་གླུ་གཏོར་བཟིག་འདུ་འདུ་བོ།

A: You aren't competing with me. I know English script. How's that, boy?

ཀ། ཁྱོང་མི་འགྲན་གི ངས་དབྱིན་ཇི་རྒྱལ་ཁབ་གི་ ཡི་གེ་ཤེས་ཡ། ཅི་མོ་རེད། ཞི་ཡི།

B: Hoya! I know it even without studying it.

ཁ། ཧོ་ཡ། ངས་དེ་བཟོ་མ་བསླབ་ན་ར་ཤེས་གི་ཡ།

---

15 In Tibetan tradition, there are five greater and five lesser sciences. Five greater sciences are craftsmanship (Tib. བཟོ་རིག་པ།), logic (Tib. གཏན་ཚིགས་རིག་པ།), grammar (Tib. སྒྲ་རིག་པ།), medicine (Tib. གསོ་བ་རིག་པ།), Dharma or "inner science" (Tib. ནང་དོན་རིག་པ།), and five lesser sciences are synonyms (Tib. མངོན་བརྗོད།), mathematics and astrology (Tib. སྐར་རྩིས།), drama (Tib. ཟློས་གར།), poetry (Tib. སྙན་ངག), composition (Tib. སྡེབ་སྦྱོར།).

16 A *torma* is a cake, usually made of barley flour and used in rituals. Here the speaker rhymes Burma and *torma*.

17 *Lutor* is a type of *torma* specifically offered to the nagas.

2. Boasting

A: Is that even possible?

ཀ དེ་མོ་བཟིག་ར་ཡོད་ནི་ཨེ་རེད།

B: And then, I started university at fifteen!

ཁ དེ་ན། ང་ལོ་བཅོ་ལྔའི་ཐོག་ནས་སློབ་གྲྭ་ཆེན་མོར་ཞུགས་ག་ཡ།

A: [dismissively] Heh, I graduated from university at fifteen!

ཀ ཧེ། ལོ་བཅོ་ལྔའི་ཐོག་ནས་ང་བརྫོ་སློབ་གྲྭ་ཆེན་མོ་མཐར་ཕྱིན་སོང་ད།

B: By the age of ten I had gone to school overseas!

ཁ ང་ལོ་བཅུ་ཐམ་པའི་ཐོག་ནས་ཕྱི་རྒྱལ་ལ་སློབ་སྦྱོང་ད་སོང་སྦྱོང་ད་ཡ།

A: I graduated from all schools at age five, and perfected all scripts.

ཀ ང་ལོ་ལྔ་གི་ཐོག་ནས་སློབ་གྲྭ་ཡོད་ཡོད་གོ་མཐར་ཕྱིན་ནས། ཡིག་རིགས་ཡོད་ཡོད་གོ་བྱང་ཆུབ་སོང་ད།

B: I served the people and made contributions to the country at the age of three.

ཁ ངས་ལོ་གསུམ་གི་ཐོག་ནས་མི་དམངས་ད་བུ་བ་སྒྲུབ་བས། རྒྱལ་ཁབ་བ་བྱུས་རྗེས་བཞག་ནི་ཡ།

A: My hair became grey as soon as I was born.

ཀ ང་སྐྱེས་མ་ཐག་ཏུ་མགོ་དཀར་བོས་ལོག་སོང་ད།

B: That's not possible. I am not only great at learning, I'm also excellent at sports!

ཁ དེ་མོ་བཟིག་ཡོད་ནི་མ་རེད། ང་རིག་གནས་དར་ནོ་ཁེར་མོ་མིན། རྩལ་སྦྱོང་གི་ཕྱོགས་ནས་ར་དར།

A: I'm excellent in that too!

ཀ དེ་ང་ར་དར།

B: I can run 400 to 500 kilometers in one hour.

ཁ ང་དུས་ཚོད་གཅིག་གི་ནང་ད། སྲ་ལེ་དབར་བཞི་བརྒྱ་ལྔ་བརྒྱ་བཟིག་ག་རྒྱགས་ཐུབ་བ།

A: I can run 1000 kilometers in half an hour!

ཀ ང་དུས་ཚོད་ཕྱེད་ཚ་བཟིག་གི་ནང་ད་ས་ལེ་བར་སྟོང་བཟིག་ག་རྒྱགས་ཐུབ་བ།

B: You can't compete with me! I can get out of the country in five minutes.

ཁ ཁྱོད་ད་མི་འགྲན་གི་ང་སྐར་མ་ལྔ་གི་ནང་ད་རྒྱལ་ཁབ་གི་ཕྱི་སོར་འབུད་ཐུབ་བ།

A: You don't compare to me! I can run around the earth in a single minute!

ཀ ཁྱོད་ང་མི་འགྲན་གི་ངས་སྐར་མ་གཅིག་གི་ནང་ད་འཛམ་གླིང་ད་སྐོར་ར་རྒྱག་ཐུབ་བ།

B: I don't believe you. ཁ། དའི་རྣར་མི་འགྲོ་གི

A: I'm boasting. ཀ། ངས་ལབ་རྒྱག་གོ་ནི།

B: Uh, I can carry 500 pounds of grain. ཁ། ཨ། ངས་འབྲུ་རིགས་རྒྱ་མ་ལྔ་བརྒྱ་ཁྱག་ག་ཡ།

A: You can't beat me. I can lift 600 pounds of gold with one hand. ཀ། ཁྱོང་མི་འགྱུན་གི ངས་གསེར་རྒྱ་མ་དྲུག་བརྒྱ་ལག་ཡས་གི་ཁྱག་ག་ཡ།

B: You can't compete with me. I can carry 1 pound of wool on my back and walk. ཁ། ཁྱོང་མི་འགྱུན་གི ངས་བལ་རྒྱ་མ་གང་ཁུར་རས་འགྲོ་ཐུབ་བ་ཡ།

A: Oh, by the *Yum* if you can't do that.[18] ཀ། ཨོ། དེ་ད་ཡུམ་མི་ཐུབ་གི་ན།

B: Uh, *ala*. ཁ། ཨེ། ཨ་ལ།

A: In my area, it's ok if I don't wash my clothes for three years. How's that? ཀ། དེ་བཟོའི་ས་ཆ་ནས་ལོ་གསུམ་མ་གོན་རྒྱ་མ་བགྱུས་ན་ཆོག ཅི་མོ་རེད།

B: That's nothing. In my area, it's ok if we don't wash our faces for three months. ཁ། དེ་བཟོ་ཅང་མ་རེད། དེ་བཟོའི་ས་ཆ་དེ་ནས་ཟླ་བ་གསུམ་མ་ཁ་ལག་མ་བགྱུས་ན་ཆོག

A: That's nothing. In my area, we don't wear clothes except for at weddings, and we don't wash our faces except at New Year. ཀ། དེ་བཟོ་ཅང་མ་རེད། དེ་བཟོའི་ས་ཆ་ནས་སྟོན་མོ་མིན་ནས་གོས་མི་གོན། ལོ་སར་ར་མིན་ནས་དོ་མི་བཀྲུ་ཡ།

B: In my area, having lice is considered an omen that you'll get rich. ཁ། བྱུང་གི་དེ་བཟོའི་ས་ཆ་དེ་ནས་ཤིག་བདབ་བདད་ན་རྒྱ་མགོ་འབྱུད་རྒྱུའི་རྟེན་འབྲེལ་རེད་ཟེར་ར།

---

18 The "Yum" is short for *yumdumpa* and refers to the *prajnaparamita* "perfection of wisdom." In Amdo, the text is mentioned as an oath. By negating the oath, the speaker is affirming the previous statement.

2. Boasting

A: Well then, in my area, they say it's a sign of your merit if you're oily.[19]

ཀ༽ ནོ་ན་དེ་བཟོའི་ས་ཆ་དེ་ནས། ཚོ་ཆགས་བཏང་ན། བསོད་ནམས་ཡོད་དིའི་མཚོན་རྟགས་རེད་ཟེར་ར།

B: Oh, well, in my area, some comrades have wild yaks walking single file on their heads.[20]

ཁ༽ ནོ་ན་དེ་བཟོའི་ས་ཆ་ནས་གྲོ་མཐུན་ལ་ལའི་མགོ་ན་འབྲོང་གཉར་གི་ར་ཡོད།

A: Well then, in my area, some comrades shine.

ཀ༽ ནོ་ན་དེ་བཟོའི་ས་ཆ་ནས། གྲོ་མཐུན་ལ་ལའི་ཕྱོག་ན་འོད་རྒྱགས་གི་ར་ཡོད།

B: Huh? What's wrong with that?

ཁ༽ ཨེ། དེ་ཆེ་བཟིག་མ་ཉན་ཐལ།

A: Oh, that is, their clothes are oily, the golden sun shines on it, and it radiates a conch-coloured light.

ཀ༽ ཨོ། དེ་ད། ལུ་གི་ཕྱོག་ག་ཚོ་ཆགས་གས། ཚོ་གི་ཕྱོག་ག་གསེར་མདོག་གི་ཉི་མ་འཕྲོས་ཡས་དང་མདོག་གི་འོད་ཟེར་འབུད་གོ་ནི་རེད་ཡ།

B: [dismissive] Heh. Yes. Yes. My place has people like that, too.

ཁ༽ ཧེ། རེད། རེད། དེ་བཟོའི་ས་ཆ་ན་ར་དེ་མོ་ཡོད།

A: Uh. In my area, people speak a mix of Tibetan and Chinese.

ཀ༽ ཨུན། དེ་བཟོའི་ས་ཆ་ནས་རྒྱ་སྐད་བོད་སྐད་འདྲེས་མ་བཏད་ལ།

B: We also speak like that in my area.

ཁ༽ དེ་དེ་བཟོའི་ས་ཆ་ནས་ར་དེ་ཡས་བཏད་ལ།

A: How do people in your area speak?

ཀ༽ ཁྱོ་བཟོའི་ས་ཆ་ནས་ཆེ་ཡས་བཏད་ལ།

B: Uh, how should I say it?

ཁ༽ ཨུན། ད་ཆེ་ཡས་བཏད་རས།

A: I have an idea.

ཀ༽ ང་བློ་བཟིག་ཡོད་གི

B: Yeah?

ཁ༽ ཡ།

---

19 Referring to skin and hair that is dirty and oily, and that this gets on your clothes as well.

20 Here the "wild yaks" are lice, and they walk in a line like yaks climbing a narrow mountain path.

A: Uh, let's say two old acquaintances have just met up, one from my area and one from your area.

B: That's fine.

A: They have met now.

B: Sure.

A: Yeah, come on.

B: Ah! Ok! I haven't seen you for ages **bei**[21], *wei*!

A: Don't talk **nonsense** (*hu* 胡). I only **contact with** (*dajiaodao* 打交道) and deal with my **side hustle** (*gaofuye* 搞副业) these days. Who says I can find the **time** (*shijian* 时间) to just stand there?[22]

B: Really? If you say so *aro*, now that you are running a **side hustle**, are you becoming the father of **renminbi** (人民币)?[23]

A: Take pity on me, getting **reminbi** is not **easy** (*jiandan* 简单).

B: Really? What's up?

---

21   *Bei* is a feature of the dialect of Chinese spoken in Qinghai.
22   Readers of both Chinese and Tibetan will notice that the verbs *da* and *gao* in the borrowed phrases "*dajiaodao*" and "*gaofuye*" respectively have been placed at the end to fit with conventions of Tibetan grammar.
23   *Renminbi* (literally "people's money") is one commonly used term for the Chinese currency. Becoming the "father" of *renminbi* would suggest that he is becoming wealthy.

2. Boasting

A: This morning, uh, my **tractor** (*shou fu* 手扶) **broke** (*huai* 坏) down and in the afternoon I went to have it **welded** (*han* 焊).

ཀ དེ་རིང་སྔ་དྲོ། ཨུ། ངེག་ཚོའི་ (手扶) དཔེ་ (坏) ཡས་བཏང་དེ། ཕྱི་རོ་ཡང་སོང་ནས་ཧན་ (焊) བརྒྱག་ཡས་བཏང་ངས་ཡོང་ང་ཡ།

B: Your **tractor**'s faults (*maobing* 毛病) really aren't **small** (*buxiao* 不小), huh?

ཁ ཁྱོའི་ཆིག་སྟོའི་ (手扶) དེ་ར་བབ་གི་མོ་ཡིན་པོ་འོ་ (毛病不小) ཡིན་ན།

A: **Small faults** (*xiao maobing* 小毛病) are ok.

ཀ ནོ་མོ་ཡིན་བཟོ་དེ་ར་དུག་ཀྱོའི་རེད་བཟེ་ན།

B: Yup.

ཁ ཡུན།

A: If **big faults** (*da maobing* 大毛病) **occur** (*chu* 出), what **solution** (*banfa* 办法) do you have other than just lying down.

ཀ ཏྲ་མོ་ཡིན་ (大毛病) བཞིག་ཐོའི་ (出) ཡས་བཏང་དུས་དུ་རོ་མ་གཞལ་ནས་འདུག་རྒྱུ་མིན་ན་ད་པན་ཧྥ་ (办法) བཞིག་གང་ན་ཡོད།

B: Truly, if a **big fault occurred**, your **income** (*shouru* 收入) would really be **interrupted** (*danwu* 耽误), aro!

ཁ ཨོ་ད་རོ་འམས། ཏྲ་མོ་ཡིན་ (大毛病) བཞིག་ཐོའི་ (出) ཡས་བཏང་རས། ཁྱོའི་ཆིག་རོའི་ (收入) གི་ཐོག་ག་རོ་འམས་ཏུན་བོའི་ (耽误) ཡས་བཏང་ནི་རེད་གོ་ཨ་རོ།

A: That broken **tractor** of mine needs **major repairs** (*daxiu* 大修), but now I don't have the **means** (*tiaojian* 条件).

ཀ ངའི་ཆིག་ཆག་དེ་ཏྲ་ཞིག་ (大修) བཞིག་ད་ཡོད་དགོ་གི་ར། ད་བར་ཡང་ཐོའོ་ཅན་ (条件) དེ་ར་མེད་གི་ཡ།

B: [dismissively] *Ayaya*, your **maternal uncle** (*jiujiu* 舅舅) is like a **landlord** (*dizhu* 地主). [He] is a **box** (*xiangzi* 箱子) of **renminbi**. Why don't you borrow some?

ཁ ཨ་ཡ་ཡ། ཁྱེད་གི་ཅིག་ཅིག་ (舅舅) ཧྱིས་གྱོའུ་ (地主) འདྲ་མོ་རེད་གོ། རིན་མིན་པིས་གི་ཞང་ཚི་ (箱子) རེད་གོ་ཚ་ཚིག་བསྐྱིས་བཏང་ན་མི་ཆོག་ནས་འོ།

A: [scoffing] Heh, you really **don't understand** (*bu liaojie* 不了解) my **uncle's temper** (*piqi* 脾气). When he's in a bad **mood** (*xinqing* 心情), he comes, breaks all the **furniture** (*jiaju* 家具) in the home, and then leaves. Do you think it is okay to borrow from him?

ཀ། དེ། ཁྱོས་དེད་ཀའི་ཇོའུ་ཇོའུ་གི་ཕིས་(脾气) དེ་ད། ཌོ་མས་པོའུ་ལེའོ་ཅེ་ (不了解)། ཞིན་ཆེན་(心情)མེ་ཏུ་དས་བ་ཚོ། ཡོང་དས་ཁྱིམ་གྱི་ཅ་དོའུ་(家具) ཚ་པོར་ཀྲོག་བཏང་དས་བུད་འགྲོ་གི་ར། དེ་ཏུ་ར་ཅིག་སྐྱི་ཉན་རྒྱུ་ཨོ་རེད།

B: [sighing] Huh, right. right. It's a lot of **trouble** (*mafan* 麻烦) for a small **matter** (*shiqing* 事情). Yeah?

ཁ། ཧུ། རེད། རེད། ཏི་ཆེན་(事情)ཆུང་ངུང་མ་ཧྥན་(麻烦)མང་གི་ཡིན་ན།

A: Ah, karmically wicked one, **all of society** (*zhengge shehui* 整个社会) is like that.

ཀ། ཨ། ལས་ངན་གོ་གྱིན་གྱི་ཏི་དས་(整个社会)ད་ལོས་ཡིན་ད།

B: Uh...

ཁ། ཨུན།

A: Our **family relations** (*jiating guanxi* 家庭关系), uh... uh... are **really difficult to talk about** (*hennanshuo* 很难说).

ཀ། ཨུ་བཟོའི་ཅ་ཐེན་བགན་ཞིས་(家庭关系)འདི་ར། ཨུན། ཨུན། ཉིན་ནན་ཏོ་(很难说) ཡ།

B: That's the **truth** (*shihua* 实话)!

ཁ། ཏི་ཏུ་ཨོ། (实话哦)

A: The longer we went on the more Chinese it became.

ཀ། ཡུན་གྱི་ཡུན་གྱི་ཡོང་ན་ད་རྒྱ་སྐད་གྱི་ལོག་ཐལ་བཞེ།

B: *Olé*, truly.

ཁ། ཨོ་ལེ་བཞེ་ན།

A: Oh, that is understandable. I don't have any objections.

ཀ། ཨོ། ད་དེ་ར་ཆེ་ཁག་རྒྱུ་ད་བསམ་འཆར་དེ་ར་མེད།

B: Then, to what do you have objections?

ཁ། དེ་ན། ཁྱི་ཆེ་བཞིག་ག་བསམ་འཆར་ཡོད་ནས།

2. Boasting

A: These days, some intellectuals who claim to be serving the people, doing the work for the ethnicity, who are the role models for future generations...

ཀ ད་སྐབས་ཀྱི་དུས་འདི་བཞིག་ག་མི་དམངས་ ང་ཞབས་འདེགས་ཞུ་བོ་ཡིན་དུ། མི་རིགས་ག་ བྱ་བ་ལས་ནོ་ཡིན། མི་རབས་གཞུག་མའི་མིག་ དཔེ་བཙས་པོ་ཡིན་ཟེར་ནས་མཁས་པ་སྐྱོར་ བཞིག་གིས་...

B: [agreeing] Uh-huh.

ཁ ཨུན།

A: ...they throw the affairs of the nationality into the bottom of a sombre well, and communicate unnecessary things in unintelligible speech. I not only get angry but want to bite them.

ཀ མི་རིགས་ཀྱི་ལས་དོན་ཤུན་ནག་གི་དོང་ ཞབས་བ་ཏུ་བཏང་ངས། མི་དགོ་ནས་དོན་ དག་མི་གོ་ནི་སྐད་ཆ་དུང་ངས་བཤད་ན་ད། ངོ་མ་ཁུ་བཟི་སྟོ་ལངས་ནས་ནང་ནས་ར། སོ་ བཞིག་བཏབ་བཏང་ན་འདོད་གི་ཡ།

B: Hehe, how do they speak, aro?

ཁ ཧེ། ཧེ། དི་ཚེ་ཡས་བཤད་ནི་རེད། ཨ་རོ།

A: Alas, it is like this.

ཀ ད་ཐལ་ར་ཅིག་གི་འདི་མོ་བཞིག་རེད་ཡ།

B: Yes.

ཁ ཡ།

A: [hiccup sounds]

ཀ ཨུ་འི། ཨུག་གི།

B: What was that?

ཁ དི་ཆེ་བཞིག་ཡིན་ནས།

A: Isn't it me coming to your home drunk again?

ཀ ཡང་བཟི་ཡས་ཁྱེད་ཁ་ཐོན་བཏང་ནི་མིན་ནས།

B: Oh, right. right.

ཁ ཨོ། དི་རེད། དི་རེད།

A: [hiccups] Ayo'e, you didn't open the door quickly. What **terrible thing** (*duibuqi* gi *shiqing* 对不起གི事情) did I do to you?

ཀ ཨུ་ཨུ། ཨ་ཡོ་འེ། ཁྱིས་ང་རེམ་མ་སློ་མི་ཕྱེ་ནོ། ངས་ཁྱོ་བདས་པོའུ་ཆིས་གི་ཏི་ཆིན་(对不起 གི 事情) ཆེ་བཞིག་ལས་བཏང་།

B: What?

ཁ ཨ།

A: What?

ཀ ཨ།

B: Oh, it's you.

ཁ ཨོ། ཁྱོ་ཡིན་ནས།

A: What?

ཀ ཨ།

B: I'm really **sorry** (*duibuqi* 对不起)! Come in, come in!

ཁ ངོ་མ་བཏུས་པོ་ཉི་ཆེས། (对不起)ཡ། ཡ། ནང་དགོག་ནང་དགོག

A: [agreeing] Uh-huh.

ཀ ཨུན།

B: Come in and drink some tea. Ah, karmically wicked one, you came here after **setting off** (*za* 炸) a **grenade** (*shouliudan* 手榴弹),[24] *ba*?[25]

ཁ ནང་དགོག་ག་ཇ་བཞིག་འཐུང་ད། ཨ། ལས་དན་གོ། ཡང་ཅིག་བཞིག་ནས་ཉིག་ལིག་དན་ (手榴弹)བཞིག་ཙ(炸)་ཡས་ཏང་ནས་ཡོང་བཞིག་པ།

A: If I have **"cash"** (*qian* 钱) money, why not drink the nectar liquor,[26] eh **little brother** (*laodi* 老弟)?

ཀ ཆན(钱)་སྟོར་མོ་ཡོད་ན། ཆང་བདུད་རྩི་མི་འཐུང་ད་ཆེ་ཡེད་རྒྱུ། ཨ། ལོ་ཏིས(老弟)།

B: [inquiringly] Huh?

ཁ ཨ།

A: Tonight, we two bottles of people threw back one liquor.

ཀ དེ་དགོང་ད། ང་མི་དོ་གི་ཆང་རྒྱ་མ་ཅིག་གསུག་བཏང་།

B: What did you say?

ཁ ཆི་བཞེ།

A: Oh no, I am saying I single handedly drank two bottles of **grain alcohol** (*liangshi baijiu* 粮食白酒).[27]

ཀ ཨོ་མ་རེད། ང་མི་ཅིག་གིས་ཡུང་ཏི་པེ་ཅིག་ (粮食白酒)་རྒྱ་མ་དོ་འཐུང་བཏང་ད་བཞེ་ནི་ཡ།

B: [surprised] Ah, ah! Wow! Is your **alcohol tolerance** (*jiuliang* 酒量) sky-high these days?

ཁ ཨ། ཨ། ཡ། ད་བར་ད་ཁྱོ་ཅིག་ཡུང་(酒量)་གནམ་མ་ཐོན་ནས་བསྡད་ཡོད་ནི་མིན་ན།

---

24 A euphemism for finishing an entire bottle of liquor.
25 *Ba* is a particle appended at the end of sentences, and is believed by many to have been borrowed from Chinese.
26 Here, he uses the alliteration and rhyme for the Chinese *qian* "cash" and the Tibetan *chang* "liquor."
27 *Baijiu* is the clear, distilled liquor frequently drunk throughout China.

2. Boasting

A: It is not bad. But It's **nothing** (*cha de yuan le* 差得远了) **compared** (*bi*比) with Drakpa's.[28]

ཀ ཅིག་ཅིག་མཚན་གི་རེད་དུ། གྲགས་པ་ཡིས་ (比) བཟིག་ཡས་ན་ཁ་དེ་ཡོན་ལ (差得远了)།

B: Ok, fair enough.

ཁ ཡ། དེ་བཟེ་ར།

A: [dismissively] Huh, Drakpa is also nothing **special** (嚼头).[29]

ཀ ཧུ། གྲགས་པ་ར་ཚོ་ཐིག (嚼头) དེ་ར་མེད་ལ།

B: [confirming] Uh-huh.

ཁ ཡིན་ཡུ།

A: He cooks a pound of noodles right after throwing back a pound of liquor.

ཀ ཆང་རྒྱ་ལུ་གང་གཤུག་ནོ་ར། ཁོ་རྒྱ་མ་གང་བསྐོལ་ནོ་བོ་ཐུག་རེད་མོ།

B: *Aro aro*, what is the **meaning** (*yisi* 意思) of "cooking a pound of noodles"?

ཁ ཨ་རོ། ཨ་རོ། ཁོ་རྒྱ་མ་གང་སྐོལ་ཡས་བཟེ་ནོ་ཅེ་བཟིག་གི་ཡིས་སི (意思) རེད།

A: [sighing dismissively] *Aiya*, fool, you are **truly** a fool, I'm saying that when he's drunk, he throws it back up.

ཀ ཨ་ཡ། སློའུ་དུ་ཏི་ཏུ (实话) སློའུ་རེད་ཡ། ཆང་འཐུང་ན་བཟེ་ཡས་བསྐྱུག་བཏང་ནོ་བཟེ་ནི་ཡ།

B: Oh that's right. That's right.

ཁ ཨོ་དེ་རེད། དེ་རེད།

A: Well, "little brother."

ཀ ཡ། ལོ་ཊིས། (老弟)

B: Yes?

ཁ ཨ།

A: Um, if you have liquor, put it in front of me. Be quick!

ཀ ཨུ། ཆང་བཟིག་ཡོད་ན་སྨྱུན་ན་ཞོག་རོ། རེམ་ར།

---

28 This may refer to a specific person, but it also may be used to create assonance in the phrase here.

29 嚼头 literally means, "something that can be chewed for a long time without losing taste." With the negation 没 in front, it metaphorically refers to something not worth considering. Thus, Menla Jyab suggests that Drakpa's tolerance is not great.

B: [sighing] *Aiya*. Unfortunately, by your flesh if I even know what liquor looks like.[30]

A: Hehe, **forget it** (*suanleba* 算了吧). You, you're an **alcohol** (*jiu* 酒) drinker yourself. I don't believe you can endure not drinking it. [hiccups]

B: *Aiya*, if there's even a **whiff** (*weidao* 味道) of **liquor** in my house, then you can say I didn't want to pour you some.

A: Well then, don't **play** (*kai wanxiao* 开玩笑), bring some quick.

B: Huh, [I] truly don't have any, otherwise I would offer you some. Um, let me tell you.

A: Yeah?

B: Don't drink any more tonight.

A: [agreeing] Uh-huh.

B: Go get some sleep.

A: [hiccup]

B: You have to go to **work** (*shang ban* 上班) again tomorrow.

---

30   The speaker is suggesting that he has no liquor at home.

2. Boasting

A: [unhappily] Do you **care** (*guanxin* 关心) about my **work**?[31] If you want to pour me some then do it. If you don't, then **I'll be off** (*zou la* 走啦)!

ཀ། ངའི་རུང་པན་(上班)་ད་ནུ་པན་(下班)་བརྩི་བཀན་ཞིན་(关心)་ཡོད་རྒྱུ་རེད་ལ། ད་སྦུད་ན་འདོད་ན་ལུད། མི་སྦུད་ན། ཚོ་ལྷ་(走啦)།

B: Hey! Don't be angry.

ཁ། ཡ། ད་དོ་མ་སློ་བཞིག་མ་ལངས།

A: **Cut the bullshit** (*shao feihua* 少废话), you!

ཀ། ཉི་རྫས་དུ། (少废话) ཁྱོ།

B: Hey, [in frustration] **honestly**!

ཁ། ཡ། ད། ཉི་དུ་(实话)།

A: Forget about it (*suanla* 算啦).

ཀ། བསན་ལྷ་(算啦)།

B: Well then, then, **beat it** (*gun* 滚).

ཁ། དེས་ན་ད། དེས་ན་ད། བཀོན་(滚)།

A: [no longer pretending to be drunk] So is this good behaviour? Is the speech pleasant? Does anyone understand it?

ཀ། ད་བྱ་སྤྱོད་ཨེ་ཡག་གི་སྐད་ཆ་ཨེ་སྙན་གི་རང་ང་ཅིག་གི་ཨེ་གོ་གི

B: *Olé*, if it continues like this, won't our Tibetan language become a **hybrid language** (*zazhong hua* 杂种话) in the end.

ཁ། ཨོ་ལེ་བཞིན་ར། ད་འདི་ཡས་ཅིག་སོང་རས་ད། མཐའ་མཇུག་ཏྲ་མ་བཞིག་ག་ཨུ་བཟོ་བོད་གི་སྐད་ཆ་འདི་ཚ་སྤྱོང་དུ། (杂种话)་གི་ལོག་རྒྱུ་མིན་ནི་ཨེ་རེད་བོ།

A: [Catching B in his hypocrisy] Ohoho! You weren't careful and you spoke it too.

ཀ། ཨོ་ཧོ་ཧོ། ཉམས་མ་བཞག་ག་ཁྱོ་རང་གིས་ར་བཤད་ལ་བཞེ།

B: Hey! *aro, aro*, we forgot to boast.

ཁ། ཡུ། ཨ་རོ། ཨ་རོ། ལབ་རྒྱག་རྒྱུའི་བརྗེད་ཐལ།

A: Oh, true. True. True. Now let's boast. Let's boast. Let's boast. I'm a tall person.

ཀ། ཨོ་བདེན་གི་བདེན་གི་བདེན་གི་ད་ལབ་རྒྱག་ད་ལབ་རྒྱག་ད་ལབ་རྒྱག་ད་སྒྱི་གཟུགས་རིང་ཡིན།

B: I'm also tall.

ཁ། ད་ར་གཟུགས་རིང་ཡིན།

---

31 Literally, in my getting on and getting off work (*shang ban* and *xia ban*).

A: My body is three armspans tall. ཀ ངའི་གཟུགས་ན་འདོམ་པ་གསུམ་ཡོད།

B: My body is six armspans. I'm the taller of us. ཁ ངའི་གཟུགས་ན་འདོམ་པ་དྲུག་ཡོད། ཨུ་གཉིས་གའི་ང་རིང་གི

A: I'm taller. My body is nine armspans. ཀ ང་རིང་གི་ ངའི་གཟུགས་ན་འདོམ་པ་དགུ་ཡོད།

B: I'm taller. My body is twenty armspans. ཁ ང་རིང་གི་ ངའི་གཟུགས་ན་འདོམ་པ་ཉི་ཤུ་ཡོད་པ།

A: I'm taller. My body is fifty armspans. ཀ ང་རིང་གི་ ངའི་གཟུགས་ན་འདོམ་པ་ལྔ་བཅུ་ཐམ་པ་ཡོད།

B: I'm taller. My body is one hundred armspans. ཁ ང་རིང་གི་ ངའི་གཟུགས་ན་འདོམ་པ་བརྒྱ་ཡོད།

A: I'm taller. My body is incalculable with armspans. My head is above the clouds. ཀ ང་རིང་གི་ ངའི་གཟུགས་འདོམ་པ་གིས་འཇལ་མི་ཐུབ། ངའི་མགོ་སྤྲིན་གི་ཡན་ན་བྱུད་ལས་བསྡད་ཡོད།

B: Hmph, even so I'm taller. ཁ ཧུན། དེས་ན་ར་ང་རིང་གི

A: Really? ཀ ཡ།

B: My head is among the stars. ཁ ངའི་མགོ་སྐར་མའི་གསེང་ན་ཡོད།

A: I'm taller. The earth is turning under my feet.[32] ཀ ང་རིང་གི་ སའི་གོ་ལ་བརྫེ་ངའི་རྐང་འོག་ན་འཁོར་གི་ར་ཡོད།

B: Um, I am taller. ཁ ཨུ། ང་རིང་གི

A: Really? ཀ ཡ།

B: My head reaches the sky and feet on the earth. The sun and moon are under my armpits, how is that, *aro*? ཁ ངའི་མགོ་གནམ་མ་ཐུག་གས། རྐང་བ་ས་ཐུག་ཡོད། ཉི་ཟླ་གཉིས་ཀ་ངའི་མཆན་ན་ཡོད། ཅི་མོ་རེད་ཨ་རོ།

---

32 Here he is suggesting he is so huge that the earth is like a ball under his feet.

2. Boasting

A: I...	ཀ	ང་།
B: I'm the taller of us.	ཁ	ཉུ་གཉིས་གའི་ང་རིང་ག
A: I'm bigger.	ཀ	ང་ཆེ་གི
B: Really?	ཁ	ཡ
A: I...	ཀ	ང་།
B: Yes?	ཁ	ཡ
A: I...	ཀ	ང་།
B: Yes?	ཁ	ཡ
A: I'm bigger.	ཀ	ང་ཆེ་གི
B: Ok.	ཁ	ཡ
A: My upper lip reached sky, lower lip touches the earth, and teeth are in the middle. I am bigger, am I not? Hehe!	ཀ	ངའི་ཡ་ཁ་གནམ་མ་ཐུག་ཡོད། མ་ཁ་སར་ཐུག་ཡོད། དུང་སོ་སུམ་ཅུ་བར་ན་ཡོད། ད་ང་ཆེ་ནི་མ་ར་ཆེ་རེད། ཧེ་ཧེ།
B: Then where is your face, karmically wicked one?	ཁ	འ་ལས་དན་པོ། དེས་ན་ཁྱོའི་ཏོ་གང་བཞག་ན་ཡོད་ནས་ཨོ།
A: Huh? [dismissively] Heh, we boasters and liars don't need face at all.	ཀ	འ ཧེ། དི་བཟོ་ལབ་རྒྱུ་གཤོབ་རྒྱུ་མཁན་རིག་ག་བྱུང་གི་ཏོ་མི་དགོ
B: You don't need face? If you don't need face, then what do you need?	ཁ	ཏོ་མི་དགོ་ཏོ་མི་དགོ་ན་ཁྱོ་ཆེ་བཞག་དགོ་ནས།
A: I need alcohol! Hiccup!	ཀ	ཆང་དགོ་ཡ། ཤུག་ལོས།
B: Oh, haha!	ཁ	ཨུ་ཧ་ཧ།

3. The Dream རྨི་ལམ།[1]

A: Dear members of the audience! Firstly, look at my face.

ཀ། མཛའ་བརྩེ་ལྡན་པའི་ལྟད་མོ་བ་རྣམ་པ། སྔོན་ན་ཆོད་མས་ངའི་དོར་གཅིག་ལྟོས་གོ

B: You're not that beautiful.

ཁ། ཡག་བཏང་རྒྱུ་མེད་ཀ

A: In particular, look at my eyes.

ཀ། ལྷག་པར་དུ་མྱིག་ག་གཅིག་ལྟོས།

B: [as if suddenly realizing] Oh, your eyes are probably different sizes.

ཁ། ཨཾ། མྱིག་གཉིས་ཀར་ཆེ་ཆུང་བཟིག་ཡོད་ན་ཐང་གི

A: Then, *aro*, please lookest at my ears!

ཀ། དེའི་འཕྲོར་ད་ཨ་རོ། རྣ་བ་གཅིག་གཟིགས་རོགས་གནོང་།

B: Oh, your nose is very long, indeed.

ཁ། ཨོ། སྣ་ད་དེས་དེས་ཅིག་རིང་གི་ཡ།

A: What nose? Ear! Ear! Ear! I said ear![2] Only people with congested noses care about noses.

ཀ། སྣ་བདོག་གོ་རྣ་ན་ན། རྣ་འབྱོག་ཟེར་ནི་ཡ། སྣ་འཆང་མ་འཚང་འདིས་ད་སྣ་གི་ཐོག་ག་སེམས་ཁུར་ཡས་བསྟད་ཡོད་མོ།

B: Oh! There is nothing special about your eyes and ears. What is there to look at?

ཁ། ཨོ། ཁྱོའི་མྱིག་ར་རྣ་གཉིས་ཀ་ཁྱད་པར་བ་བཟིག་མ་རེད་མོ། དེར་བལྟ་རྒྱུ་ཅི་བཟིག་ཡོད་གི།

---

1   A is performed by Menla Jyab and B is performed by Phagmo Drashi. This performance makes extensive use of humilific and honorific registers. To see these marked explicitly, see https://yeshe.org/the-dream/

2   Ear and Nose are homophones in the dialect spoken by Phagmo Drashi (B), hence the misunderstanding.

A: [disagreeing] *Hang! hang!* Why would the Three Ancestral [Dharma] Kings of Tibet award me a Nobel Prize if my eyes and ears are not unique?³

ཀ ཧང་ཧང་། ངའི་མྱིག་ར་རྣ་འཕྱོག་གཉིས་ཀ་ཁྱད་པར་བ་བཞིག་མིན་ན་བོད་ཀྱི་མེས་དབོན་རྣམ་གསུམ་གྱི་ནོ་འབེར་གྱི་བྱ་དགའི་རྟགས་མ་སྟེར་རྒྱུ་ཨེ་རེད།

B: Hey, you karmically wicked one! When did you meet the Three Ancestral Kings of Tibet?

ཁ ཨ་ལས་ངན་པོ། ཁྱོ་བོད་ཀྱི་མེས་དབོན་རྣམ་གསུམ་བཟོ་ནམ་བཞིག་ལ་ཐུག་ནི་ཡིན།

A: Um, the night that I flew into the sky.

ཀ ཨང་། གནམ་ལ་འཕུར་གྱི་དགོང་མོ།

B: The night you flew into the sky?

ཁ ཁྱོ་གནམ་ལ་འཕུར་གྱི་དགོང་མོ།

A: *Olé,* the night I requested some time off and flew into the sky.

ཀ ཨོ་ལེ། གནང་བ་ཞུས་གནམ་ལ་འཕུར་གྱི་དགོང་མོ།

B: Which night was that?

ཁ དེ་ནམ་གྱི་དགོང་མོ་རེད།

A: [pityingly] Ah, you don't understand anything, do you? On the auspicious New Year's Eve night, I went sightseeing in the sky after asking permission to drink the nectar-liquor from the strict chief of the household, Namtsokyi.⁴

ཀ ཨ། ཁྱོ་འདིར་གོ་བ་བཞིག་མེད་ནོ། དུས་བཟང་བོ་རྒྱ་ལོའི་གནམ་གང་གི་དགོང་མོ། ཁྱིམ་བདག་མོ་བཙན་པོ་གནམ་མཚོ་སྐྱིད་ལ། ཅང་བདུད་རྩི་འཕྱང་གི་གནང་བ་ཞུས་དགུང་ནམ་མཁའི་དབྱིངས་ནས་ལྟད་མོར་སོང་ང་ཡ།

B: I do not understand what you are saying.

ཁ ངས་ཁྱོའི་དེའི་ཏུ་མི་གོ་གི

---

3 The three ancestral kings of Tibet are Songtsen Gampo (སྲོང་བཙན་སྒམ་པོ།), Tri Songdetsen (ཁྲི་སྲོང་ལྡེ་བཙན།), and Tri Tsukdetsen (ཁྲི་གཙུག་ལྡེ་བཙན།). They are credited as the three kings who brought Buddhism to Tibet.

4 Here Menla Jyab imitates traditional oratory, opening each line with a set of three syllable formulae.

3. The Dream

A: Oh, If I tell you clearly, on New Year's Eve night last year, I drank some alcohol and spilt a bowl of noodles after my wife fed me a bowl of noodles.

ཀ། ཨོ། ད་ངྟོ་ལ་གསལ་པོ་ཡས་ནས་བཤད་ན། ན་ནིང་རྒྱ་ལོའི་གནམ་གང་གི་དགོང་མོ་ཅང་བཟིག་འཐུང་ངས་ཁྱེར་རས་ཁྱན་མོས་ཁོ་གང་སླུད་བོའི་ཁར་ད་རུང་ཁོ་གང་སླུགས་བཏང་ཡ།

B: Ew, you vomited?

ཁ། ཏི། བསྐྱགས་བཏང་ནས།

A: At the time, the earth and sky were spinning in my eyes, and after a while, I flew into the sky, *aro*.

ཀ། སྐབས་དེར་དའི་དརྒྱིག་ལམ་ན་ར་གནམ་ས་འཁོར་གོ་གི་ར་ཅིང་མ་འཁོར་ར་གནམ་ས་མ་ར་འཕུར་ཐལ། ཨ་རོ།

B: Oh? How did you fly?

ཁ། ཨོ། ཅི་གི་འཕུར་ཐལ།

A: Uh, I was curled up in bed caring for my son, and suddenly, wings grew on me, and I was flown out.[5]

ཀ། ཨ། ཉལ་སའི་ནང་ནས་རུམ་གི་ཞི་ལིར་སེམས་ཅུང་བཟིག་ཡས་ནས་ཀད་པ་བསྐྱམས་ནས་བསུད་ཡོད་ད། ད་གློ་རྒྱག་ག་གཤོག་པ་ཐོགས་གས་འཕུར་རས་བྱུད་ཐལ།

B: Hahaha, that's amazing!

ཁ། ཧ་ཧ་ཧ། དི་ཡ་མཚན་རེད་ལ།

A: Uh, chased by the wind, slashed by the rain, dust swirling, hit with the heat, I suffered tremendously before reaching the sky.

ཀ། ཨ་ད་རྐྱུང་གིས་དེད་ནིར། ཚར་གིས་གཅར་ནིར། ས་རྫུབ་ཡོད་ནིར། ཚ་བས་གསུར་ནིར། ནམ་མཁའ་ཐོན་རགས་གོ་ད་ངས་ཅིག་ད་ག་བཏང་ད་ར།

B: [sarcastically] Sure, um, if you say so.

ཁ། དི་ད་མིན་ནས་ད། ཤུན། ད་ཡིན་རྒྱའི་རེད།

---

5   There is unusual grammar here, with the phrase *wud ta* (བྱུད་ཐལ།) usually reserved for third-person phrases. When used for oneself it gives the sense that someone is not in control of the action.

A: In any case, ever since I was a child who did not know how to eat *tsampa* I have thought of viewing the mat of the eight-petaled-lotus-earth from the eight-spoked-wheel-sky.[6]

ཀ གང་ལྟར་ཡང་། གནམ་འཁོར་ལོ་རྩིབས་བརྒྱད་ཀྱི་གནམ་དོག་ནས་པདྨ་འདབ་བརྒྱད་ཀྱི་གདན་སྟེང་དུ་ལྟད་མོ་གཅིག་བལྟ་རྒྱུའི་དངས་པ་པ་རྩམ་ལོག་ཟ་མི་ཤེས་དུས་བཟུག་གི་དུན་སྙིང་ད།

B: Is that believable?

ཁ ངར་འགྲོ་ནི་བཟིག་ཨེ་རེད།

A: I didn't want to abandon my wife and son, but since I have already grown wings, flown into the sky, and overcome all those suffering, I should take a look at the external container world, right?[7]

ཀ དའི་ལི་མ་བུ་གཉིས་ཀ་སྤོས་གི་མི་སྡོངས་གི་ར། མི་སྡོངས་རུང་གཤོག་པ་སྒྲོགས་བཏང་བཟིག་ནམ་མཁའ་འཕུར་བཏང་བཟིག་སྡུག་ར་བཅུས་བཏང་བཟིག་ད་ངར་ཕྱི་སྣོད་འཇིག་རྟེན་གི་ཁམས་འདིར་ལྟད་མོར་ཅིག་བལྟ་དགོ་ག

B: Hmph, utter bullshit! Oh, what shape is this world?

ཁ ཉུན། རྫུན་གཏམ་ཁོ་ན། ཨོ། འཇིག་རྟེན་ཁམས་འདིའི་ཆགས་དབྱིབས་ཆེ་མོ་བཟིག་རེད།

A: Uh, have you ever been to Tsongonpo Lake?[8]

ཀ ཨ། ཁྱོ་མཚོ་སྔོན་པོར་སོང་ཨེ་མྱོང་།

B: Yes, I have.

ཁ མྱོང་ད།

A: Well, it is like that.

ཀ ཨོ། དེ་མོ་བཟིག་རེད།

B: Really?

ཁ ཨ།

---

6   These are two epithets for the earth and sky in Tibetan oral literature, eight-spoked-wheel-sky (གནམ་འཁོར་ལོ་རྩིབས་བརྒྱད།) and the eight- petaled-lotus-earth (ས་པདྨ་འདབ་བརྒྱད།), very likely originating from India/Buddhism.

7   There is a Tibetan categorisation of the world that divides the universe into "the world of the external vessel" (ཕྱི་སྣོད་ཀྱི་འཇིག་རྟེན།) and "the inner contents of sentient beings" (ནང་བཅུད་ཀྱི་སེམས་ཅན།); here, it is talking about the former.

8   Tsongonpo, is the Tibetan name for Koknor (in Mongolian) or Qinghai Lake (青海湖) in Chinese, one of the highest salt lakes in the world, and a major geographic feature of Amdo.

3. The Dream

A: As the Tsonyang Mahadeva's head protrudes from Tsongonpo Lake.[9]

ཀ། མཚོ་སྨྱོན་ཁྲི་ཤོར་རྒྱལ་མོའི་ཀློང་ན་མཚོ་སྙིང་མ་ཧཱ་དེ་ཝ་མགོ་བཟོ་འབུར་རས་བསྡད་ཡོད་ཀ་བཞི།

B: [dissatisfied] Heh.

ཁ་ ཧེ།

A: Mount Sumeru is also erected in the middle of the ocean like a millrind.[10]

ཀ་ རིའི་རྒྱལ་པོ་རི་རབ་ར་རྒྱ་མཚོ་ཆེན་པོའི་དབུས་ན་རང་འཐག་གི་ལྟེ་བ་ལྟ་བུའི་ཡམ་བཅུད་ངས་བསྡད་ཡོད་ཀྱི་ཨ།

B: [unimpressed] Heh, Such an ugly metaphor.[11]

ཁ་ ཧེ། དེ་མོ་དཔེ་འཛིག་སྟེ་བོ།

A: [scoffing] Heh, do not look down on Mount Sumeru, boy!

ཀ་ ཧེ། ཁྱོས་རིའི་རྒྱལ་པོ་རི་རབ་བ་མཐོང་ཆུང་མ་ཡེད་གོ་ཞི་ལི།

B: You shut up. Why would I look down on Mount Sumeru?

ཁ་ དཀྱོ་ཁ་རོག་ག་སྡོད་ལ་ཐོངས། ངས་ཚེ་བཞག་ག་རིའི་རྒྱལ་པོ་རི་རབ་བ་མཐོང་ཆུང་ཡེད་དགོ་ནི་རེད།

A: Then I looked carefully and saw, in the east of Mount Sumeru, the continent of Pūrvavideha, with its two minor continents, shaped like a scythe.

ཀ་ དེ་ནས་ད་ངས་ཞིབ་གི་གཅིག་བལྟས་ར། རིའི་རྒྱལ་པོ་རི་རབ་ཀྱི་ཤར་ཕྱོགས་ན་ཤར་ལུས་འཕགས་གླིང་སྙིང་ཕྲན་གཉིས་དང་བཅས་པ་ཟོར་བ་བཞིག་ག་རིག་གི

B: Scythe? Say it's the shape of a crescent.

ཁ་ ཟོར་བ་བདོག་གོ་ དབྱིབས་ཟླ་གམ་ལྟ་བུ་བཟེ་རོ།

---

9   Tsonyang Mahadewa (མཚོ་སྙིང་མ་ཧཱ་དེ་ཝ།) is an island in the heart of Tsongonpo Lake.
10 Unlike the commonly found four-armed iron support, Tibetans use a wooden peg in the centre of the bed-stone of the hand mill, which is usually known as the te (ལྟེ།) "navel."
11 Here and in ensuing turns of speech, Menla Jyab begins with descriptions of Tibetan cosmology that will be familiar across the region because of their inclusion in secular oratory, but ends with hyperlocal metaphors. When Phagmo Drashi corrects him, he suggests the conventional simile for Tibetan poetry.

A: Um, It's okay. In the south, the continent of Jambudvīpa, with its two minor continents, is shaped like the teeth of a *wakshel*.[12]

ཀ། ཨ། ཆོག་ནི་ར། ལྷོ་འཛམ་གླིང་ན་ལྷོ་འཛམ་བུ་གླིང་སྟེང་ཕན་གཉིས་དང་བཅས་པ་བག་གད་བཟིག་གི་ཁ་རིག་ག

B: Say it's the shape of the teeth of a saw.

ཁ། སོག་ལེ་ཁ་ལྟ་བུ་བཟེ་རོ།

A: In the west, the continent of Aparagodānīya, with its two minor continents, round like the bread cooked in ash.[13]

ཀ། ནུབ་ཕྱོགས་ན་ནུབ་བ་ལང་སྤྱོད་ཀྱི་གླིང་གླིང་ཕན་གཉིས་དང་བཅས་པ་གོར་གོར་གོ་རེ་ཐལ་བསྲེག་མ་འདྲ་བཟིག་རེད་ལ།

B: [dismissively] Heh!

ཁ། ཧེ།

A: In the north, the continent of Uttarakuru, with its two minor continents, is square-shaped like a napkin.

ཀ། ཨ་བྱང་ཕྱོགས་ན་བྱང་སྒྲ་མི་སྙན་གྱི་གླིང་གླིང་ཕན་གཉིས་དང་བཅས་པ་གྲུ་བཞི་ལྟ་ཕྱིས་འདྲ་འདྲ་བཟིག་རེད།

B: Hey! Enough, enough. You are going to ruin it with all these metaphors. How about you give us an account of our snowy Tibetan regions instead.

ཁ། ཡད་ཆོག་གི་ཆོག་གི་ཁྱོས་དཔེའི་འཇོག་ཡས་རྫོང་རྒྱ་རེད། དེར་བསླས་གི་རང་རེ་བོད་ཁ་བ་ཅན་གྱི་ཁ་བརྡ་བཟིག་བྱོས་ར།

A: [as if beginning an oration] Oh, white stupa-like snow mountains surround this snowy Tibetan Pureland of ours; it is a place where the rivers with eight qualities run melodiously;[14] a place where the silk-like grasslands glitter; a place where the three types of livestock—white, black, and multi-coloured—prosper speedily.[15]

ཀ། ཨོ། རང་རེ་བོད་ཁ་བ་ཅན་གྱི་ཞིང་ཁམས་འདི་ད། རི་གངས་དཀར་མཆོད་རྟེན་གྱི་ར་བས་བསྐོར་བ། རྒྱ་གཅན་མོ་ཡན་ལག་བརྒྱད་ལྡན་གྱི་འགྱུར་ཁུགས་སྙན་ས། སྤང་གོས་ཆེན་སྤྲིན་མོའི་འོད་མདངས་གསལ་ས། ཕྱུགས་དཀར་ནག་ཁྲ་གསུམ་གྱི་འཕེལ་ཁ་མགྱོགས་ས།

---

12   A wooden tool with teeth used for softening sheepskin in Amdo.
13   This is a type of bread, common in Amdo. The bread is thin and circular in shape and cooked in smouldering ash. The ash and burned parts are scraped off before consuming.
14   The eight qualities of water are sweet, cool, pleasant, light, clear, pure, not harmful to the throat, and beneficial for the stomach.
15   Herders in Amdo often use this phrase in oral literature to refer to all of their livestock.

B: So you are going to do a thorough praise.

| ཁ གཉིས་གྱི་བསྟོད་པ་བཟིག་ཡིན་རྒྱུ་རེད་ལ།

A: *Olé.* It is a place where all the people are strongly religious; a place where even lice receive life-release practices;[16] a place where both young and the old are with great endurance; a place where even if you jumped over their heads, they would have no complaints; a place where even a one-year-old is compassionate; a place where there are many honorifics in the speech... Oh, it should be said that our snowy Tibetan land is where archaic terms are not changed in the written texts; old black yak hair tents over our heads are not changed; the primitive old traditions are not changed; where the syllable *Om* are not changed in our minds.[17]

ཀ ཨོ་ལེ། ཁྱི་ཡར་སྐྱེས་ཐམས་ཅད་ཆོས་དད་ཆེ་ས། ཤིག་སོ་མད་ཡིན་རུང་ཚེ་ཐར་གཏོང་ས། ཁ་ཀན་གཞོན་གཉིས་ཀ་བཟོད་བསྲན་ཆེ་ས། མགོར་བྲྱིད་ནས་སོང་རུང་བསམ་འཁར་མེད་ས། ཆུང་ལོ་གཅིག་ཡིན་རུང་སྱུང་སེམས་ལྡན་ས། ཁའི་གསུང་གཏམ་ནང་ན་ཞེ་ཆིག་མང་ས། ཨོ། ད་ཡིག་ཕོག་གི་བརྡ་རྙིང་མ་འགྱུར། མགོ་ཕོག་གི་སྦྲ་རྙིང་མ་འགྱུར། ཡ་ཕོག་གི་སོལ་རྙིང་མ་འགྱུར། སེམས་ཕོག་གི་ཨོཾ་ཡིག་མ་འགྱུར་ར། ཡོད་ནོ་ད། རང་རེ་བོད་ཁ་བ་ཅན་རེད་ཟེར་རྒྱུ།

B: *Lakso! Lakso!*[18] This is what probably should be said.

ཁ ལགས་སོ། ལགས་སོ། དདེ་ཟེར་དགོ་ནི་ཡིན་རྒྱུའི་རེད།

A: While I was fascinated by the beautiful mountains and rivers and lovely folk cultures, suddenly a robust swirling wind came, and I was turned like a spindle wheel, *aro!*

ཀ བོད་ཀྱི་མཛེས་སྡུག་ལྡན་པའི་རི་རྒྱ་ར་ཡིད་དུ་འོང་བའི་དམངས་སྲོལ་ལ་མཆར་རས་བསྡད་ཡོད་དུས། སོྲ་རྒྱག་ག་ཀྲུང་ནག་འཁྲུབ་མ་བཟིག་ཕོན་ནས་ཁྲིད་ཡོད་དས་ང་བཟེ་ནོ་འཕང་ལོ་བསྒོར་བསྒོར་ཡིད་བཏང་ཐལ། ཨ་རོ།

---

16 *Tsétar* (ཚེ་ཐར།), translated here as "life-release" refers to the practice of freeing animals to gain merit. Pastoralists, for example, will promise not to kill certain livestock from their herds. Menla Jyab uses providing life-release for lice sarcastically, as an absurdly extreme version of the practice.

17 This whole turn is a critique of how pious, patient, but also cowed he believes Tibetans to be.

18 This is a common affirmation phrase that the orator receives from the audience while delivering a speech in Amdo.

B: Then you fell back to the ground, didn't you?

ཁ་ དེ་ནས་ད་ཕྱིར་ར་ཐང་ལ་ལྷུང་སོང་ནི་མ་ར།

A: At some point, everything disappeared from my sight, and there was something on my head. I touched it, and it was something velvety. It might have been a cloud or a *khatak*, and probably was my blanket. I was utterly baffled, *aro*.

ཀ་ མཚམས་བཞིག་ག་ད་དའི་མྱིག་ལམ་ནས་ཡོད་ཚད་ཀྱི་ཡོད་ཚད་གོ་ཡལ་ཐལ། མགོ་བཞིག་ན་ཅིག་ཡོད་ཀྱི་ཅིག་ལྡངས་ར་ར་འབའ་བེ་འབོད་བེ་བཞིག་རེད། སྤྲིན་བཞིག་ཡིན་ནི་འདུ་འདུ། ཁ་བཏགས་བཞིག་ཡིན་ནི་འདུ་འདུ། ཡང་ད་རང་གི་ཉལ་ཐུལ་ཡིན་ནི་འདུ་བཞིག་གྭ་ར་རེད། ད་བབ་གི་མགོ་ཉོག་ཐལ་ཨ་རོ།

B: You were probably lost.

ཁ་ ད་མགོ་འཁོར་སོང་བཞིག་ག

A: I gave it some thought, and things were really bad. If I had left my wife, lost my son, and wandered off, I'd be finished.

ཀ་ འདུད་བཞིག་བརྒྱབ་བ་ར་བབ་གི་འགྲིག་གི་མེད་ཀྱི་བུད་མྱིད་བསྐྱུར་བཏང་དས། བུ་ཕྱུང་བོར་བཏང་དས། རང་གི་སྟོམ་སོང་ན་བྱུང་གི་ཚར་སོང་བཞིག་གོ

B: Well, then what should you do?

ཁ་ ཨོ། ད་ཅི་བཞིག་ཡེད་དེ།

A: At that point, suddenly, a star fell in front of me.

ཀ་ སྐབས་དེར་ད་གློ་བུར་གའ་དའི་སྔུན་ན་སྐར་མ་བཞིག་ལྷུང་དས་བུད་ཐལ།

B: A star?

ཁ་ སྐར་མ་བཞིག

A: Uh, not a star. It might have been the kettle from our home or your household's white tent.

ཀ་ ཨ། སྐར་མ་བཞིག་ར་མ་རེད་མ་རེད། དེད་ཁའི་ཐབས་དེས་ཡིན་ནི་འདུ་འདུ། ཁྱེད་ཁའི་རས་གུར་ཡིན་ནི་འདུ་འདུ།

B: You are going to tell lies again.

ཁ་ ཡང་གཡོབ་གཏམ་རྒྱུ་རེད་ལ།

A: Oh, it was a UFO, so he came to pick me up.

ཀ་ ཨོ། UFO བཞིག་རེད་ཡ། སྨྱི་ལེན་གི་ཐོན་བཏང་བཞིག

B: Who?

ཁ་ སུ།

A: Uncle Tongtsen.

ཀ་ ཨ་ཁུ་སྟོང་བཙན།

3. The Dream

B: Who is "Uncle Tongtsen"?

A: You do not know Gar Tongtsen, the chief minister of the Tibetan king Songtsen Gampo?

B: You are going to lie again.

A: [accidentally agreeing] *Olé*... [realizing his mistake] No! King Songtsen Gampo was very fond of him since Gar Tongtsen went to receive the ladies of China and Nepal and escorted sacred statues in the past. So, he was sent to collect me today.[19]

B: Really? What quoth he?

A: He immediately recognized me and said, *aro*, "**Hello**, buddy!"

B: "Buddy"?

A: It would take too long to talk in detail about how about the sorts of things Gar Tongtsen and I discussed, Tibetan ancestors welcomed me, how the Three Ancestral Kings offered me beer and all the things I heard and saw on this trip. So if were to speak briefly about the things I heard and saw.

---

19 Later Tibetan historical accounts mention the critical role Gar Tongtsen played in bringing the two princesses Gyaza Kongcho (རྒྱ་བཟའ་ཀོང་ཇོ་) and Balza Tritsun (བལ་བཟའ་ཁྲི་བཙུན་) from China and Nepal respectively to Tibet as wives for the King Songtsen Gampo in the seventh century. Histories also recount that these two princesses brought two statues of the Buddha, and people believe they are housed in Jokhang and Ramoche temples in Lhasa to this day, attracting thousands of pilgrims annually.

B: [scoffing] Hmph, again you're going to tell a bunch of lies.

ཁ། ཨད། ཡང་གཏོབ་ལུང་བ་གང་སྒྲིག་རྒྱུ་རེད་ལ།

A: People like us are sleeping here, but our Tibetan ancestors are already in a world of science, *aro*!

ག དུ་འུ་བཟོ་ཅན་པོ་ཤུལ་ན་གཉིད་ལས་བསད་ ཡོད་ནོ་མིན་ནས་བོད་ཀྱི་མེས་པོ་རིགས་ག་ད་ སྟེ་ཚན་རིག་གི་འཇིག་རྟེན་བཞག་ག་ཐོན་ནས་ བསད་ཡོད་ཀྱི ཨ་རོ།

B: How do you know that?

ཁ། དེ་ཁྱེ་ཡས་ཤེས་ཀྱི

A: They have computers, and the internet is widely available.

ག གློག་ཐིག་ཆེས་འཁོར་ཡོད་ཀྱི་ཤེས་ཚན་དུ་རྒྱ་ མང་གི

B: [disbelieving] Huh?

ཁ། ཨ།

A: Motorcycles are their rides; they live in skyscrapers, gates are electric and automatic, doors have electric doorbells, and they watch electric television and listen to symphonies. And for the home goods, there are electric beds, electric food storage, electric stoves, electric pots, and electric food.

ག ཞེན་པ་མོ་ཊོ་རེད། བཞུགས་ས་ཐོག་ཁང་རེད། ཉི་སོ་གློག་སོ་རང་འབྱེད་རེད། ནང་སོ་གློག་གི་ བང་ཅན་རེད། ལྟ་རྒྱུའི་གློག་གི་བརྙན་འཕྲིན་ རེད། ཉན་རྒྱུའི་མཐུམ་གློག་རོལ་མོ་རེད། ད་ ནང་གི་ཅ་ལག་ར། གློག་གི་གཟིམ་ཁྲི། གློག་ གི་ཟས་སྣམ། གློག་གི་ཐབ་ཀ གློག་གི་བ་མ། གློག་གི་ཟ་མ།

B: You... What did you say? Electric food?

ཁ། ཁྱོས། ཁྱོས་ཚེ་བཟིག་བཟེ། གློག་གི་ཟ་མ།

A: No, no, no! Except for food, everything is electric.

ག མ་རེད། མ་རེད། མ་རེད། ཟ་མ་མིན་ནས་ད་ ཡོངས་རྫོགས་ག་གློག་གི་ཧྲས་ཧྲག་ཧྲག་རེད་ ཡ།

B: [disapprovingly] *Ang ang*, you are telling some funny lies.

ཁ། ཨང་ཨང་། གཏོབ་བཟིག་ག་སྐྱིད་པོ་ཧྲག་ཧྲག་ གཏམ་གི

3. The Dream

A: Uh, then the Three Ancestral Kings threw a banquet for me. All the Tibetan ancestors danced, Thonmi Sambotha performed a poetry recitation,[20] Sakya Pandita Kunga Gyeltsen played the piano,[21] and Uncle Thangdong Gyalpo performed a **disco** dance.[22]

ཀ། ཨ། དེ་ནས་དབོད་རྒྱལ་མེས་དབོན་རྣམ་གསུམ་གྱིས་ང་སྟོན་མོ་ཡས་ཐལ། ཕྱུར་རྒྱལ་མེས་པོ་ཡོངས་རྟོགས་གར་ར་བོང་ཐལ། ཐོན་མི་སམ་བྷོ་ཊ་ཚང་གིས་སྙན་ཚིག་བྱེར་འདོན་ཡས་ཐལ། ས་པཎ་ཀུན་དགའ་རྒྱལ་མཚན་གྱིས་རོལ་རྩེད་རོལ་དབྱངས་དགོད་ཐལ། ཨ་ཁུ་ཐང་སྟོང་རྒྱལ་པོས་བརྩེ་ Disco ཞེས་བྱོ་བརྒྱུབ་ཐལ་ཡ།

B: Um, if you say so…

ཁ། ཨ། ད་ཡིན་རྒྱུའི་རེད།

A: The *derkha*[23] in front of me was also fabulous.

ཀ། ད་སྤྱན་གྱི་སྡེར་ཁ་ར་དར་གི

B: The *derkha*?

ཁ། སྡེར་ཁ།

A: *Olé*.

ཀ། ཨོ་ལེ།

B: What was there to be eaten?

ཁ། ཅི་བཟིག་ཟ་རྒྱུ་ཡོད་གི

A: Um, there was meat, butter, and cakes. There was churned tea and sweet tea. There was barley liquor and wine. There was modern beer, candies, and **sunflower seeds** (*guazi* 瓜子).

ཀ། ཨ། ཤ་མར་སྦྱུད་གསུམ་ཡོད་གི དགུགས་ཇ་མངར་ཇ་ཡོད་གི ནས་ཆང་རྒུན་ཆང་ཡོད་གི དེང་རབས་སྤུ་ཆང་ཡོད་གི ཀ་ར་ཀུ་ཙེ (瓜子) ཡོད་ག

B: [dismissive] Huh! Those are just things that you like.

ཁ། ཧྱ། ཁྱོད་དགའ་ནི་ཏག་ཏག་རེད་ལོ།

---

20 Tibetans credit Thonmi Sambhota with creating the Tibetan script during the seventh-century reign of Songtsen Gampo.
21 Sakya Pandita Kunga Gyeltsen (1182–1251) is a famous Buddhist scholar known for his writings on philosophy, music, and poetry.
22 Thangdong Gyalpo is a fourteenth-century architect and artist known for founding Tibetan opera performances and iron suspension bridges.
23 Derkha is food such as meat, fruits, candies, bread, sunflower seeds, and peanuts in display put into plates and bowels during the festivals such as New Year and weddings in Amdo.

A: This time I found that our ancestors are not only great but are probably boasters as well, *aro*!

ཀ དེ་རིངས་དུ་ངས་གཅིག་བསླབ་ར་ཤུ་བཟོའི་མེས་པོ་རྣམས་པ་བཟོ་རྣབས་ཆེན་ཏག་ཏག་གཱ་རེད་དུ། ལབ་རྒྱལ་ཏག་ཏག་ར་ཡིན་ནི་འདུག་བཟིག་རེད་ཡ། ཨ་རོ།

B: Really?

ཁ ཡ།

A: They all told me about how they ruled Tibet, how they learned from the good qualities of others, how they built temples for subduing the border and further borders,[24] how they invited foreign translators, how they translated countless texts into Tibetan, and how they edited and finalized them, how they established the legal code, and many more.

ཀ ཚང་མས་ཅིག་ཁྱེར་ཚོས་བོད་ཀྱི་སྲིད་དབང་བསྒྱུར་སྟོལ། གཞན་གྱི་ལེགས་ཆ་བསྒྱུར་སྟོལ། མཐའ་འདུལ་ཡང་འདུལ་གྱི་གཙུག་ལག་ཁང་བཞེངས་སྟོལ། ཕྱིའི་ལོ་ཙཱ་བ་དཔོན་འདོ་ལོ་ཙཱ་བ་མང་པོ་སྤྱན་དྲངས་ནས་གཞུང་རྟོགས་མེད་བོད་ལ་བསྒྱུར་སྟོལ། གཏན་ན་ཕབ་སྟོལ། དཀ་བཅོས་ཡམ་སྟོལ། ཁྲིམས་སྟོལ་བཙུགས་སྟོལ། མང་ང་མང་ང་བཤད་གོ་གི

B: [unimpressed] *Hang*, read the historical records! That is true!

ཁ ཧང་། ཁྱོས་ལོ་རྒྱུས་ཡིག་ཆར་ལྟོས་ར། དེ་བདེན་གྱི་མོ།

A: It is not that. They only talked about those things to give me a hard time. They say we haven't surpassed what they have done, and we have been left behind in the current era.

ཀ མ་རེད་ཡ། ཁྱེར་ཚོས་དེ་སྒྲིང་དོན་ཡང་ང་གསེག་འབུ་གི་ཡོད་ནི་རེད་ཡ། དེད་སང་ཤུ་ཚོ་ཁྱེར་ཚོས་ལས་དོའི་ཕན་ན་བརྡ་ཐུབ་གི་མེད་གི་དུས་རབས་གི་རྟ་ལྱུས་ཐལ་ཟེར་གོ་ནི་ཡ།

B: Hmmm, those are also words of concern.

ཁ ཡུང་། དེ་ར་ཁ་བའི་ཚིག་རེད་མོ།

A: Uh, the Seven Wise Men also told me an entire valley of things, *aro*.[25]

ཀ ཨ། བོད་ཀྱི་མཛངས་མི་མི་བདུན་གྱིས་ར་ང་ལུང་བ་གང་བཤད་བཏང་བལ། ཨ་རོ།

---

24 Tibetan mythology describes the land of Tibetan as a giant demoness. In order to subdue the demoness and make Tibet a Buddhist land, the King Songtsan Gampo had 108 temples built at key points of the Tibetan region.

25 "The Seven Wise Men" (མཛངས་མི་མི་བདུན་།) were a group of Tibetan sages credited with significant technological contributions to Tibetan culture during the Tibetan Imperial period (618–842AD).

3. The Dream

B: What did they say?

ཁ ཅི་ཟེར་གི

A: They said the gold, silver, copper, and iron they found are still rusting away in our time.

ག ད་ཁིར་ཚོའི་རིང་ད་རྙེད་ནོའི་གསེར་དངུལ་ཟངས་ལྕགས་ཁྲོ་ཚོའི་རིང་ད་ད་དུང་བཙའ་ཆགས་ནས་བསྡད་ཡོད་གི་ཟེར་གི

B: They are correct.

ཁ བདེན་གི་མོ

A: They said the wooden ploughs from their time are still being dragged by the yaks in our time.

ག ཁིར་ཚོའི་རིང་གི་ཤིང་གཤོལ་ཁྲོ་ཚོའི་རིང་ད་ད་དུང་གཡག་གིས་ཚོས་དྲུད་ནས་འགྲོ་གོ་གི་ཟེར

B: Isn't it correct?

ཁ རེད་མོ

A: Uh, they said that in their time they made nomadic lives sedentary, but people are climbing back up the mountains in our time.[26]

ག ཨ ཁོ་ཚོའི་རིང་ད་འབྲོག་སྡེ་སྒྲོང་སྡེ་གི་བཏང་ད་ར་ཁྲོ་ཚོའི་རིང་ད་ཕྱིར་ར་རི་མགོར་འགོ་གོ་གི་ཟེར

B: Of course, they are right.

ཁ དེ་ད་མིན་ནས་ད

A: *Aro*, Songtsen Gampo alone had more than three hundred ministers. Pity my ears if I let them all say whatever they want.

ག ཨ་རོ འདི་ཡས་བཞག་ཆོད་ལ་བཞག་གི བཞག་བཏང་ན་སྲོང་བཙན་སྒམ་པོ་གཅིག་པོར་བློན་པོ་སུམ་བརྒྱ་ཆིག་ཡོད་ཀྱི་ར་ དའི་ན་འགྱོག་གཞིས་ཀ་སྙིང་མ་རྗེ

B: [disagreeing] *Ang*, when someone points out our shortcomings, if what they said is true, then we should acknowledge it.

ཁ ཨང་ ད་སྐྱོན་ན་མཛུབ་གུ་བཙུགས་ན་བདེན་ན་བདེན་གི་ཟེར་དགོ་ནི་རེད

---

26 In critiquing those who "climb back up the mountains," Menla Jyab appears to stand in support of policies aimed at resettling pastoralists.

A: Uh, they spoke about how nowadays, both the peaceful and wrathful internal conflicts are serious for Tibetans; for the peaceful, how anger and envy are making them less united; for the wrathful, how they have internal killings due to conflicts over caterpillar fungus and winter pastures.[27] After saying so many things, they conveyed that they were disturbed, *aro*.

ཀ། ཨ། དབོད་ལ་ཞི་དྲག་གཉིས་ཀྱི་ནང་འཁྲུག་ཚབས་ཆེ་སོལ། ཞི་བ་ཞེ་སྡང་ར་ཕྲག་དོགས་ཀྱི་ནང་མི་མཐུན་སྒྲིག་མིན་སོལ། དྲག་པ་དབྱར་རྩྭ་ར་དགུན་ས་བཅད་ལས་ནང་མི་དམར་གསོད་ཡས་སོལ། བཤད་ཀྱི་བཤད་ཀྱི་ཁོ་ཚོ་ར་འདུག་གི་མི་འཇོག་ཞེ་འདྲ་བཟིག་བཤད་ཀྱི་ཨ་རོ།

B: What did they say?

ཁ། ཅི་བཟིག་ཟེར་གི

A: They said, "there are many old minds, and new concepts are few. There are many Lamas and leaders and those passionate about Tibet are few. Many wear yellow and red robes, but genuine monks are few. Moton Phakgo is rich and superstitious people are poor.[28] You guys degraded the true dharma we have brought by superstitiously believing in it."

ཀ། དད་བར་བྱད་པ་རྙིང་པ་མང་གི་ལྟ་བ་གསར་པ་ཉུང་གི བླ་མ་དཔོན་པོ་མང་གི་བོད་འདང་ཆེ་ནི་ཉུང་གི་སེར་ཁ་དམར་ཁ་མང་གི་བཙུན་པ་རྣམ་དག་ཉུང་གི་མོ་སྟོན་ཕག་མགོ་ཕྱུག་གི་ལྐོངས་དད་མཁན་བཟོ་སྦུག་གི་དེ་ཡིན་ན་ད་ཁོ་ཚོས་སོལ་བདོད་དོའི་དམ་པའི་ཆོས་བདོག་གོ་ཁྲོ་ཚོས་རློངས་དད་ཡས་བརྫུད་བཏང་ཐལ་ཟེར་ཡ།

B: [agreeing] *Ang*, how true!

ཁ། ཨང་། ཅི་མ་བདེན།

A: However, the Three Ancestral Kings praised me so much, *aro*.

ཀ། རེད་ད། བོད་ཀྱི་མེས་དབོན་རྣམ་གསུམ་གྱིས་ང་བསྔོ་གཞེས་ཀྱི་བསྟོད་པ་ཡིད་གོ་ཀི་ཨ་རོ།

B: Oh? How didst they speak it?

ཁ། ཨོ། ཅི་གི་གསུང་གི

---

27 Note that for Menla Jyab, "internal killings" is not only meant to include violence within families or communities but extends to the entire Tibetan population more generally.

28 Moton Phakgo is a well-known folktale character who pretends to be a fortune-teller and comes up with prophecies by using a pig head as the prop, hence the name "pig-head fortune-teller" (མོ་སྟོན་ཕག་མགོ).

3. The Dream

A: [as one of the kings] *Ya*, noble son, your right eye sees the good; your left eye sees the bad; your right ear hears the good; your left ear hears the bad. In addition, your mouth is perfect for performing *khashag*, pay attention with your left on the way back and you will get some benefit from it. *ndendendendenden*[29]

ཀ། ཡ། དུ་རིགས་ཀྱི་བུ། སྨྱིག་གཡས་པས་བཟང་རིག་གི་སྨྱིག་གཡོན་པས་དན་རིག་གི་རྣ་གཡས་པས་བཟང་གོ་གི་རྣ་གཡོན་པས་དན་གོ་གི་དེའི་སྟེང་ད་ཁྱོའི་ཁ་དེ་ཁ་ཤགས་བཤད་སྤྲོད་གོ་མཚན་ཨེ་འདུག་གི་ཕྱིར་ར་འགྲོ་དུས་གཡོན་པས་མཉམ་ཞོགས་ག་སོང་ར་ལག་ཡོད་ཕན་ཚམ་རེ་ཡོད། འདེ་འདེ་འདེ་འདེ་འདེ་འདེ།

B: What did they give you?

ཁ་ ཅི་བཞིག་སྤྲེར་གི

A: *Ha*, the Nobel Prize.

ཀ། ཧ། ནོ་འབེར་བུ་དགའི་ཏགས་མ།

B: Bullshit. What did the Nobel Prize look like?

ཁ་ ཁྱོའི་ཕྱི་གཏམ་ད། ནོ་འབེར་བུ་དགའི་ཏགས་མ་བདག་གོ་ཅི་མོ་བཞིག་རེད།

A: Uh, there was an eight-spoked wheel on the rim, eight-auspicious symbols in the middle, and eight-petaled lotus at the bottom.

ཀ། ཨ། ཁ་ན་འཁོར་ལོ་རྩིབས་བརྒྱད་ཡོད་གི་བར་ན་བཀྲ་ཤིས་ཏགས་བརྒྱད་ཡོད་གི་ཞབས་ན་པད་འདབ་བརྒྱད་ཡོད་གི

B: It was probably a porcelain bowl.

ཁ་ དཀར་ཡོལ་བཞིག་ཡིན་ས་ཡོད་གོ

A: Uh, in it, the nectar...

ཀ། ཨ། ནང་ན་བདུད་རྩི།

B: Huh?

ཁ་ ཨ།

A: Uh, no, no, no. There was nothing inside it; there was nothing inside it.

ཀ། ཨ་མ་རེད་མ་རེད་མ་རེད། ནང་ན་ཅང་མེད་གི་ནང་ན་ཅང་མེད་གི་ཡ།

B: You don't even know how to lie properly.

ཁ་ གཡོབ་ར་གཏམ་མི་ཤེས་གི་ར།

---

29 Said once, the syllable *nde* (འདེ།) would be perceived as terse or an order. Spoken many times (as done here), it suggests that they are giving or handing him something.

A: Uh, then the Three Ancestral Kings sent a message to the young Tibetan boys and girls in the form of a *dunglen* song.[30]

ཀ། ཨ། དེ་ནས་ད་མེས་དབོན་རྣམ་གསུམ་གྱིས་ བོད་ཀྱི་གསར་བུ་གསར་མོ་ཚོར་སླ་སྙན་དུང་ ལེན་གྱི་ལམ་ནས་སྐད་བཟིག་སྐུར་གྱི

B: Then sing it!

ཁ། ཡ། ཁྱོས་ཅིག་ལོངས།

A: *Ye*, the lady with the feminine body and boy's hair:

ཀ། ཨེ། སྨན་བུ་མོ་མོ་ལུས་པོ་མགོ་ཅན།

When you go away, it is unattractive, and

པར་སོང་ན་སྙིག་ག་སྡུག་སྤྱད་རེད།

When you come back, you upset people.

ཚུར་ཡོང་ན་རྣམ་ཏོག་ཟ་སྤྱད་རེད།

I feel relieved when you are gone.

ཁྱོ་མེད་ན་སེམས་ནས་དགེ་བ་རེད།

Ye, the young man with a liquor bottle in his hands:

ཨེ། སྐྱག་ཕར་ར་ལག་ན་ཆང་པང་ཅན།

When you go away, it is shameful, and

པར་སོང་ན་སྙིག་ག་སྟོན་སྤྱད་རེད།

When you come back, you instigate fights.

ཚུར་ཡོང་ན་གྱོད་ཁ་གཏུག་སྤྱད་རེད།

It is a relief for the neighbours when you are gone.[31]

ཁྱོ་མེད་ན་ཁྱིམ་མཚེས་དགེ་བ་རེད།

B: That is something believable.

ཁ། དེ་བཟོ་རྣར་འགྱོ་ནི་བཟིག་རེད།

---

30 Dunglen is a popular form of music in Amdo since the 1980s accompanied either by mandolin or Tibetan lute known as Dranyen (སྒྲ་སྙན།).

31 The tune follows an older version of the Amdo *dunglen* song known as Akhu Padma (ཨ་ཁུ་པདྨ།) popularized by Palgon, a *dunglen* singer from Machu in Amdo. Menla Jyab changes the lyrics in order to critique the behaviours of young men and women.

3. The Dream

A: Then I took the prophecy of the Three Ancestral Kings in mind and paid attention to the bad on the way back and......

ཀ དེ་ནས་ད་ངས་མེས་དབོན་རྣམ་གསུམ་གི་ལུང་བསྟན་ཡིད་ལ་བཟུང་ནས་ངན་གི་སྟོར་ར་མཐམ་བཞག་གས་ཡོང་ད་ར།

B: Did you get anything out of it?

ཁ ལག་ཡོང་བཞིག་ཨེ་ཡོད་གི

A: Oh, I got a lot out of it. I went from the Headless and Tailless Village to the Tell-Everything Village and heard some stunning things.

ཀ ཨོ། ད་ཡོད་གི་ཡ། མགོ་མེད་གཞུག་རྡུམ་སྟེ་བ་ནས་བྱུད་ལས་མི་བཤད་དགུ་བཤད་སྟེ་བ་རགས་གོར་ཡོང་ད་ར་སྐད་ཆ་ཡ་མཚན་ཏུག་ཏུག་གོ་གི

B: Ya, what did you hear?

ཁ ཡ། སྐད་ཆ་ཅི་བཞིག་གོ་གི

A: When they speak, my stomach aches; when they swear, my ears burn; when they scold, my legs tremble.

ཀ ཨ། ཁ་བརྒྱགས་ན་ཁོག་ནས་ཁོའུ་གི་མནའ་བསྐྱལ་ན་རྣ་འབྱུག་ཚོ་གི་བཤིགས་བཏང་ན་སྐྱིད་པ་འདར་གི

B: So, you are saying that it's all frightening words?

ཁ ཨོ། སྐད་ཆ་འཇིགས་གོ་ཏུག་ཏུག་རེད་བཟེ་ནས།

A: Olé, firstly if I talk about how they give me a stomach-ache when they speak: the words from their mouths are dirty.

ཀ ཨོ་ལེ། ད་དང་པོ་ཁ་བརྒྱགས་ན་ཁོག་ནས་ཁོའུ་སྒུལ་བཟོ་གཅིག་བཤད་ན་ཁ་ནང་གི་སྐད་ཆ་སྦེ་གི

B: Ya, how do they speak?

ཁ ཡ། ཅི་གས་བཤད་གི

A: For example, when I arrived at the Headless-Tailless Village and went to Uncle Complaint-mouth's home, this old man's speech disgusted me.

ཀ ད་དཔེ་བཞག་ན་ང་མགོ་མེད་གཞུག་རྡུམ་སྟེ་བ་ཕེན་ནས་ཨ་ཁུ་སྨུག་སྟེ་ཁ་ཚང་ད་ཅིག་སོང་ད་ར། རྒད་པོ་དེའི་སྐད་ཆམས་ད་ཞེན་ཁ་བརྗོགས་བཏང་ཐལ།

B: Ya, what did this Uncle Complaint-mouth say?

ཁ ཡ། ཨ་ཁུ་སྨུག་སྟེ་ཁ་བདོག་གོས་ཅི་ཟེར་གི

A: Uh, there was not one good word from his mouth, *aro*. He said, "*Aro*! *Ya*, karmically wicked one, you came. Let's go inside our tent and drink some tea.[32] The unlucky one, when did you come? Hey, demon dog, ghost dog, sorcery dog, one whose head should be tied to the ground. *Wei*, bad dog, your mouth should be directed to your father and mother, consuming all the dead and long-dead. I guess the dog saw all those who had died and disappeared."

B: What was that?

A: Wasn't it him scolding their family dog for barking at me, *aro*?

B: *Pee!*[33] Truly, he just speaks disgusting words.

A: *Aro*, that is a wealthy family, and possessions are decent too. But the names are all "torn" and "broken."

B: *Oh*, what does that mean?

A: Uh, talking about containers and things, they are broken cabinet, broken cauldron, broken pot, broken porcelain bowl, bad bowl, broken ladle, bad ladle, torn mat, bad mat, ripped stove, and bad stove.

---

32 In this, Menla Jyab uses humilific forms of "come," "tent," "drink," and "tea," the speaker lowering himself in relation to the speaker.

33 This interjection suggests that the speaker is dismissing a phenomenon or thing when the speaker is disgusted by it.

B: So, everything was broken and torn?

A: Of course not! It was their local speech. And when speaking ornamental language, *aro*: things which should be attached to a corpse, things which should be laid on the road, something which should hit one's heart with, things which should be used for a dog bowl, funeral bowl, items should be thrown in the *gto*,[34] there are so many.

B: Pee! *Lalala*.[35]

A: For clothing: ripped coat, torn pants, ripped lambskin robe, torn sheepskin robe, bad hat, torn sash, torn shoes, *gto* clothing, and dog clothing. For food and cuisine: corpse-food, *gto* food, dog-food, ghost-food. One would not dare to eat when hearing these names, *aro*!

B: That's really filthy speech, *aro*.

A: Then I arrived at the Horse-Herder Village. People were cursing the horses, and it was terrifying too.

B: Gosh.

---

34 A ritual of ransom.
35 *Lalala* is an expression of surprise or awe.

A: The one that should be skinned, the one that should be made into a corpse, the one that should be driven away by bandits, the one that should be made into an inflatable raft, the one whose tail should be cut, the one whose mane should be sheared, the one that should carry corpses (which I didn't even understand)! When I arrived at the Yak-Herder Village, they were cursing the yaks, *don*-yaks,[36] ghost-yaks, sorcery-yak, disappearing-yaks, the one that should contract rinderpest, the one that should die from *sakyon* disease,[37] the one who should no longer leave footprints. There were so many.

ཀ ད་ཅིག་རྟ་གོ་བཞུ་རྒྱུའི། རྟ་རོ་ཡེད་རྒྱུའི། ཇག་པས་འདེད་རྒྱུའི། སྒྱུ་བ་ཡེད་རྒྱུའི། ཇ་མ་གཅོད་རྒྱུའི། རྡོག་མ་འབྲེག་རྒྱུའི། རོ་མ་ཡེད་རྒྱུའི་ད་ར་མི་གོ་གི་ནོར་རྫི་སྡེ་བར་ཕྱིན་ན་ར་ཡང་ནོར་ལ་སྨྱགས་གོ་གི་ཡང་གདོན་ཟོག་འདྲེ་ཟོག་བྱད་ཟོག་ཡལ་ཟོག་གོར་ནག་ཡོང་རྒྱུའི་ས་སྐྱོན་གྱི་འཆི་རྒྱུའི། རྗེས་ཆད་རྒྱུའི་ད་མང་གི་ཡ།

B: Most likely they were hurt by the milk and yoghurt that they drank.[38]

ཁ དའོ་ནོ་འཐུང་ནོ་མ་བཟང་ནི་ཡིན་རྒྱུའི་རེད།

A: When I arrived at Goat and Sheep Herder Village, there were even more. Ones that should contract *za* disease,[39] the ones that should contract head-worms, ones that should have diarrhoea, ones that we should sweep up after,[40] ones that should be handed to a butcher.

ཀ ར་མ་ལུག་རྫིའི་སྡེ་བར་ཕྱིན་ན་ར་ཡང་མང་གི་གཟའ་ན་རྒྱུའི། མགོ་འབུ་འདེབ་རྒྱུའི། ཆུང་ཡོང་རྒྱུའི། ཤུལ་སྡུད་མས་རྒྱག་རྒྱུའི། ཤན་པའི་ལག་ལ་འཛོག་རྒྱུའི།

B: They were the butchers themselves!

ཁ ཤན་པ་ཁོ་ཚོ་རང་གི་རེད་མོ།

---

36   A type of harmful spirit.
37   This disease occurs in yaks and cattle; once contacted, the animal would die in less than a few hours after groaning loudly.
38   This sarcastically suggests that the yaks didn't do enough by giving their milk.
39   This is a common disease occurring in sheep where the contacted animal would have balance issues.
40   Meaning that they are sold and the ground should be swept to leave no trace of their existence.

3. The Dream

A: Then I arrived at Primitive Village, people swore some strange oaths.

ཀ ཨ། ཡ་ཐོག་སྟེ་བར་ཐོན་ན་ར་མནའ་བཟིག་ག་ ཡ་མཚན་དག་དག་སྐྱེལ་གོ་གི

B: How did they swear?

ཁ ཅི་གས་སྐྱེལ་གི་ཡོད་གི

A: By generations of ancestors! By all the scriptures that have been written and chanted! By the one and only Mani! By the twelve volumes of the Yum![41] By all the pure virtues! By Kumbum![42] By Shachong![43] By Kanjur and Tenjur![44]

ཀ དུ་སྦྱི་རིང་སྦྱི་རྒྱུད། བྲིས་པ་བཏོན་པ། མ་ཎི་ ཁེར་པོ། ཡུམ་དུམ་པ་བཅུ་གཉིས། དཀར་པོ་ དགེ་བ། སྐུ་འབུམ། བྱ་ཁྱུང་། བཀའ་འགྱུར་ བསྟན་འགྱུར།

B: Oh my, oh my!

ཁ ཨང་ཨང་།

A: By all the dharma on this earth, then followed by, by having nine bites at my father's raw liver!

ཀ ས་ཁ་ས་ཐོག་གི་ཆོས། དེ་ནས་མར་ཡོད་ན་དེ་ ཨ་བའི་མཆིན་པ་རྗེན་པར་སོ་དགུ་བཏབ་བོ།

B: *Lalala.*

ཁ ལ་ལ་ལ།

A: By having nine gulps of my mother's blood after killing her! By spreading my son's bones to nine different places after smashing them! It was endless, *aro.*

ཀ ཨ་མ་བསད་ལས་ཁྲག་ག་དུན་དགུ་ཡམ་ནོ། ཞི་ལིའི་རུས་པ་བཏུང་དས་ས་ཆ་དགུར་སྦྱོ་ནོ། དུ་ཚར་རྒྱུ་མེད་ནི་བཟིག་ཡོད་གི་ཨ་རོ།

B: Oh my goodness! That's utterly terrible.

ཁ ཨང་ཨང་ཨང་། དུ་དོ་མ་གཅིག་བཙོག་གི་གོ

A: Don't fret; there are even worse things yet to come.

ཀ དུ་ཁྱོ་མ་བྱེལ་ར་དེའི་ར་བཙོག་གོ་དེའི་གཞུག་ ན་ཡོད་ཞིར་ཡ།

B: There's even worse than that?

ཁ དེའི་བཙོག་ར་ཡོད་ཞིར།

---

41   Name used in Amdo for the twelve volumes of the "Perfection of Wisdom Sutra" texts, and a popular oath.
42   One of the largest monasteries in Amdo.
43   An important monastery (and also the name of a mountain deity) in Amdo.
44   The foundational texts of Buddhism, the Kanjur is the sayings of the Buddha, and the Tenjur is collected commentaries from great teachers.

A: Of course, from Black-Nose Black-Tongue Village to the Tell-Everything Village it was all about cursing people.

ཀ ཨ་ལོས་ཡོད། སྣ་ནག་ལྕེ་ནག་སྡེ་བ་ནས་བྱུད་ལས་མི་བཤད་དགུ་བཤད་སྡེ་བ་རགས་གོ་ད་ཁྱེར་སྙིགས་སོལ་རེད་ཡ།

B: *Ya*, how do they curse people?

ཁ ཡ། ཁྱེར་ཆེ་ཡས་སྙིགས་ནི་རེད།

A: Uh, at first, they will express their wish that everything goes wrong for you.

ཀ ཨ། དང་ཐོག་ཁྱོད་ཀྱི་དོན་བྱ་མི་འགྲུབ་ནའི་ཁ་གཡང་བཟིག་འབོད་ནི་རེ།

B: Gosh.

ཁ ཨད།

A: The one whose endeavours should go wrong, the one whose works should be carried away by the Guchu river,[45] the one who should never have any prosperity, the one whose merits should be tied to a dog's neck, the one who should never see happiness, the one whose mouth should be smeared with ash, the one whose head should be put in a bag, she who should be widowed for nine times, there's enough to fill a whole valley.

ཀ དབྱ་ལམ་མ་མི་འགྲོ་རྒྱུའི་བྱ་དགུ་ཆུར་འདྲེས་རྒྱུའི་ཁ་ཡར་ར་མི་འགྲོ་རྒྱུའི་བསོད་ནམས་ཁྱིའི་སྐྱེར་འདོགས་རྒྱུའི་སྐྱིད་སྙིག་གིས་མི་རིག་རྒྱུའི་ཁ་ཐལ་གིས་གཏོད་རྒྱུའི་མགོ་སྙེ་གིས་བཏུམས་རྒྱུའི་ཡུགས་ས་ཐེངས་དགུར་འབྱུད་རྒྱུ། དགུང་བ་གང་ཡོད་ནི་རེད་ཡ།

B: Oh my goodness.

ཁ ཨད་ཨད་ཨད།

A: Uh, then they will pray for you to have an unhealthy body.[46]

ཀ ཨ། དེའི་འཕྱོར་ད་ཁྱོད་ཀྱི་སྐུ་ལུས་མི་བདེ་བའི་སྨོན་ལམ་བཟིག་འདེབས་རྒྱུ་རེད།

B: Geez.

ཁ ཨད།

---

45 This is the name of the main river in Rebgong, a tributary of the Yellow River (རྨ་ཆུ།).
46 Interestingly, the word used here for "body" is an honorific term.

A: The one who should get a goitre, the one who should become mute, the one who should get lockjaw, the one who should go blind, the ones whose tongue should fall out, at the same time, they use things like voracious, big-belly, ever-hungry at their convenience. *Aro*, you know that, right?

B: *Pee! Pee!* What a terrible thing.

A: After that, they will tell you to leave this human world.

B: Oh?

A: Uh, the one whose face should never be seen, the one whose speech should never be heard, the one whose name should never be called, the one whose happiness should be diminished abruptly, the one whose life should follow the setting sun. Uh, after that, the one whose head should be buried under a rock, the one who should be dumped into a well, and the one over whose head dirt should be shovelled. *Ayoshe*, I can't finish listing them here, *aro*.

B: Goodness, who wants to listen to those?

A: Ah, they will pray like: All the dead people from your family! All the dead people from the past and now! Your father and your mother! The corpse of your father and mother! The heads of your father and mother! Nine freshly dead corpses still warm! *Aro*, are you disgusted?

ཀ སྐེ་སྐྲངས་བྱུང་རྒྱུའི། དཀའ་འབྱིར་རྒྱུའི། ཁ་དཀས་རྒྱུའི། སྨྱིག་ཨར་རྒྱུའི། ལྕེ་ཅད་རྒྱུའི། དུ་བོར་ཐུར་ར་བདའ་ཁན། ཕོ་ཆེ། བཀྱགས་མེད། བློ་རྒྱལ་ཅན་གོ་ཁ་ནང་ད་བདེ་ཕྱོགས་ག་སྟོད་རྒྱུའི་རེད་གོ ཨ་རོ། དེ་ཁྱོས་ཤེས་ག་བཟེ།

ཁ ཕིས་ཕིས། ཅིའི་ཐན་ལུས་བཟེག་རེད།

ཀ དེའི་འཕྱོར་ད་ཁྱོ་འཛིག་ཧེན་མི་ཡུལ་འདི་ནས་ད་ཐུད་ལ་སོང་ཟེར་རྒྱ་རེད་ཡ།

ཁ ཨོ།

ཀ ཨ། དུ་དོ་ཞྱིག་གིས་མི་རིག་རྒྱུའི། སྐད་ན་གིས་མི་གོ་རྒྱུའི། མིང་གིས་མི་འཇེན་རྒྱུའི། སྐྱིད་ཀེད་པས་ཅད་རྒྱུའི། ཚེ་ཉི་མའི་རྟ་འགྲོ་རྒྱུའི་ཨ་དེའི་འཕྱོ་ད། མགོ་རྡོ་འོག་ག་འཇུག་རྒྱུའི། ས་འོག་དོང་ནས་ལ་འཕེན་རྒྱུའི། མགོ་ར་ས་ལྷག་རྒྱུའི། ཨ་ཡོ་ཤེ། ད་དས་བཟད་ལས་ར་མི་ཆར་གི་ཨ་རོ།

ཁ ཨང་ཨང། ད་ཉན་ན་འདོད་ས་ཨེ་ཡོད་གི།

ཀ ཨ་ད་ད་རུང་ཁྱེད་གི་ཕྱི་ཕི་ཡལ་ཡག་གནན་ཤི་ད་བརྒྱུད། ཨ་བ་ཨ་མ། ཕ་རོ་མ་རོ། ཕ་མགོ་མ་མགོ ཨ་རོ། ནག་དགུ་བརྗེགས་དགུ་པོ་ར་ད་རུང་རྔས་པ་ཚན་པོ་སོ་མ་ཞི་དྲུང་གི་དེ་བཞེ་སྦོན་ལམ་འདེབས་རྒྱ་རེད་ཡ། ཨ་རོ། ད་ཁྲམ་ཧོག་ཨེ་ལངས་གི།

B: *Lalala*, those are truly disgusting words. They really need to be changed.

ཁ ལ་ལ་ལ། དྭོ་མ་སྐད་ཚ་སླེ་པོ་ཧག་ཧག་དི་དྭ་དྭོ་མ་གཅིག་བསྒྱུར་དགོག

A: Uh, I had never heard this type of speech before. I bet this is the benefit the three ancestral kings said I would get out of it, *aro*!

ག ཨ། དྭ་བྲེདས་མིན་ནས་སྐད་ཚ་འདིའི་རིགས་དས་གོ་མ་མྱོང་། མེས་དབོན་རྣམ་གསུམ་གྱིས་ད་འདྲ་ཕྱོགས་ཀྱི་ལག་ཡོད་ཡོད་བཟེ་ལུང་བསྟན་ནོ་དི་ད་འདི་ཨེ་ཡིན་ན་ད་འདོད་ཀྱི་ར། ཨ་རོ།

B: Yeah, probably!

ཁ ཨེ། ཡིན་རྒྱུ་རེད་གོ

A: They said those are not [the gains in the prophecy].

ག མ་རེད་ཟེར་ཡ།

B: Who said that?

ཁ སུས་མ་རེད་ཟེར་གི

A: Some herders came and said I misunderstood them, and they did not have such ways of swearing oaths and cursing.

ག ཟོག་རྫི་སྨྱོར་བཞིག་ཡོང་དས་ཁྱོས་ཁྱེར་ཚོ་བཀན་ལོག་ཡོད་བཏང་ནི་རེད། མནའ་སྐྱེལ་སྐྱོལ་ར་སྨྱིགས་སྐྱོལ་དི་མོ་མེད་ཟེར་གི

B: What did you say?

ཁ ཁྱོས་ཅི་བཟེ།

A: I told them, "I am saying all this for your own good, You have them! By your flesh if you don't." They said, "we don't." I said, "you do!" And they said, "We don't!" *Aro*, my blood was boiling and I pushed one of them, and there was a "bang" sound.

ག དས་ན་ཚ་ཡམས་བཞད་གོ་ནི་རེད། ཡོད་ཀྱི་ཁྱོའི་ཤ་མེད་ཀྱི་ན་བཟེ་ར། མེད་ཟེར་གི་ཡོད་ཀྱི་བཟེ་ར། མེད་ཟེར་གི་ཨ་རོ། ཁྱག་བཟེ་ཁོལ་ནི་བཞིག་རེད། གཅིག་ག་ཕུད་རྒྱག་བཞིག་ཡོད་བཏང་ར་སྨྱིག་སེ་བྱུད་ཐལ།

B: What was it?

ཁ ཅི་བཞིག

A: My son had been sleeping with me and I had kicked and pushed him to the ground.

ག རྫམ་གི་ཞི་ལེར་ཉལ་བས་གཅིག་བརྒྱབ་བས་ཐང་ལ་འཕང་དས་བཞག་ཡོད་ཀྱི་ཡ།

3. The Dream

B: After all that, it was all just your dream. Oh, your son was all right, right? What did he say?

ཁ བཤད་བཤད་གི་ཧ་མ་དེ་ཚང་མ་ཁྱོད་ཀྱི་རྨི་ལམ་རེད་མོ། ཨོ། ཞེ་ལྱེར་ཅིང་བཅོས་མེད་ལ། ཆེ་ཟེར་གི

A: He said, "Father and Mother! By all the dharma on the earth! Who threw me to the ground?"

ཀ ཨ་བ་ཨ་མ། ས་ཁ་ས་ཕྲོག་གི་ཆོས། ང་བརྡ་ལ་འཕེན་ནོ་སུ་ཡིན། དེ་ཟེར་ཡ།

A and B: Hahaha.

ཀ ཁ ཧ་ཧ་ཧ།

4. All-good Menla སྨན་བླ་ཀུན་བཟང་།[1]

A: *Ya*, Uncle Menla!	ཀ	ཀ ཡ། ཨ་ཁུ་སྨན་བླ།
B: Call me Kunzang!	ཁ	ཀུན་བཟང་བཟེ།
A: *Ya*, Uncle Kunzang!	ཀ	ཡ། ཨ་ཁུ་ཀུན་བཟང་།
B: Menla! Menla!	ཁ	སྨན་བླ། སྨན་བླ།
A: *Ya*, Uncle Menla, you…	ཀ	ཡ། ཨ་ཁུ་སྨན་བླ། ཁྱོ།
B: No, no! Kunzang.	ཁ	མ་རེད་མ་རེད། ཀུན་བཟང་།
A: *Ya*, so, are you actually Menla or Kunzang?	ཀ	ཡ། ད་དོན་དོ་མས་ཁྱོ་སྨན་བླ་ཡིན་ནི་ན་ཀུན་བཟང་ཡིན་ནས།
B: Menla Kunzang	ཁ	སྨན་བླ་ཀུན་བཟང་།
A: *Lalala*. Kunzang on top of Menla, is it fitting for you?[2]	ཀ	ལ་ལ་ལ། སྨན་བླ་དེའི་ཁ་ལ་ཀུན་བཟང་དེ་བཟོ་ཁྱོ་ཨེ་མཛད་གི།

---

1 In this performances, Phagmo Drashi is in the "A" position, while Menla Jyab voices "B."

2 Here Phagmo Drashi takes the name literally: Menla being the name of the medicine Buddha and *kunzang* literally meaning "all good," and suggests that such a name is inappropriate for him.

©2025 Jyab (text)
Thurston & Samdrup (Trans. & Notes), CC BY-NC 4.0   https://doi.org/10.11647/OBP.0452.04

B: That's what they call me, even if it's not fitting. | མི་མཛའ་ན་ར་ཐོགས་སོང་བཞིག་ག་བཟེ།

A: Oh, I hadn't heard that. | ཀ ཨོ། ངས་མ་གོ

B: Truly, you wouldn't believe how much I have suffered since being called Menla Kunzang! | ཁ དོ་མ། དའི་སྙིང་ད་སྨན་བླ་ཀུན་བཟང་བདགས་གས་ཕྱིར་རས་ད་ངས་ཆིག་དག་བདང་ནོ་ད་བཤད་ལས་རྣར་མི་འགྲོ་ཡ།

A: If I wouldn't believe it then you must be lying. | ཀ བཤད་ལས་ན་མི་འགྲོ་དུས་ད་གཤོག་གཅུམ་གོ་ནི་ཡིན་རྒྱུའོ་རེད།

B: No way no way. I am telling the truth. There isn't even a lie the size of a louse's leg. | ཁ ཆེ་ཡིན་ཆེ་ཡིན། དོ་མ་བཤད་གོ་ནི་ཡིན། རྫུན་བཞིག་ག་དཤིག་གི་ཤུག་ཏི་འད་བཞིག་ར་མེད།

A: Then you tell me. | ཀ འོ་ན་ཁྱོས་དགོད་ར་ཡ།

B: [with unwilling laughter] Ahihi, I am not going to tell you. You are not going to believe me. | ཁ ཨ་ཧི་ཧི། ད་མི་བཤད་ནི་ཡིན། ཁྱོའི་རྣར་འགྲོ་རྒྱུ་མ་རེད།

A: If I don't believe, then I don't believe you! Just tell me. | ཀ དའི་རྣ་མ་སོང་ན་མ་སོང་། ཁྱོས་དགོད་མོ

B: Are you going to believe me? How about you tell me that. | ཁ ཁྱོའི་རྣར་འགྲོ་རྒྱུའེ། ཡ་ད་དི་བཟེ་ར།

A: [surprised] *Ala*, how would I know if I believe you or not if you don't tell me. | ཀ ཨ་ལ། རྣ་འགྲོ་རྒྱུ་བཟེ་ཁྱོས་མ་བཤད་ལ་ངས་ཤེས་ནས།

B: Isn't it me signing a contract before telling you? So when you don't believe me after I've finished, either you don't have ears, or you have them but you're deaf, or you're an utter fool. Otherwise, what do you do with those ears? | ཁ ངས་ར་མ་བཤད་གོང་ད་གན་རྒྱ་འཛོག་གོ་ནོ་མིན་ནས། བཤད་བཏང་ཚར་རས་ད་ནྭ་མི་འགྲོ་ནི་ཡོད་དུས་དེར་ནྭ་འབྱོག་མེད་ནི་ཡིན་རྒྱུའོ་རེད། ཡོད་རུང་འོན་པ་ཡིན་ནི་ཡིན་རྒྱུའོ་རེད། ཡང་མིན་ན་བབ་གི་སློའུ་བཞིག་ཡིན་ནི་ཡིན་རྒྱུའོ་རེད། དི་མིན་ན་ནྭ་དིག་རེ་བབ་གི་ཆེ་ཡོད་རྒྱུ།

4. All-good Menla

A: Oh, though I may not believe, I still need to fix my attention and listen to it as though I'm listening to folktales.

ཀ ཨོ། དངོས་མི་འགྱོ་ན་ར་རྣམ་ཤེས་གཏད་ལས་ གནའ་གཏམ་མ་ཉན་ཉན་བཞིག་ཡེད་དགོ་ བཏང་ནི་རེད།

B: Oh, when you believe me, my story is as different from an ordinary folktale as the earth is from the sky, *aro*.

ཁ ཨོ། དངོས་བྱད་སོང་དུས་ཐད་སོ་དང་ཁས་ གི་གནའ་གཏམ་བཞིག་ག་བསྟུན་ན་ད་གནམ་ ས་གི་ཁྱད་པར་ཡོད་རྒྱུའི་རེད་གོ་ཨ་རོ།

A: What's important is that I would listen closely if you were to tell it.

ཀ གཙོ་བོ་ཁྱོས་ཅིག་བཤད་བཏང་རྒྱུ་ན་ངས་ གཞིས་གི་ཉན་རྒྱུ་རེད་མོ།

B: If I tell it, it's going to take too long.

ཁ ད་བཤད་ན་སྐད་ཆ་རིང་འགྱོ་གི

A: Well then then tell a short version.

ཀ འོ་ན་ཐུང་ཐུང་བཞིག་ཤོད་ར་དེ་རེད།

B: Uh, if it's short no one will like it.

ཁ ཨ། ཐུང་ན་ཐམས་ཅད་མི་དགའ་གི

A: Then tell a version that's neither short nor long.

ཀ དེ་ན་ད་ཐུང་རྒྱུ་རིང་རྒྱུ་མེད་ནི་བཞིག་ཤོད།

B: If I tell it neither short nor long, then I'm not an elder who tells folktales, not a scholar who can tell modern stories, not a *lama* who knows the next life, not a leader who doesn't need an inside man.

ཁ རིང་ཐུང་མེད་པའི་གཏམ་བཞིག་བཤད་ན། ང་ གནའ་གཏམ་བཤད་གི་གནའ་སྒྱི་མ་རེད། ད་ གཏམ་བཤད་གི་མཁས་པ་མ་རེད། ཕྱི་མ་ མཁྱེན་གི་བླ་མ་མ་རེད། ནང་མ་མི་དགོ་དཔོན་ པོ་མ་རེད།

A: Oh, now it has turned into a wedding speech. Say, "first, it's difficult for my snow-white mind to manifest it," *aro*![3]

ཀ ཨོ་ད་སྟོན་བཤད་གི་ལོག་ཐལ། དང་པོ་འི་ གངས་དཀར་སེམས་མ་འཆར་དཀའ་གི་ཨ་རོ།

B: First, it's easy for my snow-white mind to manifest it.

ཁ དང་པོ་འི་གངས་དཀར་སེམས་མ་འཆར་ སྟུ་གི

---

3 In the previous turn, speaker B has riffed on a formula common to Tibetan speeches, and speaker A extends that here. The speech style continues through to the next page.

A: Oh?

ཀ ཨོ།

B: It is easy to loosen the knots of the silky tongue. It is easy to speak from between the 30 teeth of my mouth. It is easy for you to listen to it from boxy-machines.[4] These days my *khashag* and advice are cheap.

ཁ ལྕེ་དར་མའི་མདུད་པ་བཀྲོལ་སྟབས་གྱི་ཁའི་དུང་སོ་སུམ་བཅུའི་བར་ནས་བཤད་སྟབས་གྱི། ཁྱོས་འཕུལ་སྒམ་གྱུ་བཞིའི་ནང་ནས་ཉན་སྟབས་གྱི། དའི་ཁ་བཤགས་ལ་ལ་ཁ་སང་དེ་རིང་ད་གོང་སྟབས་གྱི།

A: *Lalala*. Nothing is difficult for this guy!

ཀ ལ་ལ་ལ། འདིར་དཀའ་མོ་བཟིག་བབ་གི་མེད་གི་སེ།

B: I, the one with a cheap straw hat, bear this difficulty only out of concern for the snow-white goddess.[5] This time I wrote this play causing all sorts of laughter because I need cash.[6]

ཁ སྭ་མོ་རྗེ་ཞུ་ཅན་གིས་དཀའ་མོ་འདི་གདས་དགར་ལྷ་མོ་བསམས་མས་ཁུར་ནི་ཡིན། གད་མོ་སྣ་ཚོགས་སློང་བའི་ཅེད་མོ་འདི་ད་ཐེངས་སློར་མོ་དགོ་ཡས་བྱིས་ནི་ཡིན།

A: Oh, then it's certain that it won't be worth listening to.

ཀ ཨོ་དེ་ཉིན་རྒྱུ་མེད་ཁོ་ཐག་རེད་ཡ།

B: I'll say, "Bearded uncles above, don't say they're bad omens and meaningless chatter. Young ones in the middle with pens don't say it's glib and easy to listen to. Powerless women below don't say 'ha ha ho ho[7] it's a lie!'"

ཁ གོང་གི་ཨ་ཁུ་སྨྲ་ར་ཅན་ཚོས་ཐན་ལྷས་ར་ཁ་འབུལ་མ་ཟེར། བར་གི་གསར་བུ་སྨྱུག་གུ་ཅན་ཚོ་ཁ་བདེ་ར་སྨྲ་བདེ་མ་ཟེར། ཞོལ་གི་མ་སུ་དབང་མེད་མ་ཚོས་ཧ་ཧ་ཧོ་ཧོ་རྫུན་གཏམ་རེད་མ་ཟེར་ཟེར་རྒྱུ།

A: There's no need! There's no need.

ཀ མི་དགོ་མི་དགོ

B: [disbelievingly] "No need?" *Wei*!

ཁ མི་དགོ་བདོག་གོ་སེ།

---

4   In the context of Amdo in the 1980s and 1990s, this refers specifically to radios.
5   "Snow white goddess" appears to be a reference to Tibet and likely draws its imagery from a poem by Jangbu that was popular around this time. See https://www.tibetcm.com/contemporary/pfv/2014-12-11/4007.html
6   In this line "B" repeats the syllable "*mo*" several times in a form of traditional language play.
7   A laugh that women in Amdo use to express disbelief or derision.

4. All-good Menla

A: You replaced difficult with easy, so I replaced *lakso* with "no need."

B: You can't say there's no need. If you say there's no need, then I'll have nothing more to say.

A: And you can't say, you won't speak. If you don't speak, then I'll have nothing more to listen to.

B: Ah, I'll speak if you'll have me speak. Speaking truthfully, there's really not that much to say. It was last year after I was named Menla Kunzang.

A: *Ya*, then get on with it.

B: One day, my wife blew up, saying "Menla Kunzang! Just writing your *khashag*, don't you have to fill your mouth? Go collect some firewood."

A: Then go collect firewood!

B: Hmph, though I am a good person, it's not ok for the wife to be giving me orders. I was very angry and ran and grabbed the ground...

A: You didn't pick up a big rock, did you?

B: ... I picked up an axe and brought it [with me]...

A: *Ala*. you can't hit with an axe!

B: ... I put the axe through my sash and dashed out.

ཁ སྟ་རེ་སྐག་ག་དངས་བཏང་ནས་ཕྱུར་སེ་བཏང་བཏང་ང་།

A: [scornfully] Heh, I thought you were going to beat your wife.

ག དེ། ངས་བྱིས་ཀུན་མོར་གཅར་རྒྱུ་རེད་འདོད་ལ།

B: By the *Yum*! It is difficult to go collect the firewood, let alone on foot. So I secretly rode the old horse that was so thin it was about to fall over.

ཁ ཡུམ་བཟེ། ཆ་མ་འཐུ་གི་སོང་ངས་མ་ཚོག་རྐང་ཐང་ང་སོང་ངས་བཟོ་མ་ནི་རེད། ཏུ་རྐན་བསྐ་བོ་ལོག་ལ་ཁད་བཞིག་ཡོད་ནོ་ཁ་རོག་ག་ཞོན་ནས་ཕྱད་སོང་།

A: So even that had to be ridden secretly?[8]

ག དེ་ར་ཞེས་གི་མ་བཞག་ག་ཞོན་དགོ་ནི་ཨེ་རེད།

B: I rode and rode, and at some point, I paid some attention and realized that the old horse was just bouncing up and down in one spot as if it was dancing.

ཁ སོང་སོང་ངས་བར་བཞིག་ག་མཐམ་བཞིག་བཞག་ཐུས་ཏུ་ཀུན་ཁ་མ་ཕྱིར་བོ་ཅིག་བོ་བཞིག་འདུ་བཞིག་བྱིད་ངས་བསྡད་ཡོད་གི

A: [dismissively] Oh, oh, that must be your Dudu Disco.[9]

ག ཨོ་ཨོ། དེ་ད་ཁྱོད་གི་ཏུའུ་ཏུའུ་disco་བདོག་གོ་ཡིན་ནི་ཡིན་རྒྱུའི་རེད།

B: I bent over from atop the horse and looked, and something was wrong, *aro*.

ཁ རྟ་གོང་ནས་མར་ར་བསྒུར་རས་ཅིག་བལྟས་ར་བྱ་ལས་མ་སོང་མེད་གི་ཨ་རོ།

A: What had happened?

ག ཅི་བཟིག་ཡས་བཏང་བཞིག

B: Uh, the axe tucked in my sash had fallen out and had broken one of the horse's legs.

ཁ ཨུན། ངའི་སྐག་གི་སྟ་རེ་ཕྱུང་ངས་ཁྱིར་རས་རྟ་ཀུན་གི་སུག་ཏི་གཅིག་བཅག་གས་དང་བཏང་བཞིག

A: As if it was made of red clay.[10]

ག ས་དམར་གིས་ལས་ནི་ཡིན་ས་ཡོད་དུ།

---

8   This implies that B's wife is very strict and controls what he can and cannot do.
9   Dudu would be the sound people make when feeding horses.
10 Red clay (ས་དམར་) is used in Amdo to make animal sculptures and *tsha tsha* moulded images used as offerings.

4. All-good Menla

B: So what could I do? It's certain that a horse with three legs can't take me anywhere.

ཁ དེ་ཅི་བཟིག་ཡིན་རྒྱུ། རྐང་ལག་གསུམ་ཅན་གྱི་རྟ་བཟིག་གིས་རྐང་ཚིགས་གོམ་ཞིག་མི་ཐུབ་ནོ་ཁོ་ཐག་རེད་རེ།

A: If it could then you should ride a tripod.[11]

ཀ དེ་ཐུབ་ན་དུ་ཧྲེར་རྐང་གསུམ་མ་ཞོན་ནས་མི་འགྲོ།

B: I was left with no choice, so I cut a tree branch and implanted it as the horse's leg and set off and I tell you that my horse was faster than before!

ཁ རང་ད་སྤྱུག་ག་ཕྱུག་གས་སྡོང་བོའི་ར་ལག་བཟིག་བཅད་ལས་ཡོང་དངས་རྟ་རྐན་གྱི་རྐང་བའི་ཕྱལ་བ་སྤྱད་བཏང་དངས་བྱད་སོང་ད་ར། རྟ་རྐན་དང་མ་གི་དེའི་ར་མགྱོགས་རེད་བཟེ་ནས་ཡ།

A: Oh, I hope it was like that.

ཀ ཨོ་ད་ཡིན་འགྱོ་རེད།

B: At some point, the horse was not moving again.

ཁ བར་བཟིག་ག་ཡང་རྟ་རྐན་ན་འགུལ་རྒྱུར་མེད་གི།

A: It must have been tired.

ཀ ད་ཚད་བཏང་ནེ་ཡིན་རྒྱུའི་རེད།

B: I turned back and looked and my gosh......

ཁ ཁ་ཕྱིར་ར་འཁོར་རས་ཅིག་བལྟས་ར། ཨ་བུ་དེ་ན། བུ་ནེ།

A: Something else was wrong?

ཀ ཡང་བུ་ལས་མ་ལས་ནས་སོང་མེད་ག

B: That tree branch had grown into the sky and my horse and I were like toys at the foot of the tree.

ཁ སྡོང་བོའི་ར་ག་དེ་སྡོང་རྐན་གྱི་བཟིག་གི་ལོག་གས་ནམ་མཁའ་གྱེན་ན་སྐྱེས་བཏང་ནོ་རྟ་རྐན་དེད་གཉིས་ཀ་བཟེ་ནོ་སྡོང་རྩ་ན་ཅིག་གི་ཅེད་ཕྲུད་བཟིག་ག་རིག་གི་བཟེ་ནེ་ཡ།

A: They're probably your wife's toys.[12]

ཀ དེ་ཁྱེད་ཀྱི་རྐན་མོའི་ཅེད་ཕྲུད་ཡིན་ནེ་ཡིན་རྒྱུའི་རེད།

---

11 This is likely a reference to tripods that government survey teams placed on mountains in the 1980s and 1990s.

12 Here A continues to suggest that B is under his wife's thumb.

B: Uh, *ya* so I thought I must go into the sky and have a look around. There wouldn't be anything wrong with that. So I climbed up the tree.

A: [scoffing] *Ang*, so climb then!

B: After, eighty-one days, I finally reached sky. The sky was absolutely delightful, *aro*.

A: What was it like?

B: It is utterly blue.

A: So being blue is delightful?

B: It was so delightful that I completely forgot to collect firewood.

A: Of course, you had seen all the blue.

B: After wandering around for some time and when the afternoon sun was setting, I was so hungry my insides hurt.

A: Your insides were probably stuck together.

B: I thought about going home for a meal and looked down and *ahawonahawo...*

A: Now what had happened?

B: The tree I climbed was nowhere to be seen.

A: It didn't fall down did it?

B: My horse dragged it to somewhere else, after all it was his prosthetic leg.

A: Then, sit there blissfully in the utterly blue place!

B: I gave a thought and remembered people saying that there are gods and goddesses in the sky. I thought "*Ya*, I should look for them." I went on and on and finally arrived in front of a temple.

A: Was it the Mani Temple in your village?

B: I looked inside from door gap for a bit. Yep! I tell you they were all sitting in the sun picking each other's lice.

A: Were they the elders from your village?

B: Of course not! Gods and goddesses! I prostrated eighty-one times 'til my forehead was numb from it, *aro*.

A: That's probably because your forehead has not received the training yet.

ཀ   ལྷོག་སོང་ནི་མིན་ན།

ཁ   རྟ་ཀུན་གྱིས་སྡིང་པོ་དྲུད་ལས་བྱུད་སོང་བཞག་
    ཡ། ཅི་ཁག་རེ། ཁོ་གི་ཞིང་ཀང་རེད་མོ།

ཀ   དཀྱི་དགས་སྟོན་པོ་སྟོན་པོ་ནས་སྐྱིད་པོ་སྐྱིད་
    པོ་བྱོས་ཡ་སྡོད་ཡ།

ཁ   འདྡ་བཞིག་བཀུབ་པ་ར་སེམས་ཅན་གྱིས་
    བཤད་རྩུལ་ཡིན་ན་ནམ་མཁའ་ན་ལྷ་ལྷ་མོ་
    བདོག་གོ་ཡོད་ནི་ཟེར་གི་ཡ་དི་ཚ་བོ་ཅིག
    བཙལ་གི་འགྲོ་དགོ་གི་འདོད་ལས་སོང་སོང་ང་
    ང་ར་དུ་ལྷ་ཁང་བཞིག་གི་མདུན་ན་ཐོན་ཐལ།

ཀ   ཁྱེད་ཚོ་བོའི་སྤྲེ་བའི་མ་ཎི་ཁང་རིག་བཏང་ནི་
    མིན་ན།

ཁ   སྒོ་སྦུབ་ནས་ཡུན་གྱིས་ཅིག་བལྟས་ར། རེད་གོ་
    ཅང་མ་ཉེ་མ་གཞིས་ཡེ་ཤིག་འཕྲུས་ཡེ་བསྡད་
    བཞག་ཡོད་གི་བཟེ་ནས་ཡ།

ཀ   ཁྱེད་ཚོ་བོའི་སྤྲེ་བའི་ལོ་ལོན་ཚ་ཡིན་ནི་མིན་ན།

ཁ   ཅེ་ཡིན་ཅེ་ཡིན། ལྷ་དང་ལྷ་མོ། ཁོ་ཚ་བོར་
    དབུགས་ཐེངས་གཅིག་གིས་ཕུག་དགུ་དགུ་
    བཀྱུད་རྒྱུ་གཅིག་འཚལ་བཏང་ང་ར་ཐོད་པ་
    བཟོ་བེར་རེ་རེ་ཡོད་གི་རང་ང་།

ཀ   ཁྱོའི་ཐོད་པ་ད་རུང་སྦྱང་བ་ཐོབ་མེད་ནི་ཡིན་
    རྒྱུའི་རེད།

B: I said, "*Om mani padme hum.* Gracious ones, people say that food and clothing are self-arising in heaven, but none have arisen for me, please quickly put something self-arisen in my stomach. Quickly!"[13]

ཁ ཨོཾ་མ་ཎི་པདྨེ་ཧཱུྃ། དྲིན་ཅན་ཚ་གོ། སེམས་ཅན་གྱིས་བཤད་ནོ་ཡིན་ན་ལྷ་ཡུལ་ན་ཟས་རང་འབྱུབ་ར་གོས་རང་འབྱུབ་དག་གོ་ཡིན་ནི་རེད་ཟེར་གྱི་རེད། ང་ཅིག་ང་ར་མ་འབྱུབ་ཐལ་ཕོ་གི་གདང་ང་རེམ་མ་རང་འབྱུབ་བཟིག་རེམ་མ་ཕྱོངས་བཟེ་ར།

A: What did they say?

ག ཅི་བཟིག་ཟེར་གི

B: [disappointedly] Ha! I tell you they didn't even look at me.

ཁ ད། སྟེ་ཚ་བོས་ང་ཅིག་གིས་ཅིག་བལྟ་ཁ་མི་ཤན་གི་བཟེ་ན།

A: Maybe you are too ugly to look at.

ག དེ་ཁྱེད་དགོ་བལྟ་སྦོལ་མེད་ནི་ཡིན་རྒྱོ་རེད།

B: One of them told me the truth.

ཁ གཅིག་གིས་ད་དྲང་མོར་བཤད་བཏང་ཐལ།

A: What did he say?

ག ཅི་ཟེར་གི

B: He said, "Ah, karmically wicked one, as you can see we are just skin and bones. Few people prostrate these days, and those who make offerings are especially few. We don't have anything to eat ourselves. What should we give you?"[14]

ཁ ཨ་ལས་དན་གོ་དེད་ཚ་བོ་ར་ཕྲ་ཟད་ལས་རུས་པར་ཕྱག་གས་བསྟད་ནོ་འདི་རེད། ད་བར་དཕྱག་འཚལ་ནི་ར་མང་བ་མེད་གི་མཚོད་འབུལ་ཡོད་ནི་ལྷག་པས་ཉུང་གི་དེད་ཚ་བོ་རང་གེར་ཟ་རྒྱུ་མེད་ནི་བཟིག་གི་ཁྱོ་ཅི་བཟིག་སྤྱེར་རྒྱུ་ཟེར་གི་ཡ།

A: What did you say?

ག ཁྱོས་ཅི་བཟིག་བཟེ་ཨ།

B: I said, "Ah, don't lie to me! I heard in the human world that you guys have some things that we don't have."

ཁ ཨ་ད། ཁྱེད་དགོས་གཡོབ་གཏུམ་གྱི་འདུག་གི་མི་དགོ་ནས་མི་ཡུལ་ནས་གོ་ནི་རེད་ཁྱེད་ཚ་བོར་ད་མི་ཡུལ་ན་མེད་ནི་ཏག་ཏག་ཡོད་ནི་རེད་དི་བཟེ་ར།

---

13 "Self-arising" (རང་བྱུང་།) is a term commonly used in religious language to suggest something that appears without effort. We maintain the religious register that Menla Jyab uses here.

14 In traditional Tibetan religious practice, burnt offerings are thought to provide sustenance to those in the heaven realms.

4. All-good Menla

A: And what did he say to that?

ཀ དེ་བཟེ་ན་ཆེ་ཟེར་གི

B: "Ah, do we have merit like the human world? These days, people don't believe in gods. People have faith in people. In the human world, how great are the offerings received when people chant, even those who don't know the dharma! We have nothing."

ཁ ཨ། མི་ཡུལ་གི་བསོད་ནམས་དེ་མོ་ཡོད་ནས། ད་བར་དུ་སྐྱེ་ལ་དད་པ་ཡོད་ནི་མ་རེད། སྐྱེ་སྲིད་དད་པ་ཡོད་ནི་རེད། མི་ཡུལ་ནས་ཆོས་མི་ཤེས་ནི་ཚོས་ཅིག་བཏོན་བཏང་ན་ར་འབུལ་བ་ཆེ་ར་ཡོད་ཀི དེད་ཆ་བོ་ཅིང་ར་མེད་ལ།

A: And then?

ཀ དེ་ནས།

B: Then I looked carefully and they were also so hungry they were barely breathing, aro! ...

ཁ དེ་ནས་དངས་ཞིབ་ཏུ་ཅིག་བལྟས་ར་ཁོ་ཚ་བོ་ར་ལྟོགས་བཏང་ནས་དོ་མ་དབུགས་བཞིག་ལེན་གོ་ནོ་དེ་ཁེར་རོ་རེད་ཨ་རོ།

A: Oh!

ཀ ཨོ།

B: ...I cannot bear hunger like them. I didn't know that the happiness of heaven was like that. Now I've seen the other side of the mountain, and learned that that the wild yak's head was bare.[15]

ཁ ཁོ་ཚོའི་ལྟ་ཡས་བཟུན་ནས་བཟོད་མི་བ་གི ལྷ་ཡུལ་གི་བདེ་སྐྱིད་བདོག་གོ་དེ་མོ་བཞིག་ཡིན་ནོ་མ་ཤེས། ད་ཁ་ཡག་པར་ནང་རིག་སོང་ནས། འབྲོང་མགོ་རྗེན་ནོ་ཤེས་སོང་ནས།

A: Used up the only proverb you know?

ཀ གཉས་དཔེ་ཁེར་རོ་ར་ཡར་འཛོག་ཡོད་བཏང་ནས།

B: Lamenting I went to look for a way down and I found one!

ཁ སྒུག་སྟེ་བཞིག་བཏོན་བཏང་ནས་མར་ར་འགྲོ་ཐབས་གི་ལམ་བཞིག་བཙལ་ཡས་ཡོད་གོ་ར་འགྲིག་ཐལ།

A: Was the horse dragging the tree back?

ཀ རྟ་ཉན་གིས་སྡོང་བོ་དུད་ལས་ཕྱིར་ར་ཐོན་བཏང་ནི་མ་ར།

---

15 This seems similar to the English phrase "the grass isn't always greener on the other side."

B: No! Among those with bad karma mine is better, out of nowhere a pillar of ice appeared hanging straight down from the sky. Hugging it, I slid down.

ཁ། མ་རེད། ང་འདི་ལས་ངན་ནང་གི་ལས་ཆེན། མ་བསམ་ས་ནས་དར་གི་ཀ་བ་བཟིག་ཆགས་གི་ནམ་མཁའ་ནས་མར་ར་དུང་མོ་ཡས་དཔུང་ངས་བཞག་ཡོད་གི་དེར་འཐམས་མས་མར་ར་ཤུད་བཏང་ར།

A: So have you arrived on the earth?

ག ས་ཐོག་ག་ཐོན་བཏང་ཐལ།

B: Who knew that the pillar did not touch the ground. I almost lost the pillar in my hand and made a scene. I couldn't climb up or go down, and so I just stayed there holding tight.

ཁ། ག་བ་དེ་མར་ར་ས་ཐོག་ག་ཕྱུག་མེད་ནོ་ཤུས་ཤེས་རེ། ཅིག་མིན་ན་ལག་ནས་ཀ་བ་འོར་རེ། བྱུས་དག་བཟིག་ཡེ་བཏང་ཐལ། ཡར་ཡར་ར་འགྲོ་མ་ཐུབ་མར་མར་ར་ཡོང་མ་ཐུབ། ག་བ་འབྱར་རས་ད་བསྡད་ནི་རེད།

A: Oh, so you just hung there like a spider?[16]

ག ཨོ། དུ་ཁྱིད་དགེ་ཤ་ཡེ་འཕངས་འཁིལ་གི་ལྟ་ཡས་སྡོད།

B: I thought for a bit, and it seemed ok.

ཁ། འདད་བཟིག་བརྒྱབ་བ་ར་དག་རྒྱུའོ་དག་གི

A: You mean dropping down?

ག མར་ར་ཤྱིང་བཏང་ན་ཡིན།

B: Of course not. It was autumn then, so grabbing the stalks blown from the threshing ground by the wind, I twisted them into a rope, tied it to the pillar and slid down.

ཁ། ཆེ་ཡིན། སྐབས་དེར་སྟོན་ག་རེད། གཡུལ་ཕུར་ས་བོ་ནས་རླུང་གིས་ཁྱེར་ཡོང་ནོའི་གྱི་མ་བཟུང་ངས་བསྡད་ལས་ཐག་པ་བཟིག་བརྒྱབས་བཏང་ངས་ཀ་བ་མཐུད་བཏང་ངས་ད་མར་ར་ཤུད་བཏང་།

A: [disbelieving] Hm... That's quite a rope! There's no way that would break.

ག ཨུན། དཐག་པ་བདོག་གོ་རེད། ཆད་རྒྱུ་བཟིག་ཆེ་ཡོད།

---

16 Literally "the old lady with a spindle," this refers to a spider in Amdo that hangs from a single strand of web. We have been unable to identify its Latin name.

B: Unfortunately, while sliding along well, a huge gust of wind blew up, and cut the straw rope, and I plummeted like a shooting star.

|ཁ ཐལ་ར་ཅིག་གི་འིབ་ཆེན་བཟིག་བྱུད་ལས་ཡོང་གོ་དུས་རྡུང་ཆེན་བཟིག་གཡུགས་གས་ཕྱིར་རས་རྩྭ་ཐག་བཅད་ལས་ཉྱད་བཏང་ནོ་ང་བཟེ་ནོ་སྐར་མདའ་ལྟུང་ལྟུང་ཡས་བཏང་ད་ར།

A: *Ohoho*! That's a good simile!

ཀ ཨོ་ཧོ་ཧོ། དཔེ་འཇོག་བཟེ་ཡག་གི

B: As soon as I thought about it would take to reach the ground, with a zzzz sound I not only hit the ground but burrowed underneath. Fortunately, my head was above the ground.

|ཁ དས་ཐོག་ག་ཐོན་རྒྱུའི་ཚེ་མོ་བཟིག་ཡོད་ནི་ན་འདོད་ལས་འདད་བརྒྱབ་མ་བརྒྱབ་ག བཟེར་ཟུ་བཟིག་གུགས་གི་ར་ང་ས་ཐོག་ག་ལྟུང་ནིའི་མི་ཆད་ས་འོག་ག་འཐུལ་སོང་ནོ། ཡག་ཡག་ག་མགོ་ཐུ་ས་ཁ་ན་ཡོད་གི

A: You were probably stopped by your nose.

ཀ དེ་ཁྱོའི་སྣ་འཐོགས་ནི་ཡིན་རྒྱུའི་རེད།

B: I moved a little and everything seemed ok.

|ཁ ཅིག་འཕགས་ག་ར་དུག་གི་གོ

A: Could you get out of the ground?

ཀ ས་ཁར་འབྱུད་ཐུབ་ག

B: When I had almost gotten out, an earthquake sent me tumbling back in up to my eyes.

|ཁ ས་ཁ་བུད་ནི་བུད་ནི་ཡིན་དུས་ས་འགུལ་བཟིག་བརྒྱབས་གས་ཕྱིར་ར་ས་འོག་ག་འཐུལ་སོང་ནོ། མིག་གི་མཆམས་རགས་གོ་མ་ཐོགས་ཐལ་གོ

A: Oh, this time even your nose was underground.

ཀ ཨོ། དཐེངས་ད་སྣ་ར་ས་འོག་ག་བསྣུས་བཏང་བཟིག་ག

B: I looked around at ground level, and yep! a drunk, black thing was stumbling closer and closer.

|ཁ དས་ར་ཁད་མཆམས་ནས་ཅིག་བསྣུས་ར། རེད་གོ ཆང་འཐུང་ནག་ལོག་ག་བཟིག་རེ་ནི་ར་རེ་ནི་རེད།

A: Who was it?

ཀ སུ་རེད།

B: It was a crippled ant.

|ཁ གྲོག་མ་གྱོལ་བོ་བཟིག་རེད།

A: Heh, I thought he was a real drunkard.

ཀ ཧེ། ང་བཟི་དོ་མ་ཆད་འཐུང་བཞིག་ཡིན་ནས་ན་འདོད་ལ།

B: Yes, I tell you the bastard was completely drunk.

ཁ རེད། བུ་བསད་གོ་བཟི་ཡམས་བསྟད་ཡོད་ཀྱི་བཟེ་ནས་ཡ།

A: I bet.

ཀ ད་ཡིན་རྒྱུའི་རེད།

B: The ant said "Alala. Your blanket is so thick! Hehe, are you covering your head with it? Ya! Get up and drink." Pulling me by several of my hairs, he got me out up to my throat.

ཁ ཨ་ལ་ལ། ཁྱོད་ཀྱི་ཉལ་གོས་མཐུག་ག དེ་དེ། མགོ་རུམ་མ་བཏང་ངས་བསྟད་ཡོད་ནས། ཡ་ཡར་ར་དགྱེ་ར་ཆང་འཐུང་ཞིན་ན་ཅིག་ཟེར། ངའི་སྐྲ་ཉག་ཆ་ཅིག་གིས་འཐེན་བཏང་ནོ་ཤྱིད་ཐག་གི་མཚམས་རག་གོ་ཡར་ར་ས་ཁར་ཕྱུང་ངས་བཞག་བཏང་ཐལ།

A: Now you'll really drink.

ཀ ད་གཉིས་གྱི་འཐུང་རྒྱུ་རེད་ལ།

B: The moron stumbled and stepped on my head, and I was pushed completely back underground.

ཁ དོ་རྟོགས་རྒྱུའོ་འཁྱལ་ཡམས་ཁྱེར་སོང་ངས་དའི་མགོར་ཅིག་སློས་བཏང་ནོ། ང་ཕྱིར་ར་ས་འོག་ག་བརྫངས་ཡག་ག་བརྫངས་བཏང་ནོ།

A: Oh, if an ant could flatten you, just thrash about.[17]

ཀ ཨོ། ད་གྲོག་མ་བཞིག་གིས་སྙབས་འཛོག་ན་ད་འཕགས་ར་བྱོས་ཡ།

B: I thrashed, and things got worse. I completely slid away.

ཁ འཕགས་ར་ཡམས་བྱེད་རས་ད་མ་འགྱིག་ནི་རེད་ཡ། བག་གི་ཤུད་ལས་ཕོར་ཐལ་ར།

A: Where did you slide to?

ཀ གང་ད་ཕོར་ཐལ།

B: Perhaps it was the next life, and I landed with a thump.

ཁ ད་ཚེ་ཕྱི་མ་བདོག་གོ་ཡིན་ནས་ན། ང་ཅིག་ག་ལྡུང་སེ་ལྡུང་ཐལ།

A: Oh, so you'll see eighteen levels of hell.

ཀ ཨོ། ད་དམྱལ་ཁམས་བཅོ་བརྒྱད་བདོག་གོ་མཇིག་གིས་རིག་རྒྱུ་རེད་ལ།

---

17 This is an unusual turn of phrase and only works in the context of Menla's fantastic comedy. The implication is that if he is so weak that an ant can flattened him, then he is on his own.

4. All-good Menla

B: Well, I don't know whether it was eighteen or nineteen, but I decided to go see if Shinjé Chojya was home.[18]

A: Was he?

B: He wasn't, but his wife was.

A: [disbelievingly] *Ang*.

B: The wife of this so-called Shinjé Chojya just doesn't watch the dog.[19]

A: Hehe. As if she's "Mrs. ne'er-do-well" from your village.

B: I stared down the old dog and went in the house. The she got up half-heartedly and greeted me.

A: Oh, she's worse than "Mrs. Ne'er-do-well"

B: "*Aro*, where'd your husband go?" That's what I said.

A: Where did she say he'd gone off to?

B: She said, "Who knows? He's been out visiting people since yesterday, and he probably got drunk again."

---

18 *Tshad ke* (ཚད་ཀེ) gives a sense that someone is doing something purposefully, particularly for the purposes of making a joke. Shinjé Chojya is the Lord of Death in Tibetan Buddhist cosmologies.

19 When guests arrive in Amdo, it is custom for someone to mind the watchdog to ensure the guest's safety. The fact that she fails to do this suggests that she is lazy.

A: As if he's your village's "Mr. Never at home." ཀ ད་དེ་ཁྱོ་ཚའི་སྡེ་བའི་ཀུན་པོ་རེ་བོར་ཡིན་ས་ཡོད་ད།

B: I suffered through the one bowl of tea I drank at their home. ཁ ད་དེ་བ་ནས་ཇ་གང་འཐུང་ནོ་ད་ཤྱིད་ལ་མ་སོང་ང་ཅིག་དག་བཏང་།

A: *Ya*, was it too strong? ཀ ཡ། ཇ་ཁ་ནི་མ་ར།

B: What a messy woman. The sash around her waist wipes everything except her feet. ཁ ཅི་འདུ་འདུའི་ཨ་ཡེ་སྐྱག་རྟོགས་བཟིག་སྐྱག་གི་ཀྲེད་རགས་དེས་ད་ཀྲད་བ་མིན་ནས་ད། མི་ཕྱི་ནི་བཟིག་མེད་གི

A: [with surprise] Ah? ཀ ཨ།

B: She wiped a glob of snot the size of a dog's corpse, folded the sash over and then wiped the butter lamp bowl and put it up high. She wiped the bowls and put them low. She picked up the pot with it and moved it over there, folded some cash and knotted it in it, then she said, "our home has nothing," and wiped her tears with it.[20] ཁ སྣ་ཁྱི་རོ་འདུ་བཟིག་ཕྱིས་ནེ་སྟེ་གཏུད་བཏང་དས། མཆོད་ཀོང་ཕྱིས་ཡར་ར་བཞག་བཏང་དས། དཀར་ཡོལ་ཕྱིས་ཡས་མར་ར་བཞག་བཏང་དས། ཟངས་ད་སྟྱིད་བས་པར་ར་ཕོག་བཏང་དས། སྒོར་ཞེའུ་འགའ་སྟྱིད་བས་ཁྱག་ག་མདུད་བཏང་དས། ད་ཁྱོད་གི་ཅང་ཡོད་ནི་མ་རེད་ཅན་གོ་བཞད་ལས་ད་སྤྱིག་ཚུ་ཕྱིས་བཏང་ཐལ།

A: Oh, that sash is really useful! ཀ ཨོ། ད་རོ་མ་ཀྲེད་རགས་དེས་རོ་མ་གོ་བདོག་གོ་ཆོད་གི

B: When I was heading off, she ripped off a piece of her sash and said, "tie things with this!" ཁ ད་རུང་ང་ཡོང་ཁ་ཀྲེད་རགས་གི་སྟེ་ནས་ཅིག་བཤགས་གས་དངོས་པོ་སྟོམ་སྱུད་སྟོས་ཟེར་ཡ།

A: Is all that true? ཀ ད་དེ་འདུ་བཟིག་བཟོ་ཨེ་བདེན་ན།

B: And then I went to the neighbour's house, and the so-called Shinjé Chojya was in their home! ཁ དེ་ནས་ཁྱིམ་མཚེས་ཚང་ད་ཅིག་སོང་ད་ར། གཤིན་རྗེའི་ཆོས་རྒྱལ་ཡིན་ན་དེ་དི་བ་ན་ཡོད་གི

---

20 At this point, he is describing (in somewhat grotesque detail) that she does not adhere to Tibetan standards of spiritual purity and bodily hygiene.

4. All-good Menla

A: What was he doing?

ཀ ཅི་བཟེག་ཡོད་གོ་གི

B: He said he was hung over and looking foolish with nine layers of sleep in his eyes, putting both feet into the stove's ash catcher, and letting ash collect on his feet.

ཁ ཆང་གནོད་བཏང་ནས་བདོག་གོ་བཟེ་དཀྱུག་སྨུག་རིམ་པ་དགུ་ཆགས་གས་སློ་ངོ་བཟེག་ཡས་ཐལ་དོང་ནང་ང་ཀང་བ་གཉིས་ཀ་ཏུང་ངས་ཐལ་སློག་གས་ད་བསྡད་ཡོད་གི

A: Oh, an image of a dirty old man has appeared before my eyes.

ཀ ཨོ དུ་ཀྱུག་ལམ་མ་ཀྲན་པོ་སླེ་བོ་བཟེག་ཤར་རས་ཁྱེར་རས་ཐོན་ཐལ་གོ

B: It was disappointing. I don't know whether he was Uncle Chojya or Uncle Drinker but I said, "Having arrived here, am I dead?"

ཁ ཡིད་བརོ་ཆད་ནི་བཟེག་རེད ཨ་ཁུ་ཆོས་རྒྱལ་བདོག་གོ་ཡིན་ནས་ན་ཨ་ཁུ་ཆང་རྒྱལ་དགའ་གོ་ཡིན་ནོ་བརོ་མི་ཤེས་གི་ར ང་འདི་བཟེག་ག་སློན་ནས་བསྡད་ཡོད་ནོ་ཨི་སོང་ནི་ཨེ་རེད་བཟེ་ར

A: What did he say?

ཀ ཅི་ཟེར་གི

B: He said, "No way, no way. Among all those who come before me, you are the only one who is not handsome. Go back!"

ཁ ཅི་ཡིན་ཅི་ཡིན ང་ཡོད་སར་ཡོང་ཡོང་གོ ནོའི་ནང་ནས་པོ་སློ་མེད་ནི་བཟེག་ཡོད་ནོ་ཁོ་གཅིག་གོ་རེད ཁྱོད་གི་ཕྱིར་ར་སོང་ཟེར་གི་བཟེ་ནི་ཡ

A: He gave it to you straight!

ཀ སྟེ་གིས་དྲང་མོར་བཤད་བཏང་ཐལ

B: And I spoke directly too.

ཁ ངས་ར་དྲང་མོར་བཤད་བཏང་།

A: *Ya.*

ཀ ཡ

B: *Olé.* I said, "It would give me tons of trouble if you sent me into my next life before I found a wife."

ཁ ཨོ་ལེ ངའི་ལག་ག་ཀྲུན་མོ་མ་ཡོང་གོང་ང་ཆེ་ཕྱི་མར་ཡོང་གི་བརྒྱག་བཏད་དུས་ད་ར་ར་ཏུབ་བཏང་ནི་རེད་ནི་བཟེ

A: Didn't he say, "Rest easy. Even if you go back you won't find a wife?"

ཀ སེམས་བདེ་མོ་བྱོས ཕྱིར་ར་སོང་དུང་ར་ཀྲན་མོ་ལག་ག་ཡོང་ནི་མ་རེད་མི་ཟེར་ག

B: And he spoke straight, too.

ཁ ཁོ་དགེས་ར་དྲང་མོར་བཤད་བཏང་ཐལ

A: What did he say?

ཀ ཅི་ཟེར་གི

B: He said, "You are the uglier of us, but you are more appreciated among people than I am. Nowadays it seems you are more famous than me. So go back and keep it up!"

ཁ ཉུ་གཉིས་ཀའི་ཁྲི་བཅོག་གོ་ཁྱོ་ཡིན་ནོ་མིན་ནས་སེམས་ཅན་གྱི་འདང་ཅན་གོང་བསླས་ན་ཁྱོ་རེད། ད་བར་ད་བསླས་ན་ཁྱོ་ཅིག་གྱུག་གོ་ཁ་བཞིག་རེད། ཕྱིར་ར་སོང་ད་ཉི་རེ་བཞིག་བྱོས་ཟེར་གི

A: [dismissively] Hmph, you are a fluent boaster. What do you have to keep doing?

ཀ ཞུན། ད་ལབ་བདོག་གོ་འཐྲོགས་རྒྱ་བཞིག་མེད་གི ཉི་རེ་ཅི་བཞིག་ཡེད་དགོ་ནི་རེད།

B: He said, "If making people happy is the [practice of the] dharma, you make them happy by being funny. There's no one who is as dirty and funny as you. Go back and make everyone laugh."

ཁ སེམས་ཅན་དགའ་ན་ཆོས་ཡིན་ནས་ན། དགའ་སྦྱད་གོ་དགོད་སྦྱད་རེད། ཁྱོ་འདྲ་འདུའི་མེ་གོ ཁྱོ་འདྲ་འདུའི་དགོད་སྦྱད་བཞིག་མེད་གི ཕྱིར་ར་སོང་ད་ཅང་མ་དགོད་གི་རྒྱགས་ཟེར་གི

A: That should be true.

ཀ ད་ཡིན་རྒྱུའི་རེད།

B: And that I went on and on, and in a valley, and as soon as I got out of the valley, I had arrived, aro.

ཁ དེ་ནས་ད་ཡུང་བ་བཞིག་གི་ནང་ད་སོང་སོང་སོང་ད་ར། ཁ་བྱུད་ནོ་ར་ཕོན་ནོ་ཕོད་ཕྱག་རེད་ཨ་རོ།

A: Where had you arrived?

ཀ གང་ད་ཕོན་བཏང་བཞིག

B: I had arrived in America and the old horse was waiting for me.

ཁ ཨ་མེ་རི་ཁར་ཕོན་བཏང་བཞིག རྟ་རྒན་གྱིས་བསྒུག་གས་བསྡད་ཡོད་གི

A: There's no doubt that wooden legged horse of yours could have reached America.

ཀ ཁྱོའི་ཞིང་རྐང་དི་ད་ཨ་མེ་རི་ཁར་ཨེ་ཕོན་མི་ཕོན་མེད།

B: It wasn't a problem that it has a wooden leg, but the old horse had given birth and it gave me tons of trouble.[21]

ཁ ཤིང་རྐང་ཡིན་ནོ་སྐྱོན་མེད་གི་ར། རྟ་རྒན་སྦྲུག་བཏང་ངས་ད་ཅིག་ཐབ་བཏང་།

A: Believing you is killing me.

ཀ དཀར་འགྲོ་ཡི་ཤི་འགྲོ་གི་ཨ་རོ།

B: Riding the old horse and leading the foal, I was heavy and broke its back, I left the old horse, and rode the foal and it was like flying.

ཁ རྟ་རྒན་ཞོན་བཏང་ངས་རྟེའུ་ཁྲིད་བཏང་ད་ར། ང་ལྗིད་ནི་གི་ར་རྟ་རྒན་གྱི་སྒལ་ཚིགས་བཅོ་གཏོར་རས་བཞག་བཏང་ཐལ། རྟ་རྒན་བསྐྱུར་བཏང་ངས་རྟེའུ་ཞོན་བཏང་ད་ར་འཕུར་བཏང་ནི་བཞིག་ག་རིག་གི

A: Probably! It was born from the peg-legged one.

ཀ དཱ་ཡིན་རྒྱུའོ་རེད། ཤིང་རྐང་གིས་སྐྱེད་ནི་རེད་མོ།

B: And at some point the foal wouldn't move.

ཁ བར་བཞིག་ག་ཡང་རྟེའུ་འགྲོ་རྒྱུ་ར་མེད་གི

A: It had probably broken a leg again.

ཀ ཡང་རྐང་བ་བཅག་བཏང་ནི་ཡིན་རྒྱུའོ་རེད།

B: It hadn't broken its leg, but bubbles were coming from its mouth.

ཁ རྐང་བ་བཅག་མེད་གི་ར་ཁ་ནང་ན་ལྦུ་བཞིག་འཕྱུར་རས་བསྡད་ཡོད་གི

A: Oh, so it must be the old peg-leg horse's foaming foal.

ཀ ཨོ་ དེ་རྟ་རྒན་ཤིང་རྐང་གི་རྟེའུ་ཕུག་ལྦ་འཕྱུར་བདོག་གོ་ཡིན་ནི་ཡིན་རྒྱུའོ་རེད།

B: It was thirsty from all the running. So I put its mouth in the Gulf and made it drink, and it was never quenched. I turned back and looked. Of course!

ཁ རྒྱགས་ནི་གི་ར་སྐོམ་བཏང་བཞིག་ཡ། ཁ་མཚོ་ཁུགས་ག་གཏད་ལས་ད་འཐུང་གི་བཅུག་བཏང་ད་ར་འགྲངས་རྒྱ་བཞིག་ནི་མེད་ཐལ། ཁ་ཕྱིར་ར་འཁོར་རས་ཅིག་བལྟས་ར། ཆི་ཁག་རེ།

A: Ya?

ཀ ཡ།

B: I tell you they were fighting a war there.

ཁ དེ་ན་དམག་འཁྲུག་རྒྱག་གོ་ནི་རེད་ལ་བཟེ།

---

21 This likely suggests that he then had to take care of or carry the foal.

A: Ok.

B: A passing rocket had broken off my old horse's hindquarters.[22]

A: Oh, it must have been a "thief" brand rocket.

B: I rode the front half of the horse to look for the hindquarters, but weren't the hindquarters eating grass in a desert, *aro*?

A: So let it eat!

B: [to the horse] How can you be eating grass? Picking some wild onion, I joined both upper and lower halves and sewed them together with it. It became a handsome foal, but its blood pressure was a bit low. So I peed in its mouth and rode it, and it made a *whoosh*-ing sound.

A: I bet. You'd peed in its mouth!

B: Running over the water and crossing the ocean, kicking up a cloud of white and red dust behind us. Without knowing it, we'd arrived in Shanghai.

---

22 In discussing the gulf and the war there, he is talking about the Gulf War (1990–91). Also, there is a logic error here. Menla seems to have misused the term "old horse" when he was now riding the foal.

A: That's understandable! The ocean's dust had probably made you foolish.[23]   ཀ། ཚེ་ཁག་རྒྱུ། རྒྱ་མཚོའི་རྡུལ་གྱིས་གློའུ་གི་བཏང་ནི་རེད།

B: So I couldn't go home emptyhanded, right?   ཁ། ད་ལག་སྟོང་པ་ཕྱལ་ལ་སོང་ཐེར་རྒྱུ་མེད་གི་རེ།

A: [agreeing] Un.   ཀ། ཡུན།

B: There were some stray yaks at the Shanghai Theatre Academy, I drove them and I had a fun trip.   ཁ། དྲུང་དྲེ་བྲོས་གར་སློབ་སྦྱོང་ན་ནོར་ལྷྱམ་ དུས་ གཡུ་བཟིག་ཡོད་ནི་རེད་ལས། ད་སྙིད་པོ་ཡོད་ནི་རེད།

A: Oh, having yaks to drive from Shanghai must be fun.   ཀ། ཨོ། ད་དུང་དེ་ན་ནོར་དེད་ལས་ཡོད་རྒྱ་ཡོད་ དུས་ད་སྙིད་པོ་ཡིན་རྒྱའོ་རེད།

B: Just driving a couple of yaks is nothing. There are many barefooted people back home,[24] so I loaded them with forty- to fifty-thousand pairs of Black-Yak-Lip shoes,[25] went through the Loess Plateau, Stoneless Valley, putting one pouch-full of stones in the pouch of my tight shirt and hitting on the horns of polled yaks, which was enjoyable.[26]   ཁ། རང་ན་ནོར་ཚ་ཅིག་དེད་ལས་ར་ཡོད་རྒྱ་ཅིང་མེད་གི་ཕ་ཡུལ་ན་ཁང་རྟེན་མང་ནི་ར་བཟེ། རྒྱ་སློམ་ནག་དོང་ནོར་ཁ་བཟིག་གི་ཁྲི་ཚོ་བཞི་ལྔ་བཟིག་བཀལ་བཏད་དས། དུས་སེར་མཚོ་སློང་ནས་བྱད་ལས་རྡོ་མེད་ལུང་པ་བརྒྱུད་ལས། ཚེ་ལེན་ཁ་འབྱར་གོའི་ནང་ད་རྡོ་རུམ་གང་འཁུས་བཏད་དས་གཡག་མགོ་རོ་རེག་ག་ར་རྡོ་བྱད་ལས་ཡོད་ད་ར་ད་ཅིག་བསོ་གི།

A: It probably would be enjoyable to think ridiculous thoughts.   ཀ། ད་འདྲ་མདོ་མེད་བརྒྱུབ་ན་བསོ་ནི་ཡིན་རྒྱའོ་རེད།

---

23 He's foolish because he didn't realize he'd arrived in Shanghai.
24 The Tibetan word *pha yul* (ཕ་ཡུལ།), literally "fatherland" and translated here as "home" could refer to one's own community or to a much larger region. The numbers given afterward seem to speak to general poverty of the Tibetan region in the early years of the post-Mao era.
25 This refers to a style of black shoes with a layer of cotton or wool between two pieces of cloth that was popular in the early 1980s and 1990s, mostly for wearing in winter.
26 This statement is intentionally ridiculous. There is no pouch in a tight shirt, and polled yaks have no horns.

B: My wife was also waiting for me... ཁ ད་ཀུན་མོས་ར་བསྒུག་གས་བསྡད་ཡོད་གི

A: *Ah? Aro aro*, hold up, *aro*! Didn't you not have a wife? ཀ ཨ། ཨ་རོ་ཨ་རོ། ཁྱོ་སྡོད་ཨ་རོ། ཁྱོ་ཀུན་མོ་མེད་ནི་མིན་ནས།

B: Who told you I didn't have a wife? ཁ ཁྱོ་མེད་གི་ཟེར་ནོ་སུ་རེད།

A: *Ona*, when you met Shinjé Chojya you told him you didn't have a wife. ཀ ཨོན་ཁྱོ་གཤིན་རྗེའི་ཆོས་རྒྱལ་ཕྲུག་དུས་ཀུན་མོ་མེད་ཟེར་ནོ།

B: *Ona*, I told you earlier that my wife sent me to collect firewood. ཁ ཨོན་དེའི་སྔུན་ན་ངའི་ཀུན་མོས་ང་ཚ་མ་འཛུ་གི་མངགས་ག་བཟེ་ནོ།

A: *Olé*, you did say that. ཀ ཨོ་ལེ་ དེ་བཟེ་ནས།

B: I also said that as well.[27] ཁ ངས་ར་དེ་བཟེ་ནས།

A: *Ona*, in reality, which is true? ཀ ཨོན་དོན་དོ་མ་གང་བདེན་ནས་ཨོ།

B: The truth, well, what my wife said was the truth. ཁ བདེན་རྒྱུ་འོ་ད་དེད་ག་འི་ཀུན་མོས་བཤད་ནོ་བདེན་ནི་རེད་ཡ།

A: *Ya*? ཀ ཡ།

B: Uh, after I got home, and had three pots of noodles and that took the edge off my hunger and had a chat, and my wife said..... ཁ ཨ། ཡུལ་ཐོན་ནས་ཐུག་པ་ཟངས་ད་གསུམ་འཐུང་བཏང་ནས་ལྟོགས་མགོ་ཆིག་མནན་བཏང་ནས་ཁ་བརྡ་བཟིག་ཡས་ར་ད། ཀུན་མོས་བཤད་གི་བཟེ་ནས་ཡ།

A: What did she say? ཀ ཅི་ཟེར་གི

---

27 Agreeing with "A" that he had told the Shinjé Chojya that he had no wife.

4. All-good Menla

B: ... It's better to listen to nonsense from you and Hwala Kunzang[28] than to listen to the mumblings of a confused person holding a meeting. But I have a complaint about you.

ཁ། ཁྱི་ད་རུ་ཧུར་རེ་བཟིག་གིས་ཚོགས་འདུ་བསྲུས་ནི་བཟེ་ལྷུ་རུ་བསྒྲོལ་ནོ་ཉན་རགས་གི་ད། དཔའ་ལ་ཀུན་བཟང་ཡིན་ནས་ན་དེ་ར་ཕྱེད་གཉིས་ཀའི་གཤོབ་བ་ཉན་ནིའི་དགའ་གི་ར། ཡང་ང་ཁྱོ་བསམ་འཚར་བཟིག་ཡོད་གི།

A: What was it?

ཀ། ཅི་བཟིག་ཡིན་ནས་ན།

B: She said, "Hwala Kunzang lies endlessly, and you eat endlessly."

ཁ། དཔའ་ལ་ཀུན་བཟང་བཟོ་སྟེ་གཤོབ་གཏམ་བཏང་དུས་ཞབས་བཟིག་མེད་གི་ར། ཁྱོད་ཟས་འཕྱོང་བཏང་དུས་ར་ཞབས་བཟིག་མེད་གོ་ཟེར་ཡ།

A: Oh!

ཀ། ཨོ།

---

28 Hwala Kunzang seems to be a fictional name, and likely is used to parallel the name Menla Kunzang.

5. Elders' Conversations ལོ་ ལོན་ཚོའི་ཁ་བརྡ།[1]

A: *Ya*, comrade Phagmo! According to some people, we perform these *khashag* trying to be eloquent. But what's your take on this?	ཀ། ཡ། རྟོ་མཐུན་ཕག་མོ། ཁྱི་ལ་ལས་བཤད་ན། ཉུ་ གཞིས་གས་ཁ་བདེ་ཡས་ནས་ཁ་ཤགས་བརྡོག་ གོ་བཤད་ཀྱི་ཟེར་གི་འདིའི་ཐད་ལ་ཁྱོ་ལྟ་ཆུལ་ ཅི་བཞིག་ཡོད་གི།
B: In my opinion, well I don't know about you, but I think it's true that I am eloquent.[2]	ཁ། ངས་བསྲས་ན་ད་ཁྱོ་བཟོ་ཅི་གོ་ར། ངའི་ཁ་བདེ་ ནོ་བདེན་གི་འདོད་ཀྱི།
A: I think if one says we are eloquent, that's no different from scolding us.	ཀ། ངས་བསྲས་ན་ཁ་བདེ་གི་བཞི་བཏང་ན། ཉུ་ གཞིས་ག་ཁ་ལོག་བཞིག་བརྒྱབ་བཏང་ནི་ར་ ཁྱད་པར་མེད་ཀྱི།
B: *Ya*? Why's that?	ཁ། ཡ། དེ་ཅི་བཞིག་ག
A: It's a sign that they do not recognize *khashag* arts.	ཀ། དེ་ཁ་ཤགས་སྒྱུ་རྩལ་ཁས་མ་བླངས་ནོའི་རྟགས་ རེད།
B: *Ya*?	ཁ། ཡ།

---

1 Menla Jyab is "A" and Phagmo Drashi is "B."
2 *Khabde* (ཁ་བདེ།, literally "good mouth") is translated here as "eloquent," though it can also mean quick-witted. The implication here is that there are many who meet these criteria.

©2025 Jyab (text)
Thurston & Samdrup (Trans. & Notes), CC BY-NC 4.0 https://doi.org/10.11647/OBP.0452.05

A: Think about it. If this new form of *khashags*, this *khashag* art form, is so simple that anyone with a mouth, anyone who is eloquent, can speak them, then would we get the chance?

B: *Olé*! It would fall into the hands of the leaders first.

A: Based on this, it's not right to say that the kings of *khashag* are eloquent.

B: *Ona*, what is it ok to say we're good at?

A: First, our meaningful watchers are good.

B: "Meaningful watchers"?

A: I'm saying our eyes are good!

B: Who, not having good eyes in their head, would throw them into the trash heap?

A: If a *khashag* is to become like a mirror of life at that time, then first you have to examine life with the meaningful watcher.

B: First, you have to look for the materials for the composition.

A: And next, our producing happiness when heard is good.

B: Producing happiness once heard? Are there many people hiding in your body? *Aro*, they're all personal names![3]

A: I'm saying it's not enough to have good eyes. You also need to have good ears.

B: Who, not having good ears on the sides of their head, would stitch them to the soles of their boots.

A: If a *khashag* is to become like a record of major issues, the producing happiness once heard must eavesdrop on real life to assist the meaningful watcher.

B: If you need to look for the material for the composition, you must have broad hearing range, and you must have an expansive field of vision.

A: And next our processing factories must be good.

B: Processing factory? Oh, there are also the names of companies.

A: Uh, seeing and hearing is not enough. I'm saying you also need a good brain.

---

3   Joy when heard (ཐོས་པ་དགའ།) is the childhood name of the famed ascetic Milarepa. "Producing happiness" (དགའ་སྐྱེད།), also features in one of Menla Jyab's pennames: "Pleasure producing snow child" (གངས་བུ་དགའ་སྐྱེད།).

B: Who, not having a good brain on top, would go around carrying it on their back?

ཁ༽ སུ་བཟིག་གིས་འོ་གཙུག་གི་ཀླད་པ་མ་བདེ་རང་གི་རྒྱབ་བ་ཁུར་རས་འགྲོ་གི་གི།

A: If you want to artistically portray a *khashag* composition that has been found in real life, you must use your brain to compose it out of what you've seen and heard.

ཀ༽ ཁ་བཤགས་བརྩམས་ཆོས་བཟིག་འཚོ་བ་ལས་རྙེད་ལས་སྒྱུ་རྩལ་གྱིས་མཚོན་དགོ་ན། རང་གི་མཐོང་ཐོས་ཡོད་ཚད་ཀླད་པ་འགུལ་ཡས་གསར་རྩོམ་ཡེད་དགོ་གི་ཡ།

B: I would have known that even if you hadn't said it.

ཁ༽ དེ་ད་ཁྱོས་མ་བཤད་ན་ར་ཤེས་ནི་རེད་ད།

A: Uh, there are some that don't know this and say that the mouth that can't do anything other than being the food importing company and the breath exporting company also think that it is the production site for *khashag*, and so say that we're eloquent.

ཀ༽ ཨུ། དེ་མི་ཤེས་ནི་ཡོད་ལས་ད། ཟ་མ་ནང་འདྲེན་ཀུང་སི། ཁ་རླངས་ཕྱིར་གཏོང་ཀུང་སི་གི་གོ་མིན་ནས་མི་ཆོད་ནོ་གི་ཁ། ཁ་བཤགས་ཐོན་རྫས་ཐོན་ས་རེད་འདོད་ལས་ད་ཁ་བདེ་གི་བཟེ་ནི་རེད་ཡ།

B: Um, and so, it's worse than scolding, it's an accusation.

ཁ༽ ཨུན། དེ་ད། ཁ་ལོག་བཟིག་བཀྱུབ་ནི་གི་ར་ཧྲ་རེད་ཡ། བགད་ལོག་ཡས་བཏང་ནི་རེད།

A: Ah, even accusing and scolding, some people call us eloquent, I say that the thing that cannot be silenced is our *khashag*.

ཀ༽ ཨ། བགད་ལོག་ཡས་ཁ་ལོག་བཀྱུབ་རུང་། ཁ་ཁེར་གིས་ཁ་བདེ་བཏགས་རུང་། ཁ་རོག་ག་འདུག་མི་ཉན་ནོ། ཉ་གཉིས་ཀའི་ཁ་བཤགས་རེད་ལ་བཟེ།

B: It goes without saying.[4]

ཁ༽ ཅི་བཤད་རྒྱུ།

A: And then, in this short *khashag*, how about if we imitate elders who are like the setting sun in the land of snows?

ཀ༽ དེ་ན་ད། ཁ་བཤགས་ཐུང་ཐུང་བོ་འདིའི་ནང་ནས། ཉ་གཉིས་ཀས། བོད་གངས་ཅན་ཕྱུལ་གི་ལ། ཁའི་ཉི་མ་ལྟ་བུའི་བོ་ལྡན་ཆ་བོའི་ཁ་བཟེའི་ལད་མོ་བཟིག་ཡས་ན་ཅི་ཡེད་ཀི།

---

4   Here Menla (A) adopts an oratorical style, prompting Phagmo (B) to provide the appropriate response required of audiences in this genre: "of course" or "it goes without saying" (ཅི་བཤད་རྒྱུ།).

5. Elders' Conversations

B: Of course.

A: Uh, in that case, our capacity for examining and eavesdropping on life will be revealed.

B: Of course.

A: Say something instead of just repeating "of course."

B: Heh, in my opinion, elders have nothing to discuss other than holding their young ones and assembling at the door of the Manikhang to chant some mani. So what should I say?

A: Ah, karmically wicked one. As for whether or not they have conversations, let's mimic their conversation, and then you'll know. *Ya*, let's begin!

B: *Ya*.

A: *cough* *cough*

B: What was that, *aro*?

A: Heh, don't elders have to cough?

B: Heh, I thought that a gnat had gotten in your throat.

A: Must a gnat have gotten into my throat?

B: Ok, ok, Now begin, begin.

A: Ok. Begin.

A: *cough* Ya, Uncle Phagmo! You're not in pain?[5]

ཀ། ཨུ་ཧི། ཡ། ཨ་ཁུ་ཕག་མོ། ཁྱོ་ཟུང་མ་ཁོལུ།

B: If I was, would I be able to come here?

ཁ། ཁོ་ན་གོ་ན། འདིར་ཡོང་ཐུབ་ནི་ཨེ་རེད།

A: Uh, ye, where are you going today?

ཀ། ཨུ། ཡེ། དེ་རིང་གང་ང་འགྲོ་གོ

B: I'm not going anywhere.

ཁ། ཅང་ང་ར་མི་འགྲོ།

A: Well then, will you stay here?

ཀ། དེས་ན་འདི་ནས་འདུག་རྒྱུ་ནས།

B: I'll stay. That's for sure.

ཁ། འདུག་རྒྱུ། ཁོ་ཐག་ཡིན།

A: Uh, what will you do here?

ཀ། ཨུ། བསྡད་ལས་ཅི་བཟིག་ཡོད་རྒྱུ།

B: Why do you ask?

ཁ། ཅི་ཡོད་ལ་བཟེ་ནས། ཁྱོ།

A: [scoffing] Heh, is there an elder like this? Can't carry a conversation at all.

ཀ། ཧེ། དེ་མོ་ལོ་ལོན་བཟིག་ཨེ་ཡོད་ལ། བབ་གི་ཁ་བཏང་ཡོད་ས་མི་འགྲོ་གི་ར།

B: What!? I don't look like an elder?

ཁ། ཅི་རེད། ལོ་ལོན་བཟིག་གཱ་མི་རིག་གཱ།

A: You do! You look like a young man who is constantly looking for trouble.

ཀ། རིག་གི། གསེག་འདྲུས་མ་བྱེད་ལ་ཡོད་ནས་གསར་བུ་བཟིག་གཱ་རིག་གི་ཡ།

B: [scoffing] Heh, I didn't know the chats of elders were unique. So what should we do now?

ཁ། ཧེ། ངས་ལོ་ལོན་གི་ཁ་བརྡ་དོག་གོ་ཁེར་རེ་བཟིག་ཡིན་ནོ་མ་ཤེས། ད་ཅི་བཟིག་ཡོད་རྒྱུ།

---

5   Asking (in the negative) if someone is not sick, or not in pain, or (in the positive) has eaten is a common form of greeting in Amdo.

5. Elders' Conversations

A: Uh, elders' conversations are full of information about social life in their time. When you know how to listen, you will know their take on that place's situation, that village's affairs, that family's members, and that character's mental state. Now you should know how to voice them.

ཀ། ཨ། ལོ་ལོན་གྱི་ཁ་བརྡའི་ནང་ན་སྐབས་དེའི་སྤྱི་ཚོགས་འཚོ་བ་ཡོད་ནི་རེད། ཉན་ཤེས་སོང་ན། ས་ཆ་དེའི་གནས་ཚུལ། སྡེ་བ་དེའི་དོན་དག ཁྱིམ་ཚང་དེའི་བཟའ་མི། མི་སྣ་དེའི་སེམས་ཁམས། ཅང་མ་བྱུར་དུ་ཤེས་ཐུབ་ནི་རེད། ད་ཁྱོས་བཤད་ཤེས་དགོ་ནི་རེད་ཡ།

B: I don't know how to voice them. Would a young man like me know what thoughts elders hold in their hearts.

ཁ ངས་བཤད་མི་ཤེས་གི་ ལོ་ལོན་བཟོས་ཁོག་ག་ཅི་བཟིག་དུན་གོ་ནི་ད་གསར་བུ་བཟིག་གིས་ཤེས་ནས།

A: I put this to you: I'll be an elder, and you be a young one, and we'll chat, that ok?

ཀ ངས་ཁྱོ་བཤད། ད་ལོ་ལོན་བཟིག་ཡིན་ལ། ཁྱོ་ཆུང་ཆུང་བཟིག་བྱོས། ཨུ་གཉིས་གས་ཁ་བརྡ་ཡིན་དི་ད་ཚོག་ག

B: Oh, that's fine.

ཁ ཨོ་ དི་ད་ཚོག་གི་ཡ།

A: Uh, I'll be a mother-in-law and you be her daughter-in-law.

ཀ ཨུ། ང་ཨ་ནེ་ཡིན། ཁྱོ་མནའ་མ་བྱོས།

B: Heh, are we being two women again?

ཁ དེ། ཡང་ཨ་ཡེ་གཉིས་ཡིན་ནི་ཨེ་རེད

A: Let's begin!

ཀ མགོ་ཙོམ་གོ

B: Go ahead.

ཁ མགོ་ཙོམ།

A: Daughter-in-law!

ཀ མནའ་མ།

B: Yes?

ཁ ཤུན།

A: For Tibetan daughters in law, being hard working is not enough.

ཀ བྱུང་ཨུ་བཙོའི་བོད་གི་མནའ་མ་བཟིག་ཡིན་ན། ཡག་ལས་ག་འཛོམས་ནས་ཚོག་ནི་མ་རེད།

B: *Ona*?

ཁ ཨོ་ན།

A: We have to respect our husbands as if they are *lama*s.

ཀ རང་གི་ལོ་སྐྱེས་བླ་མ་གི་ལྟ་ཡས་བགྱུར་དགོ་ནི་རེད།

B: There's no way.

བ་ནི་མ་རེད།

A: We mustn't speak first in public. It's especially bad to go on blah, blah, blah when the men are chatting.

སྐྱེ་མང་ནང་ནས་ཁ་སྔ་མི་ཉན། ལྷག་པར་དུ་ཞི་མི་ཚོའི་ཁ་བརྗོད་ནང་ད་པ་ར་ར་ཅིག་བཤད་དུས་ད་བྱ་ལམ་མ་མ་སོང་ནི་རེད།

B: What would happen?

ཅི་བཞིག་ཡས་འཇོག་ནི་རེད།

A: [emphatically] *Un un*, wouldn't it echo in mountains and valleys?[6] Next, you mustn't visit others in the camp too much.

ཨུན། ཨུན། རི་ལུང་བ་གཉིས་ཀ་གྲགས་མི་འགྲོ་ནས། དེའི་འཕྲོད། རུ་སྒོར་ར་ཤུལ་གི་འདུག་མི་ཉན།

B: [disapprovingly, as himself] *Un*, so they won't let her go out.

ཨུན། ད་སྒོར་འགྲོ་གི་འདུག་རྒྱ་མ་ར།

A: I'm not saying that you're like that, but you must always be careful about things like this. Do you hear, daughter-in-law?

ངས་ཁྱོ་ནི་མོ་བཞིག་རེད་བཟེ་ནི་མིན་ད། འདི་མོ་འདི་རྒྱུན་དུ་མཉམ་པར་འཛོག་དགོ་ཨེ་གོ་ཐལ། མནའ་མ།

B: [as the daughter-in-law] I hear you, *Ane*.[7] I'll have a difficult time in your house.

གོ་ཐལ། ཨ་ནེ། དཁྱིད་ཁ་ནས་དགའ་རྒྱ་རེད།

A: Just look at the bride in the family over there.

དཕྱིས་གན་བ་ཚང་གི་མནའ་མ་ལྟོས་ར།

B: Which family?

སུ་བ་ཚང་གི།

---

6 Suggesting that people will gossip about her.
7 *Ane* means "mother-in-law" here.

5. Elders' Conversations

A: That one over there. She has no limits. Every day she wolfs down a big helping of *tsampa*, bullshitting, whoever she meets she just *chagchagchag*. *Phe*! There's no daughter-in-law like that.[8]

B: *Ona*, how must a daughter-in-law be, mother-in-law?

A: When I was young and came to this house, I didn't even dare to make a peep. I was even embarrassed to pee in a place where my father-in-law might see.

B: You must have found it difficult to pee then.

A: In truth, this is what's meant by "time and eras have changed." A daughter-in-law from my time would be so rare these days.

In those days when I was sent as a bride,[9] I couldn't say things like the girls these days these days say, like, "I'll go to this family, I won't go to that family."

> "All braided ladies go out as brides."[10]

---

8   *Chagchagchag*, is the sound of running her mouth, and *phe* is a vocable that is meant to be dismissive and suggest disapproval.
9   Tibetans prefer patrilocal marriage, and the phrase "sent as a bride" (གནས་ལ་བྱིན་) suggests that a woman moves (literally, "is given") to the groom's home.
10 Nearly every Tibetan woman braids her hair, and so this short proverb is meant to suggest that every woman gets married into another family.

If one doesn't listen to their parents, who will they listen to?

ཕ་མའི་ཁ་མི་ཉན་ན་སུའི་ཁ་ཉན་རྒྱུ།

B: Mother-in-law, that's an old, traditional way of thinking. I don't accept it.

ཁ ཨ་ནེ། ཁྱོད་དེ་སྔོལ་རྒྱུན་གྱི་བསམ་བློ་བྱེད་པ་རེད། ངས་ཁས་མི་ལེན།

A: It's good if in real life a daughter-in-law can speak to her mother-in-law like that.

ཀ འཚོ་བའི་ནང་གི་མནའ་མས་ཨ་ནེར་དེ་ཡས་བཤད་ཐུབ་རྒྱུ་ན་དགའ་གི་ར།

B: [speaking as himself] Do I look like a daughter-in-law?

ཁ ང་མནའ་མ་བཟིག་ག་འེ་རིག་གི

A: You do. But, it isn't particularly clear from your speech whether you are a daughter-in-law beneath her mother-in-law or her son who is in the university.

ཀ རིག་གི་རེད་དུ་སྐད་ཆ་བཤད་ཕྱོགས་ཨ་ནེ་དེའི་མཐའ་འོག་གི་མནའ་མ་ཡིན་ནི་ན། དེ་བ་ཅོང་གི་སློབ་གྲྭ་ཆེན་མོན་ཡོད་དེའི་ཞི་ལི་ཡིན་ནི་ན་ཨ་ཇ་བཟིག་མི་ཤེས་གི་ཡ།

B: Heh, you're saying that I don't look like the daughter-in-law.

ཁ ཧེ། ད་དེ་མནའ་མ་དེར་མི་རིག་གི་བཟེ་བཏང་ནི་རེད་མོ།

A: Our primary topic is the conversations of elders. It's ok if you don't look like a daughter-in-law as long as I look like a mother-in-law. Come on, let's keep chatting.

ཀ བརྗོད་བྱ་གཙོ་བོ་ལོ་ལོན་གྱི་ཁ་བརྡ་རེད་མོ། གཙོ་བོ་ཨ་ནེར་རིག་བཏང་ན། མནའ་མར་མ་རིག་ནར་སློན་མེད་གི་ཡ་འགྲིག་གླུ་མཐུད་དུ་ཁ་བརྡ་ཡོད་མོ།

B: Ya, mother-in-law! Your daughter-in-law is listening.

ཁ ཡ། ཨ་ནེ། མནའ་མས་ཉན་ནས་བསྡད་ཡོད།

A: Ayoshe, this is me here stepping into the next life.

ཀ ཨ་ཡོ་ཞུ། ང་ད་ཚེ་ཕྱི་མའི་ཡུལ་ལ་གོམ་པ་བསྒྱེང་ནས་བསྡད་ཡོད་ནི་འདི་རེད།

B: I do not see it, but it must be true.

ཁ ངས་མི་རིག་གི་ར། ད་ཡིན་རྒྱུའི་རེད།

5. Elders' Conversations

A: In general, I shouldn't worry about anything other than chanting Mani, but our youngest daughter, with nothing better to do, went to school in inner China,[11] and I am not going to see her again even when I die.

ཀ སྤྱིར་གྱི་མ་ཎི་ཚ་རེ་འདོན་རྒྱུའི་མིན་ནས་ཚེ་བསམ་ར། བུ་གཞིའི་ཞི་མོ་ཆུང་བ་གོ་ཡང་ཀྱོང་རྒྱུ་མེད་ལ་རྒྱུ་ཁོག་ཕྱུར་ར་སློབ་གྲྭ་སོང་ནི་བཟེ། ཐ་མ་ང་འཆི་དུས་བཟེག་ག་དོ་ར་ཐུག་རྒྱུ་མ་རེད་ཡ།

B: I'm here even if you do not see her, mother-in-law!

ཁ ད་མ་ཐུག་ན་ར་ང་ཡོད་ཁྱི་མོ་ཨ་ནེ།

A: Ah, daughter-in-law, when a person gets old, what I say to that girl is like farting in the water. At the time, I tried to stop her from going but couldn't.

ཀ ཨ། མནའ་མ། སྐྱི་བོ་གིས་ཕྱུབ་སོང་ན་ད། ཞི་མོ་དེར་ངས་བཤད་ནོ་བཟོ་རྒྱུ་ནང་ང་གཡག་བཀང་ནོ་རེད། དེ་རས་ཅིག་བཀག་ག་ར་མ་ཁུག་ཐལ།

B: You deserve it!

ཁ ཁྲིགས་སེ་རེད།

A: I say, it wouldn't have been like this if her father were still alive.

ཀ མོ་དགེའི་ཕ་ཀན་འཛིག་ཧེན་ཆེ་དོགས་ན་ཡོད་རྒྱུ་ན་ད་དེ་མོ་བཟེག་ཆེ་ཡིན་བཟེ་ར།

B: If father-in-law hadn't died, he'd have been more strict.

ཁ ཨ་མྱེས་བདོག་གོ་ཡང་ཞི་མེད་རྒྱུ་ན་ཅིག་བཙན་ས་ཡོད་ག

A: In the old society,[12] we had a musket and he carried it to go bandit. He suffered a lot in order to feed me and my children. Back then, I didn't even have a full butter lamp to offer after the deceased passed.[13] [crying] Hu hu.

ཀ འཛིག་ཧེན་རྙིང་བའི་རིང་ང་ཨུ་གོ་སྨན་བོའུ་བཟེག་ཡོད་ནོ་ཁུར་རས་ཧག་ག་སོང་དས། ངའི་མ་བུ་ཚའི་བོའི་ཁ་རྒྱབ་གྱི་དོན་ན། ཏུ་ཏུ་ཆེ་ར་མ་དག་བཟེག་ནས། ངས་ཕྱི་བོ་དེའི་ཛྭ་ཕྱར་ར། ང་དེ་རས་མཆོད་མེ་སྐོང་རིལ་གང་འཛིག་ཕྱུད་ར་གང་ན་ཡོད་རྒྱུ། ཧུ་ཧུ

---

11   Tibetans often refer to Han dominated lowlands outside of the Tibetan plateau as "Inner China" (རྒྱ་ཁོག or རྒྱ་ནང་།).
12   The "old society" refers to Tibetan life before 1958.
13   When a Tibetan dies, it is common to offer butter lamps, and sometimes much more. Not being able to offer a full butter lamp suggests extreme poverty. Additionally, Tibetans consider it taboo to say the name of a deceased person (with some exceptions for famous historical personages).

B: [crying sound] Uh, uh.

A: [as himself] *Aro aro*, what's she doing?

B: [as himself] The daughter-in-law is sad.

A: Heh, I tell you what: you're not acting like a daughter-in-law, *aro*.

B: You were doing the easier role of the mother-in-law, and gave me daughter-in-law who is not allowed to speak up. I can't stay here putting up with your bullying, *aro*.

A: *Ya, ya*, if the mother-in-law is easier, I'll give it to you, and I will be an old man, and I'll come by to talk to you. Now see if it's easy!

B: Oh, I love it. I've learned exactly what the old mother-in-law is like.

A: *Ya*, let's begin!

B: Let's begin!

A: *Ya*, Ane Phagko, you're home?

B: Yes, yes. I can't get anywhere, so what can my bag of bones do other than stay at home.

A: Are you doing better after the recent illness I heard about?

B: Uh, it's still there a bit, but death just won't have me. *Ya*, let's go inside, let's go inside.

5. Elders' Conversations

A: [as himself] *Ya, ya*, the mother-in-law this time is done well, *aro*.

B: I said it was easier, but you didn't believe me.

A: *Ya*, old lady, tell me, are your son and daughter-in-law on good terms?

B: At the moment they are, but...

A: Ok.

B: It's said "People these days, and the colour of yellow amber..." Right?[14]

A: Indeed.

B: So there's no trusting it.[15]

A: That's true, unfortunate lady! What these of the younger generation think in their hearts changes like the weather. My rotten daughter-in-law does all her chores with utmost efficiency, but you never see a smile on her face.

B: She must be full of resentment.

A: *Un un*, you say she's full of resentment, even a bowlful of tea given by her is really telling, *aro*.

---

14 This is an abbreviated version of a proverb, suggesting that people these days are unreliable (an observation), and the metaphor that amber changes colour over time.

15 This refers to the relationship between the boy and his wife, which is good for the moment but can't be trusted.

B: Oh, well I've been constantly pressuring my daughter-in-law, and there's no sign of disobedience for now.

ཁ ཨོ་ད་དེད་ཁའི་མནའ་མ་བཙོད་དས་མགོ་མནན་མནན་ན་བསྡད་ནི་ར། ད་ལྟ་བཙོད་ད་མགོ་ཡར་ར་འགྱོག་ཀྱིའི་ཚུགས་ཀ་མེད་གི་གོ

A: The main thing is that your son is good, old lady. My good for nothing son can't wait to kick us out.

ཀ གཙོ་བོ་ཁྱེད་ཁའི་ཞི་ལི་དུ་སོང་ནི་རེད། རྐན་མོ། དེད་ཁའི་བླ་བསང་ད་འབྱུད་རྒྱུའི་ད་དེད་བཟའ་འདུས་གཉིས་ཀ་ཁེར་རེ་འཕུད་ན་འདོད་ལས་བ་གི་བཟིག་མེད་ཡ།

B: Daughters-in-law are outsiders, we don't know them. If our own sons don't take care of us before our bones turn to dust, then who will?

ཁ ད་མནའ་མ་བཙོ་གཞན་གྱི་རེད། ཤེས་རྒྱུ་ཡོད་ནི་མ་རེད། རུས་བོ་ཚ་བོས་འཐིམ་རགས་གོ་རང་གི་བུས་རང་གི་མི་གསོ་སུམ་གསོ་རྒྱུ།

A: My son would beat us to death before he would take care of us.[16]

ཀ དེད་ཁའི་ཞི་ལིས་ད་རྡུང་མ་རྡུང་ཡས་གསོད་རྒྱོའི་མ་ཡས་ན། གསོ་རྒྱུའི་བཙོ་ད་དུ་རིའི་ལ་དགུ་རེད་ཨ་རོ།

B: *Ala*, why don't you give him a mouthful of pee?[17]

ཁ ཨ་ལ། ཁྱོས་དེའི་ཁ་ནང་ད་མར་ར་རྫང་གང་བཏང་དས་བཞག་མི་འཛོག་ག

A: I couldn't, he would pee at me before I could pee at him.

ཀ མི་ཐོངས་གི་དི། ཕར་ར་གཏོང་རགས་གོ་སྤྱི་གི་ཚུར་ར་གཏོང་རྒྱུ་རེད་ཡ།

B: [pityingly] Ah, ah!

ཁ ཨ། ཨ།

A: He isn't ashamed of beating his own mother. Old age has vanquished me, and I am not strong enough to stand up to him.

ཀ ཨ་མ་གཅར་རྒྱའི་རོ་མི་ཚའི་གི་ད་ལོ་ནས་སས་ཐུབ་སོང་ནི་རེད། ཤེད་ལ་མི་འདང་ད།

---

16 The Tibetan ཕ་རིའི་ལ་དགུ, literally "nine mountain passes away" is a common expression in Amdo suggesting that something being far from reality or extremely unlikely to happen.

17 With this phrase, B figuratively suggests that A should beat his son.

5. Elders' Conversations

B: *Olé, Olé*. If we don't close our eyes soon, it is difficult to say what these children will do, right?

A: You can say that again, karmically wicked lady. *Aro*, by the way, did you hear that yesterday a girl and a boy committed suicide in "Old brain" Village?[18]

B: *Atsi, Atsi*[19] something is wrong with "Old Brain" Village, as well?

A: You said it. Every year, someone is taken by ghosts. This time, perhaps something even worse has taken them.

B: Oh.

A: Oh, they tied their necks together with a rope and were hanging from either side of a branch like saddle bags.

B: Ah, *Jetsunma!*[20] Oh what happened to those two?

A: It's said it was nothing big, they wanted to get married, but their families didn't agree, that was the trigger.

---

18 དེ་བཞིན་བདེན་ཡ། is commonly used to start a conversation or change the topic.
19 *Atsi* is an interjection Tibetans use to express surprise.
20 This common injection refers to the Boddhisattva Jetsun Drolma (རྗེ་བཙུན་སྒྲོལ་མ།), and functions similarly to the English "Oh my God!"

B: Oh, right, right. Then it was probably karmic retribution for not listening to their parents.

ཁ། ཨོ། དེ་རེད། དེ་རེད། ད་ཕ་མའི་ཁ་མ་ཉནས་ནོའི་རྣམ་སྨིན་འཁོར་ནི་མིན་ནས་ད།

A: They say that the boy was the one who tried to be eloquent, telling us not to fight when we fought over the grassland a little while ago.

ཀ ཞེ་ལེ་བདོག་གི་འདང་ཕྱིས་ཤུ་ཚོས་རྒྱ་ས་བཀྱད་དུས་ཐ་ཚོ། རྟང་རེས་མ་ཡེད་བཟེ་ཁ་མགས་བཟིག་བཅས་བསྲུད་ཡོད་གི་ཟེར་ནོ་དེ་རེད་ཟེ་ཡ།

B: Ya, he was the one that everyone called a coward.

ཁ ཡ། གན་ཚ་བོས་སྣུག་པོར་བཟིག་རེད་ཟེར་གོ་ནོ་དེ་རེད་ལོ།

A: Ang, that's too bad. That's who it was.

ཀ ཨང་། ད་སྙིང་མ་རྗེ་ར། ད་དེ་རེད་ཟེ་ཡ།

B: These kids won't give us peace of mind.

ཁ དན་ཡས་འདི་ཚ་བོས་སེམས་བདེ་གི་འཇུག་རྒྱུ་མ་རེད།

A: Kids these days don't respect their beloved parents. They don't chant mani or the refuge prayer. The degenerate age when people only live ten years is probably here.

ཀ ད་དེང་སང་གི་ཞ་ཡས་འདི་ཚ་བོས། དྲིན་ཆེན་ཕ་མ་མི་བཀུར་གི་མ་ཎི་སྐྱབས་འགྲོ་མི་འདོན་གི་དུས་འདན་ཚོ་ལོ་བཅུ་བ་བདོག་གོ་ར་ཕོན་གོས་ཡོད་གི་གོ།

B: Hehe, olé.

ཁ ཧི་ཧི། ཨོ་ལེ།

A: There is nothing to be laughed about, unfortunate lady, I am telling the truth. If it was in the old society, when a boy is around fifteen or eighteen, he would be able to go be a bandit with the other men even though he wouldn't be able to race horses alone. Who would think of committing suicide?

ཀ ད་བཞད་ར་ཅིག་དགོད་ན་མིན་ནས། ཨ་ལས་དན་མ། ངས་དོ་མ་བཟེ་ནས། སྔོན་འཇིག་རྟེན་རྙིང་བ་ཡིན་རྒྱུ་ན། ཕོ་ལོ་ལྔ་གསུམ་བཅོ་བརྒྱད། དྲུག་གསུམ་བཅོ་བརྒྱད་སློག་པས་བཞག་གས་ད། རྟ་འདིའི་གོང་ནས་ཁེར་རྒྱགས་མིན་རུང་། ཕ་ཨ་ཁྱིའི་ཇག་གི་དཕུང་ཡ་མི་ཤུན་ནས། སྲིབས་རྒྱོའི་བཟེ་ཡིད་ལ་དྲན་ནས།

B: Yeah, yeah. People in the past were real heroes.

ཁ ཨོ་ལེ། ཨོ་ལེ། དོ་མ་འཇིག་རྟེན་གན་འགྱི་དི་རིགས་པ་ད་དཔའ་བོ་བདོག་གོ་རེད་དས།

5. Elders' Conversations

A: *Un un,* your deceased husband and I were best bandit-buddies. He should have been re-born in a Pureland. He was a real marksman.

ཀ ཨུན། ཨུན། ཁྱོའི་ཕོ་སྐྱེས་ང་བསད་གོ་དེད་གཉིས་ཀ་ཡང་རྐག་རོགས་ཡོད་ལ་མེད་ལ་བོ་རེད། དགའ་པའི་ཞིང་ནས་ཅིག་སྐྱེས་བོའུ་སླེ་བདོག་གོ་ད་དེ་ཡིན་ཡ།

B: That's what they say.

ཁ ཟེར་གི་མོ།

A: One day, we drove some of Drongtsa's horses.[21] We arrived at the *labtse* pass when the sun was about to set,[22] and the posse wasn't far behind.

ཀ ཉིན་ཚིག་ཡང་། དུ་གཉིས་ཀས་འབྲོང་ཚ་གི་ལ་བོ་ཚ་བོ་དེད་ལས། ཉི་མ་འཛད་ལ་ཁད་བཞིག་ད་ལབ་ཙེ་ཤུག་ཁ་ཕྱིན་ཐ་ར། ད་ར་མདའ་ར་དེད་ཚ་བོའི་བར་ན་ར་ཚང་བཞིག་མེད་ཁི་གོ

B: *Un, un, un.*

ཁ ཨུན། ཨུན། ཨུན།

A: Even then, those from Drongtsa had a contingent of strong young men, and the strong lads were riding a team of equally strong horses. May the three jewels bless me, they were after us like shooting arrows.

ཀ དེ་རས་བཞིག་གི་འབྲོང་ཚ་གན་ཚ་པོ་གསར་གྱུབ་ཡོད་ཡ། དགསར་བུ་ཇ་ན་མ་ན་དག་དགའི་རྟ་ཇ་ན་མ་ན་དག་དག་ཞོན་ནས། དགོན་མཆོག་གསུམ། དེ་གཉིས་ཀ་འི་ཟུར་ར་རང་ད་མདའ་ཧུད་ནི་འདུ་བཞིག་རེད།

B: *Hawo hawo*, now what?

ཁ ཧུ་བོ། ཧུ་བོ། ད་ཅི་བཞིག་ཡིན་རྒྱུ།

A: The deceased one was not an unfit person.

ཀ ད་བླ་བསད་གོ་གྱི་བདེ་བོ་མིན་ནི་མ་རེད་དུས།

B: *Un, un.*

ཁ ཨུན་ཨུན།

A: I didn't know how he jumped off the horse, but by the time I saw, he had already set up the rifle's bipod before I could even dismount.

ཀ རྟ་གོང་ནས་ཚ་ཡམ་ཕྱིངད་ནི་མ་ཤེས་ཐལ་ར། ངས་གཅིག་རིག་དུས་ད། ང་ཐད་ད་མ་བབས་གོང་བཞིག་གི་སྟེ་གི་པོའུ་རུ་ས་བཙུགས་གས་བཞག་ཡོད་གི

B: *Un.*

ཁ ཨུན།

---

21 Drongtsa is the name of a fictional pastoral community from which they have taken the horses.

22 *Labtse* (ལབ་ཙེ) are traditionally found atop mountains, cairns filled with large wooden arrows that are the weapons of local protector deities.

A: "*Aro*, look at the one riding the white horse at the front," as soon as he had said this, there was a *tsag*,[23] and *Om mani padme hum* didn't he make both horse and rider collapse in a cloud of dust.

ཀ ཨ་རོ། སྔུན་གི་ཏ་ར་ར་ཞོན་ནོ་ལྟོས་གོ་བཟེ་མ་བཟེ་ཚག་སེ་བཏང་དས་བཞག་བཏང་ཐལ་ར། ཨོ་མ་ཎི་པདྨེ་ཧཱུྃ། མི་ཏ་གཉིས་ཀ་ཅིག་ཏུལ་ལྟོག་སེ་བཏང་དས་བཞག་མི་འཛིག་ན་ད།

B: Ah, ah, Jowo Rinpoche!

ཁ ཨ། ཨ། ཇོ་བོ་རིན་པོ་ཆེ།

A: It was just like killing the mother of the wolf pack. Of course it would be like that.

ཀ ད་ཡིན་ན་ར་ལོས་ཡིན་ད། ད་རོ་མ་སྱང་ཚོགས་ནད་ནས་སྱང་མ་བསད་ནི་བཟེག་ག་རེག་གི་གོ

B: *Un*.

ཁ ཨུན།

A: With a cry of either a *ki* or a *hi*, they rushed toward us,[24] and we didn't know who to shoot at. A mother's son riding a black horse raced towards us.[25]

ཀ གི་རེར་ཟེར་དགོ་ནི་ན། ཧེ་རེར་བཟེག་ཡས་ཞོགས་བཏང་ནོ་གང་ད་རྒྱག་དགོ་ནི་ར་མི་ཤེས་གི་ཨ་མའི་བུ། ཏ་ནག་ནག་ཞོན་ནི་བཟེག་ཡང་ཕྱིར་རས་ཕྲོན་ཐལ།

B: *Un un*, it would have been better to flee.

ཁ ཨུན། ཨུན། ད་ཧར་ར་བྲོས་ནས་ལོས་དགའ།

A: He was completely calm and said "*Ya aro*! That one riding a black horse is yours." My goodness. Ah, unfortunate lady.

ཀ སྟེ་ལྟོད་ལ་བབས་བས་བསྱད་བཏང་དས། ཡ། ཨ་རོ། ཏ་ནག་ནག་ཞོན་ནོ་གན་ད་དེ་རིང་ཁྱོའི་ལག་གི་ལྷ་བསད་རེད་ལ་ཟེར་གི་ར། བུ་འདི་ན། བུ་འདི། ཨ་ལས་ད་མ།

B: *Un*.

ཁ ཨུན།

A: I was still young then.

ཀ ད་དེ་རས་ལོ་ར་ཆུང་ནི་རེད་ད།

B: *Un, un*.

ཁ ཨུན་ཨུན།

---

23 Onomatopoeia for the crack of a musket firing.
24 *Ki* is a sound that might be made as a part of spurring people on in a fight, *hi* suggests a loud wail.
25 "Mother's son" (ཨ་མའི་བུ།) is an exclamation of praise used for a hero.

5. Elders' Conversations

A: I messed it up. My hand was shaking like a prayer flag, as people do when they're nervous. There was no way I could light the fuse. As I watched, the black horse and rider closed in.

ཀ ངས་ཅིག་བརྫོད་ནོ་ད། ཆུ་བོ་འདི་འཆབ་བངང་ན། དའི་ལག་པ་ཇེར་ནོ་འདར་རས་དར་ལྕོག་གཡུག་གཡུག་ཡས་བདང་ངོ། སྣན་བོ་ཨ་ད་མ་བོ་ཆུ་བཞིག་གང་ནས་བསྐྱུབ་རྒྱུ་བསླས་བསླས་རིག་རིག་ག་ཆུ་ནག་ཏ་ནག་ཅན་གོ་དེ་ཙིབས་བ་བདད་བདང་ཚར་ཐལ།

B: *Ahawo*, my goodness, what to do?

ཁ ཨ་ཏ་གོ་བྱ་དི། ད་ཅི་བཞིག་ཡིད།

A: At that moment, he fired, *kag!*

ཀ དའི་ཚད་ལ་ཡང་སྟེ་གི་སྨག་སེ་བདང་ངས་བཞག་བདང་ཐལ།

B: Again one fell over.

ཁ ཡང་བརྫོགས་བདང་།

A: Of course. Would he have missed? At that time, after all that shaking, I pulled the trigger once. A single bullet flew, and these days in Drongtsa village there's "Dent-head" Thubten.[26]

ཀ མིན་ནས་ཚོ། དས་འཆོར་ནས་རིམས་དེ་ང་ཅིག་འདར་འདར་རས་ཁེར་བཞིག་མཐན་ནོ། བོའུ་རྗེའུ་ཁེར་བོ་ད་དེད་སད་གི་འབྱོང་ཚོ་སྟེ་བའི་ཐུབ་བསྟན་བོད་བོ་ཡིད་ཁ་བཞི།

B: Yes.

ཁ རིད་མོ།

A: That was his forehead.

ཀ གན་གི་ཐོད་པ་གན་རིད་ཡ།

B: People say that. (as himself) *Ya*, ok ok. How is my imitation of their conversations?

ཁ ཇེར་གི་བཞེ་ན། ཡ། ད་ཚོག་གི་ཚོག་གི་ངས་ཁ་བཛད་འད་མོ་ཡས་ནོ་ཆེ་མོ་རིད།

A: Ah, amazing! It looks like you really became that old man! You deserve an award![27]

ཀ ཨ། དཔའ་མིད་ཁྱུ། པོ་བོན་དའི་ཁོག་ག་འཇུལ་བདང་ནི་བཞིག་ག་རིག་གི་དགའ་རྟགས་འབབ་གི

B: What are you going to give me?

ཁ ཅི་བཞིག་སྟེར་རྒྱུ།

---

26 "Dent-head" is a nickname referring to the wound that man received in the skirmish.

27 Literally, the language reads that he really "went into that old man's chest."

A: I have nothing to give, I will say a prayer that you will get old quickly.

ཀ སྦྱིར་རྒྱུ་ཅང་མེད། ཁྱོ་རིམ་མ་ལོ་ལོན་རྒྱུའི་ཁ་གཡང་བཟིག་བོས་ནི།

B: Your skull![28] I don't want to get old that soon, *wei*!

ཁ མགོ་སྐོག་བཟོད། ང་བཟོ་ལོ་ལོན་ན་མི་འདོད་ཀི་སྟེ།

---

28 This is a curse. Perhaps like "Screw you!" in this context.

6. Please, Dear Leader དཔོན་པོ་མཁྱེན།[1]

A: The three of us have to speak this three-person *khashag*. But before that, let me introduce these two.	ཀ སུམ་བཞད་ཁ་ཤགས་འདི་ངེད་ཚ་བོ་གསུམ་པོས་བཞད་དགོ་རྒྱུ་རེད། དེའི་ན་ནས་ཁེར་གཉིས་ཀ་མཚམས་སྦྱོར་བཟིག་ཡིན།
B: Yeah, well then, introduce me first.	ཁ ཡ། དེས་ན། སྔོན་ན་ང་མཚམས་སྦྱོར་བྱོས།
C: Introduce *me* first.	ག སྔོན་ན་ང་མཚམས་སྦྱོར་བཟིག་བྱོས།
B: This is my first time at the evening variety show, *Aro*! Introduce me first!	ཁ ང་ད་བྲེངས་གི་འདི་རིག་རྩལ་དགོངས་ཚོགས་ག་ཞུགས་ནོ་བྲེངས་དང་པོ་ཡིན་གོ་ཨ་རོ་ སྔོན་ན་ང་མཚམས་སྦྱོར་བྱོས།
C: With the exception of this time, I've never been to an evening variety show. *Aro*. Introduce me first.	ག ང་ད་བྲེངས་མིན་ནས་རིག་རྩལ་དགོང་ཚོགས་ག་ཞུགས་མ་མྱོང་། ཨ་རོ། སྔོན་ན་ང་མཚམས་སྦྱོར་བཟིག་བྱོས།
A: [to one] You don't be hasty… [to the other] And *you* don't be eager. I have a condition for who I will introduce first.	ཀ ཁྱོར་མ་བྲེལ། ཁྱོར་མ་ཧམ། སྔོན་ན་སུ་མཚམས་སྦྱོར་ཡེད་རྒྱུའི་ཆ་རྐྱེན་བཟིག་ཡོད།
C: What condition?	ག ཆ་རྐྱེན་ཆི་བཟིག

---

1 In this three-person *khashag*, Menla Jyab is "A", "B" is Phagmo Drashi, and "C" is a comedian/emcee named Phurwa.

©2025 Jyab (text)
Thurston & Samdrup (Trans. & Notes), CC BY-NC 4.0   https://doi.org/10.11647/OBP.0452.06

A: Uh, whichever one of you is higher ranking, that one will be introduced first.   ཀ ཨ། སྱིའི་དཔོན་ས་མཐོ་ན་དེ་བདོག་གོ་སྔོན་ན་མཆམས་སྟོར་ཡོད།

B: You must like leaders.   ཁ ཁྱོ་རང་གི་དཔོན་པོར་དགའ་ས་ཡོད་ཀི་མོ།

A: I would say that it's the only good quality I have.   ཀ ང་བཟང་བཟིག་ཡོད་ནོ་ད་དེ་གཅིག་པོ་ཡིན་ནི་རེད་བཟེ་ན།

B and C: You even say it's a good quality, wei!   ཁ ད་རུང་བཟང་ཡིན་ཟེར། སེ།
ག

A: I have a question: Which of you two makes a higher salary?   ཀ ང་འདི་རྒྱ་བཟིག་ཡོད་ཀི་ཁྱོ་གཉིས་གའི་སྱིའི་ཟླ་ཕོགས་མཐོ།

B: What's the point of asking our salaries?   ཁ ཟླ་ཕོགས་དྲིས་ཡས་ཆེ་རྒྱུ།

A: Uh, whoever's salary is higher should be a higher-ranking leader.   ཀ ཨ། སྱིའི་ཟླ་ཕོགས་མཐོ་ན་དེའི་དཔོན་ས་མཐོ་ནི་རེད་མོ།

C: I make 150 every month.   ག ང་ཟླ་རེར་བརྒྱ་ར་ལྔ་བཅུ་ཡོད།

A: Ya? You make 150,   ཀ ཡ། ཁྱོ་བརྒྱ་ར་ལྔ་བཅུ།

B: I make less than he does.   ཁ ང་ཁོ་དགི་བསྣས་ན་ཅིག་དམན་གི

C: Ya, how much do you make?   ཀ ཡ། ཁྱོ་ད་ཡོད་གི

B: I make 200 minus 50.   ཁ ང་ཉིས་བརྒྱ་ལྔ་བཅུ་གིས་མི་ལོངས་གི

A: That's the same. Which of you is more famous?   ཀ དེ་གཅིག་ར་གཅིག་རེད་མོ། ཡ་ད་ཁྱོ་གཉིས་གའི་སྙིང་ཅན་པོ་སུ་ཡིན་ནས།

C: In Tibetan regions, there's not a single one who hasn't heard my name.   ག བོད་རིགས་ས་ཁུལ་ན་འདི་སྙིང་གོ་མ་སྐྱོང་ནི་གཅིག་ག་ར་མེད།

B: Oh, if we're speaking of names, all Tibetans have heard my name.   ཁ ཨོ། སྐྱོང་བཤད་ན་ད། འདི་སྐྱོང་བོད་བཟིག་ཡོད་ཡོད་པོས་གོ་སྐྱོང་ང་།

A: *Ya*, it's the same again. *Ya*, what do you guys use for getting around?

ཀ། ཡ། ཡང་གཅིག་ར་གཅིག་རེད། ཡ། དཁྱོ་གཉིས་ཀ་ཧུར་ཆུར་ར་འགྲོ་སྒྱུད་གོ་ཆེ་བཟིག་ཡིན།

C: Even if I go one span, I have never not taken a car.[2]

ག ང་ས་མཐོ་གང་ད་སོང་ན་ར། རྣངས་འཁོར་ར་ཁ་གར་མ་སྨྱོང་།

B: I drive a car to go pee!

ཁ ང་གཅིན་ཕོག་ག་སོང་ན་ར་རྣངས་འཁོར་བསྐོར་རས་སོང་ནས།

A: Ha! These two are probably a pair of chauffeurs. *Ya*, let's not argue over who's first and who's next. Let's introduce you first. Don't move. *Un*, Give me a straight answer to whatever I ask. What's your name?

ཀ ཧྡུ། འདི་གཉིས་ཀ་ཁ་ལོ་བ་གཉིས་ཡིན་ས་ཡོད་གོ ཡ། ད་སྔ་གལུག་མི་ཚོད་ནི་ཐོས། ད་སྔོན་ན་ཁྱོ་མཚམས་སྦྱོར་ཡེད་རྒྱུའི་བྱ། མ་འགུལ། འུན། ངས་ཆེ་བཟིག་དྲིས་ན་ཁྱོས་དྲང་མོ་ཐོས་ལན་ཐོབས། ཁྱོའི་མིང་ད་ཆེ་ཟེར་ར།

C: My name is Phurwa.

ག ངའི་མིང་ད་ཕུར་བ་ཟེར་ར།

A: And what was your name originally?

ཀ དྲང་མ་ཁྱོའི་མིང་ད་ཆེ་ཟེར་ར།

C: Uh, originally? Originally I was called Phurwa.

ག ཨ། དྲང་མ། དྲང་མ་ར་ཕུར་བ་ཟེར་ར།

A: [dismissively] Heh, Phurwa, Hurwa, such an uncomfortable name in the mouth, it almost breaks your tongue.[3]

ཀ ཧེ། ཕུར་བ། ཧུར་བ། དེ་མོ་མྱིད་ཁ་ནང་ད་མི་བདེ་ནི་བཟིག་ལྕེ་བཟོ་གཅོག་ལ་ཡེད་གི

C: Your tongue is probably a piece of wood.

ག ཁྱོའི་ལྕེ་དེ་ཤིང་ཏོ་བཟིག་ཡིན་ས་ཡོད་ད།

---

2 A *mtho* མཐོ། is the distance from the thumb to the tip of the middle finger. We have used the English "span" because it is a similar measurement, though slightly different in that the English span is the measure from thumb to pinky finger.

3 Asked to suggest that Phurwa is not his real name. Hurwa uses the Amdo practice of pronouncing *pha* as *ha*. Hurwa, however, refers to tent stakes, while Phurwa is pronounced in Amdo for names and ritual daggers.

A: And you now, how old are you?

C: Thirty-three.

A: [scoffing] Heh, you look like someone who is sixty-six.

C: Do I look that old?

A: How long have you been in your job?

C: Thirteen years.

A: So this is the result of working for thirteen years?

C: It is mainly because I haven't had any free time.

A: In my opinion, it's mainly because you've been wasting your days.

C: That is not it. It's mainly because I was installed as leader and the workload was heavy: meetings and trainings, trainings and meetings everyday.

A: Ah? Hold up. Thou art a leader?

C: *Olé*.

A: Ah, that's just like me. When I was young, my mom used to say that my left eye had a problem. That was true. *Aro*, how could I not know that thou art a leader? Thou mustn't be angry with me! Uncle Phurwa.[4]

ཀ། ཨ། ང་འདི་ད་འདི་མོ་བཞིག་ཡིན་མོ། ཆུང་རས་བཞིག་གི་ཨ་མམ་ཁྱིའི་ཤྱིའི་གཡོན་པ་དེ་གེས་བཞིག་ཡོད་ཀྱི་ཟེར་ར། དོ་བདེན་གི་ཨ་རོ། ཁྱེད་གི་དཔོན་པོ་ཡིན་ནོ་མི་ཤེས་སྤོལ་བཞིག་ད་ཡོད་ནས། ཁྱེད་ག་ཐུགས་རྒྱལ་བཞེངས་མི་ཉན་གོ ཨ་ཁུ་ཕུར་བ།

C: Uncle? Aren't you older than me?

ག ཨ་ཁུ། ཁྱིད་འདི་ཆེ་བོ་མིན་ནས།

A: Thou art a higher-ranking leader than me. I'll introduce thee again: What's thy appellation?

ཀ ཁྱེད་ག་ང་བསྡན་ན་དཔོན་ས་མཐོ་གི་མོ། ངས་འོར་གེས་མཆམས་སྟོར་ཡེད། ཁྱེད་གའི་མཚན་ན།

C: Appellation? Oh, my name, right? I'm called Phurwa.

ག མཚན། ཨོའི་སྒྱིད་ང་ཡིན། ཕུར་བ་ཟེར་ར།

A: Oh, Look! The *phar* for the word 'promotion'![5] What an appellation. Amazing!

ཀ ཨོ། ལྟོས། གོས་ཡར་འཕར་གི་འཕར། མཚན་བདོག་གོ་རེད། དཔེ་བཞིག་མེད་གི

C: Not amazing at all! Isn't it a name so uncomfortable for the mouth that it breaks the tongue?

ག ཐལ་ར་ཅིག་གི་དཔེ་མེད་ནས། ཁ་ནང་ང་མི་བདེ་ལྟེ་གཅིག་སྤྱད་གོའི་མྱིད་མིན་ནས།

A: Oh, my apologies, my apologies. Thy appellation wasn't to blame. It's the fault of my useless tongue.[6] What thou sayest was not wrong. This tongue of mine; this inflexible, piece of wood, it should be cut and thrown into a urinal.

ཀ ཨོ། ཐུགས་རྒྱལ་མ་བཞེངས། ཐུགས་རྒྱལ་མ་བཞེངས། དེ་ཁྱེད་གེས་མཚན་ལན་ནི་མ་རེད། ལམ་མ་སྤྱར་རྒྱུའི་འདའི་ཁ་ནང་གི་ལྟེ་མ་འགྲིག ནི་རེད། དི་ང་ཁྱེད་གེས་གསུངས་ནོ་ནོར་མེད་གི་ངའི་ལྟེ་འདི་ད་ཤིང་རྡོ། གྱིད་རྡོ། བཅད་ལས་ཆབ་ཏོ་གི་ནང་ད་ཧེན་རྒྱ་བཞིག་རེད།

---

4 In Amdo, a speaker might use the word *akhu* "uncle," to speak respectfully to elders and monks.

5 *Phar* (འཕར།) in "promotion" (གོས་ཡར་འཕར།) and the character's name Phurwa (ཕུར་བ།) are pronounced similarly in Amdo dialect.

6 Literally "the tongue in my mouth that should be thrown out on the road" (a dirty place, where many will step on and over it).

C: You will cut out your tongue for me.   ག   དའི་དོན་ན་ཁྱོའི་ལྕེ་གཅོད་རྒྱུ་རེད་ལ།

A: What is thine age?   ག   ཁྱེད་ཀ་དགུང་ལོ་ག་ཚོད་ཡིན།

C: 33   ག   སུམ་ཅུ་སོ་གསུམ།

A: 33?   ག   སུམ་ཅུ་སོ་གསུམ།

C: *Olé.*   ག   ཨོ་ལེ།

A: I don't believe it. You look twenty-three.   ག   མ་རེད་མོ། ཉི་ཤུ་རྩ་གསུམ་བཟིག་ག་རེད་དོ།

C: Don't I look older?   ག   བསླས་ན་རྒས་བསྡད་མེད་ག

A: No way, no way. There's a saying, "a man shouldn't be called old in his thirties." You still have to be leader for thirty more years. Moreover, you have to keep moving up.   ག   ཆེ་ཡིན་ཆེ་ཡིན། ཁ་དཔེ་ར། ཕོ་ལོ་སུམ་ཅུར་རྒས་མིང་མེད་ཟེར་ག དུ་རུང་བཞི་ད་ལོ་སུམ་ཅུར་དཔོན་པོར་འདུག་དགོ་རྒྱུ་རེད། དེའི་མི་ཚད་རྫེ་མཐོར་འགྲོ་དགོ་ནི་རེད།

C: If I move up my workload will be unbearably heavy!   ག   ད་རྫེ་མཐོ་བཟིག་སོང་དུས། ངས་བུ་བ་ཁུར་ཐུབ་རྒྱུ་མ་རེད།

A: Really, as you go higher and higher in rank, you have more and more to do. As you do more and more things, your responsibilities get heavier and heavier.   ག   དོམ། དཔོན་ས་རྫེ་མཐོ་སོང་གི་སོང་གི་བྱ་བ་རྫེ་མང་རྫེ་མང་ཡིན་ནི་རེད། བྱ་བ་རྫེ་མང་ད་སོང་གི་སོང་གི་འགན་འཁུར་རྫེ་ལྕི་རྫེ་ལྕི་ཡིན་ནི་རེད།

C: That's difficult.   ག   ད་དཀའ་ག

A: Really difficult. Extremely horrible. There's nothing to be done. It's difficult for a regular person, but they couldn't find anyone able to go higher than thou.   ག   དོམ་དཀའ་གི་གཉིས་གི་ཐུ་གི་བཀོད་པ་མེད་གི་རང་ད་སྐྱི་བཟིག་གིས་དཀའ་གི་ཡིན་ནའང་ཁྱེད་ག་མིན་ནས་རྫེ་མཐོ་འགྲོ་ཁུབའི་སྐྱི་བཟིག་བཚལ་ཡས་མི་རྙེད་ལ།

C: It'd be the same for anyone.   ག   དི་སུ་ཡིན་ན་ར་གཅིག་རེད་མོ།

6. Please, Dear Leader

A: *Un*, no way, no way. It's fundamentally different. If thou didn't go higher and another did, then the people's lives would get worse, the livestock's strength would decrease, and the heads of grain would be scattered.

ཀ ཤུན། ཆེ་ཡིན། ཆེ་ཡིན། དི་རྩ་བ་ནས་འདུ་ནི་མ་རེད། ཁྱེད་ཀ་རྗེ་མཐོར་མ་སོང་ད་གཞན་པ་བཞིག་སོང་དུས་མང་ཚོགས་ཀྱི་འཚོ་བ་རྗེ་སྡུག་ག་བུད་འགྱོ་ནི་རེད། ཕྱུགས་ཟོག་གི་ཤ་མེད་ལྱང་འགྱོ་ནི་རེད། འབྲུ་རིགས་ཀྱི་སྟེ་མ་འཐོར་འགྱོ་ནི་རེད།

C: Wouldn't that be a poison?

ཀ དི་བདོག་གོ་དུག་བཞིག་ཡིན་ནི་མ་ར།

A: Ah, leader, for thee it's like the saying of teaching *ka* and *kha* to the Buddha.[7] There are poisons to thy right and left. Be careful! If thou takest the wrong step, putting aside the loss it would be for the people, it would also cause me lifelong suffering.

ཀ ཨ། དཔོན་པོ་ཁྱེད་ག་སངས་རྒྱས་ག་ཁ་གི་དཔེ་རེད་ད། ཁྱེད་གའི་གཡས་དང་གཡོན་ན་དུག་དང་དུག་འདུ་བ་མང་ད་ཡོད་ནི་རེད། གཟབ་གཟབ་བྱོས། གལ་ཏེ་ཁྱེད་ག་སྤུངས་མི་ལེགས་པ་རེ་བྱུང་བཏང་དུས། མང་ཚོགས་ཀྱི་གྱོང་གུད་ཡིན་ནོ་ཕར་ར་ཞོགས་ར། ང་ར་ཚེ་གང་གི་སྡུག་བསྒྲལ་བཞག་བཏང་ནི་རེད།

C: Why for you?

ཀ ཁྱོ་ཆེ་བཞིག་ག

A: Leader thou knowest without being told, but since we are relatives, of course I would like to speak the words of my heart.

ཀ དཔོན་པོ་ཁྱེད་ག་ཞུ་ཆེ་དགོ་མཁྱེན་ནི་རེད། ད། ཨུ་གཉིས་ག་ཨ་ཁུག་ཡིན་ནོའི་སྟེང་ནས་ར་ངས་སེམས་གཏམ་རེ་ད་བཤད་ན་འོས་འདོད།

C: In what way are we relatives? *Wei*!

ཀ ཨུ་གཉིས་ག་ཆེ་ཡས་ཉེ་ནི་རེད། སྨེ།

A: Uh, just by looking at me, of course thou wilt know that a person like me cannot be thy relative. It's because of the paternal cousins again.

ཀ ཤྱུ། ང་འདུ་བཞིག་ཁྱེད་ག་གི་སྨྱུན་མིན་ནོ་ད་བལྟས་ན་ར་ལོས་ཤེས་ར། ཡང་པ་སྨྱུན་དེའི་ཅེན་གི་ནོ།

C: [surprised] Paternal cousins?

ཀ པ་སྨྱུན།

---

7 "Teaching *ka* and *kha* to the Buddha" is a saying suggesting that one does something unnecessary. *Ka* and *kha* are the first two consonants of the Tibetan alphabet, and refer to the whole of the Tibetan alphabet. Teaching the enlightened Buddha such fundamental knowledge is completely unnecessary.

A: Oh, Of course I know that our fathers were not brothers. The two fathers of our two fathers, if we trace back to *their* fathers, then there was the problem.

ཀ ཨུ་གཉིས་ཀའི་ཕ་གཉིས་ཀ་སྤུན་མིན་ནོ་ད་ལོས་ཤེས་ར། ཕ་གཉིས་ཀའི་ཕ་གཉིས་ཀ་དེའི་ཕ་གཉིས་ཀ་དེད་ལས་ཡོང་ན་ཡང་འགྲིག་ཡོད་ནི་མ་རེད་བཟེ་ན།

C: What was wrong?

ཀ ཅི་བཟེག་ཡས་བཞག་ཡོད་ནི་རེད།

A: They were said to be paternal cousins!

ཀ ཕ་སྤུན་ཡིན་ནི་རེད་ཟེར་གི་བཟེ་ན།

C: Who says that?

ཀ དེ་སོ་བཟེག་སུས་ཟེར་གི

A: My father.

ཀ དེད་ཀའི་ཨ་ཕ།

C: That's just idle talk.

ཀ དེ་རང་ང་བཞད་གོ་ནི་རེད།

A: Thou must speakest thus. I know that. That's a demand of your job.

ཀ ཁྱེད་གིས་དེ་ཡས་གསུང་དགོ་ནི་རེད། ངས་ཤེས་ནི་རེད། དེ་བྱ་བའི་དགོས་མཁོ་རེད།

C: This has a bearing on my job?

ཀ དེ་བྱ་བར་ཅི་བཟེག་གི་འབྲེལ་བ་ཡོད་གི

A: If thou trace relations and family and differentiate between the important and the unimportant, then could you honestly lead the broad masses of the people? Could you continue to preserve your magnificent leadership position?

ཀ ལོས་ཡོད་བཟེ་ར། གལ་ཏེ་ཁྱེད་ཀས་ན་ཉེ་ར་ཤ་ཁྲག་དེད་ལས། རོ་ཆེན་ར་རོ་མེད་བཏོད་བཏང་ན། རྒྱ་ཆེ་བའི་མང་ཚོགས་དྲང་བདེན་གི་འཁྲིད་ཐུབ་ནས། རྣམས་ཆེ་བའི་དཔོན་ས་སུ་མཐུད་དུ་སྐྱོང་ཐུབ་ནས།

C: That last bit is your own idea.

ཀ གཞུག་གི་ཆིག་དེ་ཁྱིའི་བསམ་པ་རེད།

A: If you ask my father the story of how we're related, you'll know. But when I was two years old, my father went abroad. If you ever need anything from abroad, just ask. So keep me in thy heart.

ཀ ཨུ་གཉིས་ཀ་ག་ཁྲག་ཡིན་ནོའི་ལོ་རྒྱུས་དེད་ཀའི་ཨ་ཕ་གཅིག་འདྲི་རྒྱུ་ན་ད་ཤེས་ནི་རེད་ད། ཡང་ང་ལོ་གཉིས་ཡིན་རས་ཐད་ཚོ་ཨ་ཕ་ཕྱི་རྒྱལ་ལ་བྱུད་སོང་ནི་རེད། གཞུག་ཕྱོགས་ཕྱི་རྒྱལ་ན་དགོ་ནི་ཡོད་ན་ཆིག་གཅིག་ཡིན། ཐུགས་ག་ཅིག་ཟུངས་གོ་ད་ད།

6. Please, Dear Leader

C: You're nothing like the person you were before.

ག དེང་མ་གི་ཁྱེད་མ་རེད།

A: I'm speaking the truth, I'll say "yes" to whatever thou sayest. After all, thou are not an ordinary person like him!

ཀ ངོ་མ་བཤད་ནས། ཁྱེད་གས་ད་ཅི་བཤད་ན་ཡང་ཡིན་ནས་ཡིན་ན་ཅང་མེད། ཁྱེད་ཀྱི་ཁེར་གི་འདུ་འདྲོ་རང་ཁམས་གི་ཁྱུ་མ་རེད་མོ།

B: What have I done, *wei*?

ཁ ངས་ཅི་བཟིག་ཡས་བཏང་ནི་རེད། ཝེ།

A: *Un*, I ask you, what's your name.

ཀ ཨུན། ངས་ཁྱོ་འདྲི། ཁྱོའི་མྱིང་ད་ཅི་བཟིག་ཟེར་ར།

B: Phagmo Drashi

ཁ ཕག་མོ་བཀྲ་ཤིས།

A: What was your name last year?

ཀ ན་ནིང་ཁྱོའི་མྱིང་ད་ཅི་ཟེར་ར།

B: Last year I was also called Phagmo Drashi.

ཁ ན་ནིང་ར་ཕག་མོ་བཀྲ་ཤིས།

A: He, "She-pig," Phagmo, a she-pig among all the pigs, such an awkward name, it almost tears my throat.

ཀ ཏེ། ཕག་མ། ཕག་མོ། ཕག་གི་ནང་ནས་ར། ཕག་མ། དི་མོ་མྱིང་སྒྲོར་ལོག་བཟིག་ཁྱེད་ཐག་བཟོ་གཤག་ལ་ཡོད་ཀ

B: Your throat is probably made of paper.

ཁ ཁྱོའི་མྱིད་ཐག་དི་ཤོག་བུ་བཟིག་ཡིན་ས་ཡོད་གི་ར།

A: Ya, then how old are you this year?

ཀ ཡ་ད་ཁྱོ་ད་ལོ་ལོ་ད་ཨིན།

B: 50 even.

ཁ ལྔ་བཅུ་ཐམ་པ།

A: It's finished.

ཀ ཚར་སོང་ནི་རེད།

B: What's finished?

ཁ ཅི་བཟིག་ཚར་སོང་ནི་རེད།

A: It's not long before you go to the next life.

ཀ ད་ཚོ་ཕྱི་མ་འགྱོ་རྒྱུའི་ཅིང་བཟིག་མེད་ལ།

B: Since they've dumped leadership responsibilities on my shoulders, I have no choice but to bust my ass till I die.

A: Hold on! Thou art also a leader?

B: *Un.*

A: *Ya*, I am completely blind. Even when I was young, my teacher would say "your eyes are terrible." He would tell me I should wear a pair of +900 glasses. That was really true, *aro*. How could I not have recognized thee? My apologies, Uncle Phagmo!

B: Uncle? Aren't you my senior?

A: Thou art higher ranking than me. I'll introduce again. What's thy appellation?

B: My name is Phagmo Drashi.

A: Listen, the *phag* in the word for "promotion," *Un*, Could such an appellation be found in Geshe Chodak?[8] Amazing!

B: Wasn't it not only not amazing, but an awkward name that tears the throat?

---

8   This is referring to a dictionary compiled by Geshe Chodak, a Buryati monk who studied in Sera Monastery in the first half of the twentieth century. See Dge bshes chos grags 1957.

6. Please, Dear Leader

A: That wasn't thy appellation's fault. My poor-quality throat was to blame. But what thou sayest wasn't wrong. My throat is made of paper, gray paper, single ply gray paper used for rolling cigarettes.

ཀ། དེ་ཁྱེད་ཀའི་མཚན་ལན་ནི་མ་རེད། རྒྱ་སྒྲུབ་མེད་ནོ་དེད་ཁའི་སྙིད་ཐག་ལན་ནི་རེད། དེ་ར་ཁྱེད་ཀས་གསུངས་ནོ་ནོར་མེད་གི་ དའི་སྙིད་ཐག་འདི་ད། ཤོག་གུ་སྒྱ། ཤོག་སྐྱ། ཤོག་སྐྱ་ར་ཁེར་ཆེབ་དོ་སློན་སྡུད་གོ་དེ་རེད་ཡ།

B: You'll burn your throat for me.

ཁ། ཁྱོས་ངའི་དོན་ན་སྙིད་ཐག་ཚིག་ལེག་གི

A: *Ya*, what's thy age?

ཀ། ཡ། ཁྱེད་ཀ་དགོང་ལོ་ད་ཡིན།

B: Fifty even.

ཁ། ལྔ་བཅུ་ཐམ་པ།

A: Fifty even, *un*, no sign of aging, *aro*!

ཀ། ལྔ་བཅུ་ཐམ་པ། ཨུན། རྒས་ཉམས་བཟིག་མེད་ནོ་ཨ་རོ།

B: I'm not finished?

ཁ། ཚར་རས་བསྡད་མེད་ཀ

A: Of course not. As the saying goes, "Fifty is an age when your belly swells with experience." You still have to bear the responsibility of leadership for many years. Not only that, but you have to keep moving up too.

ཀ། ཆེ་ཡོད་བཟེ་ར། ཁ་དཔེ་ར། ཕོ་ལོ་ལྔ་བཅུ་ཉམས་མྱོང་གི་གསུམ་པ་རྒྱས་པའི་དུས་ཡིན་ཟེར་ག དུང་བརྩོད་ལོ་མང་བ་དཔོན་པོ་འཁུར་དགོ་ནི་རེད། དེའི་མི་ཚད་རེ་མཐོར་འགྲོ་དགོ་ནི་རེད།

B: If I move up, my body won't be able to cope.

ཁ། ད་རེ་མཐོ་ཆིག་སོང་དུས་ཕུང་པོ་གིས་ཚུགས་རྒྱ་ཨེ་རེད།

A: Really, as you go higher and higher in rank, you have more and more to do. As you do more and more things, your responsibilities get heavier and heavier.

ཀ། ངོ་མ་དཔོན་ས་རེ་མཐོ་སོང་གི་སོང་གི་བྱ་བ་རེ་མང་རེ་མང་ཡིན་ནི་རེད། བྱ་བ་རེ་མང་ང་སོང་གི་སོང་གི་འགན་ཁུར་རེ་ལྗི་རེ་ལྗི་ཡིན་ནི་རེད།

B: That's difficult!

ཁ། ད་དཀའ་ག

A: Really difficult. Extremely horrible. There's nothing to be done. It'd be difficult for a normal person, but they couldn't find anyone able to go higher than thee.

ཀ ཏོ་མ་དགའ་གི་གཞིས་གི་ཧྲུ་གི་བགོད་པ་མེད་གི་རང་ང་ཅུ་བཟིག་གིས་དགའ་གི་རེད་དུ་ར་ཁྱེད་ཀ་མིན་ནས་རྗེ་མཐོ་འགྲོ་རྒྱུའི་ཅུ་བཟིག་བཙལ་ཡས་མི་སྲིད་ལ།

B: It'd be the same for anyone.

ཁ དི་སུ་ཡིན་ན་གཅིག་རེད་མོ།

A: No way. No way. That's completely different. If you didn't get promoted but another did, then the earth wouldn't be able to turn. The sun wouldn't shine on the snow mountains. The Tibetan masses wouldn't be awakened.

ཀ ཆེ་ཡིན། ཆེ་ཡིན། དི་རྩ་བ་ནས་འདྲ་ཉི་མ་རེད། ཁྱེད་ཀ་རྗེ་མཐོ་མ་སོང་གཞན་པ་རྗེ་མཐོ་བཟིག་སོང་ཚུལ་སའི་གོ་ལ་བྱུང་གི་འཁོར་ཁ་ཤུན་ཉི་མ་རེད། གངས་རིའི་སྟེང་ང་ཉི་མ་འཆར་ཉི་མ་རེད། བོད་རིགས་མི་དམངས་ང་སད་རྒྱུ་ཡོད་ཉི་མ་རེད།

B: It wouldn't be such a big hindrance, aro!

ཁ དི་བདོག་གོ་བར་བགེགས་བཟིག་ཡིན་ཉི་མ་ར། ཨ་རོ།

A: Ah, leader, thou hast taught the buddha's ka and kha. But there are many who create obstacles and interruptions for thee inside and out. Be careful! If a misfortune falls on thee, it goes without saying that it would be a loss for the Tibetan ethnicity, it would also make me shed tears for thee.

ཀ ཨ། དཔོན་པོ་ཁྱེད་ཀ་སངས་རྒྱས་ཀ་ཁ་གི་དཔེ་ཡིན་ཉི་རེད་དུ། ཁྱེད་ཀའི་གཡས་དང་གཡོན་ན་བགེགས་དང་བར་ཆད་ཡེད་ཉི་མང་ང་ཡོད་ཉི་རེད། ཧྲགས་གཟབ་གཟབ་ཆོས། གལ་ཏེ་ཁྱེད་ཀ་སྦྲམས་མི་ལེགས་ག་རེ་བྱུང་བདང་ན་བོད་རིགས་གི་གྱོང་གུད་ཡིན་བོད་མ་བཤད། ད། ང་ར་ཁྱེད་ཀའི་དོན་ན་ཤྲིག་རྒྱུ་བཞུར་གི་བཞག་བཏང་ཉི་རེད།

B: Why would you?

ཁ ཆྱུ་ཆེ་བཟིག་ག

A: Leader thou knowest without being told, but since we are relatives, of course I would like to speak the words of my heart.

ཀ དཔོན་པོ་ཁྱེད་ཀ་ཞུ་ཆེ་དགོ་མཁེན་ཉི་རེད། ད། ཨུ་གཉིས་ཀ་པ་ཁྲག་ཡིན་ནོའི་སྟེང་ནས་ར་ངས་སེམས་གཏམ་རེ་བཤད་ན་ལོས་འདོད།

B: Bullshit! In what way are we relatives?

ཁ ཆྱི་གཏམ། ཨུ་གཉིས་ཀ་ཆི་ཡས་པ་ཁྲག་ཡིན་ཉི་རེད།

6. Please, Dear Leader

A: Though it's certain that we're not tracing back to the Rock demoness mother,[9] but again the maternal cousins...

ཀ། ཐག་སྲིད་མོ་ནས་བརྒྱུད་ལས་འདེད་གི་མེད་ནོ་དཁོ་ཐག་ཡིན་ནི་རེད་དཱ། ཡང་མ་སྨྱུན་དེའི་རྗེན་གི་...

B: Maternal cousins?

ཁ། མ་སྨྱུན།

A: *Un*, of course I know that our mothers were not sisters. The two mothers of our two mothers, if we trace back to their mothers, then there was the problem.

ཀ། ཨུན། ང་གཉིས་ཀའི་མ་གཉིས་ཀ་སྤུན་མིན་ནོ་ད་ལོས་ཤེས་ད། ང་གཉིས་ཀའི་མ་གཉིས་ཀའི་མ་གཉིས་དེའི་མ་གཉིས་ཀའི་མ་གཉིས་ཀ་དེད་ལས་སོང་ན་ཡང་འགྲིག་ཡོད་ནི་མ་རེད་བཟེ་ན།

B: What was the problem?

ཁ། ཅི་བཟེག་ཡས་བཞག་ཡོད་ནི་རེད།

A: *Un*, it's said that they're cousins.

ཀ། ཨུན། མ་སྨྱུན་ཡིན་ནི་རེད་ཟེར་གི་བཟེ་ན།

B: Who says that?

ཁ། སུས་དུ་ཟེར་གི

A: My mother.

ཀ། དེད་ཁའི་ཨ་མ།

B: That's just idle talk.

ཁ། དི་རང་ད་བཤད་གོ་ནི་རེད།

A: Thou must speakest thus. I know that. That's a demand of your job.

ཀ། ཁྱེད་ཀས་དེ་ཡས་གསུང་དགོ་ནི་རེད། ངས་ཤེས་ནི་རེད། དི་བྱ་བའི་དགོ་མཁོ་རེད།

B: How is it related to my job?

ཁ། དི་བྱ་བ་ཅི་བཟེག་གི་འབྲེལ་བ་ཡོད་གི

A: If thou trace relations and family and differentiate between the important and the unimportant, then could you honestly lead the broader masses of the people? Could you preserve your magnificent leadership position for long?

ཀ། གལ་ཏེ་ཁྱེད་ཀས་ནུ་ཏེ་ར་བ་ཁྱག་དེད་ལས། རྟོ་ཆེན་ར་རོ་མེད་བཏོད་བཏང་ན། རྒྱ་ཆེ་བའི་མང་ཚོགས་ན་ཏེ་ལྷུར་སྐྱོང་ཐུབ་ནས། གཟི་བརྗིད་གི་དཔོན་ས་སྨུན་རིང་ད་འཛིན་ཐུབ་ནས།

B: That last bit is your own idea.

ཁ། གཞུག་གི་ཅིག་དེ་ཁྱེའི་བསམ་ཚུལ་རེད།

---

9 A reference to the Tibetan origin myth that posits humanity being the children of a union between an enlightened Boddhisattva monkey and a rock demoness.

A: If you ask my father about the story of how we're related, you'll know. But when I was two years old, my father went abroad. If you ever need anything from abroad, just ask. So keep me in thy heart.

C: That's enough. Let me ask you: What's thy appellation?

A: Ah, well, let's say "what's your name" instead of "thy" and "appellation"

C: *Ya*, what's your name?

A: Leader, thou decide what my name is and that'll be it.

C: How can you make someone decide your name?

A: Uh, if the leader decides my name, I can just use it, right?

C: How's that possible, *aro*?

A: Well then, see if thou canst guess my name, leader.

C: See if I can guess?

A: *Olé*. I think you definitely can guess it.

C: *Un*, I think your name is "Sweet Talker."

A: Sweet Talker?	ཀ ཁ་ཡག
C: Did I guess it?	ག ཨེ་བྱེད་ཐལ།
A: *Un*!	ཀ ཨུན།
C: I said, did I guess it? *Wei*!	ག ཨེ་བྱེད་ཐལ་བཟེ་ནི་ཡ། སྟེ།
A: *Un*, you guessed it! You guessed it! My name is Sweet Talker.	ཀ ཨུན། བྱེད་ཐལ། བྱེད་ཐལ། ངའི་མྱིང་ད་ཁ་ཡག་ཟེར་ར།
C: Which two syllables are they?	ག ཡི་གེ་གང་གཉིས་ཀ་ཡིན།
A: *Un*, leader, it's whatever two syllables thou say they are.	ཀ ཨུན། དཔོན་པོ་ཁྱེད་གྱིས་བཤད་གོ་ནོའི་ཡི་གེ་དེ་གཉིས་ཀ་ཡིན།
C: How do you write them?	ག ཆི་ཡས་བྲིས་ནི་རེད།
A: *Un*, writing them is not difficult. The *kha* for "*ka, kha, ga, nga*" and the *yag* for "really beautiful."[10]	ཀ ཨུན། བྲིས་བཏང་ན་ར་དགའ་བཏང་རྒྱུ་མེད། ཀ་ཁ་ག་ང་གི་ཁ། ཏུ་ཅང་མཛེས་པ་གི་ཡག
C: Sweet Talker!	ག ཁ་ཡག
A: Uh, yes. Sweet Talker as in "flattery."[11]	ཀ ཨུན། རེད། ཁ་ཡག་དོ་དགའ་གི་ཁ་ཡག
B: *Aro*! Wait! Wait! I heard it said that your name isn't 'Sweet Talker.'	ཁ ཨ། ཨ་རོ། སྡོད་སྡོད། ངས་གོ་ནོ་ཡིན་ན་ཁྱོའི་མྱིང་ད་ཁ་ཡག་མི་ཟེར་གི་མོ།
A: What dost thou think my name is?	ཀ ཁྱེད་གྱིས་བསམས་ན་ངའི་མྱིང་ད་ཆི་བཟིག་ཟེར་གི

---

10   With many homophones in Chinese and Tibetan, it is common to ask someone how to write their name. Speakers may, in turn, tell you the syllables by their connection to other words. Here, *kha yag* literally means "sweet talker" or sycophant.

11   These lines play on the repeated use of ཡག "pretty" or "beautiful." Someone with a "pretty mouth" might be called a "sweet talker," hence the link to flattery.

B: From what I heard, your name was Ugly Chest. ཁ ངས་གོ་ན་ཡིན་ན་ཁྱོད་ཀྱི་མིང་ད་ཁོག་རྩོག་ཟེར་གི

A: Sweet Talker Ugly Chest. It can't be true, aro?[12] ཀ ཁ་ཡག་ཁོག་རྩོག་དེ་འདུག་བཟིག་ར་ཨེ་བདེན་ན་གོ་ཨ་རོ།

B: I think you're called Ugly Chest, did I guess it? ཁ ངས་བསམས་ན་ཁོག་རྩོག་ཟེར་གི་ཨི་བྱེད་ཐལ།

A: *Un*. That's... ཀ ཨུན་དེ་ད་

B: I said is that it? ཁ ཁྱོ་ཨི་རེད་བཟེ་ནི་ཡ།

A: *Un*, yes, yes. My name is Ugly Chest. ཀ ཨུན་རེད་རེད་ངའི་མིང་ད་ཁོག་རྩོག་ཟེར་ར།

B: Which two syllables are they? ཁ ཡི་གེ་གང་གཉིས་ཀ་རེད།

A: When your chest hurts, *ayo, uh uh*. ཀ ཁོག་ག་ཁོའུ་ན། ཨ་ཡོ། ཨུ་ཨུ།

B: Just say it. ཁ ད་མར་ར་ཤོད་ད་བཟེ་ན།

A: *Un*, when your chest hurst, the chest for your chest hurts. And the ugly for not so pretty. ཀ ཨུན། ཁོག་པ་ཁོའུ་ན། ཁོག་པ་ཁོའུ་ནོ་གི་ཁོག་དེ་ར་ཡག་རྒྱུ་མེད་ནོ་གི་རྩོག

B: Ugly Chest. ཁ ཁོག་རྩོག

A: *Un*, yes. The "ugly chest" for ugly mind and ugly chest. ཀ ཨུན་རེད། བསམ་རྩོག་ཁོག་རྩོག་གི་ཁོག་རྩོག

C: No! I think your name is Sweet Talker! ག མ་རེད་མོ། ངས་བསམས་ན་ཁྱོའི་མིང་ད་ཁ་ཡག་ཟེར་གི

A: Yes. My name is Sweet Talker. ཀ རེད། ངའི་མིང་ད་ཁ་ཡག་ཟེར་ར།

B: I think your name is Ugly Chest. ཁ ངས་བསམས་ན་ཁྱོའི་མིང་ད་ཁོག་རྩོག་ཟེར་གི

---

12 This name is so ridiculously unflattering, that his acceptance is utterly ridiculous.

6. Please, Dear Leader

A: My name is Sweet Talker, and also Ugly Chest.

ཀ ངའི་མྱིང་ད་ཁ་ཡག་ར་ཟེར་ར་ར་ཁོག་རྫོག་
    ར་ཟེར་ར།

C: Why's that?

ག དེ་ཅི་བཟིག་ཡིན་ནས། ཨ་རོ།

A: *Un*, some call me "Sweet Talker," and some call me "Ugly Chest."

ཀ ཡུན། ཁ་ཡས་གིས་ངའི་མྱིང་ད་ཁ་ཡག་ཟེར་
    ར། ཁ་ཡས་གིས་ངའི་མྱིང་ད་ཁོག་རྫོག་ཟེར་
    ཟེར།

B: What's that supposed to mean?

ཁ དེ་བདོག་གི་ཅི་བཟེ་ནི།

A: *Un*, it's useful for you to identify which is which.

ཀ ཡུན། ཁྱེད་རྣམ་པ་ཚོས་མི་འཁྲུག་རྒྱུ་འོ་གོ་
    ཚོད་གི་མོ།

C: Right. Let me ask you a question.

ག རེད། ངས་ཁྱི་ཅིག་འདྲི།

A: *Un*, what do you want to ask, please?

ཀ ཡུན། ཅི་བཟིག་འདྲི་རྒྱུ་ལགས།

C: How old are you?

ག ཁྱི་ལོ་དུ་ཡིན།

A: Give me a hint for how old I am.

ཀ ང་ལོ་དུ་ཡིན་ནས་ཁྱེད་གས་བརྡ་བཟིག་རྐྱོབས།

C: So there's a hint to be given for how old you are?

ག ལོ་དུ་ཡིན་ནི་དེ་བརྡ་བཟིག་རྒྱག་རྒྱུ་ཡོད་ནི་
    ཞེ་རེད།

A: How old dost thou need me to be?

ཀ ཁྱེད་ག་ལོ་ན་ཚོད་ཅི་མོ་བཟིག་དགོ་ནས།

C: Tell me straight how old you are.

ག ལོ་དུ་ཡིན་ནས་དྲང་མོ་ཤོད་མོ།

A: How about thou guesseth how old I am.

ཀ ཡང་མིན་ན། ང་ལོ་དུ་ཡིན་ནས་ཁྱེད་གས་ཞེ་
    ཁྱེད་གི་ཅིག་རྩོས།

C: *Un*, I think you are eighty years old.

ག ཡུན། ངས་བསམས་ན་ཁྱི་ལོ་བརྒྱད་བཅུ་ཐམ་
    པ་རེད།

A: I am.

ཀ ང་ཡིན།

C: *Olé*.

ག ཨོ་ལེ།

A: I'm eighty.   ཀ བརྒྱད་ཅུ་ཐམ་པ་ཡིན།

C: Really?   ག ཨེ་རེད།

A: *Un*, yes, yes.   ཀ ཨུན། རེད་རེད།

B: Ah! so it's whatever number he says!   ཁ ཨ་དི་བཟེ་ན་དུ་རེད་ལ།

A: This eminent leader is really quite wise. He took one glance and knew that I am eighty years old.   ཀ དཔོན་པོ་འདི་བ་ཚང་ངོ་མ་མཁས་པ་འདོག་གོ་རེད། དཀྱིག་གིས་ཅིག་གནའ་ནོ་ར་ལོ་བརྒྱད་ཅུ་ཡིན་ནོ་ཤེས་ཡས་བྱུད་ཐལ།

B: *Aro*, are you eighty years old?   ཁ ཨ་རོ། ཁྱོ་ལོ་བརྒྱད་ཅུ་ཡིན་ནས།

A: Ya, of course! I'm eighty. I just had my eightieth birthday party yesterday.   ཀ ཡ། བོས་ཡིན་བཟེ་ན་བརྒྱད་ཅུ་ཐམ་པ་ཡིན། ཁ་སང་སོ་མ་གྱུ་སྟོན་ཡས་ནོ།

B: I think you're not eighty years old.   ཁ ངས་བསམ་ན། ཁྱོ་ལོ་བརྒྱད་ཅུ་མ་རེད།

A: To you, mine age, uh, no, how old am I?[13]   ཀ ཁྱེད་གས་བསམ་ན་ང་དགུང་ལོ། ཨུན། མ་རེད། ནོ་ལོ་དུ་རེད།

B: I think you're no more than eight years old. Am I right?   ཁ ངས་བསམ་ན་ཁྱོ་ལོ་བརྒྱད་གི་ཆེ་བཟིག་མ་རེད། ཨེ་རེད།

A: *Un*, right, right. I am eight years old.   ཀ ཨུན། རེད་རེད། ང་ལོ་བརྒྱད་ཡིན།

B: Are there any eight-year-olds who look so old?   ཁ ལོ་བརྒྱད་ཅན་བཟིག་ག་འདི་མོ་ལོ་ལོན་བཟིག་ཨེ་ཡོད་ལ།

---

13 Here Menla Jyab inappropriately uses the honorific for himself. This may be merely for humour, or a subtle note that many in Amdo are less comfortable with honorifics, not using them much in everyday speech.

6. Please, Dear Leader

A: Heh, As the saying goes: Young kids with underdeveloped brains and old people with feeble minds are one and the same.[14]

C: *Aro*, you're no longer eighty?

A: *Un*, no way. No way. I'm eight. But I'm also eighty. I'm both an underdeveloped kid and a feeble-minded old person.

C: It's so hard to follow this guy. *Ya*, let me ask you: *Aro*, are you a boy or a girl?

A: Oh, well this. It's really difficult to say. Thou decidest and that will be it.

C: How can that be?

A: *Un*, if the leader says I'm a boy, then I'm a boy. If the leader says I'm a girl, then I'm a girl.

C: Is that possible, *aro*?

A: *Un*, or else Leader, see if thou canst guess if I'm a boy or a girl.

C: *Un*, I think you're a boy, right?

A: Yes. I'm a boy.

---

14 Suggesting that young people and elders sometimes share similar mental capacities and understandings.

B: No. I think you're a girl. Did I guess it?

A: Did you? Yes, yes. You guessed it. You guessed it. Look! Leaders' eyes are unlike others'. Do you see that he identified me correctly with just one look? If you trace me back to my origins, I am a girl.

C: If you say that, then was I wrong?

A: *Un*, of course not. Of course not. You weren't wrong.

B: *Ya*, so what I said was wrong!

A: Of course not. Both of you weren't wrong.

C: Well then who was wrong?

A: I was wrong.

B: How were you wrong?

A: *Un*, mainly I was born a hermaphrodite, that was the problem.

C: So in reality are you a boy or a girl?

A: *Un*, right after I was born, I was a girl. But after a few days, I became a boy. Now I'm a boy, and I'm also a girl.[15]

---

15 In these lines, the Tibetan term ཧྲུའུ་ལོག (pronounced *shoolog*) refers to a Tibetan conception of someone who is born a girl and becomes a boy a few days after

C: [as if unsatisfied with the answer] ག ཨ་ཧ།
A ha!

B: Wait! Come here! ཁ སྡོད་དུ། འདིར་ཤོག

A: Un. ག ཨུན།

B: Let me ask you. ཁ ངས་ཁྱོ་ཅིག་འདྲི།

A: Ya. ག ཡ།

B: You're not sick or in pain, are you? ཁ ཁྱོ་ཁོའུ་རྒྱུ་ན་རྒྱུ་མེད་ལ།

A: Even my teeth have never had an ache. ག སོ་ཁོའུ་བཟིག་ར་བྱུང་མ་མྱོང་།

B: Un, I think you're not quite well. Is it true? ཁ ཨུན། ངས་བསམས་ན་ཁྱོ་ཅིག་བདེ་གི་མེད་གི། བདེན་གི

A: Un, that's true. There is some pain. What dost thou think hurts? ག ཨུན། བདེན་གི་མོ། ཁོའུ་རྒྱུའོ་ཁོའུ་གི་ཆེད། གས་བསམས་ན་ཆེ་བཟིག་ཁོའུ་གོ་གི

B: I think you have appendicitis. ཁ ངས་བསམས་ན་ཁྱོ་རྒྱུ་ལྷག་ཡོད་གི

A: Un, I do. I have my appendix.[16] ག ཨུན། ཡོད། རྒྱུ་ལྷག་ཡོད།

B: How big is it? ཁ ཆེ་མོ་བཟིག་ཡོད།

A: Un, it can't be more than one or two arm-spans long. ག ཨུན། འདོམ་པ་གང་དོ་བཟིག་གི་ཆེ་བཟིག་ད་ མེད་རྒྱའོ་རེད་ད།

C: I think you have no illnesses. Right? ག ངས་བསམས་ན་ཁྱོ་ནད་གཅིག་ར་མེད་གི་ཨེ་ རེད།

A: Oh, that's also right. Yes. I think I don't. ག ཨོ། དེ་ར་རེད་རེད། ངས་བསམས་ན་ར་མེད་གི

---

birth. This can also work in the reverse.

16 This appears to be an intentional misunderstanding. The term རྒྱུ་ལྷག can be either appendix or appendicitis. A (voiced by Menla Jyab) clearly has no idea what the appendix is.

B: I think you do, right?

A: Right, I seem to have a disease but when I think about it again I don't.

C: *Ya*, then what I said was wrong?

B: What I said was also wrong?

A: No, no. You both aren't wrong. I was wrong. I have a terrible disease. I feel ill sometimes and feel really good sometimes.

C: Ah, do you take medicine?

A: I eat it like *tsampa*.

B: I think you don't take a single dose.

A: Right. I don't.

C: It's fine if you do. It's ok if you don't. We are the only ones who have the cure for what ails you.

A: What is it?

B: You have to be promoted to a leadership position.

A: Oh, well then, keep me in mind, dear leaders!

C: But, at present, this medicine is not in our hands. Neither of us is a leader!

6. Please, Dear Leader

A: Then? ཀ ཨོ་ན།

B and C: We are speakers of *khashag*! ཁ ག ཁ་ཤགས་བཤད་ནོ་ཡིན་ཡ།

A: [dismissively] Heh! ཀ ཧེ།

7. The Telephone ཁ་པར།[1]

A: So what should we do now?

ཀ ད་ཨུ་གཉིས་གས་ཅི་བཟིག་ཡེད་དགོ་གི་ར།

B: It's up to you. Whatever you say.

ཁ ཁྱོ་དགེ་གསལ་གོ ཁྱིས་ཅི་བཟེ་ན་དི་ཡིན།

A: Well, I'll say something. Instead of sitting here silently, let's speak a *khashag*. But before we speak a *khashag* let me look at your mouth.

ཀ ད་ངས་བཤད། ཨུ་གཉིས་ཀ་ཁ་རོག་ག་འདུག་རགས་གོ་ཁ་བཤད་བཟིག་བཤད། ཁ་བཤད་མ་བཤད་གོང་ད་ངས་ཁྱོའི་ཁ་གཅིག་བལྟ།

B: I am young and I've just lost a tooth.[2]

ཁ ཁ་ད་རུང་ཆུང་ར། སོ་ཞིག་བཟིག་སོ་མ་ལོག་སོང་ཨ།

A: That's not a problem. When I look at your mouth, I can see into your chest.

ཀ དེར་སྨྱོན་མེད་ཀི་ར། ཁྱོའི་ཁ་བལྟས་ན་ངས་ཁྱོའི་ཁོག་རིག་གི་ཡ།

B: How is it? My chest is full of art.

ཁ ཅི་མོ་རེད། ངའི་ཁོག་ག་སྒྱུ་རྩལ་གིས་གང་ངས་བསྡད་ཡོད

A: I don't see any art, but there are a lot of guts.[3] There is also tripe.

ཀ སྒྱུ་རྩལ་བཟོ་མི་རིག་གི་ར་རྒྱུ་ཆོག་མང་གི་ཤྱོད་ཕུ་བཟིག་ར་ཡོད་ག

---

1   In this performance, Menla Jyab plays "A", while Phagmo Drashi is "B."
2   Pastoralists in Amdo tell the age of livestock by looking at their teeth. Here, the speaker assumes Menla Jyab wants to look into his mouth for this reason. Chos bstan rgyal (2014) for more information describes this practice in detail.
3   Here, Menla Jyab plays on the similar pronunciations of སྒྱུ། and རྒྱུ།.

B: What did you say? I have tripe?[4]   ཁ་ ཅི་བཟེ། ད་གྲོད་པུ་ཡོད་ཀི།

A: Oh, just kidding. But your mouth is especially good for one thing...   ཀ་ ཨ་ལ་ཀུ་རེ་ཡིན་དུ། ཁྱོད་ཀི་ཁ་ད་ཕྱོགས་ཁེར་བཟིག་ག་ད་ཞེ་གི་མཛའ་གི་ཡ།

B: It's a mouth made for speaking *khashag*.   ཁ་ ཁ་བཤགས་བཤད་སྟུད་ཀོའི་ཁ་ད་ཡིན།

A: Uh, it's a mouth made for making phone calls.   ཀ་ ཨ། ཁ་པར་རྒྱག་སྟུད་ཀོའི་ཁ་རེད་མོ།

B: Ah? Made for making phone calls?   ཁ་ ཨ། ཁ་པར་རྒྱག་སྟུད་ཀོ

A: *Olé*! Look at your mouth. Such a comfortable mouth, such a round mouth, one would think it's absolutely going to say "*Wei!*"[5]   ཀ་ ཨོ་ལེ། ཁྱིས་ཁྱོད་ཀྱི་ཁ་ལྟོས་དཱ། དེ་མོ་ཁ་བསོ་མོ། དེ་མོ་ཁ་གོར་གོར། རང་ད་སླེ་བཟེ་ལོས་འཛིག་འདོད་ག

B: So you can't make phone calls unless your mouth is round?   ཁ་ དེས་ན་ཁ་གོར་གོར་ཚན་བཟིག་མིན་ན་ཁ་པར་རྒྱག་ཤུན་རྒྱུ་མ་རེད་པ།

A: Oh, you can make calls if your mouth is square or triangular. The main thing is that a *khashag* speaker also has to look in the mouths of those making phone calls.   ཀ་ ཨོ་ཁ་གྲུ་བཞི་ཡིན་ནས་མི་ཆོག་ཟུར་གསུམ་ཡིན་ན་ར་ཁ་པར་བརྒྱབ་ན་ཆོག་གི་རེད། གཙོ་བོ་ཁ་བཤགས་བཤད་མཁན་བཟིག་ཡིན་ཕྱིན་ཁ་པར་རྒྱག་ནི་ཚོའི་ཁ་ནང་ད་ར་བལྟ་དགོ་ནི་རེད་ཡ།

B: So you must have looked in them carefully.   ཁ་ ཁྱིས་དེར་ཞེ་གི་ཅིག་བསླབས་ཡོད་ས་ཡོད་ཀི་མོ།

A: Oh, would you believe it if I told you that I could write an entire *khashag* just about telephone conversations?   ཀ་ ཨོ། ངས་ཁ་པར་གི་ཁ་བརྡ་ཁེར་རེས་ཁ་བཤགས་བཟིག་བྱིས་འཛོག་ག་བཟེ་ན་ཁྱོའི་རྩར་ཨེ་འགྲོ

---

4   The term translated here as "tripe" (གྲོད་པུ།) is used for livestock but not humans, hence Phagmo Drashi's confusion.

5   "Wei" is a common way of answering the phone across China.

B: I would if it's true. But not if it's not true.

ཁ	བདེན་ན་ཉར་འགྲོ། མི་བདེན་ན་ཉར་མི་འགྲོ།

A: That may be, but now I'll tell you the truth.

ཀ	དེ་མོ་བཞག་ད་ཡིན་རྒྱུའི་རེད་ད། ད་ངས་ཁྱོ་དྲང་མོར་བཤད་དེ།

B: If you didn't tell me the truth, would I believe it?

ཁ	དྲང་མོར་མ་བཤད་ན་ངའི་ཉར་འགྲོ་ནས།

A: Truthfully, I would sit silently less if asked to guard the telephone than if I was made to speak khashag.[6]

ཀ	དྲང་མོར་བཤད་ན། ང་ཁ་ཤགས་བཤད་གི་འཇུག་རྒྱུའི་བསླབས་ན་ཁ་པར་སྲུང་གི་གཞུག་བཏང་ག་དཀའ་རོག་ག་འདུག་ནི་མ་རེད་ཡ།

B: So what would you do?

ཁ	ད་ཁྱོས་ཅི་བཞག་ཡོད་ནི་རེད།

A: My hand would not stop making phone calls, my mouth would not stop making conversations. I would not know from where the sun rises and to where it sets.[7]

ཀ	ད་ལག་རང་བསྐྱད་མེད་ལ་ཁ་པར་རྒྱག་ནི་རེད། ཁ་རང་བསྐྱད་མེད་ལ་ཁ་བརྗེ་ཡེད་ནི་རེད། ཉི་མ་བཙོ་གང་ནས་ཤར་རས་གང་ད་འཇའ་ནས་ར་ཤེས་རྒྱུ་མ་རེད།

B: Of course it rises from the east and sets in the west.

ཁ	དེ་ཤར་ནས་ཤར་རས་ནུབ་བ་ནུབ་ནི་ཡིན་རྒྱུའི་རེད།

A: Aro! It hasn't been long since the telephone appeared in the land of snows, but there's a lot to be learned from a single phone.

ཀ	ཨ་རོ། ཁ་བ་ཅན་ན་ཁ་པར་དར་རས་ཆང་མ་འགོར་བཞིག་ར། ཁ་པར་བེར་རོའི་སྟེང་ན་ཤེས་བྱ་མང་ད་བཞིག་ཞེས་རྒྱུ་ཡོད་གི་མོ།

B: That may be so.

ཁ	དེ་བཟོ་ཡིན་ན་ཐང་།

A: There are all sorts of telephone conversations. For example, one time, someone was calling home from the hospital. That one was unique.

ཀ	ཁ་པར་ནང་གི་ཁ་བརྗེ་རྣམ་པ་སྣ་ཚོགས་རེད། དཔེ་བཞག་ན་རེབ་ཆིག་ཅིག་གིས་སྨན་ཁང་ནས་ཕྱིར་ཡུལ་ཁ་པར་རྒྱག་གོ་གི་ར་ད། དེ་ཡང་ཁྱེར་རེ་བཞིག་རེད་ཡ།

---

6   At this time, the telephone was a new technology in Amdo, and there would likely be someone whose job was to mind and answer the phone. The word "guard" is likely used for humorous effect.

7   This is to suggest that he would lose all track of time.

B: *Ya*, what did he say? ཁ ཡ་ཅི་ཟེར་གི

A: You are going to laugh. Let's act it out. ག ཁྱོད་དགོད་མི་དགོད་མེད། ཉུ་གཉིས་ཀས་ལད་མོ་བཟིག་ཡེད་གོ

B: [agreeing] *Ya*. ཁ ཡ།

A: [shouting] *Wei, aro*! ག ཝེ། ཨ་རོ།

B: What's that? It sounds like someone's shouting from a mountaintop. ཁ དེ་ཅི་རེད། སྐང་ན་འབོད་གོ་ནི་བཟིག་ག་རིག་ནོ།

A: Ah, having lived for too long in the mountains, he speaks with a loud voice wherever he goes. ག ཨ། སྐང་ནས་འདུག་རྒྱུའོ་མང་སོང་ངས་གང་ནས་བཟད་ན་སྐད་མགོ་མཐོ་ནི་རེད།

B: Then that's fair enough. Ok, let's go again. ཁ དེ་ན་ཁག་མེད་གི་ཡ་འོར་གི་ཡོང་།

A: [shouting again] *Ya*, let's go again: *Wei, aro*! ག ཡ་འོར་གི་ཡོང་། ཝེ། ཨ་རོ།

B: [shouting back] *Wei, Ah*! ཁ ཝེ། ཨ།

A: *Aro*! Are you Phagmo? ག ཨ་རོ། ཁྱོད་ཕག་མོ་ཨེ་ཡིན།

B: *Aro*! I am, I am. ཁ ཨ་རོ། ཡིན་ཡ་ཡིན།

A: Are you certain? ག ཁོ་ཐག་ཡིན་ནས།

B: I'm certain! ཁ ཁོ་ཐག་ཡིན།

A: Yeah, we were completely wrong! ག ཡེ་བབ་གི་ཅིག་མ་འགྲིག་བཟིག་ཡ།

B: *Ya*, what is it? ཁ ཡ་ཅི་བཟིག་རེད།

A: *Ya*, it's ok if you don't come back. It won't take long. ག ཡ་ཁྱོ་ཕྱིར་ར་མ་ཐོན་ན་ཆོག་གི་མོ། དུ་ཅིང་བཟིག་འགོར་རྒྱུ་མ་རེད།

B: *Oh* that's great. I was planning to come with a whole month's provisions.

ཁ ཡ་ད་ཏུ་སོང་ནི་རེད། ངས་ཟླ་ཚིག་གི་ལྟོ་བཟང་ངས་ཡོང་རྩིས་ཡོད།

A: *Aro*! You needn't bring any meat. Mom's going to go under the knife tomorrow.[8]

ཀ ཨ་རོ། ད་ཤ་ཁྱེར་རས་ཡོང་མི་དགོ་གི ཨ་མ་ནངས་ག་བཤའ་རྒྱུ་རེད།

B: [laughingly] *Ya ya ya ya ya ya.*

ཁ ཡ་ཡ་ཡ་ཡ་ཡ།

A: [in normal voice] You refused to believe me when I told you you would laugh.[9]

ཀ ཁྱི་དགོད་ལ་བཟེ་ན་ཏུ་མི་ཐང་ག་བཟེ།

B: Though I understand it, it is funny, *aro*.

ཁ གོ་རྒྱུའི་གོ་གི་ར། དགོད་རྒྱུ་ཡོད་གི་གོ་ཨ་རོ།

A: *Aro*, there are also phone calls that make you want to cry.

ཀ ཨ་རོ། ད་དུང་དུ་རྒྱུ་ཡོང་ཉེས་ཁ་པར་བཞིག་ར་ཡོད་ཡ།

B: So they're probably speaking while crying.

ཁ ད་ཧ་ཞིར་ར་བཤད་གོ་ནི་ཡིན་རྒྱུའི་རེད།

A: The speaker doesn't cry, but the listener will burn with embarrassment.

ཀ བཤད་ནོ་ཧུ་ནི་མ་རེད་ད། ཉན་ནོ་ངོ་ཚ་ཡས་འབར་འགྲོ་གི

B: How so?

ཁ དེ་ཅི་མ་ཉན་ནི་རེད།

A: Some girls these days who don't know their own value and become different people when they make phone calls.

ཀ རང་གི་རིན་ཐང་མི་ཤེས་ནིའི་ཁ་སང་དེ་རིང་གི་བུ་མོ་ཁར་ཁེར་ཁ་པར་བརྒྱབ་བཏང་ན་ཁེར་རེ་བཞིག་ཉན་ནས་བྱད་འགྲོ་གི

B: *Ya*, act it out!

ཁ ཡ་ལད་མོ་བཞིག་སྟོས་ར།

---

8   In the Tibetan, the term བཤའ། literally meaning "slaughter." Some pastoralists in Amdo use this term for undergoing surgery, as seems to be the case here.

9   *Hamithang* (ཧུ་མི་ཐང་།) means "difficult to convince." With a *no* at the end, it can mean "maverick" or "rebel."

A: *Ring ring.*

ཀ ཀྲིང་ཀྲིར་......

B: *Wei!*

ཁ སྦེ།

A: [in a feminine voice] Hello!

ཀ Hello

B: *Wei*, who is it?

ཁ སྦེ། སུ་ཡིན།

A: [coyly, in a feminine voice] *Un*.

ཀ ཨུན།

B: What was that?

ཁ དེ་ཅི་བཟིག་ཡིན་ནས།

A: Don't pretend like you don't know!

ཀ མ་ཤེས་ཁུལ་བོ་མ་ཡེད་དོ།

B: You're Drolma, right?

ཁ ཁྱོ་སྒྲོལ་མ་རེད་མོ།

A: **Annoying** (*taoyan* 讨厌) You know and pretend like you don't.

ཀ ཐའོ་ཡན་(讨厌)། ཤེས་ན་མ་ཤེས་ཁ་བོ་ཡས།

B: You want me to write you something again don't you?

ཁ ཡང་ཁྱོ་འབྲི་རྒྱུ་བཟིག་ཡོད་ནི་མིན་ན།

A: Write me a letter asking for leave.

ཀ ང་གནང་བ་ཞུ་སྨྱུད་ཀོའི་ཡི་གེ་བཟིག་ཕྱིས།

B: Where are you going with your leave?

ཁ གནང་བ་ཞུས་གང་ད་འགྱོ་གོ་ནས་......ཁྲོ།

A: This kind of job is **annoying**... I don't want to do it.

ཀ བྱ་བ་འདི་མོ་འདི་ཐའོ་ཡན་ཏེ་བཟེས་ལས་ན་མི་འདོད་གི།

B: You should say you're glad you've got a job like that. *Wei*, I have written the letter requesting leave. You come and pick it up yourself.

ཁ དེ་མོ་བཟིག་ལས་རྒྱ་ལག་ག་བྱུད་ཡོད་ནི་ཟེར་ད། སྦེ། གནང་ཞུའི་ཡི་གེ་ངས་བྲིས་བཏང་། རང་གེ་ལེན་གི་ཤོག་གོ

A: [coyly] Uh-uh.

ཀ ཨ།

B: Now what?

ཁ ཡང་ཅི་མ་ཉན་ནི་རེད།

7. The Telephone

A: With sun like this, my face will get dark, *aro*![10]

ཀ འདི་མོ་ཉི་མ་བཟིག་ཏེ་བཟོའི་ངོ་ནག་པོས་ལོག་འགྱོ་གི་ཨ་རོ།

B: *Wei*! I don't have time to come to you. Or else I'll get someone to bring it to you.

ཁ སེ། ང་ཡོང་ཁོམ་མེད། ཡང་མིན་ན་ངས་ཅིག་ག་བསྐྱུར་ར་བཏང་།

A: [in English] **Ok, bye bye**.

ཀ [in English] ok, bye bye.

B: I don't really feel like crying, but although she says "ok" with her mouth, she has no *ka* and *kha* in her chest![11]

ཁ ཏུ་རྒྱར་འདུ་རྟ་མི་ཡོང་གི་ར། ཁ་ནས་ok ཟེར་ནོ་མིན་ནས་ཁོག་ན་ཀ་ཁ་ཡོད་རྒྱུ་མ་རེད་ཡ།

A: Compared with that, the phone calls of young men these days are very interesting.

ཀ དེར་བསླས་ན་ད་བར་གྱི་གསར་ཏུ་ཚོའི་ཁ་པར་ཞེ་གི་བསོ་ནི་རེད་གོ

B: *Ya*?

ཁ ཡ།

A: Those calls are endless and never finish. Then, as soon as you understand them, they're over.

ཀ ཁ་པར་དེའི་ཏྲ་མ་མཐའ་མ་བཟིག་ག་མིན། ནས་ཚར་རྒྱུ་མེད། ཤེས་སོང་དུས་ད་ཚར་སོང་ནི་རེད།

B: That may be.

ཁ ཡིན་ན་ཐང་།

A: *Ring ring*.

ཀ ཏྲིར་ཏྲིར་...།

B: *Wei*?

ཁ སེ།

A: *Wei*? Is Phagmo the name of you?[12]

ཀ སེ། ཁྱོ་གི་སྐྱིད་ང་ཕག་མོ་ཨེ་རེད།

---

10 In China and Tibet, lighter skin is preferable, especially for women, hence the aversion to walking under the sun.

11 *Ka* and *kha* are the first two syllables of the Tibetan alphabet. Here they refer to the entirety of the Tibetan language, suggesting that the woman mixes languages and hardly speaks any Tibetan.

12 Note that in the exchange on this page, the "cadre" uses incorrect grammar and auxiliaries, hence the assumption that he must be Han Chinese. Phagmo then responds similarly.

B: [aside] He's probably Han. [in response] *Wei*, Phagmo is the name of me.

|ཁ| རྒྱ་བཟིག་ཡིན་ས་ཡོད་ཀ། སྦེ། ང་གི་མིང་ང་ཕག་མོ་རེད།

A: Your home is Jentsa.

ཀ| ཁྱོ་གི་ཕ་ཡུལ་གཙན་ཚ་རེད།

B: Wouldn't I know that?

|ཁ། དེ་ཡིན་ནོ་ངས་མི་ཤེས་ནི་ཨེ་རེད།

A: *Wei*! I'm also from Jentsa. Would you know?

ཀ| སྦེ། ང་ར་གཙན་ཚ་གི་རེད། ཁྱོ་གི་ཤེས་རྒྱུ་ཨེ་རེད།

B: I don't, but tell me and I would. Who are you?

|ཁ ཤེས་རྒྱུ་མ་རེད་ད། ཁྱོས་བཤད་ད་ཤེས་རྒྱུ་རེད། ཁྱོ་སུ་ཡིན།

A: *Ah*, I is a cadre... Is a cadre from Jentsa.

ཀ| ཨ། ང་ལས་བྱེད་པ་རེད། གཙན་ཚ་གི་ལས་བྱེད་པ་རེད།

B: There are many cadres in Jentsa! *Wei*, do you have something to say to me?

|ཁ གཙན་ཚ་ན་ལས་བྱེད་པ་ཆེ་ར་མེད་གི་ནས། སྦེ། ང་བཤད་རྒྱུ་བཟིག་ཡོད་ལ།

A: Haha, I wouldn't call if I didn't have anything to say.

ཀ| ཧ་ཧ། བཤད་རྒྱ་མེད་ན་འབོད་རྒྱ་མ་རེད།

B: Haha, I would know that too.

|ཁ ཧ་ཧ། དེ་ངས་ལ་ཤེས་རྒྱ་རེད།

A: The father of you sent some meat and *tsampa*. You need to come and get it.

ཀ| ཁྱོ་གི་ཨ་ཕ་གིས་ཤ་ར་རྩམ་པ་བསྐུར་ཡོད། ལེན་གི་ཡོང་དགོ་རྒྱུ་རེད།

B: I do. Where are you staying?

|ཁ དགོ་རྒྱུ་རེད། ཁྱོ་གང་ན་བསྡད་ཡོད།

A: *Hu*, I'm staying in the nationalities hotel. If we can't meet, I'll put it in Menla's room. Do you know Menla?

ཀ| ཧུ། མི་རིགས་མགྲོན་ཁང་ན་བསྡད་ཡོད་ཡ། ཨ་ཁོ་གཉིས་ཀ་མ་ཐུག་ན་ངས་སྨན་བླ་གི་ཁང་བ་ནང་ད་འཇོག་རྒྱུ་རེད། ཁྱོ་སྨན་བླ་ངོས་རྒྱུ་ཨེ་རེད།

B: I know him, but I'll come get it now.

|ཁ ཤེས་རྒྱུ་རེད་ད། ང་ད་ལེན་གི་ཡོང་ད།

7. The Telephone

A: [as himself] You won't find it if you go get it, *aro*!

ཀ ཨེན་གི་སོང་ར་རྙེད་ནི་མ་རེད་གོ་ཨ་རོ།

B: [now to Menla] If I don't find it, then it must still be with you.

ཁ མ་རྙེད་ན་ཁྱོའི་ལག་ན་ཡོད་རྒྱུའོ་རེད།

A: You won't know if it's there unless you call and ask.

ཀ ཡོད་མེད་ཁ་པར་རྒྱབ་བ་ཅིག་དྲིས་ར་མིན་ནས་ཡོད་འདུག་ཤེས་ནི་མ་རེད་གོ

B: Really?

ཁ ཨེ་རེད།

A: *Ring ring ring*.

ཀ ཊིར་ ཊིར་ ཊིར།

B: Are you Menla?

ཁ ཁྱོ་སྨན་བླ་ཨེ་ཡིན།

A: Uh, who am I if not Menla.

ཀ ཨ། ང་སྨན་བླ་མ་ར་སུ་རེད།

B: You are Menla.

ཁ ཁྱོ་སྨན་བླ་རེད་མོ།

A: Who told you that I'm not?

ཀ ཁྱོ་མ་རེད་ཟེར་ནོ་སུ་རེད།

B: *Aro*! Don't finish it all before I get there.

ཁ ཨ་རོ། ང་སྦྱོན་རྒས་གོ་བཟོ་ཚར་གི་འདུག་ག་གོ

A: What is it?

ཀ ཅི་བཟིག

B: Don't act like you don't know. I'm talking about the butter and tsampa.

ཁ མ་ཤེས་ཁ་མ་ཡེད་དོ། མར་དུ་རྩམ་པ་བཟེ་ན།

A: I don't know. I don't know. It was a prank that I pulled on you yesterday. But if you're coming here, buy some meat.[13]

ཀ མ་ཤེས་མ་ཤེས། དས་ཁྱོ་ཁ་སང་མ་རབ་བཟིག་བཅོས་ནོ་དི་ཡིན། འདིར་ཡོང་ན་ཡོང་ཁ་ན་བཟིག་ཉོས་ཤོག་བཟེ་ནས་ཡ།

B: So you had nothing better to do, and made fake calls.

ཁ ཁོམ་སོང་དས་ཁ་པར་རྫུན་མ་བརྒྱབ་བཟིག་མོ།

---

13 Notice how the original call convinced Phagmo that someone had brought meat for him, and now he is being asked to buy meat for Menla.

A: They are not like leaders who make real phone calls.[14] ཀ ཁ་པར་རོ་མ་བཟིག་བརྒྱབ་བས་ཁྱེད་ཚོ་དཔོན་པོ་མ་རེད་མོ།

B: Oh, leaders don't make fake calls? ཁ ཨོ་དཔོན་པོ་བཟོས་ད་ཁ་པར་རྫུན་མ་མི་རྒྱག་ནི་ཨེ་རེད།

A: Oh, the leaders speak about true things in conversations that seem fake. Those kinds of calls are difficult for unfortunate souls like you and me. You won't understand them, even if you want to listen. ཀ ཨོ་དཔོན་པོ་བཟོས་ད་ཁ་བརྫུན་མ་འདྲ་བཟིག་ཡས་དོན་དག་རོ་མ་བཟིག་བཤད་ནི་རེད་ད། ཁ་པར་དེའི་རིགས་ཁྱོ་ཉུ་གཉིས་ཀ་འདུ་འདུའི་ཁ་ལས་མི་དགོ་ནི་རིགས་གས། ཉན་ན་འདོད་རུང་དི་ར་གོ་ནི་མ་རེད་ཡ།

B: So they probably speak quietly.[15] ཁ ཁ་རོག་ག་བཤད་གོ་ནི་ཡིན་རྒྱུའི་རེད།

A: No, they don't speak quietly. ཀ ཁ་རོག་ག་བཤད་ནི་མ་རེད་གོ

B: Then? ཁ ཨེ་ན།

A: They speak gently to their superiors, in a low voice to their equals, and slowly to subordinates. ཀ གོང་ང་འཇམ་པོ་ཡས་བཤད་ནི་རེད། བར་ར་དམན་མོ་ཡས་བཤད་ནི་རེད། ཞོལ་ལ་དལ་མོ་ཡས་བཤད་ནི་རེད།

B: Oh, that's difficult. ཁ ཨོ་ད་དཀའ་གི

A: Haven't you heard it said that "If you never struggle with the difficult things, then it's difficult to reach the heights of comfort."[16] ཀ དཀའ་མོའི་དཀའ་ལས་མ་མྱོངས་ན། བདེ་མོའི་མཐོན་པོ་འཐོབ་པར་དཀའ། བཟེ་ནོ་མ་གོ་ནས།

---

14 They here is referring back to the young men whose phone calls are being imitated.
15 In the previous turn, Menla Jyab says the word *go* which can mean either "to understand" or "to hear". Phagmo Drashi chooses to interpret it as "to hear" and suggests that they speak quietly.
16 This does not appear to be a traditional Tibetan saying, but here it refers to how one must experience difficulties in order to gain promotion in the government apparatus of the day.

7. The Telephone

B: That phrase... I've not even heard it in the Elegant Sayings of Sakya Pandita.

ཁ་ དེ་མོ་ཚིག་ས་སྐྱ་ལེགས་བཤད་ནང་ནས་ར་གོ་མ་མྱོང་།

A: Those leaders have no match when they make phone calls.

ག་ དཔོན་པོ་དེ་ཚན་གོ་ད་ཁ་པར་རྒྱག་གི་རྒྱག་ར་ཁ་ཡ་བཟིག་མེད།

B: Is it so unique when they make a phone call?

ཁ་ ཁ་པར་བརྒྱབ་ན་ཁྱད་པར་བཟིག་ཡོད་ནི་ཨེ་རེད།

A: Of course it is! They have a special technique for when calling their superiors.

ག་ ལོས་ཡོད། གོང་ད་ཁ་པར་རྒྱག་རུས་ཞེབ་བཟིག་ཡོད།

B: Ya?!

ཁ་ ཡ།

A: Ring ring ring.

ག་ ཀྲིར་ཀྲིར་ཀྲིར།

B: Hehe. *Wei*, who is it?

ཁ་ ཧུ་ཧུ། སྲེ། སུ་ཡིན།

A: [to "secretary" Phagmo] It's me, Secretary Phag.

ག་ ང་ཡིན། ཕག་རུའུ་ཅི།

B: [aside] Did I become the Party Secretary? [to A] *Wei*, I know you by your voice. Do you have something to discuss?

ཁ་ ང་ཅུའུ་ཅི་ཉེན་སོང་ནི་ཨེ་རེད། སྲེ། སྐད་ལ་ཉེན་ནས་ཤེས་ཐབ། དོན་དག་ཡོད་ལ།

A: Nothing. Nothing but... as for the matter I have: I'll be fine regardless, I don't have any objection.

ག་ དོན་དག་ཅང་མེད་གོ མེད་ད། དོན་དག་བཟིག་ཡོད་ནོ། ང་ཁྱོས་ཅི་བཟེ་ན་དེ་ཡིན་ནི་རེད་གོ་བསམ་འཆར་བཟིག་མེད།

B: What?

ཁ་ ཅི་བཟིག

A: That which I called to discuss yesterday.

ག་ ཁ་སང་ཁ་པར་བརྒྱབ་ནས་བཤད་ནོ་དེ།

B: I received countless phone calls. How would I know which matter it is. *Wei*! Which matter?

ཁ་ ཁ་པར་ཁ་གྲངས་མེད་ནི་བཟིག་ཡོང་ངས། ངས་དོན་དག་གང་རེད་ཟེར་དུ། སྲེ། དོན་དག་གང་།

A: Even if I cannot go any higher, I have nothing but yes in my mind.[17]

ཀ ང་ཡར་ར་འགྲོ་མི་ཐུབ་རུང་། ངའི་ཡིད་ན་ཡ་མིན་ནས་ཅང་ཡོད་ནི་མ་རེད་གོ

B: *Ya ya ya*. Do you have anything else to say beside that?[18]

ཁ ཡ་ཡ་ཡ། དེ་མིན་ནས་ད་བཤད་རྒྱུ་མེད་ནས།

A: Hehe. Of course not. You get some sleep, Party Secretary… Take care of yourself!

ཀ ཧེ་ཧེ། ཆེ་ཡོད་བཞེ་ར། ཁྱོ་དགེ་རྒོལ་ཅུའུ་ཅི། ཕྱུང་བོར་སེམས་ཆུང་བྱོས།

B: Of course I would not kill myself. *Ya*, goodbye.

ཁ ང་གང་ང་བསད་འཛོག་རྒྱུས། ཡ་ད་བདེ་མོ།

A: Goodbye. Goodbye.

ཀ བདེ་མོ། བདེ་མོ།

B: There really is a technique, *aro*!

ཁ དོ་མ་ཞེབ་བཟིག་ཡོད་གི་གོལ་རོ།

A: When calling their equals, its relaxing.

ཀ ད་བར་ར་ཁ་པར་རྒྱག་དུས་སྟོད་བཟིག་ཡོད་ནི་རེད།

B: Likely because there's no higher and lower between them.

ཁ མཐོ་དམའ་མེད་ནོའི་རྐྱེན་ཡིན་རྒྱུའི་རེད།

A: *Ring ring ring*.

ཀ ཏིར། ཏིར། ཏིར།

B: *Wei*, who is it?

ཁ སེ། སུ་ཡིན།

A: *Wei*, bastard! You don't even know me?

ཀ སེ། དོ་རྫོགས་རྒྱལ། ང་ར་མི་ཤེས་ནི་ཨེ་རེད།

B: Who doesn't know you. How could I dare not to know you. All good?

ཁ ཁྱོ་མི་ཤེས་ནོ་སུ་རེད། ངས་མ་ཤེས་ཉན་ནས། རང་བཞིན་ཡིན་ན།

---

17 Going higher refers to promotion within government, suggesting the sort of sycophantic approaches one must take when phoning superiors.

18 Note that although this may appear impatient in the English translation, it is not so in the Tibetan.

7. The Telephone

A: *Ardzee*... absolutely all good. I solved your problem. You mustn't forget my issue.

ཀ༽ ཨ་ཙི། རང་བཞིན་ལོས་ཡིན་བཟེ་ར། ཁྱེར་གའི་དོན་དག་ངས་བསྒྲུབས་བཏང་། ངའི་དོན་དག་ར་བརྗེད་ཉན་ནི་མ་རེད་གོ།

B: I won't forget. I will be able to do it. There's not even the slightest concern about that.

ཁ༽ བརྗེད་ནི་མ་རེད། བ་ནི་རེད། བབ་གི་འདད་རྒྱག་བ་སྤུ་ཙམ་བཟིག་ར་མེད།

A: Ah, I know, I know. Keep it up!

ཀ༽ ཨ། ཤེས་ནི་རེད། ཤེས་ནི་རེད། ཤི་རེ་བྱོས།

B: *Ya ya ya*. Do you have any other issues?

ཁ༽ ཡ་ཡ་ཡ། ད་དོན་དག་ཨེ་ཡོད།

A: Of course I do. Come over to drink on Sunday. I'm boiling meat.

ཀ༽ ལོས་ཡོད། གཟའ་ཉི་མའི་ཉིན་དགར་ཆང་འཐུང་གི་ཤོག་ར། ངས་ཤ་བཙོ་ཡ།

B: By your meat if I don't come.[19] As long as you're boiling some meat. Ya, goodbye.

ཁ༽ ཁྱོའི་ཤ་ཡོང་ནི་མ་རེད་ན། ཁྱོས་ཤ་བཙོས་ན་ད། ཡ་ད་བདེ་མོ་བྱོས་གོ།

A: *Ya ya ya*. Bye bye.

ཀ༽ ཡ་ཡ་ཡ། བདེ་མོ། བདེ་མོ།

B: Now my mind is at ease.

ཁ༽ ད་སེམས་ར་བདེ་ཤོང་ནི་རེད།

A: When calling a subordinate, there is a rage.

ཀ༽ ཡང་ཞོལ་མའོ་ཁ་པར་རྒྱག་དུས་ད། ངར་བཟིག་ཡོད་ནི་རེད།

B: You will probably get heated again.

ཁ༽ ཡང་ཁ་ངར་རྒྱ་རེད་མོ།

A: *Ring ring ring*.

ཀ༽ ཊིར། ཊིར། ཊིར།

B: *Wei.*

ཁ༽ སྨྲེ།

A: *Wei.*

ཀ༽ སྨྲེ།

---

19 'By your meat' is an oath commonly sworn especially in pastoral regions. The structure of these oaths most closely approximates "I'll be damned if I..." in English.

B: Oh, oops! *Wei*? Oh no... Ah!

ཁ། ཨོ། ད་མ་འགྲིག་ཐལ། ཕྱེ། ཨོ་མ་རེད། ཨ།

A: Ah? What do you mean by "ah"? Ah?

ཀ། ཨ། ཨ་བཟེ་ནོ་ཅི་བཟིག་རེད། ཨ།

B: Ah, ah, ah, I didn't know. Um. *Ya*!

ཁ། ཨ་ཨ་ཨ། མ་ཤེས་ནི་རེད། ཨུ་་་་ཡ།

A: What's "*Ya*"? Can you get by using "*ya*" for everything, ah?

ཀ། ཡ་བཟེ་ནོ། ཡ་བཟིག་གིས་ཡོད་ཚད་ཁྱག་ག་ཨ།

B: That's right. That's right.

ཁ། དེ་རེད། དེ་རེད།

A: What's "That's right"? Ah, spineless one, Ah!

ཀ། དེ་རེད་བཟེ་ནོ། ཨ། རང་ཀླུགས་མེད་ནོ། ཨ།

B: True. True.

ཁ། བདེན་གི་བདེན་གི

A: I say it even if it isn't true, ah. Cannot even carry a conversation on this telephone of yours, eh!

ཀ། མི་བདེན་ན་ར་ངས་བཤད་ནི་ཡིན། ཨ། ཁྱུང་ཁྱེད་ཚོའི་ཁ་པར་དེའི་ནང་ནས་ཁ་བརྡ་ཡོད་ས་མི་འགྲོ་གི ཨེ།

B: Possibly. Possibly.

ཁ། ཡིན་ན་ཐང་། ཡིན་ན་ཐང་།

A: Hm. "Possibly"? Uh, if not, then am I wrong? Ah?

ཀ། ཧེན། ཡིན་ན་ཐང་། ཨ། མིན་ན་ད་འཁྲུག་སོང་ནི་མིན་ན། ཨ།

B: Ah! No way. No way. I was wrong. Tell me whatever matter you have. I'll take care of it.

ཁ། ཨ། ཆེ་ཡིན། ཆེ་ཡིན། ད་འཁྲུག་སོང་ནི་རེད། དོན་དག་ཆེ་བཟིག་ཡོད་ན་དགོངས་དགོས་ད་ངས་ཐག་གིས་གཅོད།

A: I have nothing to say. The *khashag* called "*The Telephone*" was written by a person under you. Please leave him alone.

ཀ། བཤད་རྒྱུ་མེད། ཁ་ཤགས་ཁ་པར་བཟེ་ནོ་དེ་ཁྱོའི་ཁ་ཡོག་གི་མི་བཟིག་གིས་བྲིས་ནི་རེད། ཁྱེར་གི་ཁ་རོག་ག་ཞོག་ག་ཟོངས།

B: Yes sir.

ཁ། ལགས་སོ།།

A: Stitch the mouth of the one who performed "*The Telephone*" with him.

ཀ། ཁོར་དགེའི་ཁ་ཤགས་བཤད་གྲོགས་དེའི་ཁ་ཚེམས་མ་ཟོངས།

7. The Telephone

B: Ah?   ཁ། ཨ།

A: *Olé.*   ག ཨོ་ལེ།

B: [as himself] Oh, it's difficult to listen to phone calls like that.   ཁ། ཨོ། ད་ཁ་པར་དེ་མོ་ནེ་ཉན་རྒྱོར་ར་དགའ་མོ་རེད།

A: [as himself again] Oh, well, If you're afraid of the difficult ones, there are also some that are easy. If you think it's not true, give me a call.   ག ཨོ་ད་དགའ་མོ་སྐྱག་ན་སྟུ་མོ་ར་ཡོད་ནི་རེད། མི་བདེན་ན་ཁྱོས་ད་ཁ་པར་བཟིག་ཆོབས།

B: *Ring ring ring.*   ཁ། ཏིར། ཏིར། ཏིར།

A: *Wei.*   ག ཝེ།

B: *Wei*, who are you?   ཁ། ཝེ། ཁྱོ་སུ་ཡིན།

A: Why are you asking me who I am? What do you need?   ག ཨ་ད་སུ་ཡིན་འདུག་ཁ་རས་ཆེད་རྒྱས། ཁྱོ་ཆེ་བཟིག་དགོ

B: *Wei*, is Menla there?   ཁ། ཝེ། སྨན་བླ་ཨེ་ཡོད་གི

A: I don't know. *Tak!* [sound of hanging up]. [as himself] How simple!   ག མ་ཤེས། ཐག ཅི་ར་སྟུ་གི

B: [as himself] It's too simple. It is not worth the call I made.   ཁ། སྟུ་རྒྱོ་མང་སོང་བཟིག ངས་ཁ་པར་བཏང་ནོའི་རྩ་བ་ར་མེད་གི

A: Well then, I'll do a slow one. There's nothing better than that.   ག དོ་ན་ངས་བྱི་དལ་མོ་བཟིག་ཡོང་། དེའི་ཡན་བཟིག་ད་མེད།

B: That's good. *Ring Ring.*   ཁ། དི་ད་ཏུ་གི་མོ། ཏིར། ཏིར།

A: *Wei*, you, who do you need me to call for?   ག ཝེ། ཁྱོས། ཁྱོ་སུ་འབོད་དགོ

B: *Wei*, won't you call out for Menla?   ཁ། ཝེ། སྨན་བླ་ཅིག་མི་འབོད་ལ།

A: Of course I'll call him, of course I'll call him. He's bit far away, I'll go and call him.

ཀ ཨ་ལ། ལོས་འབོད། ལོས་འབོད། ཐག་ཅིག་རིང་
ར། ང་འབོད་གི་འགྲོ་གོ

B: *Ya ya ya*. Thank you.

ཁ ཡ་ཡ་ཡ། བགའ་དྲིན་ཆེ།

A: [derisively, under his breath] Hehe, "thank you." If you need a slow [call], I'll speak with you in an hour.

ཀ ཧེ་ཧེ། བགའ་དྲིན་ཆེ། དལ་མོ་ཡས་དགོ་ན་ད་
ངས་ཁྱོ་དུས་ཚོད་གཅིག་གི་གཞུག་ནས་ད་
བཤད།

A: *Wei*.

ཀ སྟེ།

B: *Wei*.

ཁ སྟེ།

A: Ah! Are you still waiting? *Ayoshe*, I looked for him everywhere, but I couldn't find him.

ཀ ཨ། ད་རུང་བསྒུག་བསྡད་ཡོད་ནས། ཨ་ཡོ་ཤུ་
བཞིག་ར། མ་བཙལ་ས་བཞིག་མེད་ད། མ་རྙེད་
ཐལ་ཡ།

B: *Oya*! Then there's nothing we can do. Thank you!

ཁ ཨོ་ཡ། ད་བཀོད་པ་ཡོད་ནི་མ་རེད། བགའ་
དྲིན་ཆེ།

A: You needn't say "thank you!"

ཀ ད་བགའ་དྲིན་ཆེ་ད་ཟེར་དགོ་ནི་མིན་མོ།

B: [questioningly] *Ya*?

ཁ ཡ།

A: I never went to look for him!

ཀ ང་བབ་གི་བཙལ་གི་མ་སོང་ར།

B: Ah! [in surprise]

ཁ ཨ།

8. Careful Village's Grassland Dispute སེམས་ཆུང་སྡེ་བའི་ས་རྩོད།[1]

A: *Aro*! This year, I went to "Careful Village" to write a *khashag* called "The Careful Village."

ཀ ཨ་རོ། ད་ལོ་ངས་སེམས་ཆུང་སྡེ་བའི་རེར་ནིའི་ཁ་ཤགས་བཟིག་འབྲི་རྒྱུ་བཟེ་ཆེད་དུ་སེམས་ཆུང་སྡེ་བ་གཅིག་སོང་ངོ།

B: *Ya*, what was this so-called "Careful Village" like?

ཁ ཡ། སེམས་ཆུང་སྡེ་བ་བདོག་གོ་ཅི་མོ་བཟིག་རེད།

A: Ah, ah, ah... it was a village!

ཀ ཨ་ཨ་ཨ། སྡེ་བ་བཟིག་རེད།

B: If it's called "Careful Village," then it must be a village. But judging by the village's name, you'd have to be very careful when you go there, right?

ཁ སེམས་ཆུང་སྡེ་བ་རེར་གོ་དུས་སྡེ་བ་བཟིག་ད་ཡིན་རྒྱུའི་རེད་ད། སྡེ་བ་དེའི་མྱིང་ད་བལྟས་ན་ཞེ་གི་སེམས་ཆུང་ཡས་འགྲོ་དགོ་ནི་མིན་ན།

A: Ah, no, no. It's OK to let your guard down completely when you go there, *aro*!

ཀ ཨ་ཆེ་ཡིན། ཆེ་ཡིན། བབ་གི་སེམས་གློད་ཡས་བྱེད་སོང་ཆོག་གི་ཨ་རོ།

B: Ah, ah, ah. *Olémo*! You wouldn't dare go to a place where you would have to go in fear.

ཁ ཨ་ཨ་ཨ། ཨོ་ལེ་མོ། སྐྲག་དགོས་ས་བཟིག་ག་ད་ཁྱོ་འགྲོ་རོགས་མི་ཆོད་མོ།

---

1 A is voiced by Menla Jyab and B is voiced by Phagmo Drashi.

A: Uh, rather than "Careful Village" you could just as easily call it "Kind-Hearted Village." I've never seen such a hospitable village. They couldn't decide where to put me up.[2]

B: That was just them filling your belly to bursting.[3]

A: *Ah*, they weren't just hospitable with food. They also draped me in so many silk *khatak* scarves that I resembled a *labtse*.[4]

B: You got all happy and began to resemble a prayer flag.[5]

A: Additionally, my timing was excellent. Careful Village was in the middle of a land dispute.

B: So that's good?

A: One was killed over there [in the opposing village], and only three were able to be killed over here [in Careful Village].[6]

---

2   Implying that all were willing to house him.
3   In the Tibetan context, he is suggesting that this is basic hospitality and nothing special.
4   A *khatak* is a silk scarf, often white, presented to visitors, and important persons. Encouraging him to put it in his pouch suggests possible bribery. Labtse are mountaintop cairns, seen as "consecrated abodes and places of veneration for specific territorial gods" (Tsering 2016, 451).
5   This metaphor suggests that he moved excitedly, dancing like a flag flapping in the wind.
6   The verb used here, *sod* (སོད།), is in the potential form, a peculiar form can be found in Amdo and Old Tibetan expressing the ability of the action denoted by

B: Isn't three enough?

ཁ། གསུམ་ཅིག་ཉུང་སོང་ནི་མིན་ན།

A: There were also many wounded, so don't fret.[7]

ག ཨ་ད་རྡུང་རྨས་མ་མང་ནི་རེད་གོ་ཁྱོ་མ་ཐྲེལ་ར།

B: As if I was waiting to hear something like that.

ཁ། ངས་དེ་མོ་བཞིག་མ་གོ་བསྡད་ཡོད་ས་ཡོད་ད།

A: *Ah*, there are still five who look like they will die, fifty who it appears will definitely not die, and another thirty who are in great pain.

ག ཨ། ད་རུང་འཆི་རྒྱུ་ཡིན་ནི་འད་འད་བཞིག་གི་ལྔ་ མི་འཆི་ཁོ་ཐག་ཡིན་ནི་འད་བཞིག་གི་ལྔ་ བཅུ། ཚ་མོའུ་ན་མོའུ་ཅན་བཞིག་གི་སུམ་ཅུ་ ཡོད་ནི་རེད།

B: *Un*. That's plenty.

ཁ། ཨུན། ད་ཡོད་གི

A: Uh, and that was the time I arrived. Just think! Isn't that timely!

ག ཨ། དེའི་སྐབས་དེར་ད་ད་ཕྱིན་བཏང་ནི་རེད། ཁྱོས་འདད་རྒྱོབ་ར་ད་ཕྱིན་ཚད་རེད་ལ་བཟེ།

B: Maybe so.

ཁ། ད་ཡིན་ནི་ཡིན་རྒྱུའི་རེད།

A: Moreover, all I had to do was observe closely, and then write extensively about it.

ག དེ་མིན་ནས་ད། ཡང་ངས་མི་འདུ་བ་བཞིག་ བསྟུས་བཏང་དེ། མི་འདུ་བ་བཞིག་ཁྱིས་བཏང་ རྒྱོའི་དེ་རེད་དེ།

B: Your burden is light!

ཁ། ཁྱོའི་འགན་ཁུར་ལ་ཡང་གི

A: Uh, it **was** light, but with each laughing word that came out of that smiling Village Leader's mouth, my workload got heavier and heavier, *aro*!

ག ཨ། ཡང་གི་ད་ཅིག་ཡང་ནི་རེད་ད། སྡེ་དཔོན་ དགོད་ཁ་པོ་དེས་དགོད་ཞོར་ར་ཅིག་བཤད་ཀྱི་ བཤད་ཀྱི་རེ་ལྡིད་བཏང་བཏང་ཐལ་ཨ་རོ།

B: Ya, what did the village leader say?

ཁ། ཡ། སྡེ་དཔོན་གྱིས་ཅི་ཟེར་གི

---

the verb.

7   In the previous turn, the speaker said *nyungsong* (ཉུང་སོང་།), which could also mean, "too few." Though he means that three is too many, the other speaker interprets it as "too few" and assures him that plenty of others were injured.

A: [in the voice of an elderly man] "Ya, I've heard of the one called 'Menla Jyab from Amdo'[8] but I've never had an audience with him. He must be something special, an impressive guy! Hahaha!"

ཀ ཡ་མདོ་སྨན་པ་སྨན་བླ་སྐྱབས་བཟེ་ན་གོ་ནི་ ཡོད་དུ་མཇལ་ནི་མེད། རང་ད་བུ་བཟིག་ཆེ་ ཡིན། ཨ་མའི་བུ་ཧ་ཧ་ཧ།

B: [surprised] What was that?

ཁ དི་ཆེ་བཟིག་ཡིན་ནི་རེད།

A: [in normal voice] The village leader laughs with every sentence he speaks.

ཀ ཨ། སྦྱེ་དཔོན་གྱིས་ཚིག་རེ་བཤད་ལས་རེ་རེ་ དགོད་ནི་རེད་ཡ།

B: Ha! I was startled! What did he say then?

ཁ ཧེ། དེ་བཟོ་རང་ང་སྐྲག་སེ་བཏང་བཏང་ཐལ། དུ་ཅི་ཟེར་གི

A: [in the village leader's voice] "So you say you're an 'awtist.' You say you're an 'arthor'. Moreover, you say that you're a so-called 'odist.' That's a heckuva lot of titles for one person, isn't it? Hahaha!"[9]

ཀ ཨ་ད་ཁྱོད་སྦྱིད་ཅིད་པ་བདོག་གོ་ར་ཡིན་ནས་ ཟེར་གི་ རྩམ་པ་པོ་བདོག་གོ་ར་ཡིན་ནས་ཟེར་ གི་ད་རུང་སྙན་ནག་པ་བདོག་གོ་ར་ཡིན་ནས་ ཟེར་གི་སྐྱི་ག་ཅིག་གི་ཐོག་ན་པ་ལུང་བ་གཅད་ ཧ་ཧ་ཧ།

B: There it is again![10]

ཁ ཡང་ཐོན་ཐལ།

A: [as the village leader] "Well, anyway. You are exceptional. Put this *khatak* in the pouch (of your robe). Hahaha!"

ཀ གང་ལྟར། ཡོད་ལ་མེད་ལ་གོ་ཁྱོ་ལ་ཡིན་ནི་ རེད། ཁ་བཏགས་འདི་ཁྱེད་དགོས་རུམ་མ་ བསྐུམ་ཤོངས། ཧ་ཧ་ཧ།

B: He's speaking, so listen!

ཁ སྐྱེ་བཤད་ཀྱི་ཞིག་ག་རང་གིས་ཉན་ན་སྟོད་ཡ།

---

8 Using མདོ་སྨད་པ།, translated here as 'from Amdo,' as part of one's name is somewhat unusual, and really only used for famous people,

9 In the Tibetan, the Village Leader mispronounces the words "artist," "author" and "poet" (which would be new terms to him), as "person with hair on their legs," "*tsampa*-er," and "melodious black-er."

10 This refers to the Village Leader's laughter.

A: [as the village leader] "*Ah*, it's good that thou camest in general, but it's especially good that thou camest to Careful Village. Hahaha!"

ཀ ཨ་གྱིར་ཁྱེད་ཀ་ཡིབས་ནོ་དུ། དེའི་ནང་ནས་སེམས་ཆུང་སྡེ་བ་ཡིབས་ནོ་དུ། ད་ད་ད།

B: Why's that?

ཁ དེའི་རྒྱུ་མཚན་ཅི་བཟིག་ཡིན་ནི་རེད།

A: [as the village leader) "In the past, we of Careful Village weren't this timid around others. This time the weighted blackjacks all fell on our heads.[11] All the village men are over there lying on their beds. Hahaha!"

ཀ སྔང་ངེ་ཚོ་སེམས་ཆུང་སྡེ་བ་གཞན་ན་བསྒོར་ན་དེ་མོ་སེམས་ཆུང་བཟིག་མིན་དུ། དཔེ་དངས་མགོ་སྐོར་ཚོ་འགོར་ཕྱོགས་བཟིག་གིས་ཆང་མ་དེ་ཚོའི་མགོར་བབས་བཏང་ཐལ། སྡེ་ཀུན་གོ་ཉལ་ཡས་བསྡད་ཡོད་ནོ་གན་རེད། ད་ད་ད།

B: *Ya*, is that so?

ཁ ཡ། དེ་ཡིན་ན་ཡ།

A: [as the village leader] "You yourself have said that you are both Menla, and a *menpa* (doctor). It's up to you to make all these people stand again. We will run to battle as soon as we get up. Hahaha!"

ཀ ཁྱི་སྨན་བླ་ར་ཡིན་དུ། སྨན་པ་ར་ཡིན་བཟེ་རང་གིས་བཤད་གོ་གི་ཆང་མ་ཡར་ར་ཅིག་སློང་རྒྱོའི་ད་ཁྱེད་ཀ་ཅིག་གསལ། ནམ་ལངས་ན་ནམ་རྒྱགས་རྒྱ་གོ་ད་ད་ད།

B: Are you satisfied now? So what did you say?

ཁ ད་ཁྱོ་ཨེ་ཚིག་གི་ཁྱིས་ཅི་བཟེ།

A: I spoke honestly, "Dear Village leader, that would be difficult. They look badly injured, and they won't be getting up any time soon. What can I do to rouse them?" I said.

ཀ ངས་ར་དྲང་བོར་བཤད་ལ། ཨ་ཁུ་སྡེ་དཔོན་ལོ་གོ། དེ་ད་ཅིག་དགའ་གི་ཁྱེའི་གན་ཚོ་ཉལ་སློལ་བཙོག་གི་ལངས་རྒྱའི་འགོར་གི་ངས་ཅི་བཟིག་ཡས་ཡར་ར་སློང་རྒྱས་བཟེ་ར།

B: What did he say?

ཁ ཅི་བཟེར་གི

A: [as the village leader] "Hahaha!"

ཀ ད་ད་ད།

B: Now what?

ཁ ཡང་ཅི་མ་ཉན་ནི་རེད།

---

11 Translated here as "blackjack" (མགོ་སྐོར་) is a long leather strap with a piece of shaped metal attached at the end.

A: [as the village leader] "If a doctor cannot rouse his patients, then there's no way that the patients can rouse the doctor. A doctor should have a solution. Hahaha!"

ཀ སྨན་པས་ནད་པ་སློང་མི་ཐུབ་ན་ད་ནད་པས་སྨན་པ་བསླང་དགོས་ཟེར་རྒྱུ་ཡོད་ནི་མ་རེད། སྨན་པ་བཟིག་ག་བཀོད་པ་ཡོད་རྒྱུའི་རེད། ཏུ་ཧུ།

B: Now you'd better come up with something fast!

ཁ ད་རང་གིས་རེམ་མ་བཀོད་པ་འཇོན་ཡ།

A: [as himself] At the first chance I got, I said, "Dear Village Leader, I say that I am a doctor in my compositions, but if a truly wounded man was placed in my care, I wouldn't even know how to check his pulse! By Picasso!"

ཀ ད་དས་ར་བཞད་ཅེ་ཐུབ་ཡས་བཏང་། ཨ་ཁུ་སྤྱི་དཔོན་ལོ་ལོ། ངས་སྒྲུ་རྩལ་བསྐམས་ཚོས་ཀི་ནང་ན་སྨན་པ་ཡིན་བཟེ་སླུ་མོ་བཞད་གོ། ནོ་མིན་ནས། རྨས་མ་ངོ་མ་བཟིག་ལག་ག་བཞག་དུས་ད་རྩ་ར་ཅིག་སླུ་ཤེས་ནི་རེད་ན། ཡིས་ཁ་སོ།

B: [incredulously] What did you say? Picasso?

ཁ ཅི་བཟེ། ཡིས་ཁ་སོ།

A: Uh, I panicked, so I swore by a great artist.

ཀ ཨ། ང་རང་ང་འཚབ་བཏང་ངས་སྨྲུ་རྩལ་པ་ཆེན་མོ་བཟིག་མནའ་སྐྱེལ་སླུད་ཡོད་བཏང་།

B: Olé. Would he believe you if you swore an oath like that?

ཁ ཨོ་ལེ། དི་མོ་མནའ་བཟིག་བསྐུལ་ཡས། སླེ་གི་ནར་འགྲོ་ནས།

A: [as the village leader] "I believe you since you have sworn by your father!"[12]

ཀ ད་ཁྱིས་པ་རྐན་ན་ཆད་བཅུགས་གས་གཅིག་བསྐུལ་བཏང་ན་ནར་འགྲོ་ནི་རེད།

B: Oh, he believed you!

ཁ ཨོ་ནར་འགྲོ་གོ་ག

---

12 Here the Village Leader doesn't recognize the name "Picasso" and interprets it according to Tibetan conventions, in which people swear by relatives, for example "by my father's flesh" (ཨ་པའི་ཤ).

8. Careful Village's Grassland Dispute

A: [village leader's voice] "I believe that you're not a doctor, but you shouldn't keep it a secret that you are a *lama*, it's a matter for all sentient beings. Hehehehehehehe!"

ཀ སྨན་པ་མིན་ནོ་ཟེར་འགྱོ་ནི་རེད་དུ། བླ་མ་ཡིན་ནོ་ཅིག་གསང་མི་ཉན་གི། སེམས་ཅན་ཐམས་ཅད་གི་དོན་དག་ག ཧེ་ཧེ་ཧེ་ཧེ་ཧེ་ཧེ།

B: [chuckling] And you still haven't escaped.

ཁ ཡང་མ་ཐར་ཐལ།

A: [in normal voice] I was so scared that my hair stood on end. "Dear Village Leader, you're an intelligent person, so how can you say this? Look at the hair on my head, the clothes on my body, and the stubble on my face. Where is there a *lama* like me?"

ཀ ང་བཟེ་ནོ་སྐྲག་གས་མགོ་གི་སྐྲ་ཚར་ཕྱོགས་སོང་བཞིག་ཨ་ཁུ་སྡེ་དཔོན་ལོ་ལོ། ཁྱོ་ཡི་མཁས་པ་བཞིག་ག་མ་རེད་ག་ དེ་མོ་དེ་བཟད་ཉེན་ནས། ཁྱོས་ངའི་མགོ་གི་སྐྲ་ལྟོས་ར། ལུས་གི་ལུ་ལྟོས་ར། ངོ་གི་སྤུར་ལྟོས་ར། ང་འདུ་འདུའི་བླ་མ་བཞིག་ཡོད་ནས།

B: What did he say then?

ཁ དེ་བཟེ་ན་ཅི་ཟེར་གི

A: *Hehe!* He had some things to say, *aro!* [as the village leader] "I've seen faces on *tangka* paintings, and Tri Ralpachen's[13] head was like that. People say I don't know anything, but I've been around the block a few times. All those who don't like Tibetan clothes, and don't wear Chinese clothes, wear clothes like this. Whiskers grow on your face even if you are a *lama*, nobody is planting them."

ཀ ཧེ་ཧེ། སྤྱི་གི་དེའི་ཚོད་གི་བཤད་རྒྱུ་ཡོད་གི་ཨ་རོ། ངས་ཐང་ག་གི་རོ་ནས་རིག་མྱོང་ནི་རེད། ཁྲི་རལ་པ་ཅན་གི་མགོ་ར་དེ་མོ་བཞིག་རེད། མི་ཤེས་བཟེ་སྡུང་བསམ་ཤེས་རེད། ཡོད་ལུ་མི་དགའ་བོ། རྒྱ་ལུ་མི་གོན་ནོ་ཅང་མས་དེ་མོ་གོན་ཡོད་གི། ཁ་སྤུ་ཌོ་སྤུ་བཙོ་བཏབ་ནི་མ་རེད། སྐྱེས་རྒྱུའི་རེད། བླ་མ་ཡིན་རུང་ར་ཟེར་ཡ།

B: That's right. I think that's definitely true.

ཁ དེ་བཟོ་རེད། ལོས་བདེན་འདོད་གི

---

13 Tri Ralpachen (c. 805–c. 838) was one of the three dharma kings of Tibet, and the penultimate king of the Tibetan empire.

A: [in normal voice] So then I also sincerely explained, "If I were a *lama*, then my monastery would be a distillery, my monks would not have perfected the study of the "perfection of wisdom" sutra, and they would have attained perfection only in smoking cigarettes. If there is a *lama* like this, let alone in the next life, would the government[14] even accept him?"

B: That was direct. What did the village leader say?

A: [as the village leader] "Uh, I know, I know. Then swear that everyone in your work unit doesn't call you, 'Alak'"[15] [in a normal voice] he said.

B: But that's just a name your co-workers came up with themselves.

A: [normal voice] Eh, I said that too, but that old man was stubborn. [as the village leader] "So anyway,

The disputes of men are like unbreakable boulders,

The disputes of women are like juniper that doesn't rot.

---

14 The Tibetan term *gongma tshang* (གོང་མ་ཚང་།) is traditionally a way of referring to emperors and their officials. Here, however, it is used to refer to the government as it is sometimes used today.

15 Alak is a common term of respect used in Amdo for reincarnate *lama*.

For the whole business of this grassland dispute, we will entrust it to you. Hehehe."

དཔེངས་གི་ས་རྩོད་གི་དོན་དག་དེ་ད་མགོང་མ་བར་ཁྱེད་པ་ཁྱེད་ཀ་གཅིག་གཏད་རྒྱུ་ཡིན། དེ་དེ་དེ།

B: So, there's no way you can say "yes!"

ཁ་ ད་ཁྱོས་ཡ་ཟེར་ཉན་ནི་མ་རེད་གོ

A: [chuckling] I did say, "Yes."

ཀ་ ངས་ར་ཡ་བཟེ་བཏང་ཡ།

B: Ah, how could you?[16]

ཁ་ ཨ། འདི་ད་ཤི་ཐལ་ཡ།

A: Uh, I had to learn about this matter regardless—I had no choice![17]

ཀ་ ཨུ། གང་ལྟར་ངས་དོན་དག་འདིར་རྒྱུས་ལོན་བཟིག་ཡོད་དགོ་གི་བཀོད་པ་མེད་ལ།

B: It's OK to learn about it, but you can't be a fake *lama*.

ཁ་ རྒྱུས་ལོན་ཡས་ན་ཚོག་གི་ར། བླ་མ་རྫུན་མ་བཅའ་ཉན་ནི་མ་རེད་གོ

A: I thought of that too, so I spoke even better than a real *lama*!

ཀ་ ངས་ར་དེ་འདང་བསྒྲུབ་བས་ད་བླ་མ་དོ་མ་བཟོའི་ཡན་བཟིག་བཤད་བཏང་ཡ།

B: [incredulously] *Ya?!?!*

ཁ་ ཡ།

A: [in normal voice, addressing the village leader] "Uh, well, my previous incarnations thought of nothing but religion, but I'm one of those who can't even deal well with the secular."

ཀ་ ཨ། ད་སྐུ་ཚེ་སྔོན་མ་རིག་ག་བཟོ་སྟེ་ཆོས་མིན་ནས་བསམ་རྒྱུ་ཡོད་ནི་མ་རེད་ད། ད་ད་འཛིག་ཏེན་ན་ར་ཨད་ཧ་བཟིག་མི་འཁྱོངས་ནོའི་གྱུར་ཀ་དེ་རེད།

B: In saying so, you agreed that you are a *lama*.

ཁ་ བཤད་གི་བཤད་གི་བླ་མ་ཡིན་ནོ་ཁས་བླངས་བཏང་བཟིག་མོ།

A: That's right, but I kept it a secret that I'm fake.

ཀ་ དེ་རེད་ད། རྫུན་མ་ཡིན་ནོ་གསང་བཏང་ནི་རེད་ཡ།

B: That's what I was saying!

ཁ་ དེ་བཟེ་ནས་ཡ།

---

16 The Tibetan phrase *dida shi thal* (འདི་ད་ཤི་ཐལ།), literally something like "he's dead," is used to complain that someone is making a poor decision.

17 He must learn about it, because he's still planning to write a script about his trip.

A: Maybe so, but they'll figure it out in the end.

ཀ། དེ་ཡིན་རུང་མཐར་མ་བཟིག་ག་ཤེས་འགྱོ་ནི་རེད།

B: When they find out you'll be gone, and they'll be finished!

ཁ། གཅིག་ཤེས་དུས་ད་ཁྱོད་ཕར་སོང་ནི་རེད་ད། ཁེར་ཚོ་ཚར་སོང་ནི་རེད་ཡ།

A: Uh, it's not like I'm the only heartless person who has cheated these kind-hearted Careful Villagers. Put another way: I'm here only to learn and won't profit by it, *aro*!

ཀ། ཨ། སེམས་ཆུང་སྟེ་བ་སྒྲི་སེམས་མེད་ཡོང་དས་སེམས་བཟང་ཅན་འདི་མགོ་གཡོག་ནོ་ད་ཁེར་མོ་ཆེ་ཡིན། ཡང་གཅིག་བཤད་ན་ངས་རྒྱུས་ལོན་ཡོད་ནི་མིན་ནས་རྒྱ་ལེན་ནི་མ་རེད་གོ་ཨ་རོ།

B: I don't know about that... And then?

ཁ། དེ་ཤེས་ནི་མ་རེད། དེ་ནས།

A: Uh, then, pretending that I am [a *lama*], I upbraided the village leader.

ཀ། ཨ། དེ་ནས་ད་ངས་ར་ཅིག་ཡིན་ཁ་བོ་ཡས་སྟེ་དཔོན་ན་བཀའ་བཀྱོན་གནང་བཏང་།

B: You've grown bold before they've even given you any money.

ཁ། རྒྱུ་མ་འབུལ་གོང་བཟིག་གི་རྒྱུས་བ་ཉན་ཐལ།

A: Uh, "*Ah* karmically-wicked ones! Why did none of you think to contact me about this important issue until now?"

ཀ། ཨ། ལས་ངན་ཚོ། དོན་དག་འདི་མོ་ཆེ་བཟིག་བྱུང་བཏང་ངས་ད་རྒས་གོ་ད་བར་བཟིག་མི་རྒྱུག་སྦོལ་ཡོད་ནས།

B: Wouldn't you help them attack (if they asked you)?

ཁ། ཁྱོས་ར་རྒྱགས་རོགས་ཡོད་ལ་བཟེ་མིན་ན།

A: [in normal voice, to B] I can't do much, but I would help do rituals on their behalf.

ཀ། ངས་ཆེ་བཟིག་བ་ནི་མ་རེད་ད། ཆོས་རེ་བཅའ་རོགས་ཡེད་ནི་རེད།

B: You bullshit without thinking!

ཁ། ལབ་རྒྱག་རྒྱོའི་ད་འདང་རྒྱག་མི་དགོ་གི།

A: [back to the village leader] "You are the village leader! You can't rest there so comfortably."

ཀ། ཁྱི་སྦྲེ་དཔོན་རེད། བདེ་མོ་ཡས་འདུག་ས་ཡོད་ནི་མ་རེད་ཡ།

B: So, what should he do?

ཁ། ད་ཅི་བཟིག་ཡེད་དགོ་ནི་རེད།

A: "Now, you've fought though you said you wouldn't fight; and you've killed though you said you wouldn't kill. Hold a meeting tomorrow for the entire village; the *lama* will come to resolve this dispute.[18] If you're going to obey, say, 'Yes sir.' If you don't accept, then I'll go away!" I said.	ཀ ད་ས་མི་རྩོད་བཟེ་རུང་བརྩད་བཏང་བཟིག་གི་ མི་གསོད་བཟེ་རུང་བསད་བཏང་བཟིག་ནངས་ ཀ་སྟེ་བ་སྟེ་འཆོགས་རྒྱབས། ཉུད་ང་མ་གཅོད་ གི་བླ་མ་ཡོང་། བགའ་ཇི་རྒྱ་ཟེར་ན་ལགས་སོ་ བཟེ། ཁ་མི་ལེན་ཟེར་ན་ཕྱིར་ར་འགྲོ། བཟེ་ར།
B: What did they say?	ཁ ཅི་ཟེར་གི
A: [hollering] "Yes sir! Yes sir!" [normal voice] they said sounding like the Chabcha earthquake, *aro*.[19]	ཀ ལགས་སོ། ལགས་སོ། ཟེར་གི་ར་ས་ཆབ་ཆར་ ས་འགུལ་བརྒྱབས་ནི་འདུ་བཟིག་རེད་ཨ་རོ།
B: So that day was nice, but the next day must have been difficult.	ཁ དེའི་ཉིན་དགར་ད་བསོ་གི་ར། ཕྱིའི་ཉིན་དགར་ དགའ་རྒྱ་རེད་ཡ།
A: That next day, everybody gathered together: from those with white teeth to those with white hair,[20] the living and the dead!	ཀ དེའི་ཕྱིའི་ཉིན་དགར་ད་སེམས་ཅན་སྟེ་བ་གི་ སོ་དགར་ནས་མགོ་དགར་ཞི་གསོན་གཤིས་ཀ་ མཚམ་གི་འཆོགས་ཐལ།
B: [stunned] What did you say? The dead? The dead came back?	ཁ ཅི་བཟེ། ཤི་བོ་བཟེ། ཤི་བོ་བཟོ་ར་ཕྱིར་ར་འོན་ བཏང་ནི་རེད།
A: Oh... no. I was saying the mature and the immature, both the maimed and the not maimed, many of them gathered.	ཀ ཨོ། མ་རེད་གོ་རྒྱང་མ་ཡིན་མིན་གཉིས། ཀ་རྨས་མ་ཡིན་མིན་གཉིས་ཀ་མང་མ་བོ་ འཆོགས་གི་བཞག་བཏང་བཟེ་ནས་ཡ།
B: Oh, and the charlatan might also be revealed.	ཁ ཨོ་དཧུན་མ་པོ་ར་སྣང་ད་འབྱུད་གི

---

18 ང་མ་གཅོད། literally means "cut the tail," but here it is used to settle, mediate, or resolve the he dispute.

19 This is likely a reference to large earthquake in Chabcha (Ch., Gonghe) County in 1990, during which a dam broke, and that this and similar phrases below may allude to this event.

20 Here this means both young (with white teeth) and old (with white hair).

A: Uh, again the village leader went first. [in the village leader's voice] "Hey You guys! Pipe down! Pipe down! Don't push and don't crowd! We are here to worship the *lama* not to chase him away. Having come to our gate, how could we not get an audience?"

B: They will get an audience, but they'll be worshipping the wrong one.

A: In the blink of an eye, a countless amount of *khatak* were in front of me and "human heads" had fallen before me in greater number than the people there.

B: What did you say? Human heads fell before you?

A: *Olé*! The number of people on each was different, just as they have different values if you take them to a mall.

B: Oh, you're talking about money?[21] The 5s and 10s, 50s and 100s each have different images on them, and their values are different from each other. But you can't keep them.

A: Oh! [chuckling] I put them in my pouch!

---

21 This is likely a reference to the third or fourth series of Chinese RMB, both in use at the time of the performance, with the latter featuring images of different ethnic minority groups on different denominations.

8. Careful Village's Grassland Dispute

B: *Ah?* But then didn't you say that you were only there to learn, and wouldn't profit by it?

ཁ། ཨ། འོན་ཏོ་ཁྱོས་རྒྱུས་ལོན་མིན་ནས་རྒྱ་མི་དགོ་བཟེ་ནི་མིན་ནས།

A: Uh, I forgot about that as soon as I saw the riches, *aro*.

ཀ། ཨ། རྒྱུ་རིག་བཏང་ན་བརྗེད་འགྱོ་གི་ཨ་རོ།

B: I thought that you'd do that from the start.

ཁ། ངས་ར་དིང་མ་བཟིག་གི་དེ་ཡེད་རྒྱུ་རེད་འདོད་ལ་མོ།

A: Uh, then I gavest an oration.

ཀ། ཨ། ད་ནས་གསུང་བཤད་གནང་བཏང་།

B: What did you say?

ཁ། ད་ཅི་བཟེ་ནས།

A: "Uh, now all of you shut up!"

ཀ། ཨ། ད་ཚང་མ་ཁ་རོག་ག་ཅིག་སྡོད།

B: [now as an audience member] We're making no sound.

ཁ། ཁ་བཟིག་གྱག་གི་མེད།

A: "Don't make the children with bright futures cry."

ཀ། བྱ་ལམ་མ་འགྱོ་རྒྱུའི་ཞམས་དུ་གི་མ་འཁྲུག་ར།

B: Such a strict *lama*.

ཁ། དེ་མོ་བླ་མ་བཙན་པོ།

A: I'm not stunning, but I am strict. I speak little, but I would bend over under stress.[22]

ཀ། ང་ཙ་ཡ་བཟིག་མིན། བཙན་པོ་བཟིག་ཡིན། ཙུ་གེ་ཅི་གེ་བཤད་ལ། བཙར་རས་ཡོང་ན་སྒུར་ར།

B: Is that the way a *lama* should speak?

ཁ། དེ་བཟོ་བླ་མ་བཟིག་གི་བཤད་སྟོལ་ཡིན་ནི་ར་མིན་ནི་རེད་གོ

A: Uh, "but you all don't know the things I know. If you knew them, you would know whether or not I am a real *lama*."

ཀ། ཨ། འོན་ཀྱང་ངས་ཤེས་ནོ་ཁྱེད་ཆོས་མི་ཤེས། དེ་ཤེས་རྒྱུ་ན་ང་བླ་མ་ཡིན་མིན་ར་ཁྱེད་ཆོས་ཤེས།

B: So, no one knows other than me.

ཁ། དེ་ད་ངས་མིན་ནས་མི་ཤེས་གི་རེ།

---

22 Translation aims to replicate the repeated uses of *ts* sounds in the original.

A: "Uh, so if there is anyone who says that I am not a *lama*, then get out!"

ཀ ཨ་ད་བླ་མ་མ་རེད་ཟེར་ནི་ཡོད་ན་མར་བཞེག་ག་སོང་།

B: [as an audience member again] I must sit there biting my lips.

ཁ མ་ཁར་སོ་བཏབ་བས་འདུག་རྒྱུ་གོ

A: "These Tibetan land disputes are disputes over water and land. Put clearly, fights over there and fights over here and all people fighting together, they're still just fights."

ཀ བོད་ཀྱི་ས་རྩོད་ཟེར་གི་ནི་འདི་ས་རྩོད་ཆུ་རྩོད་རེད། དེ་ར་གསལ་པོ་ཡམ་བཟད་ན། ཕར་རྩོད་ཚུར་རྩོད་ཚང་མ་མཉམ་རྩོད། རྩོད་པ་རེད།

B: They know that!

ཁ དེ་ད་ཤེས་རྒྱུ་རེད་ད།

A: "Uh, this fighting is a good tradition. Uh, we fought starting from Tri Ralpachen's time. At that time, they had disputes over territory, but they didn't fight over grass. Now, they fight over grass but not territory. Although the goals were different, they were, to put it simply, fights. You need to fight, so keep fighting!"

ཀ ཨུ རྩོད་རྒྱུའི་འདི་སྲོལ་རྒྱུན་བཟང་ང་བཞེག་རེད། ཨ། ཁྲི་རལ་པ་ཅན་གྱི་རིང་ནས་བྱུང་ལམ་ད་བརྩད་ནི་རེད། སྐབས་དེར་ས་བརྩད་ནོ་མིན་ནས་རྩྭ་བརྩད་ནི་མ་རེད། ད་ལྟ་རྩྭ་བརྩད་ནོ་མིན་ནས་ས་བརྩད་ནི་མ་རེད། སོ་སོའི་དམིགས་ཡུལ་མི་གཅིག་ནོ་མིན་ནས་མདོ་རྩ་བཏད་ན་རྩོད་པ་རེད། རྩོད་དགོ་ནི་རེད། སུ་མཐུད་དུ་རྩོད།

B: So, they won't ever finish fighting?

ཁ ད་བརྩད་ལས་ཚར་རྒྱ་བཞེག་མེད་ནི་ཨེ་རེད།

A: [to B] Uh, as long as there is life on this planet, there will be fighting.

ཀ ཨ་འཛིག་རྟེན་གྱི་འཚོ་བ་མ་ཚར་ན་འཛིག་རྟེན་གྱི་རྩོད་པ་ཚར་ནི་མ་རེད།

B: But if you keep fighting, then your shepherds and goatherds will be no more.

ཁ ད་བརྩད་གྱི་བརྩད་གྱི་ཁྱེད་གྱི་ར་རྫི་ལུག་རྫི་ཚོར་ཚར་གི

A: Uh, the things that should finish must finish. This world must end. I must speak thus, and I must obtain what I seek.

ཀ ཨ། ཚར་རྒྱ་བཞེག་ཚར་དགོ་ནི་རེད། འཛིག་རྟེན་འདི་འཛིག་དགོ་ནི་རེད། ངས་འདི་མོ་འདི་བཏད་དགོ་ནི་རེད། བསམ་དོན་བཞེག་འགྲུབ་དགོ་ནི་རེད།

B: It's certain you will.

ཁ འགྲུབ་རྒྱ་ཡིན་ནོ་ཁོ་ཐག་རེད།

A: When you say it like that, now I understand something.

ཀ དེ་ཡས་བཤད་ལས་ཡོང་ན་ད་ཡང་ངས་གཅིག་ཤེས་ཐལ།

B: What is it?

ཁ ཅི་བཞིག་རེད།

A: [speaking again to the villagers] "And if I speak clearly about this grassland dispute here, it's just a dispute."

ཀ ད་ཐེངས་ཀྱི་ས་རྩོད་འདི་ར་གསལ་པོ་ཡས་བཤད་ན་རྩོད་པ་རེད།

B: They know that already.

ཁ དེ་ཁོ་ཚོས་ར་ཤེས་ནི་རེད་ཡ།

A: "Well, if there is a dispute, then there must be a reason for it. I need that reason. If you all don't tell me that reason, then I won't understand it at all. If one knows the reason, then it's easy to fight."

ཀ ཨ། རྩོད་པ་ཡས་ན་དེར་རྩ་བ་དགོ་ནི་རེད། དེའི་རྩ་བ་ཁྱོ་ཚོས་མ་བཤད་ན་ངས་རྩ་བ་ནས་ཤེས་ནི་མ་རེད། རྩ་བ་ཤེས་སོང་ན་དཀྲོད་རྒྱུའི་སླ་མོ་ཡིན་ནི་རེད།

B: You're going to sit there and say it's easy!

ཁ ཁྱོས་སླ་མོ་བཤད་ལས་བཙོག་གས་འདུག་རྒྱུ་རེད།

A: [to B] Uh, but if you think about this simple matter, then it might be difficult.

ཀ ཨ། དོན་དག་སླ་མོ་འདི་འདང་བརྒྱབ་ན་དཀའ་མོ་ཡིན་ན་ཐང་།

B: Who knows if it is a simple matter, as it's difficult even to get it out of your mouth.

ཁ དོན་དག་སླ་མོ་ཡིན་འདུག་སུས་ཤེས་ར། ཁྱོའི་ཁ་ནང་ནས་ཡོང་རྒྱུའི་ཅིག་དཀའ་གི་བཞིན་མིན་ནས།

A: [to the villagers] "You're still definitely going to fight. So, let's make some simple arrangements. If you will obey, then say 'Yes sir!' If you do not agree, I'll leave."

ཀ ད་རུང་རྩོད་རྒྱུའི་ཁོ་ཐག་རེད། ད་སྟུ་མོ་ཡེད་ལ་བཀོད་སྒྲིག་ཡོད། བགད་བཟི་རྒྱུ་རེད་ན་ལགས་སོ་བཟེ། ཁ་མི་ཡིན་ཟེར་ན་ཕྱིར་ར་འགྲོ།

B: And they probably said, "Yes sir! Yes sir!" sounding like an earthquake.

ཁ ལགས་སོ། ལགས་སོ། ཡང་ས་འགུལ་བརྒྱགས་ནི་འདྲ་བཞིག་ཡིན་རྒྱུའི་རེད།

A: Uh, "I'll ask first, and then you respond."

ཀ ཨྱུ། གོང་ནས་ངས་འདྲི། ཁྱེལ་ནས་ཁྲི་ཚོས་ལན་བློབས།

B: Now hurry up and speak.

ཁ ད་རེམ་མ་ཅིག་མྱོད་ལ་བྱོངས།

A: "First, Village Leader, stand up!"

ཀ ཐོག་མར་ཨ་ཁུ་སྡེ་དཔོན་ཡར་ར་ལོངས།

B: Will you make that old man laugh again?

ཁ ཡང་རྐྱང་པོ་དགོད་གི་འཇུག་རྒྱུ་ནས།

A: [to the village leader] "*Ya*, speak without laughing! Disputes are disputes. We need to make it easy by fighting. What's the reason that neither you Careful Villagers nor they can make it simple by fighting?

ཀ ཡ། མ་དགོད་ལ་ཤོད། རྩོད་པ་རྩོད་པ་རེད། བརྩད་ལས་སྠུ་མོ་གི་གཏོང་དགོ་ནི་རེད། ཁྱོ་ཚོ་སེམས་ཆུང་སྡེ་བ་ར་ཁོ་ཚོའི་སྡེ་བ་གཉིས་ཀ་བརྩད་ལས་སྠུ་མོ་མི་ཡོང་ནོའི་རྒྱུ་བ་གང་ད་ཐུག་ནི་རེད།

B: *Ya*, now the village leader will speak.

ཁ ཡ་ད་སྡེ་དཔོན་གྱིས་བཤད་རྒྱུ་རེད་གོ

A: [in the leader's voice] "Goodness! Starting from the old times we took turns leading off horses and killing people. Hehehe! Oh! I'm not allowed to laugh."

ཀ ཐལ་ར་ཅིག་གི་རི་ཚོས་འཛིག་རྟེན་སྟེང་བའི་རིང་ནས་བྱད་ལས་རྟ་འདེད་རེས་སྨྱི་གསོད་རེས་ཏག་ཏག་ཡམ་བསྲན་ནི་རེད། ཧེ་ཧེ་ཧེ། ཨོ། དགོད་ཉན་ནི་མ་རེད།

B: But the old world is past. We have to speak about the new society.

ཁ ད་འཛིག་རྟེན་རྙིང་པ་རྩིང་སོང་བཞིག་སྤྱི་ཚོགས་གསར་བ་བཤད་དགོ་ནི་རེད།

A: [as the village leader] "For us, there's no old and new. If it weren't for the hiatus of '58 and the Cultural Revolution,[23] more than a few people from both sides would be no more. Hehehe."

ཀ དེ་ཚོའི་བར་ར་གསར་རྙིང་གི་ཅང་དགོ་ནི་མ་རེད། ང་བརྒྱད་ར་རིག་གནས་གསར་བརྗེ་གིས་དལ་འགོར་མི་ཡོད་རྒྱུན་ཡར་ཆུར་ར་གསོད་རེས་ཡས་ཅིག་ག་གཏུགས་གས་བཞག་ཡོད། ཧེ་ཧེ་ཧེ།

---

23 1958 is the year of a revolt, the end of gradualist policies for integrating Tibet into the still-young PRC, and also a famine. Tibetans traditionally refer to 1958 as the dividing point between the "old society" and the "new society." The Cultural Revolution (1966–76) was a ten-year period of chaos that disrupted the entire nation. For more on the experience of 1958 in Amdo, see Weiner 2020.

B: Are you satisfied? You wouldn't be able to find a response to that.

A: [as himself, speaking to the village leader] "Uh, Village Leader! Speak plainly without mixing the old and new. Why did things go bad this time? There must be something to fight over," I said.

B: If there was nothing to fight about, would there be a dispute?

A: [as the village leader] "Things can't be hidden from the *lama* or from the next rebirth,[24] but the reason for the fight is no good."

B: That's probably right.

A: [as the village leader] "Do you know the household responsibility system?"[25]

B: I certainly do know it.

A: [in the voice of the village leader] "Olé! When the livestock were divided up [among individual households], and they had constructed fences in each place, and each family was allotted a mountain pass, they let their horses stray into our sheep."[26]

B: So, give them back!

---

24 This is a traditional expression suggesting that the speaker must be truthful.
25 A government policy in agricultural and pastoral communities instituted in 1978.
26 *Laha* (ལ་ཧ་) is a term used in Amdo for an extremely woolly breed of sheep that are not native to the Tibetan Plateau.

A: "Uh, how much can a few horses eat? But we can't lose our pride! We said that if they don't pay a fee, we won't return their horses."

ཀ། ཨ། ལ་ལོ་འགའ་གི་ཅི་ཟ་རྒྱུ་ར། དེ་ཚོའི་ལ་རྒྱུ་འཆར་མི་ཉན་གི་སྒླ་བཞིག་མ་བྱིན་ན་ཕྱིར་ར་མི་སྟེར་བཞེ།

B: So, they can pay it.

ཁ། དེ་ཕྱིན་བཏང་ན་ཆོག་གི་མོ།

A: "Uh, they didn't pay, so we weren't happy, and now we are at odds."

ཀ། ཨ། མ་བྱིན་ནི་རེད། མ་དགའ་ནི་རེད། ད་མ་འགྲིག་ནི་རེད།

B: Now things have escalated.

ཁ། ད་དོན་དག་རྗེ་ཆེར་བྱུད་ཐལ།

A: "From that day on, we grew accustomed to taking turns butchering any who came onto our lands."

ཀ། དེའི་ཉིན་དགར་ནས་བྱུད་ལས་ད་སུ་སུའི་ས་ཐོག་ག་སོང་ན་བཞའ་རེས་ཡེད་རྒྱུ་བཞིག་ལོབས་ཐལ།

B: [addressing the village leader] What did you say? You butchered those that came on your land?

ཁ། ཅི་བཞེ། ས་ཐོག་ག་བྱུད་སོང་ན་བཞའ་འཇོག་ནི་རེད།

A: "We butchered them! We butchered as many as we could catch. If we couldn't catch them, then they got away."[27]

ཀ། བཞའ་ནི་རེད། དུ་ཟིན་ན་དུ་བཞའ་ནི་རེད། མ་ཟིན་ན་འཕོར་འགྲོ་ནི་རེད།

B: [directly to the village leader] Oh, so if one rode a great horse one would escape.

ཁ། ཨོ། ད་རྟ་ཚ་ཡ་བཞིག་ག་ཞོན་མེད་དུས་འཆར་ནི་མ་རེད།

B: Who's saying that? Your livestock ride horses.

ཀ། ཨ། འདིས་ཆི་ཟེར། ཐོག་ཏུ་ཞོན་བཞིག་གང་ན་ཡོད་ནས་ཆི་གོ།

A: [interceding] Uh, the old man was talking about livestock!

ཀ། ཨེ། སྐྱེ་གི་རྒད་པོས་ཐོག་ཟེར་གོ་ནི་རེད་ཡ།

B: [addressing A again] Oh, I thought they would butcher people.

ཁ། ཨོ། དེ་བཞེ་ཀྱི་བཞའ་ནས་ན་འདོད་ལ།

---

27 This could refer to both villages.

A: [under his breath] That would be a hospital.

ཀ སྨན་ཁང་ཡིན་ས་ཡོད་ཀྱི་ར།

B: [to A] *Ya*, what did he say then?

ཁ ཡ་ད་ཅི་ཟེར་གི

A: [as the village leader] "*Ya*, so if you're going to butcher them, then I'll butcher them too, and let's slaughter as many as we can!"

ཀ ཡད་བཤའ་རེས་ཡེད་ན་བཤའ་རེས་ཡེད། ཞེ་བསམ་པས་བཤའ་རེས་བཞག་ཡེད།

B: It was probably a complete slaughter!

ཁ བབ་གི་རྫོགས་བཏང་ས་ཡོད་ཀྱི་གོ

A: *Ala*! Those evil ones grew more and more accustomed to butchering, and even grew accustomed to cleaving.

ཀ ཨ་ལ། དེ་རྫོགས་རྒྱུ་ཆ་བོ་བཤའ་རྒྱུའི་ལོབས་ཀྱི་ལོབས་ཀྱི་གཤག་རྒྱུ་བཞིག་ར་ལོབས་ཐལ།

B: *Aro*! Hold up! What did you say? What did they cleave?

ཁ ཨ་རོག་སྟོད་གོ་ཅི་བཞེ། ཅི་བཞིག་གཤག་བཏང་ནི་རེད།

A: Well, they weren't just cleaving cloth. Listen!

ཀ ད་རས་གཤག་གས་ཟེར་རྒྱུ་ཡོད་ནི་མ་རེད། ཉོན་ན་སྟོད་དྲ།

B: It's not that I wasn't listening, I just didn't understand.

ཁ མ་གོ་ནོ་མིན་ནས་མ་ཉན་ནི་ད་ཅི་ཡིན་དྲ།

A: [as the village leader] "uh, at one point the young men got knives in their backs while herding."

ཀ ཨ། བར་བཞིག་ད་གསར་བུ་ཚོས་ཟོག་རྫ་ནས་གྱི་དན་ཚོ་སོག་སྤུབ་ཐུར་ར་གསེབ་རེས་ཡས།

B: Oh.

ཁ ཨོ།

A: "They slashed at one of ours horizontally, and we cleaved one of theirs vertically."

ཀ ངེ་ཚོའི་གསར་རུ་བཞིག་ཐད་ཀྱི་གཤག་བཏང་ཐལ། ཁོ་ཚོའི་གསར་རུ་བཞིག་ཐུར་ར་གཤག་བཏང་ཐལ།

B: *Ah*, so now they're slashing at people!

ཁ ཨ། ད་ཐེངས་ད་སྐྱེ་གཤག་བཞིག་ཡ།

A: "Again, if you're going to slash, then I'll slash you too; and let's slash as many as we can."

ཀ ཡང་གཤག་རེས་ཡེད་ན་གཤག་རེས་ཡེད་ཞེ་བསམ་པས་གཤག་རེས་བཟིག་ཡེད།

B: So, go and slash each other to pieces![28]

ཁ དགཤག་རེས་བྱོས་ཏུ་རས་གི་ཐོངས་ད་ཐོངས།

A: "*Ala*. Those bastards got more and more used to cleaving and then ended up getting used to knocking off. But an unequal number were knocked off, and they were walking while we lay down. It's not fair, is it?"

ཀ ཨ་ལ། དོ་རྫོགས་རྒྱ་ཚ་བོ་གཤག་རྒྱའོ་ལོབས་གི་ལོབས་གི་རྫོགས་རྒྱའི་ལོབས་ཐལ། བཟོགས་ནོ་མང་ཉུང་ཕོར་ཐལ། དེའི་མི་ཆད་དེ་ཚོ་ཞལ་གྱི་བཞག་བཏང་ངས། ཁོ་ཚོ་ལངས་ངས་འགྲོ་གོ་གི། དེ་མོ་བྱ་བཟིག་ཡོད་ནས།

B: So, what are you going to do about it?

ཁ ད་ཆེ་བཟིག་ཡེད་དགོ་ནི་རེད།

A: So, he said [in the village leader's voice], "We're counting on you, wise *lama*, to pay them back with interest!"

ཀ དེ་སྟེ་གིས་བཤད་གི་ར། འདིའི་མི་ཆད་ནི་བཟིག་ཕྱིར་ར་བཅའན་རྒྱོ་ད་བླ་མ་མཁྱེན་ཟེར་ཡ།

B: So, learning about it gave you an excuse to take money, but you mustn't violate karmic law.

ཁ དརྒྱུས་ལོན་ན་ཁ་གཡར་རས་རྒྱུ་བླངས་ན། བླངས་ར། རྒྱུ་འབྲས་མེད་ནི་ལས་མི་ཉན་གོ།

A: Even if I have no money, a true thief, let alone a fake *lama*, would understand the importance of not letting this village's line be cut.

ཀ ད་ད་རྒྱུ་བརྒྱད་མེད་རུང་སྟེ་བ་འདིའི་རྒྱུད་ཆད་གི་མི་འཇུག་རྒྱོད་ད་བླ་མ་རྫུན་མ་བཟིག་མ་དགོ རྐུན་མ་དོ་མ་བཟིག་གི་ར་ཤེས་ནི་རེད།

B: Then tell them that it's an easy thing to do!

ཁ དེས་ན་ད་དོན་དག་དེ་སྟུ་མོ་བཟིག་རེད་ཟེར་དགོ་ནི་རེད།

A: Uh, I did aver that settling that affair would be easy.[29]

ཀ ཨ། ངས་ར་དོན་དག་དེ་སྟུ་མོ་བཟིག་རེད་གསུངས་བཏང་།

B: That's absolutely wrong! If that's easy, then what's difficult?

ཁ དེ་ཚ་བ་ནས་འགྲིག་ནི་མ་རེད་ཡ། དེ་སྟུ་ན་ཆེ་བཟིག་དཀའ་ནི་རེད།

---

28 དརས། refers to scraps of cloth cut from a larger piece of cloth.

29 In this line, Menla Jyab awkwardly and humorously uses honorifics to refer to the things he has said in the role of *lama*.

A: Uh, it's easy. Wipe out the other village, and then whose would their things be if not mine?

B: Well, aren't you a wolf in sheep's clothing!

A: Uh, so I will solve it beautifully!

B: [dismissively] Bullshit!

A: [to the villagers] "Uh, take a seat, Village Leader! I will call the villagers. Um, before, when the two villages fought, the losses were imbalanced. From now on, when people fight, they must be equal. In general, respect the words that the *lama* speaks, and especially, listen to the words of your parents."

B: Again, they probably said, "Yes sir!" such that, the earth and sky quaked with it more than just the earthquake! And so, who knows who will be called on first?

A: "First, that one with the long braid, stand up. [Hastily] Oh, not that one, not that one. A kid with braided hair should be catching baby birds.[30] The one behind him ... not you, not you, what old lady doesn't have a braid? The braided one behind her. Not that old man. The one young guy behind him: the one who's praying."

---

30 Meaning that he will not be calling any children forward.

B: *Ah ah ah*. There are rows and rows of people with braids!

A: "Uh, tell me! Which is better: to enjoy your own life, or to destroy your own people?"[31]

B: That's not like what a real thief would say. What did he say?

A: [in a different man's voice] "By my father's flesh, how should I know? But it must be that: 'It's better to die nobly than to live in shame for your whole life.'"

B: So he's one of those who is willing to sacrifice himself.

A: [as the *lama*] "Ah, noble son! If told to run to the paths of the dead, you will. If told to hit your father's head, you will. You are fated to defeat one who is deaf in his left ear, and who has a scar on his lip, and you're not allowed to even approach anyone else."

B: That's distinctive; there's no mistaking that!

A: [as the braided man] "Ah, my maternal uncle? Dear Alak. That's my mother's brother!" he said.

B: Oh, what do you say to that?

---

31 Here, Menla Jyab plays with the rhyme of སྲི་ཚེ་ལོངས་སྤྱོད་ "enjoying your life" and མི་རིགས་ཚར་གཅོད་, "to destroy your own people." The first and fourth syllables rhyme.

A: [Menla Jyab as himself, tersely to the braided man] "I didn't ask about that. If he's your maternal uncle, then he must be your mother's brother. Sit down! The one in front of you; the one wearing the sheepskin robe."	ཀ དེ་མོ་དེ་འདྲི་གི་མེད། ཨ་ཞང་ཡིན་ན་ཨ་མའི་སྤུན་པོ་ཡིན་རྒྱུ་རེད། མར་ར་བཙོག དེའི་སྟུན་མ་གོ སྤྱག་པ་གོན་ནོ།
B: They're all wearing sheepskin robes.	ཁ སྤྱག་པ་གོན་ནོ་ད་བཅས་མི་ཆར་ར།
A: "Uh, that one with the robe with the patch."	ཀ ཨ། སྤྱག་པ་སླན་པོ་ཅན་པོ་དེ།
B: I'm sure there are many with patched robes.	ཁ སླན་པོ་ཅན་ར་ཆེ་ར་མེད་གི་ནས།
A: "Uh, that one with the robe with a round patch sewn with black thread! Stand up!"	ཀ ཨ་སླན་པོ་གོར་གོར་སྐུད་པ་ནག་ནག་གིས་བཙེམ་ནོ་དེ་ཡར་ར་ལོངས།
B: [sounding impressed] You don't need glasses, wei!	ཁ ཁྱོས་ཆྱིག་ར་གོན་མི་དགོ་གོ་ནི།
A: Uh, I said, "Tell me!" [in a high-pitched voice] "Yes sir," he said. [in a normal voice] "But you don't have to speak," I said. [in a high-pitched voice] "Yes sir," he said. [in a normal voice] So I said, "From now on, don't say 'Yes sir' to anyone." And he said [in a high-pitched voice] "Yes sir!"	ཀ ཀྱུ། ཁྱོས་སྨོད་བཟེ་ར། ལགས་སོ་ཟེར་གི་ད་ ཁྱོས་བཤད་མི་དགོ་བཟེ་ར་ལགས་སོ་ཟེར་གི་ དེང་ཕྱིན་ཆད་སུ་ཡིན་གོ་ལགས་སོ་མ་ཟེར་ བཟེ་ར་ལགས་སོ་ཟེར་གི
B: He's an agreeable person!	ཁ མི་དྲང་མོ་བཟིག་རེད།

A: "Well, I'll speak plainly to you. If someone asks who is straight as an arrow and brave as a tiger, it's you. And if you ask who you are fated to defeat, his name is Dundul. The goal is not to defeat this side, but to defeat the other. Except for him, let alone defeating, you may not even approach anyone else."

B: And he probably said [in a slightly higher voice] "Yes sir," again.

A: He got nervous, and said, [in a high-pitched voice] "*Alak*, sir! I can't say 'Yes sir,' to that, sir."

B: What's wrong with it?

A: [in a high-pitched voice] "That man's wife is my sister! It would kill me if you told me to kill him."

B: Now that's really horrible.

A: "Uh, I didn't ask you that. In a place where you need to kill and cut people up, you can't choose who to kill. Sit down! That old, wounded man, stand up!"

B: Oh, so you won't even let the wounded sit?

A: "Uh, you're old and in the evening of life.[32] Moreover, you are now wounded. So speak sitting down!"

---

32   The original translates literally as like a sun setting behind the mountains and suggests that the elder is no longer in the prime of his life.

B: That's better.

| ཁ| དེ་བཟོ་རེད།

A: "*Ya*, old man, last time you fell into the hands of an accursed wretch, and he beat you within an inch of your life. This time, a child will fall into your hands. It's OK to kill him like a baby bird. His name is Shamtruk," I said. And the old man stood up.

| ཀ| ཡ། ཁྱད་པོ་འདང་ཡིས་ཁྱི་བུ་ལམ་མ་མི་འགྲོ་རྒྱ་བཞིག་གི་ལག་གཏོར་རས། ཕྱིར་ར་ཡོད་མི་ཐུབ་ལ་བཞིག་བཅོས་བཏང་ནི་རེད། དབྱངས་ཁྱོའི་ལག་ག་ཞུ་ཡས་བཞིག་འཆོར་རྒྱ་རེད། བྱིའུ་ཕྲུག་གསོད་གསོད་ཡས་བཏང་ཆོག ཆུང་ད་བྱམས་ཕྲུག་ཟེར་གི་བཟེ་ར། ཁྱད་པོ་རང་ད་ཡར་ར་ལངས་བཏང་ཐལ།

B: I bet the old man was happy.

| ཁ| ཁྱད་པོ་དགའ་བཏང་བཞིག་ག

A: The old man cried.

| ཀ| ཁྱད་པོ་ངུས་བཏང་ཐལ།

B: What was wrong?

| ཁ| དེ་ཅི་མ་ཉན་ནི་རེད།

A: [in the voice of the old man] "*Ah*, goodness![33] How could it come to this? I will die before my son does, for he is my son, given up for adoption, *Alak*!" he said.

| ཀ| ཨ། བུ་འདི་ན་བུ་འདི། དེ་མོ་བུ་བཞིག་གང་ན་ཡོད་ནས། ཞི་མི་འཆི་རགས་གོ་ད་ངེ་ཤོང་ན་ཤི་སོང་། ཁོར་དགེ་ནས་བུ་སྐྱལ་བྱིན་ནོ་རེད་ཡ། ཨ་ལགས། ཟེར་ཡ།

B: What else could the old man do? What father and son will fight each other?

| ཁ| ད་ཁྱད་པོ་ཅེ་ཁག་རྒྱུས། ཕ་བུ་གཉིས་གས་རྒྱག་རེས་ཡོད་གོ་ནོ་སུ་རེད།

A: "Uh, I didn't ask about that. In a place where brothers feud, how can you be free from it? Sit down!"

| ཀ| ཨུ། དེ་མོ་དེ་འདི་གི་མེད། སྤུན་ཟླ་བང་དམེ་ཡོད་ས་བཞིག་ན་ཁྱོ་ནད་ཁལ་གི་གནང་ད་བཞིག་གང་ན་ཡོད་ནས། མར་ར་བཅོག

B: Now you'll let them all die.

| ཁ| ད་ཁྱོས་ཚང་མ་འཆི་གི་འཇུག་རྒྱུ་རེད།

A: *Ya*, so I finished making arrangements for everyone.

| ཀ| ཡ། ད་ངས་ཚང་མ་བཀོད་སྒྲིག་ཡས་ཚར་གི་བཞག་བཏང་།

B: They all must be related.

| ཁ| ཚང་མ་ཕ་ཉེ་ཡིན་རྒྱུའོ་རེད།

---

33 The phrase བུ་འདི་ན་བུ་འདི། is a common expression in Amdo to express dismay.

A: *Ah*, sure are. They all descend from the Bodhisattva monkey and the rock ogress.³⁴

ཀ ཨ་དེ་ཡིན་རྒྱའོ་རེད། ཚང་མ་སྤྱུ་བྱང་ཆུབ་སེམས་དཔའ་ར་ཕྲག་སྲིན་མོ་ནས་ཆད་ནི་རེད་མོ།

B: You're really heartless.

ཁ སེམས་མེད་བདོག་གོ་རེད།

A: If Careful Village has heart, then who should care whether or not I do?³⁵ What bothered me was that the offerings they gave were too few.

ཀ སེམས་ཆུང་སྡེ་བ་སེམས་ཡོད་ན་ང་ཁེར་མོ་སེམས་ཁུར་ཆེ་ཡོད་རྒྱུས། ད་གའི་སེམས་མི་བདེ་བྱུད་གོ་ད་སེམས་ཆན་གྱི་འབུལ་བ་ཅིག་ཅིག་ཉུང་སོང་བཟིག་ཡ།

B: [reproachingly] Oh, nothing can be done (for you)!

ཁ ཨོ། ད་མ་བ་ནི་རེད།

A: I thought about it and something could be done.³⁶ I went over to Careful Village's opposing village, they offered far more than Careful Village.

ཀ འདང་བཟིག་བརྒྱབ་ར་བ་རྒྱོ་བ་གི་སེམས་ཆུང་སྡེ་བ་གི་གྱེད་ཡ་གི་སྡེ་བ་བྱུད་སོང་ར། སེམས་ཆུང་སྡེ་བ་གི་མི་ཆན་ནི་བཟིག་འབུལ་བཏང་ཐལ།

B: You're really shameless.

ཁ ད་ངོ་ཚ་རྒྱའོ་བདོག་གོ་མེད་གི

A: Uh, the work there wasn't that difficult. Just orating some sermons.

ཀ ཨ། ད་ལས་ཀ་ར་དགའ་མོ་བཟིག་མེད་གི་བགའ་ཆོས་བཟིག་གསུང་བཏང་རྒྱོའི་ད་རེད།

B: Do you know how to chant scriptures?

ཁ ཁྱོས་ཆོས་བཟིག་བཟོ་འདོན་ཨེ་ཤེས།

A: Uh, the entire village gathered, and I spoke "The essential and necessary prophecy."

ཀ ཨུ། སྡེ་བ་གོ་བསྡུས་བཏང་དས་ལྱང་བསྟན་ཁ་ཚ་དགོ་གཏུགས་མ་བཟིག་གསུངས་བཏང་།

---

34 This refers to the Tibetan creation myth, in which Tibetans are the progeny of a monkey and a demoness.

35 Here, Menla Jyab is relying on Careful Village to "have a heart" and refuse to kill relatives. His heartlessness is immaterial.

36 His partner is reproaching him, saying that he is beyond help, but Menla Jyab interprets the other literally and says there is a way to solve the problem.

8. Careful Village's Grassland Dispute

B: I've never heard a scripture like that!

ཁ། དེ་མོ་ཚེས་བཞིག་གོ་ར་མ་མྱོང་།

A: "*oM swa ra swa sti*[37] the land dispute,

ཀ། ཨོཾ་སུ་ར་སུ་སྟི་ས་རྩོད་ཀྱིས།།

oM will finish your grandchildren!

ཨོཾ་ཚ་བོ་ཚ་མོ་ཚར་རྒྱུ་རེད།།

oM swa ra swa sti the land dispute,

ཨོཾ་སུ་ར་སུ་སྟི་ས་རྩོད་ཀྱིས།།

oM will finish your grandchildren!

ཨོཾ་ཚ་བོ་ཚ་མོ་ཚར་རྒྱུ་རེད།།

oM swa ra swa sti the land dispute,

ཨོཾ་སུ་ར་སུ་སྟི་ས་རྩོད་ཀྱིས།།

oM will finish your grandchildren!"

ཨོཾ་ཚ་བོ་ཚ་མོ་ཚར་རྒྱུ་རེད།།

I chanted for the entire morning. In the afternoon, they all said that they didn't understand anything except for "quit something"[38] and "will finish something."

སྔ་དྲོ་བཞིག་གི་རིང་ང་བཏོན་བཏང་ང་ར། ཕྱི་དྲོ་ ཚང་མས་ཅིག་ཆོད། ཉིག་ཚར་རྒྱུ་རེད་བཟེ་བོ་ མིན་ནས་གཅིག་ག་ར་མ་གོ་ཐལ་ཟེར།

B: How could they?

ཁ། གོས་ཡོད་དུ།

A: Then I explained it clearly for them. I said, "This is not a prophecy that existed before, but one that has just emerged for this time. As for the meaning, it says, 'If you fight Careful Village, your village will be finished.'" And everyone was frightened.

ཀ། དེ་ནས་ད་ངས་འགྲེལ་བ་གསལ་བོ་བཞིག་ ཡས། འདི་སྔོན་ཆད་ཡོད་དིའི་ལུང་བསྟན་ བཞིག་མིན། ད་ཐེངས་བབས་དིའི་ལུང་བསྟན་ བཞིག་རེད། གད་དོན་མི་གོན་སེམས་ཆུང་སྟེ་ བར་ས་བརྩད་ན་ཁྱོ་ཚོའི་སྟེ་བ་ཚར་རྒྱུ་རེད་ བཟེ་ནི་རེད་བཟེ་ར། ཚང་མ་སྐྲག་ཐལ།

---

37 Mantra of the Boddhisattva Yangchenma (དབྱངས་ཅན་མ།).
38 This is not chanted, and likely suggests that the villagers did not understand. Menla Jyab often uses this construction to indicate someone's misunderstanding.

B: Who wouldn't be frightened by such a terrifying thing?

A: The elders spoke enough to fill a valley, and I grabbed my offerings that were enough to fill a valley and returned to Careful Village. The elders there were also speaking enough to fill a valley.

B: What were the elders saying?

A: Uh, the young folks came one after another, and said, "Mother cried. Father went crazy. A fight between relatives individually is really impossible."

B: Well then, what should be done?

A: Uh, I have a plan. If they can't fight each other individually, then let's have the villages fight. Having divined the date and time, I had both villages meet on the mountaintop.

B: Then they all went to war?

A: Then all was well.

B: *Ah?*

A: *Olé!*

B: [as if coming to a realization] *Ah,* oh, you scoundrel! Your plan is quite a plan!

A: Uh, now both villages had a peace summit, and their battle wounds were healed through marriage, and they had weddings. As for me, I had a great time going from party to party.

ཀ ཨ་སྟེ་གཉིས་ཀ་འགྲིག་ནོ་འགྲིག་སྟོན་ཡས་ནི་རེད། བྱེད་གྱི་རྨ་ཁ་གཉེན་གིས་གསོས་གཉེན་སྟོན་ཡས་ནི་རེད། ང་བཞེ་ནོ་རང་ང་སྟོན་མོ་དག་དག་གི་ནང་ནས་འཁོར་བཏང་འཁོར་བཏང་།

B: They **should** invite you to the party.

ཁ ཏོ་མ་སྟོན་མོར་བོས་ན་ཆོག་གི

A: Uh, there were so many more parties, but I had no time to attend them. When I go back, I need something to show for it. And then I set off all of a sudden. Before I left, I spoke a parting wish.

ཀ ཨུ། ད་དུང་སྟོན་མོ་མང་གི་ར་བསྲུན་ནས་འདུག་ཁོམ་མེད་གི་ད་རུང་ཕྱིར་ར་སོང་ན་སྟོན་རྒྱ་བཞིག་དགོ་གི་ཁ་མ་དེ་ནས་ལམ་མ་ལམས་བཏང་། འགྲོ་ཁ་རེ་བ་བཞིག་བཏད་ལ།

B: What wish?

ཁ རེ་བ་ཅི་བཞིག

A: "*Ah*, dear friends, since I came to Careful Village this time, I have accomplished everything I came here to do. My final hope is that you take the gifts you gave me and build a school for the children on the border of the two villages, and between both monasteries."

ཀ ཨ། སེམས་ཁོངས་གི་སྤུན་ཟླ་རྣམས་པ། ང་ད་ཐེངས་སེམས་ཆུང་སྡེ་བ་ཡོང་ནས་སེམས་དོན་ཐམས་ཅད་འགྲུབ་སོང་། མཐུག་མཐའི་རེ་བ་བཞིག་ཡོད་ནོ་དའི་འབུལ་བ་འདི་ཁ་རས་སྟེ་བ་གཉིས་གའི་མཚམས་ནས། དགོན་པ་གཉིས་གའི་བར་ནས་ན་ཡས་ཚོར་སློབ་གྲྭ་བཞིག་ཆུགས།

B: Oh, such a thing would be difficult even for a real *lama* to achieve.

ཁ ཨོ། དེ་མོ་དོན་དག་ད། བླ་མ་ངོ་མ་བཟེར་བསྒྲུབ་དགའ་ནི་རེད་གོ

A: Uh, at that moment, a small child came running over and gave me a *khatak*, and I kissed them and whispered, [as a child] "I'm not a *lama*; I'm a learner.[39] You go to school, too!" And they said, "Goodbye Uncle Menla!"

ཀ ཨ། སྐབས་དེར་ནུ་ཡས་ཆུང་ཆུང་བཞིག་བརྒྱུགས་གས་ཡོང་ནས་ཁ་བཏགས་བཞིག་འབུལ་གི་ཕྱིར་ར་ཁ་བཞིག་བསྒུལ་བཏང་ནས་ཁ་རོག་ག་ང་བླ་མ་ཡིན་ནི་མ་རེད། སློབ་མ་ཡིན་ནི་རེད། ཁྱོར་སློབ་གྲྭ་སོང་གོ་བཟེ་ར། ཨ་ཁུ་སྨན་བླ་བདེ་མོ་ཟེར་གི

---

39 Note that the original uses the word སློབ་མ། translates best as "student," but we have used "learner" to emphasize the way Menla Jyab plays with the

B: *Ya*, now hit the road!

A: Taking the narrow footpath away from Careful Village, the village leader's words echoed in my mind.[40]

B: What did the village leader say?

A: [as the village leader] "*Ya*, now that these two villages have reconciled, We plan to join both villages to have grassland disputes with another village!" he said.

B: Oh, you'll probably have to come back again!

A: *Ya*, well, anyways, goodbye, Careful Village.

B: Goodbye.

A: As dawn broke, and I was writing the end of this *khashag*, I said "Goodbye," and my wife raised her head up off our bed and said, "Where are you going?"

---

pronunciations of སློབ་མ། and བླ་མ། in the Tibetan.

40 "The Narrow Footpath" (ཀྱང་ལམ་ཕྲ་མོ།) is the title of a famous essay from modernist Tibetan author Don grub rgyal, and Menla Jyab likely expects audiences to make the connection.

9. Careful Village's Bride
སེམས་ཆུང་སྡེ་བའི་མནའ་མ། [1]

A: *Ah!* With a welcome like this, I don't know what to say or do, *aro*!

ཀ། ཨ། འདི་ཡས་དགའ་བསུ་ཡས་བཏང་ན། རང་ད་དགའ་བཏང་དས་ཅི་བཟིག་ཡེད་དགོ་ནི་ན་ར་མི་ཤེས་གི་གོ་ཨ་རོ།

B: [with a slight chuckle] Go to Careful Village again!

ཁ། ཡང་སེམས་ཆུང་སྡེ་བ་སོང་རོ།

A: Uh! I've gone to Careful Village a lot,[2] but I've never once come back with peace of mind.

ཀ། ཨ། སེམས་ཆུང་སྡེ་བ་མ་སོང་བསམ་པ་མེད་ད། སེམས་བདེ་མོ་ཡས་ཕྱིར་ར་ཡོད་དུས་བཟིག་མེད།

B: So who has you bothered this time?

ཁ། ཡང་སུས་ཁྱོད་ཀྱི་སེམས་ཁ་དཀྲུགས་བཏང་ནི་རེད།

A: If I speak my mind plainly, it's Careful Village that has me bothered. And it's Zalejyal that has Careful Village bothered.

ཀ། སེམས་གི་སེམས་གཏམ་གསལ་པོ་ཡས་བཤད་ན། ངའི་སེམས་ཁ་དཀྲུགས་ནོ་སེམས་ཆུང་སྡེ་བ་རེད་ད། སེམས་ཆུང་སྡེ་བ་དཀྲུགས་ནོ་ཟ་ལེ་རྒྱལ་རེད།

B: Zalegyal... this Zalejyal didn't kill someone, did he?

ཁ། ཟ་ལེ་རྒྱལ། ཟ་ལེ་རྒྱལ་འདོག་གོས་ཅིག་བསད་བཏང་ནི་མིན་ན།

---

1   A is voiced by Menla Jyab and B is voiced by Phagmo Drashi.
2   The Tibetan uses a double negative, which has the effect of intensifying the statement.

©2025 Jyab (text)
Thurston & Samdrup (Trans. & Notes), CC BY-NC 4.0   https://doi.org/10.11647/OBP.0452.09

A: As soon as I heard the village leader's story, I got a feeling that something wasn't quite right, *Aro*!

B: What did he say?

A: [as the village leader] "In general, Alak, it's not OK to make you tear things apart, but that Zalejyal messed up.[3] Let us gather at Goree's house with a few of Careful Village's wise elders to do some tearing, and let's make it so that there's nothing left to tear after that," he said.

B: What is that?

A: That night, I was scared and went to the Goree house, and it seemed that the elders had nothing in their hands that could be torn. What they did have were tobacco pouches.

B: Did they want to quit smoking?

A: That's what I thought, but according to the Village Leader it wasn't like that, *aro*!

B: *Ya*?

A: [as the village leader] "We've inconvenienced thee every time thou hast come. We shouldn't weary thee with resolving our external fights and internal disputes, but we have to tear Zalejyal's corpse.

---

3   The Tibetan གཏུད, translated here as "to tear," is commonly used in Amdo to mean "resolving conflicts."

9. Careful Village's Bride

B: What did you say? Zalejyal's corpse? He's dead?

ཁ ཅི་བཟེ། ཟ་ལེ་རྒྱལ་གི་རོ། ཉི་སོང་ནི་རེད།

A: [belligerently, as the village leader] "That undead one wouldn't let the elders die in peace. I don't know if it's a public quarrel or a domestic dispute, but he has started it!" he said.

ཀ འཆི་མེད་གོ་དེས་ད་ལོ་ལོན་ཚོ་ཞིབ་ཆེན་ཡས་འཆི་གི་ར་འཇུག་རྒྱུ་མ་རེད། ཕོ་གྱོད་ཡིན་ནས་ན་མོ་གྱོད་ཡིན་ནས་ར་མི་ཤེས་ནི་བཟིག་གི་ཁ་ཕྱིས་བཏང་ནི་རེད་ཟེར་ཡ།

B: Hehe, now I understand. This "tearing" and "prying" is all just a way saying that they have to resolve young Zalejyal's issue.

ཁ ཧེ་ཧེ། ད་ངས་གོ་ཐལ། གཏིད་རྒྱུ་བཟེ་གི་གཅབ་རྒྱས་བཟེ་ནོ་མིན་ནས་གསར་བུ་ཟ་ལེ་རྒྱལ་གི་དོན་དག་བཟིག་ཐག་གི་གཅད་དགོ་གི་མོ།

A: Uh, they needed to resolve it, but they couldn't resolve it.

ཀ ཨ། ཐག་གིས་གཅོད་དགོ་ནི་རེད་དུ་ཐག་གིས་ཆོད་རྒྱུ་མ་རེད།

B: What did this "Zalejyal" do?

ཁ ཟ་ལེ་རྒྱལ་བདག་གོས་ཅི་བཟིག་ཡས་བཏང་ནི་རེད།

A: They said that he found a wife, but that he found the wrong one.

ཀ བུད་མེད་བཙལ་བཏང་བཟིག་བཙལ་ནོ་འཁྲུག་སོང་བཟིག་ཟེར།

B: [surprised] Ya?

ཁ ཡ།

A: They said that she's from too far away, and her speech is unclear.

ཀ ཁ་ཐག་རིང་སོང་བཟིག་ཁ་སྐད་མི་དག་གི་ཟེར།

B: If Zalejyal understands her, isn't that what counts?

ཁ དེ་ཟ་ལེ་རྒྱལ་གི་གོ་སོང་ན་དེ་རེད་མོ།

A: Moreover, they said that her customs are different, and she's not pretty enough.

ཀ ད་རུང་ཡུལ་སྲོལ་མི་གཅིག་གི་མོ་སྦོ་མི་འོངས་གི་ཟེར།

B: But Zalejyal loves her, and that's all that matters. It's none of Careful Village's business.

ཁ ད་ཟ་ལེ་རྒྱལ་གིས་བློར་བབས་བཏང་ན་དེ་རེད་མོ། སེམས་ཆུང་སྡེ་བར་མ་བབས་ནི་བཟིག་རེད།

A: I said that too! But those elders are willful!

ཀ ངས་རང་དེ་བཞིན་ར། ཀྱད་པོ་ཚོ་གཉོད་པོ་ཏུག་ཏུག་རེད།

B: What did they say?

ཁ ཅི་ཟེར་གི

A: Uncle Tungtung was shaking his head.

ཀ ཨ་ཁུ་ཐུང་ཐུང་གིས་མགོ་ཐད་གི་གཡུག་གི་འདུག་གི

B: Judging by his name, I thought he must be like this.

ཁ མྱིང་ད་བསྣས་ན་ལོས་གཡུག་འདོད་ཀྱི

A: We take refuge in you, but thou mustn't say this.

ཀ སྐྱབས་སུ་འཚེ་ར་དེ་ད་ཅིག་གསུང་མི་ཉན་གི་གོ

B: Why not?

ཁ ཅི་བཟིག་ག་མི་ཉན་ནས་ན།

A: Um, if not from the creation of the universe, then at least from the time of our fathers and uncles, we have married girls of our own place,[4] and then raised our own families.

ཀ ཨེ་སྲིད་པ་ས་ཆགས་གས་བཞེ་ན་རེད་ད། ཨ་བ་ཨ་ཁུའི་རིང་ནས་བྱད་ལས། རང་གི་ཞི་ངན་མ་ཚོ་རང་གིས་བླངས་ནས་རང་ད་ཁ་ཁ་མོ་གསོ་ཁ་ཡས་ནི་རེད།

B: That's right.

ཁ དེ་རེད།

A: For long distance marriages, we used to "buy and sell" girls on both sides of the Yellow River.[5]

ཀ ཨོ་ད་ཐག་རིང་བརྒོ་ནས་བྱངས་སྲོལ་བཏད་ན་ར། རྨ་ཆུའི་ཕར་ཀ་ཚུར་ཀ་ཡས་ཞི་མོ་ཚོ་ཕར་ར་བཙོང་གི་ཚུར་ར་ཉོས་ནི་རེད།

B: So they consider that a very long distance.

ཁ ཨ་ཐུར་གི་ཐག་རིང་བཟིག་ཡིན་འདོད་ཀོ་ཀ

---

4 The Tibetan ཞི་དན་མ is a humilific term for the girls of their village.
5 The phrase "buying and selling" is not traditionally used in Amdo to describe the common practice of paying brideprice, but Menla Jyab uses it to critique arranged marriage.

A: "We don't know what goes on inside the heads of these empty-headed ones nowadays. But even if they don't fall in love with one from their own village, it should at least be someone from their own ethnic group."

ཀ ཨོ་ད་དེང་སང་གི་མགོ་སྟོང་བཟོ་ཁ་རྒྱ་མགོ་རྒྱུ་ཡིན་བཏང་ན། མགོ་ནང་ད་ཆེ་བཟིག་ཞུགས་གས་བསྟུད་ཡོད་ནས་མི་ཤེས་གི་ར། རང་སྡེ་ནང་ན་རང་སྐོར་འབབ་ནི་བཟིག་མེད་རུང་། རང་གི་མི་རིགས་བཟིག་ད་ཡིན་དགོ་ག་བཟེ།

B: Oh, now I get it. Zalejyal chose someone from a different ethnic group and wants to marry her.

ཁ ཨོ་ད་ཤེས་ཐལ། ཟ་ལེ་རྒྱལ་གིས་བསལ་ཡས་བསྟུད་བཏང་དས་མི་རིགས་མི་གཅིག་ནི་བཟིག་ཨིན་ན་འདོད་གོ་ག

A: That's right! That kind of ne'er-do-well wouldn't do anything other than what's inappropriate.

ཀ མིན་ནས་ད། མ་རབ་གི་རིགས་དེས་མིན་ནི་བཟིག་མིན་ནས་ལས་ནས།

B: Good, Good. So she was Han Chinese.

ཁ དུ་ནི་རེད། དུ་ནི་རེད། རྒྱ་མོ་བཟིག་ཨིན་རྒྱ་རེད་མོ།

A: She was a (foreign) girl! A (foreign) girl!

ཀ ཕྱི་མོ་བཟིག་རེད་ཡ། ཕྱི་མོ་བཟིག་རེད།

B: She couldn't be a boy, of course.[6] I meant: is the girl Han Chinese?

ཁ ཞི་ལི་བཟིག་ད་ཆེ་ཨིན་ད། ཞི་མོ་རྒྱ་མོ་རེད་ལ་བཟེ་ནི་གོ

A: "Nope, this low-life is going to make a scene by marrying a foreign girl. How can we even speak about it?" He said.

ཀ ཆེ་ཨིན་བཟེ་ར་ཤྱིག་ག་སྟོན་རྒྱུའི་འདིས་ཤྱིག་འཛད་ལས་ཕྱི་རྒྱལ་གི་ཕྱི་མོ་བཟིག་ཨིན་རྒྱུས་ཟེར་གོ་ནི་རེད། དེ་ཅིག་ག་བཤད་སོལ་ཨེ་ཡོད་གི་ཟེར་ཡ།

B: A foreigner? I can empathize with them. Did you ask what country she was from?

ཁ ཕྱི་རྒྱལ་གི་རེད། ཨ་ད་ཁོ་ཚོ་ར་ཁག་མེད་གི་གོ་རྒྱལ་ཁབ་གང་གི་ཨིན་ནས་ན་ཨེ་དྲིས།

A: Uh, I did ask, but they said that they couldn't remember on the spot.

ཀ ཨ། འདི་རྒྱུའི་དྲིས་ར། རེམ་མ་མི་དྲན་གི་ཟེར།

---

6 Here the conversation relies on B misunderstanding ཕྱི་མོ "foreign girl" as ཞི་མོ "girl," as the two terms are pronounced similarly in Amdo dialect.

B: That's also understandable. Must be hard for them to pronounce.

ཁ དེ་ར་ཁག་མེད་གི། ཁོ་ཚོའི་ཁ་ནང་ང་ར་ཡོང་རྒྱུ་མ་རེད།

A: Uncle Shepherd said that it seemed to be coming to his mind.

ཀ ཨ་ཁུ་ལུག་རྫིས་ཁོའི་ཡིད་ལ་ཡོང་ཁ་བཟིག་རེད་ཟེར།

B: I doubt it.

ཁ ད་ཅི་གོ་གོ

A: [haltingly] Let's see... Where did he say it was... It was the name of a fabric.

ཀ ག་རེད་ན། གང་བཟིག་ཟེར། རས་བཟིག་གི་མིང་ད་ཡིན་ད།

B: A fabric? Let's see. There's no country called *Buree* is there?[7]

ཁ རས་བཟིག་ག་རེ། འབུ་རས་ཟེར་ནིའི་རྒྱལ་ཁབ་བཟིག་མེད་ལ།

A: No. No. *Buree* is what I've got tied around my waist. It's the name of an expensive fabric!

ཀ མ་རེད། མ་རེད། འབུ་རས་ད་ངས་བཅངས་ངས་བསྡད་ཡོད་ནོ་འདི་རེད་ད། གོམ་པ་ཙ་ཆེན་བཟིག་གི་མིང་ཡིན་ཡ།

B: It isn't Panama, is it?

ཁ པ་ན་མ་ཡིན་ནི་མིན་ན།

A: Ah! Pa- ... Panama. Well, that ain't actually it. In the past, Careful Village's leader, the one with a great black tent, had a green-yellow Tibetan robe made of that fabric.

ཀ ཨ། པ་ན་མ། དེ་ད་ཨ་ཨ་ན་མ་ན་བཟིག་མ་རེད། སྔོན་ཆད་སེམས་ཆུང་སྡེ་བའི་དཔོན་པོ་སྦྲ་ནག་ཅན་ཆང་ང་ད་དེས་བཟོས་ནིའི་བོད་ལུ་ལྗང་སེར་བཟིག་ཡོད་ཡ།

B: America!

ཁ ཨ་མེ་རི་ཀ

A: *Ang ang ang!* Isn't that right. America! It's this so-called "A-ri." Horrible woman! Her nose was scary like an *arura* "snail!"[8]

ཀ ཨང་ཨང་ཨང་། ཆི་མ་བདེན་ནས། ཨ་མེ་རི་ཀ ཨ་རི་བདོག་གོའི་ཡིན་ཟེར་ཡ། དོ་རྫོགས་རྒྱ་མ། སྦྲ་བཟོ་འབུ་ཨ་རུ་གི་ལོག་གས་ད་ཅིག་འཇིགས་ཡ།

B: Now he's going to malign her.

ཁ ད་ཁས་རྒྱག་རྒྱུ་རེད།

---

7   The Tibetan འབུ་རས། (pronounced like *buree*) is the name of a sort of a coarse silk most often used for sashes or shirts.

8   In Amdo, the sounds for རི in ཨ་རི and རུ in ཨ་རུ་ར are pronounced similarly.

9. Careful Village's Bride

A: [as the village leader] Ahem!

ཀ ཨེ་ཧུན།

B: Who's that?

ཁ དེ་སུ་རེད།

A: Uncle Village Leader scooched forward.

ཀ ཨ་ཁུ་སྤྱི་དཔོན་སྤུན་ས་གཅིག་ཐུར་གི

B: Now he's gonna speak.

ཁ ད་བཤད་རྒྱུ་རེད་མོ།

A: [as the village leader] These modern situations are difficult to discuss like telling the Gesar epic, and are difficult to untangle like a mess of silk thread. As for Zalejyal and the young lady who cannot be separated, they don't listen when their parents speak, will they listen when the *lama* speaks? And if they still don't listen…

ཀ ཡ་ད་དེང་སང་གི་དོན་དག་འདི་བཤད་མི་ཤེས་
གེ་སར་གྱི་སྒྲུང་འདྲ་འདྲ། བཤིག་མི་ཤེས་གོས་
སྐུད་གི་དཀྲུགས་འདུ་འདུ་བཞིག་ཡིན་ནོ། ད་ཛ་
ལེ་རྒྱལ་ར་གསར་མོ་དེ་གཉིས་ཀ་སྒྱུ་མི་ཁོར་
ནོའི་སྟེང་ནས། དཔེར་ན་ཕ་མས་བཤད་ན་མི་
ཉན་གི་ར་བླ་མས་བཤད་ན་ཨེ་ཉན། ད་དུང་
མི་ཉན་ཟེར་ན།

B: Then what will they do?

ཁ ད་ཅི་བཞིག་ཡེད་རྒྱུ་རེད།

A: [as the village leader] "We would shun him before Careful Village becomes infamous. But our old fool [Zalejyal] would probably be happy about it."

ཀ སེམས་ཆུང་སྡེ་བ་སེམས་ཚན་ན་གྲགས་
རགས་གོ་སྤྱི་མི་གཅིག་བཟོ་སྟེ་གྱུབ་ནས་
ཉུད་བཏང་ན་བཟེ་ནས་ར། ཨུ་གོའི་སློབ་རྒན་
དགའ་འཛོག་ཁ་བཞིག་རེད།

B: Is it that serious?

ཁ དེ་མོ་ཚབས་ཆེན་བཞིག་ར་ཨེ་ཡིན་ན།

A: [as the village leader] "The goodness of the girls of Tibet—the land of snows—is famous everywhere, but it's unspeakable that a yak herder abandons them to take up with a bird herder?"

ཀ ད་གངས་ཅན་བོད་ཀྱི་བུ་མོ་བཟོ་ཡ་རབས་
ཡིན་ཚུལ་ཡོངས་རྟོགས་ག་གྱུགས་ཡོད་གི་དེ་
བསྐྱར་རས་ཕྱུགས་རྫི་བཞིག་གིས་བྱིའུ་རྫི་
བཞིག་བླངས་ཐལ་བཟེ་ན། ད་བཤད་སྐོལ་ཨེ་
ཡོད་གི

B: *Ah*? What's this about a "bird herder"?

ཁ ཨ། བྱིའུ་རྫི་བདོག་གོ་ཅི་ཟེར་གོ་ནི་རེད།

A: [Menla as himself] I didn't understand either. I asked for a clear reason, and old man Ada stood up and gave a detailed explanation.

B: What did Ada say?

A: [as Ada, without stopping] Well I'm not sure if it's America or Ashmerica but when did those wanderers arrive. It was last year—ah yes—in July. I don't know if it's true, but they said they were researching larks. They said that there were no larks in their land. Who knows where they flew off to!

B: Oh, so that's why they called her a bird herder.

A: [as Ada] To tell you the truth, who knows if she came to be a bird herder or if she came looking for a yak herder? Either way, Zalejyal's corpse has fallen into her hands.

B: Saying it like that makes me think that she beats him.

A: [as Ada] "Zalejyal, that weak-willed person: Initially he was teaching her pastoralist dialect, then they were accompanying each other, and finally they were together. And that's not alright, right?"

B: Everyone must have been amazed to find out about it.

A: They said that the first to find out was Uncle Toktok.

B: *Ya!* How did Uncle Toktok say that he learned of it?

A: [as Uncle Toktok] I'm a knowledgeable person. There's no way I couldn't know [about the relationship]. One acted like he understood that ghoulish language, and the other pretended like she was studying pastoralist dialect, but if you looked at their mannerisms, they were talking of living together.

B: He knew this from looking at their mannerisms?

A: [As Uncle Toktok] I thought it was wrong and told everyone, but no one believed me.

B: The elders especially wouldn't believe it.

A: [As Uncle Toktok] Are you satisfied? Then one day at a village gathering, they made a scene and let it all out of the bag.

B: Oh, what did they do?

A: [As Uncle Toktok] As soon as the foreign girl arrived, she said either "'ello" or "Hello," And I can't tell you today exactly what she did, but it was just my bad karma to see her release Zalejyal, turn around, and say [haltingly, in a woman's voice] "I … like… Zalejyal!"

B: That is probably a foreign custom to make it public.

A: [As Uncle Toktok] Uh, she didn't only want to be with him, but came right out and said it! And I was embarrassed and froze. There was nothing else I could do: I kicked Zalejyal, and fled.

ཀ ཨ་སྟེ་གིས་བསྙེག་འདོད་ནས་མི་ཚད་བསྒྲགས་བཏང་ཐལ་ར། དེ་བཟོ་ཏོ་ཚ་ནས་མི་ཚད་འཁྱེན་སོང་བཟིག་སྒུག་ག་ཕུག་གས་ཟ་ལེ་རྒྱལ་རྡོག་ཐོས་ཅིག་བརྒྱབ་བཏང་ངས་བྲོས་སོང་།

B: I'll bet!

ཁ དེ་མོ་བཟིག་ཡིན་རྒྱུ་རེད།

A: [As Uncle Toktok] If that's all they did, why should I complain again and again? Saying that it's the Tibetan custom, her team of bird-herding friends came to talk [about proposing a marriage] the next day, and we gave them a good talking to.

ཀ དེ་མོ་བཟིག་གི་ཚག་ནི་ཡས་བཏང་རྒྱས་ན་ད་དུང་ཆི་བཟིག་ག་ཏུ་པོ་ཟེར་གི་འདུག་རྒྱས། བོད་ཀྱི་ཡུལ་སྲོལ་བདོག་གོ་ཡས་ནས་བཟེ། དེའི་ཕྱིའི་ནངས་ཀ་ཡང་མོ་གི་བྱིའུ་ཏེ་འཚོ་རོགས་ཚོ་བཤད་ཀྱི་ཡོང་ཐལ། ཚད་གི་ཕྱིར་ར་བཤད་བཤད་བཏང་།

B: What did they say?

ཁ ཅི་བཟིག་བཤད་ཡོད་ནས་ན།

A: Now we spoke like this.

ཀ ད་དེ་ཚོས་འདི་ཡས་བཤད་ལ།

B: Un, un.[9]

ཁ ཨུན་ཨུན།

A: [As Uncle Toktok] "Now I am happy that you have arrived at my doorstep and are sitting at my hearth, but if any matchmakers this frightening have come here before, I'll drink Yongbha's blood![10] Oya! By my son's flesh, I won't give our boy to you, and by my daughter's neck we don't need that girl of yours. If you understand, then keep it in mind, and if you don't understand, then get the hell out! At this, they all stared dumbly at each other."

ཀ ད་ཁྱོ་ཚོ་སྒོ་ཁའི་བྱུད་ལས་གོ་ཁའི་བཅོག་ནོ་དགའ་ནི་ཡིན་དུ། དེ་རིང་བར་ར་བར་བ་འདི་མོ་འཇིགས་པོ་ཏག་ཏག་ཡོང་མྱོང་ན་ཡོང་རྒྱ་གི་ཁྲག་ག་ཁ་རག་གོ། ཨོ་ཡ། དེ་ངེད་ཁའི་ཞི་ཨི་བྱེད་ཁ་སྟེར་ན་ཞི་ཡིའི་ཤ་ར། བྱེད་ཁའི་ཞི་མོ་ངེད་ཁ་དགོ་ན་ཞི་མོའི་སྐེ། དུ་གོ་ན་ཡིད་ལ་འདི་ཟུངས། མི་གོ་ན་མར་ར་སློར་བྱུད་བཟེ་ར། གཅིག་གིས་གཅིག་གི་ངོ་བལྟས་བསྡད་ཡོད་གི་ཟེར་ཡ།

---

9 Suggests assent or agreement.
10 Yongbha is the name of one of Menla's colleagues at the dubbing office where he worked at this time. He uses the name to rhyme with ཡོང་། and སྒྱོང་།, but this is

B: They said what they should have! ཁ། ད་བཤད་རྒྱུའི་ད་བཤད་བཞག་གོ

A: [Menla as himself] Uh, Papa Cheche said he went even further.[11] ག ཨ། ཨ་ཕ་ཆེ་ཆེ་གིས་བཤད་ན་ཁོས་དེའི་ར་མི་ཚད་ནི་ཧག་ཧག་བཤད་ལ་ཟེར།

B: Ya? What did this Papa Cheche say? ཁ། ཡ། ཨ་ཕ་ཆེ་ཆེ་བདོག་གོས་ཅི་བཞིག་བཤད་བཞིག

A: Uh! Listen! ག ཨ། ཉོན་གོ

B: Ya. ཁ། ཡ།

A: [as Papa Cheche] "Now I don't know which side of the Yellow river this 'Ari' is on. You say that you came here in a bird boat [airplane], so I think you must be wealthy. Since you can come chasing birds, so I think you must have a lot of free time. And judging by the patches on your clothes, I think you must have nothing left!" ག ད་ཁྱོ་ཚོ་ཨ་རི་བདོག་གོ་རྒྱ་ཕ་རི་བཞིག་ན་ཡོད་ནས་ན་ཆུ་རི་བཞིག་ན་ཡོད་ནི་ར་མི་ཤེས་བཞེ་ནོ། ཁྱོ་ཚོ་བྱ་གྲུའི་ནང་ནས་ཡོད་ནི་རེད་བཞེ་ན་དར་རས་བསྐྱད་ཁོས་ཡོད་འདོད་གི་བཞེ་ནོ། བྱུ་བྱིའུ་བདའ་ཡམས་བསྐྱད་ཡོད་ནོ་བསླས་ན་ཁོས་མས་བསྐྱད་ཁོས་ཡོད་འདོད་གི་བཞེ་ནོ། ད་སྦུན་པ་བརྒྱབ་ནས་བསྐྱད་ཡོད་ནོ་བསླས་ན་ཚར་རས་བསྐྱད་ཁོས་ཡོད་འདོད་གི་བཞེ་ནོ།

B: Fair enough. ཁ། དེ་བཟེ་རེད།

A: [As Papa Cheche] "Now I have a message for the old men back in your 'America!'" ག ད་ངས་ཁྱེད་ཀ་ཨ་རི་ཚང་གི་ཀྲད་པོ་ཚོ་སྐད་གཅིག་གཏོང་བཟེ་ནོ།

B: That's horrible![12] ཁ། དཤི་ཐལ་ཡ།

---

also suggestive of Menla's creative play with oaths and other traditional language forms.

11   In some parts of Amdo, including Menla Jyab's home region, the Tibetan ཨ་ཕ། "father" can refer to any male of the father's generation. The word for "father," meanwhile, is ཨ་རྒྱ།.

12   This suggests he is dismissive and not approving of the elders' next statements.

A: [as Papa Cheche] "The families of Careful Village boast a long lineage. You won't understand if I say too much. We are descendants of Lhalung Hwaldor.[13] Our fathers' bones are gold, and our mothers' bones are conch. But if you bring a yellow stain on that, then we are going to fight."

ཀ དེད་ཁ་སེམས་ཅུང་སྟེ་བ་ཆང་ད་སྐྱེས་རབས་ བཤད་ན་ཁས་རབས་རེད། མང་ད་བཤད་ཉུང་ མི་གོ་གི་ དེད་ཁ་ལྷ་ལུང་དཔལ་དོར་ཆང་གི་ གདུང་རྒྱུད་ཡིན་བཟེ་ནོ། ཕ་བཟང་རུས་པ་ གསེར་ཡིན། མ་བཟང་རུས་པ་དུང་ཡིན། དེར་ སེར་ཐིག་འཐེན་རྒྱ་བཟེ་ན་གྱོད་ཡིན་བཟེ་ནོ།

B: Oh?

ཁ ཨོ།

A: [as Papa Cheche] Uh, apart from the impossibility of this marriage, we have nothing else to fight over.[14] If you still want to chase after your birds, or go collecting your bugs, you can do that as long as you let them go later. The good thing about you guys is that you won't kill them.

ཀ ཨ་ཨུ་ཚོའི་བར་ལ་གཉེན་མི་འཛིན་དོའི་ཐུན་ ཆད་ནས་དེད་ཕྱིན་ཡིན། དེའི་རྒྱུན་ཡིན། ཆ་ བོས་ད་རུང་བཟོ་བུ་བྱིུ་བདའ་ན་འདོད་ན་ འབའ་འབུ་འཛིན་ན་འདོད་ན་འཛིན་གི་ཐོག་ བཟེ་ནོ། གཞུག་ནས་བཏང་བཏང་ན་དེ་ཡིན། ཁྱུ་ཚོ་བཟང་བཟེག་ཡོད་ནོ་མི་གསོད་ནོ་ལ་ད་ གི་བཟེ་ནོ།

B: Oh, and what did he say the go-betweens said?[15]

ཁ ཨོ། བར་བ་ཚོས་ཆེ་ཟེར་གི་ཟེར།

A: He said, "It seems that they thought they had no hope, and they left saying either 'nah' or 'nor.'"[16]

ཀ རེ་བ་མེད་གི་འདོད་བཏང་ནས་ན། ན་བཟེ་གི་ ནོར་བཟེ་ཅིག་གཟུང་ཕལ་ཟེར།

B: They probably didn't understand any of it.

ཁ ཅིང་མ་གོ་ནི་ཡིན་རྒྱུའི་རེད་ཡ།

---

13 Lhalung Hwaldor is the shortened form of the name Lhalung Hwalkyi Dorje (ལྷ་ ལུང་དཔལ་གྱི་རྡོ་རྗེ།), the ninth-century monk who in 842 assassinated the final king of the Tibetan empire, Langdarma (གླང་དར་མ།).

14 This phrase is commonly used in Amdo at the conclusion of a dispute mediation.

15 In Amdo Tibetan wedding traditions, weddings are arranged through བར་བ། (pronounced *warwa* and translated here as go-betweens) who negotiate between the bride's family and the groom's.

16 These are approximations of the English word "no," and suggest that the villagers did not understand.

A: Uh, Granny Tsitsema, expressing that the old men were being reasonable, piled on.

B: *Ya*, what did Granny Tsitsema say?

A: [as Granny Tsitsema] These old men are reasonable. *Atsi*! Zalejyal must have epilepsy! If I met someone like her alone in the fields, by my mother's flesh, I'd faint.

B: That seems reasonable.

A: [as Granny Tsitsema] The human body is precious. Judging by my merit, could I say anything to anyone else?[17] Whether I say it or not, she's on full display, their bride is.

B: Let her speak! What did she say she's like.

A: [as Granny Tsitsema] Now I won't say it, *aro*. Her yellow hair is like the shining sun, her blue eyes are like a dried up spring, and her face is as pale as a coming drought. Her body is tall like a bent over tree. If they can't butcher their larks, it's certain that they'll have nothing to eat. What can I say other than *Alahoho*?"[18]

B: It's certain that nobody wants to be caught by her sharp tongue.

---

17 This is similar to, "who am I to judge?"
18 A laugh that women in Amdo make to suggest that they have made a point or to deride.

A: [Menla as himself] Uh, with that, everyone spoke at length about how they prevented this wedding, about how Zalejyal couldn't understand, and how that young lady had no way of working it out.

B: *Ya*, tell me: did that foreign girl leave or not?

A: Uh, they said she slunk away, but then something unspeakable happened.

B: What was that?

A: Zalejyal's old man who was having difficulty putting it into words,[19] finally spoke up.

B: What did he say?

A: [as the father] "Dear Alak! If I tell someone about my son's conduct and deeds, how could we ever complete our household penance.[20] But there's nothing to be done, so I'll speak." He thought for awhile, "ah, karmically wicked ones, can I say it or not?" he said.

B: Instead of asking whether he could say it or not, he just could've gone and said it!

---

19 Suggesting embarrassment.
20 Across the Tibetan Plateau, people may visit a divination specialist who will be able to tell them the rituals, chanting, and circumambulations they need to do to atone for the individual sins or their family's sins in this life (both past and future). This is called བཅའ་བ། (pronounced *jawa*), translated here as "penance."

A: [as the father] "So, if nobody says anything, the parents will speak up, *Oya*! In the matter of this demon girl, we used both the carrot and the stick with Zalejya, we've tried beating him and biting him. 'If you say you want to marry her, then we will cut you off! But if you don't marry her, we'll buy you a motorcycle.' We tried everything to no avail.

ཀ ཡ་ད་ཚང་མས་ཅིད་མི་ཟེར་ན། ཕ་མས་ཁ་
སྒགས། ཨོ་ཡ། ཞི་མོ་འདི་མོ་དེའི་དོན་དག་ག་
ཟ་ལེ་རྒྱལ་ཞི་བ་ཡས་གི་དག་པོ་ཡས། བཤའ་
ལ་ཡས་གི་འཆའ་ལ་ཡས། ཞེན་རྒྱ་བཟེ་ན་
བདའ་རྒྱས་བཟེ། མ་ཞེན་ད་མོ་ཊོ་ཊོ་བཟེ་མ་
ཡས་ཤུལ་ན་གཅིག་མེད་ད་མ་བ་ཐལ།

B: Probably.

ཁ ཡིན་རྒྱ་རེད།

A: [as the father] "It's like he has been possessed by a demon. He said that he and that girl will both live and die as one family."

ཀ ཞི་ལི་བཟེག་ཡོད་ནོ་གཞེད་གིས་བཟུང་བདང་
ནི་འད་བཟེག་རེད། ཞི་མོ་དི་ར་ཁོ་གཉིས་ཀ་
གསོན་ན་ཁྱིམ་གཅིག་ར་འཆི་ན་སྲོག་གཅིག་
ཡིན་ཟེར་གི

B: That's real love!

ཁ ཌོ་མ་བརྩེ་དུང་ཡོད་བདང་བཟེག

A: [as the father] "When they parted, he [Zalejyal] took out a silver amulet with the Buddha Shakyamuni's statue as the core and put it on her neck. As soon as she then placed something around his neck —whether it was an iron Buddha or a person, it had four limbs outstretched[21]—a blizzard wiped out many of my sheep. Ah, ill-fated ones!"

ཀ ཁ་གར་ཁ་ད་སྟོན་པ་ཤཱཀྱ་ཐུབ་པ་གཟུགས་
འཛུག་ཡས་ཉིས་དངུལ་གི་གའུ་བཟེག་ཡོད་ནོ་
དུད་ལས་གན་གི་སྐེ་བསྟོན་བདང་དངས། སླགས་
གི་སྐུ་བདག་གོ་ཡིན་ནི་ན། མི་བདག་གོ་ཡིན་
ནི་ན་ཀང་ལག་བཞི་རྐྱོང་ཡས་ནི་བཟེག་ཁོ་
གའི་སྐེ་བསྟོན་བདང་ཐལ་ར་ད་ཁ་མ་དི་ནས་
ཁངས་ཆེན་བཟེག་ག་ཁག་བཞག་གས་འདི་
ལུག་ཚོ་བཟེ་ནོ་ཏོག་ཐལ་ཨ་ལས་ཏན་ཆ་གོ

B: He pointed the finger at that [the giving of the crucifix] as the cause of that incident.

ཁ དོན་རྐྱེན་དེའི་འབྱུང་རྐྱེན་དི་ས་བསྟོར་བདང་
ཐལ།

---

21 This describes a crucifix, suggesting that the foreign woman is Christian.

A: [as the Father] "When inauspicious times come, people leave our own [Tibetan] girls who are like goddesses, and fall in love with these demon-like girls. Now he says he's going straight to America. There can be no other explanation for this. Slinking off to school was the mistake, without doubt."

B: Now he knows!

A: At that time, Zalejyal's mother stood up. [as the mother] "Your Honorable Alak, may I please say something?" She said.

B: "Of course she may!" That's certainly what you should have said.

A: [As the mother] "Though I am a nobody, I would like to speak up."

B: Of course she would.

A: [As the mother] "When I think about myself, I would like to allow my only son to do what he wants."

B: That's right. All mothers are like this.

A: [As the mother] "Uh! When I was young, I came here without any freedom. Rending two apart takes but a moment, but the suffering lasts a lifetime. As parents, we don't want to torture them with this knowledge."

B: That's right.

9. Careful Village's Bride

A: [As the mother] "Now my son's destiny is in a faraway place; and my daughter-in-law's previously accumulated karma seems to have led her to Tibet. If you, Alak, are not cruel, you will fulfill their wishes."

ཀ དངའི་ཞི་ལིའི་བོད་པའི་ཁ་ཡིག་ཐག་རིང་ན་ ཡོད་བཏང་ནི་རེད། ངའི་མནའ་མའི་སྔོན་གྱི་ ལས་དབང་བོད་ཡུལ་ན་ཡོད་བཏང་ནི་རེད། ཁྱེད་ཀ་ཨ་ལགས་འཛོག་མེད་བཟིག་མིན་ན། འདི་གཉིས་ཀའི་འདོད་ཐོག་གཅིག་འཛོག་རྒྱུའི་ དུ་ཁྱེད་ཀ་ཅིག་གསལ་ཟེར་ཡ།

B: What did you say?

ཁ ཁྱོས་ཅི་བཟེ་ཡ།

A: [Menla Jyab as himself] I said, "Use the mother's suggestion as the basis, and fulfil the young man's wishes. Call the American girl back." Then everyone said "it is just as the girl had said when she was about to leave."

ཀ ཨ་མའི་བསམ་འཆར་གཞི་མ་བྱོས། གསར་ བུའི་བསམ་དོན་འགྲུབ་གི་ཞིག །ཨ་རིའི་ཞི་མོ་ ཕྱིར་ར་བོས་བཟེ་ར། ཚང་མས་དུ་དི་རེད་ལ་མོ་དེས་ འགྲོ་ཁ་བཟད་ནོ་དེ་རེད་ལ་ཟེར་ཡ།

B: *Ya!* What did the foreign girl say?

ཁ ཡ། ཕྱི་རྒྱལ་གྱི་ཞི་མོས་ཅི་བཟེ་ནི་རེད།

A: They said that she said, [haltingly, with a high-pitched voice] "I ... goed... and I'll ...to come back!"

ཀ ང་····བུད་ཐལ···ཕྱིར་ར་···ཡོང་རྒྱུ་རེད····ཟེར་ གི་ཟེར།

10. Careful Village's Wedding སེམས་ཆུང་སྡེ་བའི་སྟོན་མོ།[1]

A: *Ya*! Now on this auspicious day; at this excellent minute! The time when good things are created! Yesterday was New Year's Eve and today is the first!

B: [Sarcastically] I also know that the day after the eve isn't the second!

A: Uh, at the good time on the first of the new year, those with wealth will show it off, those without will pretend like they have even though they lack, and when merrily dancing and singing songs, it should be said that I won't stay quiet, but will speak a *khashag*!

B: [Shouting] No need! No need! [in normal voice] This sounds like a wedding speech![2]

ཀ༽ ཡ་ད་བཀྲ་ཤིས་པའི་ཉི་མ། ཕུན་སུམ་ཚོགས་པའི་སྐར་མ། བདེ་ལེགས་འབྱུང་བའི་དུས་ཚོད། ཁ་སང་གནམ་གང་དེ་རིང་ཚེས་གཅིག་རེད།

ཁ༽ གནམ་གང་གི་འཕྲོ་ཚེས་གཉིས་མིན་ནོ་ད་ངས་ར་ཤེས་གི་ར།

ཀ༽ ཨ། དུས་བཟང་ལོ་རྒྱ་ལོའི་ཚེས་གཅིག་གི་ཉི་མ། རྒྱུ་ཡོད་ཉིས་རྒྱུ་ཆེན་རྒྱས་པ་ཡས། རྒྱུ་མེད་ཉིས་མེད་རུང་ཡོད་ཁ་ཡས། སྐྱིད་དགའ་དགས་གླུ་ལེན་གར་སྐྱེད་ཡོད་གོ་དུས། ང་ར་ཁ་རོག་ག་མི་འདུག་ཁ་ཤགས་བཤད་བཞེར་རྒྱུས།

ཁ༽ མི་དགོ་མི་དགོ་ཁྲོའི་དེ་སྟོན་བཤད་བཟིག་ག་རིག་གི་མོ།

---

1   A is voiced by Menla Jyab and B is voiced by Phagmo Drashi.
2   A more appropriate response is to say *laso* (ལགས་སོ།), which suggests assent or agreement. In saying "no need," B uses a negation inappropriate to the genre to make a joke.

A: Uh, well, it's a sign that I performed a wedding speech.

B: When?

A: The year before last, when I went to Careful Village.

B: You performed a wedding speech again, and embarrassed yourself at the wedding?

A: It's not just boasting! I don't think I gave a bad "wedding speech." After I finished speaking, Uncle Village Leader was about to cry.

B: He was distraught.

A: He was stunned. Listen to what the Uncle Village Leader said.

B: What did the village leader say?

A: [As the village leader] "*Ah, ah, ah, ah*! Knowledgeable *lama*, you knew it through and through! Such a fun wedding speech. Such a dear wedding speech, by my son's flesh!" [as himself] he said.

B: Oh! Without speaking it, I can't decide whether or not it's a dear wedding speech. I hope that it's in a language.[3]

---

3   He clearly has little hopes for the speech, being unsure if it is even in a human language.

10. Careful Village's Wedding

A: Uncle Village Leader spoke the truth! The form of my wedding speech is fresh so as to be in tune with a new era, and if you understand its meaning, it's close to real life.

ཀ། ཨ་ཁུ་སྦྲེ་དཔོན་གིས་བཤད་ན་བདེན་ནི་རེད། ངའི་སྟོན་བཤད་རྣམ་པ་སོ་མ་ཡིན་ནས་དུས་རབས་གསར་པ་མཐུན་ནི་རེད། གནད་དོན་གོ་བ་ལྡངས་ན་དངོས་ཡོད་འཚོ་བ་ནི་ནི་རེད་ཡ།

B: Is your wedding speech really so fresh?

ཁ། ཁྱོད་ཀྱི་སྟོན་བཤད་དེ་དོ་མ་དེ་མོ་སོ་མ་བཟིག་ཡིན་ནས།

A: You don't believe me? Ok, then you leave me no choice. I'll tell it again today, everyone!

ཀ། རྣར་མི་འགྱོག་ཡ་ད་བཅའ་རྒྱ་མེད་ངས་དེ་རིང་འདིར་གིས་ཅིག་བཤད་གོ་རྣམ་པ་ཚོ།

B: Do it! [addressing to the audience] Listen up, audience!

ཁ། དེ་བྱོས། ཉན་མཁན་རྣམ་པ་ཉོན་གོ

A: Why are you just sitting there listening? Applaud!

ཀ། རང་ད་ཉན་ནས་བསྡད་ལས་ཅི་རྒྱུས། ཐལ་མོ་རྡེབས་རོ།

B: [surprised that he has to ask for applause] What's wrong with him, acting like this.

ཁ། འདིའི་བྱ་འདི་རེ་ཨ་ཡ།

A: "I will say, Ya, now praise *e ma ho*[4] praise *e ma ho*,

ཀ། ཡ་ད་བསྟོད་ཨེ་མ་ཧོ། བསྟོད་ཨེ་མ་ཧོ།

Praise, praise, praise, praise the azure blue sky.

བསྟོད་བསྟོད་བསྟོད་ལ་དགུང་ཨ་སྔོན་བསྟོད།

If you don't speak praises to the azure blue sky,

དགུང་ཨ་སྔོན་འདི་མ་བསྟོད་མ་བཟོད་ན།

It is said that there is no place for satellites to be in orbit,

མེས་བཟོས་འཁོར་སྐར་ལ་འཁོར་རས་འདུག་ས་མེད་ནས་ཟེར་གི

And it is said that there's no place for these airplanes to fly.

གནམ་གྲུའི་གནམ་གྲུ་འདིར་འཕུར་རས་འགྲོ་ས་མེད་ནས་ཟེར་གི

---

4 ཨེ་མ་ཧོ། is an expression of wonder common in Tibet.

And it is said that people won't know that this earth is round."	སའི་གོ་ལ་འདི་གོར་གོར་བཟིག་ཡིན་ནོ་ར་མི་ཤེས་ནས་ཟེར་གི་ཟེར་རྒྱུ་ཡིན།
How's that?	ཅི་མོ་རེད།
B: Alright.	ཁ ཆོག་གི
A: "I will say *Ya*! Now praise, praise, praise, praise the earth.	ཀ ཡ། བསྟོད་བསྟོད་བསྟོད་ལ་ས་དོག་མོ་བསྟོད།
If we don't speak the praises to this earth,	ས་དོག་མོ་འདི་མ་བསྟོད་མ་བཟོད་ན།
It is said that there will be no place for this white snow mountain to tower imposingly.	གངས་རི་དཀར་པོ་འདི་འགྱིང་ངས་འདུག་ས་མེད་ཉེས་ཟེར་གི
It is said that there will be no place for the green meadows to stretch.	སྤང་ལྗོངས་སྔོན་མོ་འདི་འདའ་ཡམ་འདུག་ས་མེད་ཉེས་ཟེར་གི
And it is said that there's no place for herders to lie down."	ལུག་རྫི་ནོར་རྫི་ཚོ་ཉལ་ཡམ་འདུག་ས་མེད་ཉེས་ཟེར་གི་ཟེར་རྒྱུས།
How's that?	ཅི་མོ་རེད།
B: It's ok!	ཁ ཆོག་གི
A: I will say *Ya*, now praise the human world,	ཀ ཡ་ད་བསྟོད་དོ་འཛིག་རྟེན་མི་ཡུལ་བསྟོད།
and especially praise Tibet, the land of snows!	གློས་སུ་གངས་ཅན་བོད་ཡུལ་བསྟོད།
Praise the monkey bodhisattva.	སྤྲེའུ་བྱང་ཆུབ་སེམས་དཔའ་བསྟོད།
Praise the goddess mother of rock.[5]	མ་གཅིག་བྲག་གི་ལྷ་མོ་བསྟོད།

---

[5] This is a reference to the Tibetan origin myth in which humans are the children of a monkey and rock demoness.

Praise the silk knot of love.	བཅེ་དུང་དར་གྱི་མདུད་པ་བསྟོད།
Praise the long path of free marriage.	རང་དབང་རང་འགྲིག་གཉེན་ལམ་རིང་མོ་བསྟོད།
Today we also praise the weddings of Careful Village!	དེ་རིང་སེམས་ཆུང་སྡེ་བའི་སྟོན་མོ་བསྟོད་ཟེར་ཆུས།
B: So are you going to keep praising or are you going to start talking?	ཁ་ དཁྱོས་བསྟོད་ལས་འདུག་རྒྱུ་ན་བཤད་ལས་འགྲོ་ཆུས།
A: *Ya*, so, when I tell you I won't give a speech, you tell me I must.	ཀ་ ཡ་ད་གཏམ་བཤིག་མི་བཤད་བཟེ་ན་གཏམ་བཤིག་བཤད་དགོ་ཟེར་གི།
If I speak one as long as the number of hairs a caterpillar has, it's too much;	འབུ་ཕྱལ་བ་བཤིག་གི་སྤུ་གྲངས་བཤད་ན་མང་འགྱོ་གི།
and even if you, the listeners, don't get hungry, I, the speaker, will get frostbite.[6]	ཁྱི་ཉན་ནོ་མི་ལྟོགས་ན་ང་བཤད་ནོ་ཕྱིད་རྒྱུ་རེད།
A: Well, then just speak a little bit.	ཁ་ དེ་ན་ཆུང་ཆུང་བཤིག་གོད།
A: Now, when I tell you I won't give a speech, you tell me I must.	ཀ་ ད་གཏམ་བཤིག་མི་བཤད་བཟེ་ན་གཏམ་བཤིག་བཤད་དགོ་ཟེར་གི།
If I give a speech that, like a little black ant, has no beginning or end,	གྲོག་མ་ནག་ཆུང་འདུ་འདུའི་མགོ་ཇ་མེད་ནེ་གཏམ་བཤིག་བཤད་ན།
Then the listeners' heads will certainly start spinning, and the speaker will be ashamed.	ཉན་ནེ་བཟོ་མགོ་ཡུ་ལོས་འཁོར། བཤད་ནེ་བཟོ་ངོ་ཡི་ཚ་གི།
B: So speak just the right amount.	ཁ་ ད་ཚོད་དང་རན་པ་བཤིག་གོད་ཡ།

---

6   Weddings in Amdo are often held in the New Year period (in winter) when people work is light, and when people who were mourning a deceased relative in the previous year are free to celebrate again.

A: And when I tell you I won't give a speech, you tell me I must.

If I give a speech that, like a butterfly's wing, is the same on the inside and the outside.

B: Hold on, *aro*! Why are you just talking about insects?

A: Uh, it's alright, they're just metaphors

B: *Ya*, get on with it!

A: Now, if I give a speech that like a butterfly's wing is the same on the inside and the outside, I'm not an elder who speaks old speeches, I'm not an elder who speaks old speeches, nor am I a scholar of modern speeches.

B: [interjecting] Nor a *bla ma* with insights into the next life![7]

A: [aside to B] shut up!

First, it doesn't come to my mind.

Then, it doesn't come from my mouth,

And in the end it will remain in my chest.

B: If it doesn't come, then why are you still speaking?

---

7   Here "A" begins a set formula common in Tibetan oratory, and "B" has completed the set for him.

10. Careful Village's Wedding

A: So when I tell you I won't give a speech, you tell me I must.

If I give a speech of a superior man, he's like someone who does tricks while riding a good horse.

When the horse is running, he is confident that his feet won't fall out of the stirrup even as he leans over to pick a flower.

B: And if you give a speech about a mediocre man?

A: If I give a speech about the middling man, he's like someone who is taming a brown mule.

Though the mule bucks more and more violently,

he is confident that he won't lose his grip on the mule's mane.

B: Judging by the middling man's description, I wonder what an inferior man is like.

A: If I give a speech about an inferior man like me, it's like someone riding a donkey to go herding.

On level ground it must trot, on the uphill you must dismount, and you have to lead it on foot on the downhill.

B: It's better to just go on foot. Now it'll be difficult for you.

ཀ ད་གཏམ་བཟིག་མི་བཤད་བཟེ་ན་གཏམ་བཟིག་བཤད་དགོ་ཟེར་གི

སྐྱེས་པོ་རབ་བཟིག་གི་གཏམ་རེ་བཤད་ན། རྟ་འདོ་བའི་གོང་ནས་སྒྱུ་རྩལ་རོམ་འད།

རྟ་རྒྱུགས་རེས་མི་རྟོག་འབབ་རེས་ཡམ་རུང་། ཀང་སག་སྒྲམ་ཡོབ་ནས་མི་རྒྱལ་ནིའི་ཡིད་ཆོད་ཡོད་གི

ཁ སྐྱེས་པོ་འབྲིང་བཟིག་གི་གཏམ་རེ་བཤད་ན།

ཀ སྐྱེས་པོ་འབྲིང་བཟིག་གི་གཏམ་རེ་བཤད་ན། སྨུག་ཆུང་དྲེལ་ལ་ཁ་ལོ་བཏུལ་འད།

བསྒུག་གི་བསྒུག་གིས་རེ་ཐུ་ཡིན་རུང་།

རྟོག་མ་ལག་ནས་མི་འཚོར་ནིའི་ཡིད་ཆོད་ཡོད་གི

ཁ པོ་འབྲིང་གི་ཆུགས་ཀ་བཤས་ན་པོ་ངན་གིས་ཇི་མོ་བཟིག་འདག་ག་རེ།

ཀ སྐྱེས་པོ་ངན་ད་འད་བཟིག་གི་གཏམ་རེ་བཤད་ན། བོང་སྒྱུ་ལི་ཞོན་ནས་ཙོག་ཇེར་སོང་འད།

ཐང་བདེ་ས་བཟིག་ནས་འདུར་དགོ་གི ལ་གཟར་ས་སྨུག་ན་འབབ་གོ་གི ཕུར་ཕུས་ཁིལ་ན་འཁྲིད་དགོ་གི

ཁ དེར་བསྐུས་གི་དཀང་ཐང་གི་དགའ་ག དཀོས་དགའ་རྒྱུ་རེད།

A: It wasn't that the old donkey liked trotting, but the slim whip wouldn't let it be. It wasn't that I, an inferior person, liked speaking, but Careful Village wouldn't let me be.

ཀ། དབོང་རྒན་འདུར་ར་དགའ་ནི་མིན་ར་རྒྱན་ལྕག་ཕྲ་མོས་འདུག་གི་མ་བཞག་ནས། ང་སྐྱེ་དམན་བཀད་ལ་དགའ་ནི་མིན་ར་སེམས་ཆུང་སྡེ་བས་འདུག་གི་མ་བཞག་ནི་ཡིན།

B: If you speak poorly, you have a reason.

ཁ། ཁ་ནད་ང་མ་ཡོང་ན་ར་ཁག་འཛོག་ས་ཡོད་ཀ།

A: Yeah, I've been told I must speak the praises of both upper and lower [Tibet].

ཀ། ཡ་ད་སྟོད་སྨད་གཉིས་ཀའི་བསྟོད་ར་བཞག་བཤད་དགོ་ཟེར་གི།

B: Here comes the old praise again.

ཁ། ཡང་བསྟོད་པ་རྙིང་བ་བོ་ཐོན་ཐལ།

A: It's said that in the surrounding areas of the three districts of Ngari up top, there are countless pilgrims.

ཀ། དསྟོད་མངའ་རིས་སྐོར་གསུམ་གི་མཐའ་སྐོར་ན་གནས་སྐོར་བ་ཅི་ཅི་གྲངས་མེད་རེད།

It's said that in the crossroads of the four horns of U-tsang in the middle, there are countless drunkards.

བར་དབུས་གཙང་རུ་བཞི་གི་བཞི་མདོ་ན། ར་བཟི་བ་ཅི་ཅི་གྲངས་མེད་རེད།

It's said that in the six valleys of the six ranges of Amdo and Kham at the bottom, there are countless arranged marriages.

སྨད་མདོ་ཁམས་སྒང་དྲུག་གི་ཕུ་དྲུག་མདོ་དྲུག་ན་བཅུན་ཁྲིག་གི་གཉེན་ཁྲིག་ཅི་ཅི་གྲངས་མེད་རེད་ཟེར་རྒྱུས།

[to B] Is that new?

གསར་བ་ཨེ་རེད།

B: It isn't not new.

ཁ། མིན་རྒྱུ་མེད་གི།

10. Careful Village's Wedding

A: If I speak about the lineage of the leader of Careful Village—which nobody has seen but I have imagined—located in the middle of Amdo, U-tsang, and Kham: a leader was born into a great lineage, and after his birth he went to China. Employing a variety of methods, he obtained a stamp.[8] Obeying his orders, he obtained a decree. From under a white helmet he protected the four continents, defeated the four enemies with his Mt. Meru-like body, and pacified the three realms with strict commands. One should say that you are a family of leaders with an unbroken line of leaders like a beautiful mountain range![9]

ཀ དམདོ་དབུས་ཁམས་གསུམ་གྱི་དཀྱིལ་དབུས་ན་ཆགས་ནི། སེམས་ཅན་གྱིས་མ་རིག་ནིའི་རྟོག་བདགས་ཀྱི་སེམས་རྒྱུད་སྟེ་བའི་དཔོན་པོ་བརྗོའི་སྲིས་རབས་བརྗོད་བྱེད་ན། སྲི་རྒྱུད་ཅན་ན་དཔོན་པོ་སྐྱེས་བཞིན་དཔོན་པོ་སྐྱེས་ནས་རྒྱལ་གཅོང་བཞིན་ཐབས་སྣ་ཚོགས་ཀྱི་སྤྱོད་ནས་ཐམ་ག་བླངས་བཞིན་བཀའ་བྱི་བོར་བཀུར་ནས་བཀའ་འོག་བླངས་བཞིན་མགོ་ཟློག་དཀར་འོག་ནས་གླིང་བཞི་བསྐྱངས་བཞིན་སྐུ་རི་རྒྱལ་ལྷུན་པོས་དགྲ་བཞི་བཏུལ་བཞིན་བཀའ་འཆན་པོས་ཁམས་གསུམ་བདེ་ལ་བཀོད་བཞིན་ས་རི་རྒྱུད་ཡག་གི་དཔོན་རྒྱུད་མ་ཆད་ནོ་ཁྲུ་ཇ་དཔོན་པོ་ཆད་རེད་ཟེར་རྒྱུས།

B: I've heard that before in a wedding speech, but I'll allow it.[10]

ཁ དེ་ད་སྔོན་བཟད་བཞིག་གི་ཞང་ནས་གོ་ད་སྟོང་བཞིག་ར་དགོ་ནི་དྕོས་ཐོངས།

A: *Ya!* Now if I speak the of the lineage of the bride's family,

ཀ ཡ་ད་ཁྱེད་ཀྱ་འཇང་ཆང་གི་སྲིས་རྒྱུད་བརྗོད་བཞིན་ན།

you are holders of an excellent lineage:

ཁྱེད་ཀ་ཀྱི་རྒྱུད་ཅན་གྱི་བདག་པོ་ཡིན་ནོ།

A lineage of deities with white flags,

དར་དཀར་ཅན་གྱི་ལྷ་རྒྱུད་ཡིན་ནོ།

---

8 Historically, Tibetan leaders in Amdo would receive recognition of their authority from Chinese authorities (emperors or their representatives), primarily in the form of a "chop" or stamp.

9 Here Menla Jyab, praises the lineage in terms of Buddhist cosmology, with Mt. Meru being the centre of the Tibetan Buddhist cosmological word, and the continents in the four directions of the mountain, the three realms refer to the desire realm, form realm, and formless realm.

10 Meaning he'll accept that this is "new."

A lineage of *lama*s with red flags,	དར་དམར་ཅན་གྱི་བླ་བརྒྱུད་ཡིན་ནོ།
And a lineage of tantric practitioners with black flags.	དར་ནག་ཅན་གྱི་སྔགས་བརྒྱུད་ཡིན་ནོ།
If one of a cultured lineage put their mind to it	རིགས་བརྒྱུད་ཅན་གྱིས་རིག་པ་བཀོལ་བཏང་ན།
They should say that you are the bride's family and would ask for a *phata* horse like a rocket	ཕ་ཏུ་བཟོ་འཕུར་མདའ་འདུ་འདུ་དགོ་ཟེར་ནོ།
And would ask for a *mata* horse like a motorcycle,	མ་ཏུ་བཟོ་སྨོ་ཐོ་འདུ་འདུ་དགོ་ཟེར་ནོ།
and would ask for a *zhang ta* horse that reaches the North Pole![11]	ཞང་ཏུ་བཟོ་སྐྱིང་སླེ་བྱང་མ་ཐོན་ནི་དགོ་ཟེར་ནོ།
B: That's not bad!	ཁ་ ཁྱེད་ཀ་ཨ་ཞང་ཚང་རེད་ཟེར་རྒྱུས།
	ཁ་ དེ་བཟོ་མི་ཚོགས་རྒྱུ་མེད་གི་
A: *Ya*, so! If I speak of the lineage of the groom's family,	ཀ ཡ་ད། ཁྱེད་ཀ་གཉེན་ཚང་གི་སྐྱེས་བརྒྱུད་བཟོ་ ཅིག་བཤད་ན། ཁྱེད་ཀ་ཡང་།
you also, are holders of an excellent lineage:	སྐྱེ་བརྒྱུད་ཅན་གྱི་བདག་པོ་ཡིན་ནོ།
A lineage of deities with white flags,	དར་དཀར་ཅན་གྱི་ལྷ་བརྒྱུད་ཡིན་ནོ།
A lineage of *lama*s with a red flag,	དར་དམར་ཅན་གྱི་བླ་བརྒྱུད་ཡིན་ནོ།།
B: *Aro aro aro!* that's the same as the bride's family!	ཁ་ ཨ་རོ། ཨ་རོ། ཨ་རོ། དེ་ཨ་ཞང་ཚང་ར་གཅིག་ རེད་མོ།

---

11 In some parts of Amdo, there is a tradition of giving a horse to the bride's maternal uncle, called a ཞང་ཏུ། Here, Menla appears to be adding ཕ་ཏུ། "horse for the father" and མ་ཏུ། "horse for the mother," which is, to our knowledge, an innovation. He may be doing this for comedic effect to rhyme ཕ་ཏུ། with འཕུར་མདའ། which follows it, and མ་ཏུ། with སྨོ་ཐོ།.

A: Well, except for that fact that one is taking wealth, and the other is giving it, they're basically the same lineage.

ཀ། རྒྱུ་ལེན་ནི་བཞག་ར་སྟེར་ནི་བཞག་གི་ཁྱད་པར་མ་གཏོགས་རྒྱུད་རྒྱུད་ཡལ་ཆེར་གཅིག་རེད་མོ།

B: Oh, then we'll make it work.

ཁ། ཨོ། ད་ཡིན་ན་བྱོས་བྱོངས།

A: Well, so, if the excellent lineage puts their wealth into it, it should be said that you are the groom's family:

ཀ། ཡ་ད་ཤི་རྒྱུད་ཅན་གིས་རྒྱུ་སྦོབས་བགོལ་བཏང་ན།

You weigh pounds of turquoise and coral and give them.

གཡུ་བྱུར་རྒྱ་མ་ཆད་ནས་སྟེར་རོ།

Measure out ounces of gold and silver and give them,

གསེར་དངུལ་སྲང་ད་འཇལ་ཡས་སྟེར་རོ།

Measure armspans of otter pelts and woollen cloth and give them,

སྲམ་ཕྲུག་འདོམ་མ་འཇལ་ཡས་སྟེར་རོ།

And gave female yaks, and female *dzo* enough to afford a girl.

འབྲི་མོ་ར་མཛོ་མོ་བྱིན་ན་བུ་མོ་ཁྲིག་གོ།

You take both the bride and her bridesmaid together![12]

བག་མ་ར་བག་རོགས་མཉམ་གི་ལེན་ནོ་ཁྱེད་ཀ་གཉེན་ཚང་བཟང་རེད་ཟེར་རྒྱུས།

B: *Aro! Aro!* You aren't just selling the girl, but giving them her bridesmaid too?

ཁ། ཨ་རོ། ཨ་རོ། བྱིས་བུ་མོ་བཙོང་ནས་མ་ཚད་ད་རུང་བག་རོགས་ར་སྟེར་རྒྱུས་ནས།

A: Uh, even if not to that family, they have to sell her to another one. I'm simplifying things.

ཀ། དེ་བ་མ་བྱིན་རུང་། ཅིག་ག་བཙོང་དགོ་ག་ཆུ་མོ་ཡོད་ལ་བཏང་རེ།

B: Now try and keep giving your wedding speech.

ཁ། ད་ཁྱེད་ཀི་མར་ར་སྟོན་བཤད་གོ་ཞེ་ཤོད་གི་བྱོས།

---

12 This refers to the practice of the groom's family paying a brideprice.

A: *Ya*, well, if you know the nature of weddings, they are merely a worldly custom.

ཀ ཡད་སྟོན་མོ་སྟོན་མོ་བཟེ་ནོ་འདི་གནས་ལུགས་ཤེས་ན་འཇིག་རྟེན་གྱི་འགྲོ་ལུགས་ཙམ་རེད།

It should be said that I won't hide it but tell everyone today

འགྲོ་བདེ་འདུག་བདེ་ཡས་ན་ཡར་བདེ་ཆུར་བདེ་ཡིན་ནོ།

That if you give a simple wedding things will be good there and good here.[13]

སྟོན་མོ་སྟོན་མོ་བཟེ་ནོ་འདི་སྟོན་མ་ཤེས་ས་སྟོན་གནམ་སྟོན་ཡས་ན།

But if you give a lavish wedding without knowing what weddings are,

བསྟུན་ཆོར་དུས་ཐྲིག་ག་བསྟུན་ཡག་ཡིན་ནོ།

then by the end, it will be a complete embarrassment.

ངས་མ་གསང་དེ་རིང་བཤད་ཡག་ཡས་ནི་ཟེར་རྒྱུས།

B: Are you praising or are you ridiculing?

ཁ དཁྱོད་བསྟོད་པ་ཡིན་གོ་ཉེས་ན་རོ་མཆོང་འདུ་གོ་ཉེས།

A: *Ya*, of course it's praise. If I praise this *khatak* in my hand,[14]

ཀ ཡ། བསྟོད་པ་ལོས་ཡིན་བཟེ་ར། ངའི་ལག་གི་ཁ་བཏགས་འདི་བཟོ་བསྟོད་པ་རྣམ་གསུམ་རེ་འཐེན་ན།

It didn't come from the highlands, but from the lowlands.

འདི་སྟོད་ནས་མ་ཆད་སྨད་ནས་ཆད་བཞག

It came from China, the land of kings.

སྨད་རྒྱ་ནག་རྒྱལ་པོའི་ཡུལ་ནས་ཆད་བཞག

---

13 The Tibetan འགྲོ་བདེ་འདུག་བདེ། literally means going well and staying well and is used to refer to a simple wedding. ཡར་བདེ་ཆུར་བདེ། "good there and good here" parallels this, and suggests that it will be good for both families.

14 In this and several following sections, the Tibetan literally translates as "pull the three praises of." Pulling praise (བསྟོད་པ་འཐེན།) is commonly used in Tibetan wedding speeches, as does the number three. Though playing on the auspiciousness of the number three, the number of praises frequently exceeds three.

10. Careful Village's Wedding

It should be said that when this was brought to the highlands it was a ceremonial scarf for *lamas*,

འདི་སྟོད་ལ་ཁྱེར་ན་བླ་མ་བཙོའི་མཇལ་དར་ ཤིན་ན།

when this was carried to the lowlands it was a leader's judicial scarf,

འདི་སྨད་ལ་ཁྱེར་ན་དཔོན་པོ་བཙོའི་ཁྲིམས་ དར་ཤིན་ན།

and when this was brought to the gathering, it was an entertaining scarf for singers.

འདི་ཁྲོམ་པའི་གྱལ་ལ་ཁྱེར་ན་གླུ་བ་གླུ་མ་ བཙོའི་ཅེད་དར་ཤིན་ན་ཟེར་རྒྱུས།

B: Do that! Do that! Use *khatak* as playthings.

ཁ དེ་བྱོས། དེ་བྱོས། ད་ཁ་བཏགས་ཅེད་སྤྱད་བྱོས།

A: Uh, if I praise this bowl in my hand,

ག ཨ། ད་དའི་ལག་གི་དཀར་ཡོལ་འདིར་བསྟོད་ པ་རྣམ་གསུམ་རེ་འཐེན་ན།

It didn't come from the highlands but from the lowlands.

འདི་སྟོད་ནས་མ་བྱུད་སྨད་ནས་བྱུད་བཟིག

It came from the Jingdezhen in China.[15]

སྨད་རྒྱ་ནག་ཅིན་ཏེ་མཁར་ནས་བྱུད་བཟིག

The older men said, "It's worth a horse."

ཏུ་ཨ་ཁུ་འཚོགས་གས་རྟ་བཟིག་འབབ་གི་ བཟེ་བཟིག

The older women said, "It's worth a female yak."

མ་སུ་མོ་འཚོགས་གས་འབྲི་བཟིག་འབབ་གི་ བཟེ་བཟིག

The boys said, "Is it fake?" [then to B]

བུ་ཚོ་བོ་འཚོགས་གས་རྫུན་མ་ཨེ་ཡིན་ན་ བཟེ་བཟིག

Aro, I don't need to speak of the eight-spoked wheel etc. on the bowl, do I?

ད་འདིའི་ཨ་རོ་ཁ་ན་འཁོར་ལོ་རྩིབས་བརྒྱད་ ཅན་པོ་ད་བཤད་མི་དགོག

---

15 A city in Jiangxi Province. Since the Ming Dynasty (1368–1644), Jingdezhen (景德镇) has been famous centre for Chinese porcelain making.

B: There's no need for that. Just say what's in it.	ཁ མི་དགོ་གི་ནང་ན་ཆེ་བཞག་ཡོད་ནི་ཤོད་ལ་ ཐོངས་ར་དི་རེད།
A: It has the stuff you like in it!	ག ཁྱོད་ན་དགའ་དགའ་ནོ་དེ་ཡོད་རྒྱུ་རེད།
B: It should have alcohol, shouldn't it?	ཁ ཆང་ཡོད་རྒྱུ་རེད་མོ།
A: *Ya*! If praise the cool nectar in this bowl,	ག ཡ་ད་དགར་ཡོལ་འདིའི་ནང་གི་བདུད་རྩི་ བསིལ་མ་འདིར་བསྟོད་པ་རྣམ་གསུམ་རེ་ ཡས་ན།
In Upper Ngari they planted white barley,	སྟོད་མངའ་རིས་ཡུལ་ནས་ནས་དཀར་བཏབ་ བཞག
And they say that they had white barley like white conch shells.[16]	ནས་དཀར་དུང་དཀར་འདུ་འདུ་ཡོད་ནི་ཟེར་གི
In U-Tsang, in the middle, they planted blue barley,	བར་དབུས་གཙང་ཡུལ་ནས་ནས་སྔོན་བཏབ་ བཞག
And they say they had blue barley like pigeons.	ནས་སྔོན་ཕུག་རོན་འདུ་འདུ་ཡོད་ནི་ཟེར་གི
In lower Amdo and Kham they planted grey barley,	སྨད་མདོ་ཁམས་ཡུལ་ནས་ནས་སྐྱ་བཏབ་ བཞག
And they say they had grey barley like pheasants.[17]	ནས་སྐྱ་ནེ་སྐྱ་འདུ་འདུ་ཡོད་ནི་ཟེར་གི
It should be said that the essence of the three-colored barley is called cool "nectar."	ནས་ཁ་མདོག་གསུམ་གི་ཉིང་ཁུ་འདིའི་མྱིང་ད་ བདུད་རྩི་བསིལ་མ་ཟེར་ར་ཟེར་གི་ཟེར་རྒྱུས།
B: I would know it even without you telling me.	ཁ དི་ད་མ་བཤད་ན་ར་ཤེས་གི་ར།

---

16 This refers to both the size and the colour, as do the lines immediately following.
17 Likely a reference to the Tibetan eared pheasant (Crossoptilon harmani).

A: *Ya*, when you say "boil the *chang*," it is boiled like dry yak horns.[18]

ཀ། ཡ། ད་ཆང་བཙོས་ཐལ་བཙོས་ཐལ་བཟེ་དུས་ན་གཡག་རྭ་སྐམ་པོ་བཙོ་བཙོ་ཡས་བཟིག

When you say "lay out grain for *chang*!" it's like laying an eighty-year-old woman down.

ཆང་བསླལ་ཐལ་བསླལ་ཐལ་བཟེ་དུས་ན་བརྒྱད་བཅུའི་རྒན་མོ་སྒྲོལ་སྒྲོལ་ཡས་བཟིག

when you say, "scoop out the *chang*!" it's done like receiving a newborn baby!

ད་ཆང་ལོངས་ཆང་ལོངས་བཟེ་དུས་ན་གཅེས་པའི་བུ་ཕྲུག་ལེན་ལེན་ཡས་བཟིག

B: Oh, I know how to make *chang* and can also drink it.

ཁ། ཨོ། ཆང་ད་ལས་ར་ཤེས་ནི་རེད་དུ་འཐུང་ར་ཐུབ་ནི་རེད།

A: *Ya*, it should be said that if one drinks a mouthful of this *chang* their mind becomes clear like an eaglet.

ཀ། ཡ་ད་ཆང་འདི་ཧུབ་གང་འཐུང་ན་རྒྱམ་ཤེས་གསལ་ནས་བླག་ཕྲུག་གི་ལོག་འགྲོ་ཟེར་གི

If one drinks two mouthfuls, their bravery increases like a tiger cub.

ཧུབ་དོ་འཐུང་ན་སྙིང་སྟོབས་རྒྱས་རས་སྟག་ཕྲུག་གི་ལོག་འགྲོ་ཟེར་གི

If one drinks three mouthfuls, their stomach drags like a piglet.[19]

ཧུབ་གསུམ་འཐུང་ན་ཏོ་པ་ར་མི་ཁྲིག་ཏུག་ཕྲུག་གི་ལོག་འགྲོ་ཟེར་གི་ཟེར་རྒྱས།

B: That's terrible.

ཁ། དེ་ད་ཅིག་ཙོག་ག

A: It should be said that if a high *lama* drinks it, he shows signs of his spiritual attainments.

ཀ། འདི་མཆོན་པོ་བླ་མས་འཐུང་ན་གྲུབ་རྟགས་སྟོན་ན་ཟེར་གི

If a large leader drinks it, he shows signs of wisdom.

ཚོན་པོ་དཔོན་པོས་འཐུང་ན་མཁས་རྟགས་སྟོན་ན་ཟེར་གི

And if fools like you and me drink it, we show signs of madness.

བླུན་པོ་ཁྱོ་དང་ང་འདྲ་བ་བཟེ་འཐུང་ན་སྨྱོ་རྟགས་སྟོན་ན་ཟེར་རྒྱས།

---

18 This refers to the amount of time required to boil the dry yak horns.
19 Suggesting that they become fat when they drink too much.

B: *Aro*, so there's a difference based on who drinks the alcohol?

ཁ། ཨ་རོག་ཅང་ཁ་ན་བྱུད་པར་ཡོད་ནི་རེད།

A: It should be said: elders please don't drink this, or you won't see the path.

ཀ། འདི་ལོ་ལོན་བཟེས་མ་འཐུང་ལམ་སྟེ་མི་རིག

Grown ups, please don't drink this, or you won't complete your work.

དར་མ་བཟེས་མ་འཐུང་དོན་དག་མི་འགྲུབ།

Youths please don't drink this, or you won't be able to settle down.

གཞོན་པ་བཟེས་མ་འཐུང་ཁྱིམ་གཞིས་མི་ཟིན།

Cadres, please don't drink this, or you won't have a good reputation.

འདི་ལས་བྱེད་བཟེས་མ་འཐུང་ཁ་ལས་མི་དགེ

Students please don't drink this, or you won't get good marks.

སློབ་མ་བཟེས་མ་འཐུང་སྐར་མ་མི་ལོངས།

If you know how to drink this, it is medicinal nectar,

འདི་འཐུང་ཤེས་ན་བདུད་རྩི་སྨན་ཧྲས་ཡིན་ར།

But if you don't know how to drink it, it is evil poison.

འཐུང་མ་ཤེས་མ་རབ་དུག་ཧྲས་ཡིན་ཟེར་རྒྱས།

B: *Ya*! So you're saying it's ok to drink a bit!

ཁ། ཡ་དེ་བཞིན་ན་ཚོ་གི་ཅིག་གི་རེ་འཐུང་གི་བསྐྱད་ན་ཆོག་ག་བཞེ།

A: Oh! For people like you it's better to say nothing than to tell you not to drink.

ཀ། ཨོ། ཁྱི་འདུ་འདྲོ་བཞི་ཅང་མ་འཐུང་ཟེར་རགས་གོ་ཅང་མ་བཤད་ན་ཧ་ནི་རེད་ལ།

B: As if you won't drink when told to, right?

ཁ། ཁྱི་ད་འཐུང་བཞེ་ན་ར་འཐུང་ནི་མ་ར།

A: [to B] Ah, shut up! [continuing with the speech]

ཀ། ཨ་ཁ་རོག

Ya, so now if I make an offering with this ambrosial liquor, and speak the gateways of speeches,

ཡ་ད་དས་བདུད་རྩི་ཅང་གི་མཆོད་ཀ་རེ་འཕང་ནས་གཏམ་གྱི་སྒོ་མོ་རྣམ་གསུམ་བཟོ་ཅིག་བཤད་ན།

It should be said that this liquor offering is the gateway to food,	སྐྱེམས་ཕུད་ཆང་འདི་ཟས་སྒོ་ཡིན་ཟེར་གི
the thirty consonants are gateway to speech,	ཀ་ཁ་སུམ་ཅུ་དག་སྒྲ་ཡིན་ཟེར་གི
alalamo is the gateway to songs,[20]	ཨ་ལ་ལ་མོ་གླུ་སྒོ་ཡིན་ཟེར་གི
playing jokes is the gateway to conversation,	གུ་རེ་ཅེད་མོ་གཏམ་སྒོ་ཡིན་ཟེར་གི
studying knowledge is the gateway to revenue,	ཤེས་བྱ་ཡོན་ཏན་སྦྱངས་ན་ཡོང་སྒོ་ཡིན་ཟེར་གི
only raising livestock is the gateway to losses,	ཕྱུགས་ཟོག་ཁོ་ན་འཚོས་ན་ཡལ་སྒོ་ཡིན་ཟེར་གི
doing anything is the gateway to expenditure,	དོན་དག་ཅི་བཟིག་སྒྲུབ་ན་འགྲོ་སྒོ་ཡིན་ཟེར་གི
and the sure thing these days is the back door.[21]	དེང་སང་བསམ་རྒྱུ་མེད་ནོ་སྦྱག་སྒོ་ཡིན་ཟེར་གི་ཟེར་རྒྱུས།
B: *Lakso! Lakso!* I think that's definitely true!	ཁ་ ལགས་སོ། ལགས་སོ། བོས་བདེན་བསམ་གི
A: *Ya,* so if I give a speech of great things,	ཀ་ ཡ་ད་གཏམ་གི་ཆེ་བ་རྣམས་གསུམ་བརྗོད་ཅིག་བཤད་ན།
It should be said that the weddings are with great fame.	བག་ས་ར་སྟོན་མོ་སྙིང་ཆེ་གི
The invited guests are of great importance.	བོས་པའི་མགྲོན་པོ་གལ་ཆེ་གི

---

20 *alalamo* is a common set of vocables used by a singer when singing a folk song as the opening.

21 Here Menla uses the repeated use of སྒོ "door" to change from "gateway," to a sarcastic comment on the importance of "using the back door" (Ch., *zou hou men* 走后门) or using connections to get ahead in modern China.

The uninvited guests have great hopes.

མ་བོས་མགྲོན་པོར་རེ་ཆེ་གི

The bridal party have great greed,

ཨ་ཞང་ཚང་ད་ཧེབ་ཆེ་གི

The hosts have great generosity,

གཉེན་ཚང་ཚང་ད་སྟོངས་ཆེ་གི

Careful Village has a great gathering,

སེམས་ཆུང་སྡེ་བའི་ཁྲོམ་ཆེ་གི

And I—the speechmaker—have great courage!

ང་བཤད་ཀྱི་ཞི་ལིའི་སྙིང་ཆེ་གི་ཟེར་གི་ཟེར་ཆུས།

B: You're certainly not the person you were at the beginning!22

ཁ ད་དང་མ་གི་དི་མ་ར།

A: *Ya*, so if I give a speech of small things:

ཀ ཡད་གཉུམ་གི་ཆུང་བ་རྣམས་གསུམ་བཟོ་ཅིག་བཤད་ན།

It should be said that in the world, people are small.

འཛིག་རྟེན་ཁམས་ན་མི་ཆུང་གི

In Tibet—the land of snows—I'm a nobody,

གངས་ཅན་བོད་ནས་ང་ཆུང་གི

most brides are young,

བག་མ་ཕལ་ཆེར་ལོ་ཆུང་གི

and they have little power in front of their mothers-in-law.

ཨ་ནེ་སྟུན་ནས་དབང་ཆུང་གི་ཟེར་གི་ཟེར་ཆུས།

B: Tibetan girls generally have no status, so how could a new bride get power so easily?

ཁ བུད་བོད་ཀྱི་བུད་མེད་ལ་ཐོབ་ཐང་མེད་ལ་མནའ་མ་སོ་མ་བཟིག་ག་དབང་ཆ་བསོ་མོ་བཟིག་གང་ན་ཡོད་ཉིས།

A: *Ya*, so if I give a speech of the things that are many,

ཀ ཡད་གཉུམ་གི་མང་བ་རྣམས་གསུམ་བཟོ་ཅིག་བཤད་ན།

---

22 Here B points out that Menla Jyab previously says he is not brave and refers to himself as an "inferior man."

10. Careful Village's Wedding

It should be said that in Lhasa, there are many pilgrimage destinations,	ལྷ་ས་ན་མཇལ་ས་མང་ནི་ཟེར་གི་
in Ngawa, there are many businesspeople,	རྔ་བ་ན་ཚོང་བ་མང་ནི་ཟེར་གི་
in Ziling there are many scholars,	ཟི་ལིང་ན་མཁས་པ་མང་ནི་ཟེར་གི་
and in Tibet in general, there are many monks.	སྤྱིར་བོད་ཡུལ་ན་གྲྭ་བ་མང་ནི་ཟེར་གི་ཟེར་གྱུས།
B: It probably is more or less like that.	ཁ། ཕལ་ཆེར་དེ་མོ་བཟིག་ཡིན་ན་བད།
A: Ya, so if I give a speech of the things that are few,	ག ཡ་ད་འཛིག་ཏྲེན་གི་ཉུང་བ་རྣམས་གསུམ་བཤོ་ཅིག་བཤད་ན།
It should be said that there are few villages that don't have grassland disputes,	རྩྭ་ས་ཙོད་བྱེད་མེད་པའི་སྡེ་བ་ཉུང་ནི་ཟེར་གི་
there are few monasteries that maintain pure religious discipline,	ཆོས་ཁྲིམས་གཙང་མ་ཅན་གྱི་དགོན་སྡེ་ཉུང་ནི་ཟེར་གི་
there are few schools that teach culture completely and systematically,	རིག་གནས་མ་ལག་ཚང་བའི་སློབ་གྲྭ་ཉུང་ནི་ཟེར་གི་
there are few leaders who only do things for the general public,	སྤྱི་དོན་རྐྱང་རྐྱང་བསྒྲུབ་བའི་དཔོན་པོ་ཉུང་ནི་ཟེར་གི་
there are few lamas without beautiful consorts,	དྲིག་མ་ཡག་མ་མེད་པའི་བླ་མ་ཉུང་ནི་ཟེར་གི་
and there are few children these days who speak Tibetan.	དེང་སང་བོད་སྐད་ཤེས་པའི་བུ་ཕྲུག་ཉུང་ནི་ཟེར་གི་ཟེར་གྱུས།
B: Indeed! Indeed! I agree!	ཁ དེ་ཡིན། དེ་ཡིན། འཐད་པ་ཡིན།
A: Ya, so if I give a speech of things that are fitting:	ག ཡ་ད་གཉིས་གི་མཇའ་བ་རྣམས་གསུམ་བཤོ་བཤད་ན།

It should be said that it's fitting if Tibetan proverbs are spoken in the crowd today.

It's fitting if a Chinese knife hangs from the groom's waist,

it's fitting if the beautiful fur of a "three-valleys" fox is worn on the bride's head,²³

and it's fitting if the essence of this ambrosial liquor wets the orator's lips.

B: *Aro*! So aren't you wanting a dram even as you're telling people not to drink?

A: *Ya*, so if I give a speech of things that are inappropriate,

It should be said that it's inappropriate if educated cadres engage in sectarian disputes,

it's inappropriate if monks with shawls play **billiards**,

It's inappropriate if earring-wearing women are belligerent drunks,²⁴

And it is inappropriate if an eight-year-old boy smokes cigarettes.

---

23 "Three valley's fox" is a stock formula in Tibetan verbal art, and the *gya* (རྒྱ) refers to the fox's longest and best hair.

24 Literally, "act out alcohol's faults."

10. Careful Village's Wedding

B: True! Have you seen that nowadays some have cigarettes in their mouths that are longer than they are tall?

ཁ བདེན་གི་ད་བར་རང་གི་རིང་ཅུག་ཅུག་ཁ་ནང་
ང་བཅུགས་ཡོད་ནོ་མེ་རིག

A: *Ya*, so if I give a speech about respect

ག ཡ་ད་གཏམ་གི་གུས་པ་རྣམ་གསུམ་བཟོ་ཅིག་
བཤད་ན།

It should be said that among the cadres you must respect teachers,

ལས་བྱེད་ནང་ནས་དགེ་རྒན་བགུར་དགོ་ནི་
ཟེར་གི

In the village you must respect women,

སྡེ་བའི་ནང་ནས་བུད་མེད་བགུར་དགོ་ནི་
ཟེར་གི

among your family you must respect your elders,

ཁྱིམ་ཚང་ནང་ནས་ལོ་ལོན་བགུར་དགོ་ནི་
ཟེར་གི

the good daughter-in-law must respect her mother-in-law,

མནའ་མ་བཟང་པོས་ཨ་ནེ་བགུར་དགོ་ནི་
ཟེར་གི

the good groom must respect his father-in-law.

མག་པ་བཟང་པོས་ཨ་ཞང་བགུར་དགོ་ནི་
ཟེར་ཆུས།

B: Truly, it's important that everyone respects teachers!

ཁ དོ་མ་ཚང་མས་དགེ་རྒན་ཚོ་ཅིག་བགུར་རྒྱུའི་
ད་གལ་ཆེ་གི

A: *Ya*, so if I give a speech of the praises:

ག ཡ་ད་གཏམ་གི་བསྟོད་པ་རྣམ་གསུམ་བཟོ་ཅིག་
བཤད་ན།

It should be said that the auspiciousness of the New Year must be praised with weddings,

གནམ་ལོ་གསར་བའི་དགེ་མཚན་འདི་ཏྲགས་
ར་སྟོན་མོས་བསྟོད་དགོ་ནི་ཟེར་གི

the rows [of guests] in this gathering place must be praised by many singers,

ཁྱིམ་པའི་གྲལ་གི་རིམ་པ་འདི་གླུ་བ་མང་པོས་
བསྟོད་དགོ་ནི་ཟེར་གི

the wise scholars must be praised,

ཡོན་ཏན་ཅན་གི་མཁས་པ་བསྟོད་དགོ་ནི་
ཟེར་གི

the loving husbands and wives must be praised,

བཅེ་འདུད་ཅན་གྱི་བཟའ་ཟླ་བསྟོད་དགོ་ནི་ཟེར་གི

and the jealous must be praised by themselves.

ཕྲག་དོག་ཅན་གྱིས་རང་ཉིད་བསྟོད་དགོ་ནི་ཟེར་ཆུས།

B: That's an example of the bad praising themselves![25]

ཁ ངན་པས་རང་བསྟོད་ཟེར་བའི་དཔེ་རེད་ལ།

A: *Ya*, so if I give a speech about arrogance,

ཀ ཡ་དུ་གཏམ་གྱི་ཁེངས་བ་རྣམ་གསུམ་བཟོ་ཅིག་བཤད་ན།

It should be said that an incompetent monk is arrogant when a *taru*[26] is placed in his hand,

བན་ཆོས་མེད་ལག་གཱ་ཏུ་བཞག་ན་ཁེངས་ནི་ཟེར་གི

A foolish guy is arrogant when he obtains some power.

བླུན་པོའི་ལག་ག་དབང་ཆ་ཐེམ་ན་ཁེངས་ནི་ཟེར་གི

An ugly girl is arrogant when a mirror falls into her hands,

མ་ཡག་མེད་ལག་ག་དོ་ལྟ་ཕོར་ན་ཁེངས་ནི་ཟེར་གི

And if money falls into the hands of a fickle person, he is arrogant.

སྒྱི་མདོ་མེད་ལག་ག་སྒོར་མོ་ཡོང་ན་ར་ཁེངས་ནི་ཟེར་གི་ཟེར་ཆུས།

B: Many people are just plain arrogant, too.

ཁ རང་ང་རང་ང་ཁེངས་བསྡུད་ཡོད་ནི་ར་མང་ནི་རེད།

A: *Ya*, so if I give a speech about happiness.

ཀ ཡ་དུ་གཏམ་གྱི་དགའ་བ་རྣམ་གསུམ་བཟོ་ཅིག་བཤད་ན།

It should be said that if at this wedding people sing songs, dance, and don't drink, the village will be happy.

སྟོན་མོ་འདིར་ཆང་འཐུང་མེད་ལ་གླུ་ཞེན་གར་རྩེ་ཡས་ན་སྡེ་བ་དགའ་ནི་ཟེར་གི

---

25 This refers to the previous line.
26 A type of ritual drum with strikers on strings that will swing and hit the drum faces when twirled.

10. Careful Village's Wedding

The in-laws will be happy if their daughter-in-law is kind and hard-working.

མནའ་མ་བཟང་མོ་ཡིན་ནས་ལས་ཀ་ཡོད་ན་
ཨ་ནེ་ཨ་སྨྱེས་དགའ་ནི་ཟེར་གི

If the bride is beautiful and respectful, the groom will be happy.

བག་མ་མོ་སྒྲོ་ཡོད་ལས་བཅེ་སྒྲོ་སྤྱན་ན་མག་
པ་ཞི་མི་དགའ་ནི་ཟེར་གི

And if they have a child after the wedding the in-laws will be happy.

ཇ་ནས་གཉེན་སྒྲིག་ཡས་རས་བུ་ཕྱུག་སྐྱེས་ན་
ཨ་ནེ་ཨ་སྨྱེས་དགའ་ནི་ཟེར་གི་ཟེར་ཀྱུས།

B: If they're still not happy with a daughter-in-law like that, then what can be done?

ཁ་ དེ་མོ་མནའ་མ་ཡོད་ན་ད་རུང་མི་དགའ་ན་
ད་ཆེ་བཟིག་ཡེད་ཀྱུས།

A: *Ya*, so if I give a speech about joyfulness,

ཀ་ ཡ་ད་གཏམ་གི་སྐྱིད་པ་རྣམ་གསུམ་བཟོ་ཅིག་
བཤད་ན།

It should be said that if the young boy is smart and hard-working, his teacher is joyful.

བུ་རིག་པ་ཡག་གས་བཙོན་པ་ཆེ་ན་དགེ་རྒན་
སྐྱིད་ནི་ཟེར་གི

If the son is worldly and good at business, his parents will be joyful;

བུ་མཆོད་རྒྱ་ཡངས་དས་ཆོང་ད་མཁས་ན་པ་
མ་སྐྱིད་ནི་ཟེར་གི

if a woman is wise and kind to all, her husband will be joyful.

མ་ཤེས་རྒྱ་ཆེ་ཡས་ཀུན་ན་བྱམས་ན་པོ་སྨྱེས་
སྐྱིད་ནི་ཟེར་གི

If the wedding is good—with prepared meat, tea, and liquor—the guests are joyful,

ཤ་ཇ་ཆང་བསྒྲིགས་གས་སྟོན་མོ་བཟང་ན་
མགྲོན་པོ་སྐྱིད་ནི་ཟེར་གི

and if the speech is articulate and in good meter, I am joyful.

གཏམ་ཁ་ལྗེ་དག་གས་ཆིག་ཀྲང་བདེ་ན་ང་
དགེ་སྐྱིད་གི་ཟེར་གི་ཟེར་ཀྱུས།

B: By the *Yum*, if it's not.

ཁ་ ཡུམ་ཅིག་མ་རེད་ན་གོ

A: *Ya*, so if I give a speech about gatherings,

ཀ་ ཡ་ད་གཏམ་གི་འདུས་པ་རྣམ་གསུམ་བཟོ་
ཅིག་བཤད་ན།

it should be said that all have gathered on Careful Village's ground:

glorious leaders with high seats have gathered,

fake *lamas* with little money have gathered,

boastful wanderers have gathered,

and new thieves without standards have gathered.

སེམས་ཆུང་སྡེ་བའི་ས་ཐོག་ག་མ་འདུས་པ་གཅིག་ཀྱང་མེད་གི

རྒྱབ་བརྒྱག་མཐོན་པོ་ཅན་གྱི་དཔོན་པོ་བཏིང་པོ་འདུས་གི

མ་རྩ་མེད་པོ་མེད་ནི་བླ་མ་རྫུན་མ་འདུས་གི

སྐད་ཆ་རོམ་པོ་བཤད་ནི་འཁྱམ་པོ་སྦོམ་པོ་འདུས་གི

སེམས་ན་ཁ་མ་མེད་ནི་རྐུན་མ་སོ་མ་འདུས་གི ཟེར་གི་ཟེར་རྒྱུས།

B: True! They won't leave the old female yaks behind. Even the old nanny goats shouldn't be left in their sight.

ཁ ཏོ་མ་རེད། འབྲི་རྐན་མ་ཚོད་ཆེ་སྐྱུར་ར་རྐན་མ་ཚོར་རིག་ས་བཞག་ནས་འརྫོག་རྒྱུ་མེད།

A: *Ya*, so if I give a speech of the things that trot,

ཀ ཡད་གཅུམ་གྱི་འདུར་བ་རྣམས་གསུམ་བརྗོ་ཅིག་བཤད་ན།

In the azure blue sky, the little black raven trots in search of food;

དགུང་ལ་སྔོན་ཡག་གི་གོང་བ་ནས་བུ་པོ་རོག་ནག་ཆུང་གཟན་ན་འདུར་གི

From the top of the mountain with the beautiful base, my ancestors and descendants trot after livestock;

རི་རྩ་བ་ཡག་གི་རྩེ་མོ་ནས་རང་པ་རིང་བུ་རྒྱུད་ཕྲག་ཧྲིར་འདུར་གི

And today, in this auspicious age, I trot after knowledge again and again.

དུས་བསྐལ་བ་ཡག་གི་དེ་རིང་བཟོ་བོ་ཡོན་ཏན་ཤེན་གྱི་ཡང་ཡང་འདུར་གི ཟེར་རྒྱུས།

B: And you trot after money!

ཁ ཁྱི་སྦྱོར་མོ་ལེན་གྱི་འདུར་ནི་ཡིན་ད།

A: *Ya*, so if I give a speech about things that are busy:

ཀ ཡད་གཅུམ་གྱི་མི་དལ་བ་རྣམས་གསུམ་བརྗོ་ཅིག་བཤད་ན།

It should be said that when burning *suru*, your hands are busy;[27]

When riding a bike your feet are busy;

When chewing gum your mouth is busy;

And the minds of those who think of high-ranking leadership positions are busy.

B: If their minds are busy then that's what they deserve, since they aren't satisfied with an appropriate rank.

A: *Ya*, so if I give a speech about things that are harmonious:

It should be said that the sun, moon, and stars are harmonious in the sky;

tea and milk are harmonious on the stove;

thieves and bandits are harmonious on the road;

the bridal party and groom's party are harmonious at the wedding;

A speech about things that are harmonious is like that.

---

27   *Suru* (སུ་རུ་) is a species of Rhododendron used for firewood in parts of Amdo. It burns quickly, hence the suggestion that someone's hands will be busy.

B: *Ya*, enough! Enough! So do you have anything to say other than these "things that are" speeches?[28]

ཁ ཡ་ཚོག་གི་ཚོག་གི། ཁྱོད་ད་རྣམ་པ་གསུམ་ཏག་ཏག་མིན་ནས་བཤད་རྒྱུ་མེད་ནི་རེད།

A: Of course I do! *Ya*, I will praise the bride!

ག ལོས་ཡོད། ཡ་ད་ངས་བག་མ་བསྟོད་པ་ཡིན་རྒྱུ་རེད་མོ།

B: *Ya*.

ཁ ཡ།

A: *Ya*! It should be said that her skin is red like coral;

ག ཡ་ད་ཕ་རྩ་བྱུ་རུའི་དམར་ཡིན་ནོ།

her eyes are mottled like onyx;

སྤྱིག་རྩ་མཆོང་གི་ཁྲ་ཡིན་ནོ།

her teeth are white like conch shells;

སོ་རྩ་དུང་གི་དཀར་ཡིན་ནོ།

She's beautiful like Tara.[29]

མོ་སྒྲོ་སྒྲོལ་མའི་སྐུ་ཡིན་ནོ།

Today's bride,

དེ་རིང་གི་བག་མ།

Tomorrow's daughter-in-law,

ནངས་ག་གི་མནའ་མ།

the mother of the world!

འཇིག་རྟེན་གྱི་ཨ་མ་ལགས།

The elders gathered like vultures,

དཀྱུད་པོ་ཚོ་གྲོད་པོ་འཚོགས་འཚོགས་ཡས།

the matchmaker trotted around like a mountain wolf,

བར་བ་བརྗེ་རི་སྤྱང་འདུར་འདུར་ཡས།

your parents sat like distillers,[30]

ཕ་མ་བརྗེ་ཆང་མ་འདུག་འདུག་ཡས།

making plans like chess on a square board,[31]

ཁོག་རྩིས་གྲུ་བཞི་འགྱིག་འདུ་འདུ་དེད་ལས།

---

28 In traditional Tibetan oratory, many verses describe "three types" of things or people (though the actual number may not be limited to three). These are translated here as "things that are" because that phrase is most commonly used for "three types of" (རྣམ་པ་གསུམ།) is not translated literally in this text.

29 Tara is a female Boddhisattva associated with compassion.

30 Suggesting that they are paying close attention.

31 Suggesting that they examine the situation from every angle.

10. Careful Village's Wedding

having discussions that were circular like a drum,	གྱིས་ཁ་གོར་མོ་རྔ་འདྲ་འདུ་བསྒུར་རས།
And you, girl, were given as a bride.	བུ་མོ་ཁྱོ་བག་མ་བྱིན་བཏང་ནི་རེད་ཟེར་རྒྱས།
B: Of course they gave her, that's why they are having a wedding!	ཁ བྱིན་བཏང་ངས་པོ་སྟོན་མོ་ཡོད་གོ་ནི་ལོས་ཡིན།
A: *Ya* so, girl, you are probably not like this, but	ག ཡ་ད་བུ་མོ་ཁྱོ་བཟོ་དེ་མོ་ཚེ་ཡིན་དུ།
it should be said that when some unfortunate ones hit the road, they were told:	ལས་ངན་ལ་ལ་ལམ་ལ་འཕུད་གོ་དུས།
"get married and we'll give you silk and lambskin robes."	ཁྱི་གནས་ལ་སོང་ར་གོས་ཆར་གོས་ལུ་བཟོ་ཟེར་ར།
"braid your hair and we'll buy you gold, silver, turquoise and coral."	ཁྱིས་དྲུའི་སྐྲ་སྒྲེས་ར་གསེར་དངུལ་གཡུ་བྱུར་ཉོ་ཟེར་ར།
"Hit the road and you will have so many things."	ཁྱི་ལམ་མ་ལོངས་ར་ཡོད་སྟོལ་མོད་སྟོལ་བཟོ་བཤད་ལ།
"please don't cry, my dear, just go get married!"	ངའི་ལོ་ལོ་མ་ཏུ་གནས་ལ་སོང་ཟེར་ར།
And nobody except me knows that you, ill-fated one, don't have freedom over your own body.	ཁྱི་ལས་འན་རང་ལུས་རང་དབང་ན་མེད་ནོ། ང་མིན་ནས་ཅིག་གིས་ཤེས་གི་ར་མེད་གི།
B: You may know, but there's nothing you can do!	ཁ ཁྱིས་ཤེས་རུང་བཀོད་པ་མེད་ལ།
A: *Ya*, now if you, who are like Sengcham Drukmo, go get married,[32]	ག ཡ་ད་སེང་ལྕམ་འབྲུག་མོ་འདྲ་བའི་བུ་མོ་ཁྱོ་གནས་ཡུལ་ལ་སོང་ན།

---

[32] Sengcham Drukmo is the wife of the epic hero, King Gesar. In many Tibetan oral traditions, women are compared positively to Sengcham Drukmo as a paragon of feminine beauty.

It should be said that you must be wary of your mother-in-law's mouth;	ཨ་ནེ་གི་ཁ་འདིར་སེམས་ཆུང་ཡེད་དགོ
You must be wary of father-in-law's mind;[33]	ཨ་མྱེས་གི་ཁོག་འདིར་སེམས་ཆུང་ཡེད་དགོ
Be wary of your sister-in-law's ear;[34]	སྙེད་མོ་གི་རྣ་འདིར་སེམས་ཆུང་ཡེད་དགོ
You must be wary of your husband's hand;[35]	པོ་སླྱེས་གི་ལག་འདིར་སེམས་ཆུང་ཡེད་དགོ
You must be wary of your neighbour's gossip;	ཁྱིམ་མཚེས་གི་མཁན་འདིར་སེམས་ཆུང་ཡེད་དགོ
And if you're not spared despite your wariness, you don't need to stay, just come back home!	འདུག་མི་དགོ་ཁྱི་དགོ་ཕྱིར་ལ་ཐོག་ཟེར་རྒྱུས།
B: *Aro*, do you have that kind of power? And then?	ཁ ཨ་རོ། ཁྱོད་དི་མོ་དབང་ཚ་ཨེ་ཡོད་ལ། དི་ནས་ད།
A: Then I should praise the groom.	ག དི་ནས་ད་དས་མག་པ་བསྟོད་པ་ཡེད་རྒྱུ་རེད་མོ།
B: *Ya*.	ཁ ཡ།
A: *Ya*, it should be said that in robes, you're as straight as an arrow.	ག ཡ་ད་གོས་ཚ་དུའི་ནད་ནས་མདའ་སྨྱུག་གི་དང་ཡིན་ནོ།
On a horse you're light like a tuft of white wool.	རྟ་འདོ་བའི་གོང་ནས་བལ་དགར་གི་ཡང་ཡིན་ནོ།
In front of your enemies, you're quick like lightning,	དག་ནག་པོའི་སྤྱན་ནས་གློག་ཞགས་གི་ལྱུར་ཡིན་ནོ།
last year's nomad,	ན་ནིང་གི་འབྲོག་པ།

---

33   Suggesting that the father-in-law may not say much if he is unhappy, but keep it close to his chest.

34   Suggesting that the bride would be wise not to confide too much in the sister-in-law.

35   Suggesting a potential for domestic abuse.

10. Careful Village's Wedding

today's groom, | དེ་རིང་གི་མག་པ།

and a future father! | མ་འོངས་པའི་ཨ་ཕ་ཁྱོ།

From today you've gotten married. | དེ་རིང་ནས་བཟུང་དོན་དག་བཅོས་བཏང་ནི་རེད་ཟེར་རྒྱུས།

B: He has done it. | ཁ བཅོས་བཏང་ནི་རེད།

A: It should be said that your family added an old *mdzo* on top of the old horse;[36] | ཀ དཁྱེད་གས་རྟ་རྒན་ཐོག་ག་མཛོ་རྒན་བཞག་གས།

handed off your sister and took some female yaks; | སྲིང་མོ་བསྒྱལ་ཡས་འབྲི་མོ་བླངས་ནས།

exchanged all of your valuables for money; | དགའ་མོ་ཡོངས་རྫོགས་སྒོར་མོར་བརྗེས།

The reason you bought the wealth of the ocean[37] was for the purpose of getting a wife while you're still young. | རྒྱ་མཚོའི་ནད་གི་རྒྱུ་རྫས་ཉོ་དོན་ཁྱོ་ཆུང་རགས་ག་ཆུང་མ་བཞིག་ལེན་རྒྱའི་ཆེད་རེད་ཟེར་རྒྱུས།

B: He knows that. | ཁ ཤེས་ནི་རེད།

A: *Ya*, it should be said that this wife for whom you gave your wealth, isn't just your cook for life. | ཀ ཡ་ད་རྒྱུ་བྱིན་གི་ཆུང་མ་འདི་ཚེ་གང་གི་ཇ་མ་མིན་ནོ།

And that this valuable human body isn't bought at any price. | རིན་ཆེན་གི་མི་ལུས་འདི་གོང་ཆེན་གིས་ཉོ་རྒྱུ་མེད་ནོ།

And it should be said that when there isn't equal status and a balance of power, I'm not sure you'll be able to keep this wife. | འདུ་མཉམ་ར་དབང་མཉམ་མིན་དུས་ཁུན་མོ་འདི་ཁྱོ་གི་དབང་འདུག་མི་ཤེས་ཟེར་རྒྱུས།

---

36 *Dzo* མཛོ are a hybrid formed from crossbreeding a yak and cow.
37 This refers to coral, and possibly otter pelts, which were both highly valued in Tibetan communities at the time.

B: Now aren't you done giving this wedding speech yet?

ཁ། དསྟོན་བཤད་བཤད་ལམ་ཚར་སོང་ནི་མིན་ན།

A: *Ah*, what are you talking about? Listen!

ཀ། ཨ། ཁྱོ་འདིས་ཅི་ཟེར་གི་ཉོན་རོ།

B: I am listening, but it never ends!

ཁ། ཉན་ད་ཡོད་དུ། ཚར་རྒྱུ་བཟིག་མེད་གོ

A: *Ya*! To you, the dapper happy groom and the stunning beautiful bride:

ཀ། ཡ་ད་སྙིད་གི་མག་གཞིས་ཁྱོ་ལོ། ཡག་གི་བག་མ་ཁྱོ་མོ།

It should be said that what we call a life, if you know how to live it, then it's sweeter than nectar.

འཚོ་བ་འཚོ་བ་བཟེ་ནོ་འདི་རོལ་ཤེས་ན་སྦྲང་རྩི་གི་མངར་ཡིན་ནོ།

What we call a marriage, if you know how to co-exist well, then it's the happiness of the world.

བཟའ་ཚང་བཟའ་ཚང་བཟེ་ནོ་འདི་འདུག་ཤེས་ན་འཇིག་རྟེན་གི་སྐྱིད་ཡིན་ནོ།

What we call a family, if you know how to take good care of it, it will be your home for your whole lives,

ཁྱིམ་ཚང་ཁྱིམ་ཚང་བཟེ་ནོ་འདི་སྐྱོང་ཤེས་ན་ཚེ་གང་གི་ཡུལ་ཡིན་ནོ།

You both must remember this!

ཁྱེད་གཞིས་གས་ཡིད་ལ་འཛིན་དགོ་ཟེར་རྒྱུས།

B: *Laso! Laso!*

ཁ། ལགས་སོ། ལགས་སོ།

A: *Aro*, although I wanted to keep on speaking, Uncle Village Leader interrupted again.

ཀ། ཨ་རོ། ད་རུང་སྨུ་མཐུད་དུ་བཤད་འདོད་ཡོད་དུ། ཡང་ཨ་ཁུ་སྡེ་དཔོན་བར་ར་ཅིག་བཀྱབ་བས།

B: What did Uncle Village Leader say?

ཁ། ཨ་ཁུ་སྡེ་དཔོན་གིས་ཅི་ཟེར་གི

A: [as the village leader] "Compassionate *Alak*, you mustn't be angry, but if you don't stop now, the bridal party is going to hit the road," he said.

ཀ། ཨ་ལགས་ཐུགས་རྗེ་ཅན། ཐུགས་བཀྱལ་བཟིག་བཞེས་མི་ཉན་དུ། ད་མཚམས་མ་བཞག་དུས་ཨ་ཞང་ཚོ་ལམ་མ་ལངས་རྒྱ་རེད་ཟེར་ཡ།

11. Careful Village's Thief
སེམས་ཆུང་སྡེ་བའི་རྐུན་མ།[1]

A: *Aro*! This year Careful Village invited me again.

ཀ བོ་ཨ་རོ། ད་ལོ་ཡང་ང་སེམས་ཆུང་སྡེ་བས་གདན་འདྲེན་བྱས་བཏང་ངོ་།

B: And you played a fake *lama* again.

ཁ ཡང་བླ་མ་རྫུན་མ་བོ་བྱས་བཏང་བཟིག་ག

A: I wrote a *khashag* after I came back, but it still doesn't have a title.

ཀ ཕྱིར་ར་ཡོང་ངས་ཁ་ཤགས་བཟིག་བྲིས་ར་ཁ་བྱང་ད་རུང་མེད།

B: It's fine if you don't have a title. Just tell me what it's about!

ཁ ཁ་བྱང་མེད་ན་འགྲིག་གི་ར་ཁ་ཤགས་གི་ནང་དོན་ཅིག་ཤོད་དྭ།

A: The contents of the *khashag* and the reason they invited me are about the same.

ཀ ཁ་ཤགས་གི་ནང་དོན་ཁོ་ཚོས་ང་འབོད་དོན་ཕལ་ཆེར་གཅིག་རེད།

B: In that case, tell me clearly why they invited you.

ཁ དེ་བཟི་ན་སེམས་ཆུང་སྡེ་བའི་འབོད་དོན་གསལ་བོ་བཟིག་ཤོད་དྭ།

A: When I went, at first even Careful Village's leader couldn't give a clear reason.

ཀ ཨ་སོང་དུང་ད་གསལ་བོ་བཟིག་སེམས་ཆུང་སྡེ་བའི་སྡེ་དཔོན་ན་ར་བཤད་རྒྱུ་མེད་གི

B: *Ya*, what did he say?

ཁ ཡ་ཅི་ཟེར་གི

---

1   A is voiced by Menla Jyab and B is voiced by Phagmo Drashi.

A [as the village leader]: "*Ya*, now compassionate *Alak*, take a rest and sippest thou some tea!" He said.

ཀ ཡ་ད་ཨ་ལགས་ཐུགས་རྗེ་ཅན། ཐུགས་དལ་དལ་བྱོས་ང་བཞིག་བཞེས་ཟེར་ཡ།

B: Oh, anything else?

ཁ ཨོ་དེ་མིན་ནས་མེད་ནི་ཨེ་རེད།

A [as the village leader]: "Well, there are a lot of issues, I'll report at the gathering." He said.

ཀ ཨ། ད་དོན་དག་མང་གི་ར། མང་པོ་འཚོགས་ས་ནས་ཞུ་ཟེར་ཡ།

B: Were they holding another war party?[2]

ཁ ཡང་དམག་འཚོགས་བརྒྱབ་ཡོད་ནི་མིན་ན།

A: [Menla Jyab, as himself] No, no. It was a people's meeting.

ཀ མ་རེད། མ་རེད། མང་ཚོགས་གི་ཚོགས་འདུ་རེད།

B: Oh, oh, in my mind an image of people riding horses had appeared.

ཁ ཨོ། ཨོ། ང་བཟོའི་ཡིད་ལ་ཏུ་ཞོན་ཏུག་ཏུག་ཤར་བཏང་བྱལ།

A: All came on foot, and a lot were barefoot. People were trampling right over each other, *aro*!

ཀ ཚང་མ་ཀང་ཐང་རེད། དུ་རུང་ཀན་རྗེན་ར་མང་གི་ཡ། གྱི་གཅིག་ར་རྒྱུའི་བཟོ་ད་ད་ད་རེད་ཨ་རོ།

B: No place of worship is calm.

ཁ མཇལ་ས་བཞིག་ན་དེ་མོ་འཇམ་ས་བཞིག་གང་ན་ཡོད་ཞེས།

A: After all fell quiet, Uncle Village Leader stood up.

ཀ ཚང་མ་དལ་ཆག་སེར་ཅིག་བསྡད་ནི་ར། ཨ་ཁུ་སྡེ་དཔོན་ཡར་ར་ལངས་བཏང་བྱལ།

B: *Ya*!

ཁ ཡ།

A: [as the village leader] *Ya*, now count them all, young and old, without omitting a single one.

ཀ ཡ་ད་ཁ་རྒན་གཞོན་གཉིས་ཀའི་ཁེར་བཞིག་མ་སྤྱུར་ར་ཚང་ཆེས་བཞིག་བྱོས།

B: None wouldn't have come for an audience.

ཁ མཇལ་གི་ད་མི་ཕྱིན་ནི་བཞིག་མེད་ལ།

---

2 As in the case of the Grassland Dispute.

11. Careful Village's Thief

A: [as the village leader] It's good that none haven't come. Just see if there's an escape for any who won't take an oath before the *lama* today!

ཀ ད་མ་ཡོང་ནི་མེད་ན་ད་གི་དེ་རིང་ད་ཨ་ལགས་ཚང་གི་སྐུ་མདུན་ནས་སྐྱི་རེ་གི་མནའ་རེ་མ་བསྐྱལ་འཚོར་ས་ཞེ་ཡོད་གི་ལྟོས།

B: About what?

ཁ དེ་ཆེ་བཟིག་ཡིན་ནི་རེད།

A [as the village leader]: *Alak*, I am inconveniencing thee, but if I speak in detail, it's like this:

ཀ ཨ་ལགས་ཁྱེད་ག་ལོ་བཀྱལ་རེད་དུ། ཞིབ་མོ་བཟིག་བཤད་ན་འདི་མོ་བཟིག་རེད།

B: Will there be something for you to understand?

ཁ ད་ཅིག་གོ་རྒྱུ་ཞེ་ཡོད་ལ།

A: [as the village leader] The year after thou camest, a *khenpo* named Ra dzu na ma—who was fluent in both Chinese and Tibetan and seemed to be from Kham—came.[3]

ཀ དེ་ལོ་ཁྱེད་ཀ་ཕེབས་ནའི་ཕྱིར་ལོ། རྒྱ་སྐད་བོད་སྐད་ལ་ཐོགས་རྒྱུ་མེད་ནས། ཁམས་ཕྱོགས་གི་ཡིན་ནི་འདྲ་འདྲའི་མཁན་པོ་ར་ཇུ་ན་མ་ཟེར་ནི་བཟིག་ཡོང་ངས།

B: Ra dzu na ma... never heard of him.

ཁ ར་ཇུ་ན་མ། གོ་ར་མ་མྱོང་བཟིག

A: [as the village leader] We built a stupa at the mouth of Thangkoli. Some said that it was blessed, and some said that it couldn't be trusted. Some said, "If this is holy, we will worship it," and some said, "if it is demonic we will destroy it." So what should we do, thou decide. That's it.

ཀ ཐང་ཀོ་ལིའི་ཁ་ནས་མཆོད་རྟེན་བཟིག་བཞེངས་ནི་རེད། ད་ལ་ལས་བྱིན་རླབས་ཡོད་གི་བཟེ་ནི་རེད། ཡང་ལ་ལས་རྟོམ་རྒྱུ་མེད་གི་བཟེ་ནི་རེད། འདི་ལྷ་རྫས་བཟིག་ཡིན་ན་མཆོད་རྒྱུ་བཟེ་ནི་རེད། ད་གདོན་རྫས་བཟིག་ཡིན་ན་བཤིག་རྒྱུ་བཟེ་ནི་རེད། ཡང་ཅེ་བཟིག་ཡེད་རྒྱུ་ཁྱེད་ཀ་མཁྱེན་བཟེ་ནོ་དེ་ཡིན།

B: I bet you told them you wanted to tear it down quickly.

ཁ ཁྱོས་ཡང་རེམ་མ་བཤིག་རྒྱུས་བཟེ་བཏང་རྒྱུའོ་རེད།

---

3 A *Khenpo* (མཁན་པོ་) is a learned *lama* in the Nyingma tradition, or the abbot of a monastery of any sect.

A: [as himself] You make it sound like I am looking for something to tear down.

ཀ ད་བཞིན་དས་བཤིག་རྒྱུ་བཟིག་མ་རྙེད་ལ་འགྲོ་གོས་ཡོད་ད།

B: If you didn't want to tear it down, then did you want to build one as well?

ཁ བཤིག་ན་མི་འདོད་ན་ཡང་བྱིས་ར་ཅིག་ལས་ན་འདོད་ནི་མིན་ན།

A: As if I had nothing better to do!

ཀ ང་ཁོམ་མོང་བཟིག

B: So what will you do?

ཁ འོ་ན་ད་ཅི་བཟིག་ཡེད་རྒྱུས།

A: "What will I do other than speak truthfully: I've said before that I'm a student and not a *lama*. I can't say if it is blessed or not. I need you to fill me in a bit."

ཀ དང་མོ་མི་བཤད་ལ་ཅི་ཡེད་རྒྱུས། ང་བླ་མ་མིན་སློབ་སྦྱོང་མ་ཡིན་སྦྱོལ་གནན་བཞིག་གི་བཤད་བཏང་། ད་བྱིན་རླབས་ཡོད་མེད་བཟོ་བཤད་མི་ཤེས། ཁྱོ་ཚོར་བཤད་རྒྱུའི་ཆིག་འགན་ལ་དགོ

B: What should they tell you?

ཁ ཅི་བཟིག་བཤད་དགོ་ནི་རེད།

A: "First," I said, "Tell me why you needed to build a stupa. Who will tell me?"

ཀ ཐོག་མར་མཆོད་རྟེན་འདི་བཞེངས་དགོ་དོན་བཟོ་ཅིག་ཡོད། སུས་བཤད་རྒྱུ་བཟེ་ར།

B: Again I bet there was no one who could say it clearly.

ཁ ཡང་སུ་ར་གསལ་པོ་བཞིག་བཤད་རྒྱུ་མེད་རྒྱུའི་རེད།

A: There sort of was. Uncle Village Leader stood up again.

ཀ ཡོད་ས་ཡོད་གི ཡང་མ་ཁྱུ་སྟེ་དཔོན་ཡར་ར་ལངས་བཏང་ཐལ།

B: What did he say?

ཁ ཅི་ཟེར་གི

A: [as the village leader] "*Ah, ah, ah*! Dear *Alak*! You would knowest without me needing to tell you! This Thangkoli is not just some hole in the ground."

ཀ ཨ་ཨ་ཨ། ཨ་ལགས་ལོ་ལོ། ཞུ་ཅི་དགོ་ཏུ་གིས་མཁྱེན་ནི་རེད་ད། ཐང་ཀོ་ལི་ཟེར་གོ་ནོ་གན་ད་རང་ད་ཀོ་ཀོ་བཞིག་ཅི་ཡིན།

B: Then what is it?

ཁ དེས་ན་ཅི་བཞིག་ཡིན་ནི་རེད།

A: [as the village leader] "Before it was a hideout for bandits. Nowadays it is a home for thieving dogs."[4]	ཀ གན་སྔོན་ཆད་ཇག་པའི་སྒྲུང་ས་བཟིག་ཡིན། དེང་སང་ཁྲི་རྒུན་ཤུལ་ས་བཟིག་རེད།
B: How many thieving dogs can there be?	ཁ དེ་མོ་ཁྲི་རྒུན་མང་ད་བཟིག་གང་ན་ཡོད་ནས།
A: [as the village leader] "Don't say that there's so many![5] Ah, ah, ah, ah, and now they're numbers have skyrocketed, have skyrocketed. [with a pained voice] *Ayoshe*, my kidneys... *Ya*! Now one of you kids speak."	ཀ ད་མང་ངས་བཟོ་ད་མ་ཟེར་ད། ཨ་ཨ་ཨ་ཨ་ ཨ་ཁ་དར་སོང་། ཁ་དར་སོང་། ཨ་ཡོ་ཤུ། འདི་ མཁལ་མ་འདི་ད། ཡ་ད་ཞ་ཡས་ཚོའི་གཅིག་ གིས་ཤོད་ད་ཟེར།
B: And did a little kid speak?	ཁ ད་ཞ་ཡས་ཆུང་ཆུང་བཟིག་གིས་བཤད་བཏང་ ཐལ།
A: An old granny got up and spoke.	ཀ ཨ་ཡེ་ལོ་ལོན་བཟིག་ལངས་ངས་བཤད་བཏང་ ཐལ།
B: *Ya*?!	ཁ ཡ།
A: [as an old woman] "*Ala*, if the village leader is wrong, then who's right? Damn these thieving dogs. They don't even give us a chance to get a mouthful of meat down our throats.	ཀ ཨ་ལ་སྟེ་དཔོན་གི་ག་མི་བདེན་ན་གང་བདེན་ གོ་ཁྲི་རྒུན་དེ་ཚོའི་རོ་གཅིག་རྟོགས། ཤ་ཁམ་ འབུ་གང་ར་མྱིད་ལ་འགྲོ་ལོངས་མི་སྟེར་གི
B: What did they do?	ཁ ཅི་བཟིག་ཡས་བཏང་ནས་ན།
A: [as the old woman] "After taking meat off the stove and putting it down, I turned around, and when I turned back I didn't know where they had taken it."	ཀ ཤུ་བཟོས་ཁ་ཐབ་ནས་བླངས་ངས་ཐང་ད་ བཞག་བཏང་ངས་ཁ་ལོ་བཟིག་འཁོར་དུས་ གང་ད་ཁྱེར་ནས་ར་མི་ཤེས་གི

---

4 "Before" refers to the "old society," before the communist reforms of 1958.

5 This is a feature of Amdo speech, where despite appearing negative, it means that there are very many.

B: Now where would they have taken it? They would have taken it out.

| ཁ་ དགང་ད་འཁྱེར་རྒྱུས། ཐང་ད་ཕྱིར་སོན་ནི་ ཡིན་རྒྱུའོ་རེད།

A: [as the old woman] "I tell you, *Alak*! That was just an aside. But seriously, those incredible thieving dogs cannot be deterred by locks, let alone being afraid of people in the house. So what can we do?"

| ཀ་ ཨ་ལགས་བཟེ། དེ་བཟོ་བས་རང་ད་འོར་གི་ ཅིག་བཤད་ནིས། ཞེ་ཐག་གི་བཤད་ན་སྟེ་ཕྱི་ རྒྱུན་དར་བ་བོ་ཁྱིམ་གི་མྱིར་ཆེ་སྨུག་ར་སྨས་ གི་ཟ་ར་མི་ཐོགས་གི་ད་ཆེ་ཡིད་རྒྱུས།

B: So these thieving dogs probably come carrying pliers and awls!

| ཁ་ ད་འབིག་ར་སྨམ་པ་བཟུང་ནི་ཁྱི་རྐུན་བཟིག་ ཐོན་བཏང་ནི་ཡིན་རྒྱུའོ་རེད།

A: [as himself] At that time, a bald old man, covered in oil and dirt and wearing glasses with a long yak-hair string for the temple spoke up.[6]

| ཀ་ སྐབས་དེ་ད་རྒན་པོ་མགོ་རོ་སྲུམ་ལོག་ག་ཅིག་ ར་གི་ལྱུང་དུ་ཆིད་སྨུད་ཅན་བཟིག་གིས་ཁ་ བླགས་བཏང་ཐལ།

B: I think he definitely wants to speak.

| ཁ་ ལོས་གླགས་འདོད་གི

A: [as the old man] "*Aro*! By my children's blood! It is not an ordinary thing; it's like witchcraft! When those thieving dogs arrive, no one wakes up and the cattle don't scare. We don't know when they come or when they go."

| ཀ་ ཨ་རོ། ཞ་ཡིས་ཚོའི་ཁྲག ད་བུ་བཟིག་མིན་ཡ། དེ་བྱུད་བཟིག་ཡིན་ཡ། ཁྱི་རྐུན་དེ་ཚན་གོ་ཐོན་ བཏང་དུས་ཐྱེར་སད་རྒྱུ་མེད། ཐོག་ག་འདོག་ རྒྱུ་མེད། ནམ་ཡོང་ནི་མི་ཤེས། ནམ་སོང་ནི་ མི་ཤེས།

B: They wouldn't let you know when they were coming.

| ཁ་ ཤེས་ནི་ཡས་ད་མི་ཡོང་རྒྱུའོ་རེད་ད།

---

6   This description gives the sense who is not particularly careful about his personal hygiene, and probably very poor.

11. Careful Village's Thief

A: [as the old man] "If we don't know where they come from or where they go, then we don't know. If we don't know when they come and go, then we don't know. If only they had left footprints going here and there... *Ashirego*!"

ཀ དགར་ཡོང་འདིར་ཡོང་ར་མ་ཤེས་ན་མ་ཤེས། ནམ་ཡོང་ནམ་སོང་ར་མ་ཤེས་ན་མ་ཤེས། ད་གར་སོང་དེ་སོང་གི་རྐང་རྗེས་བཞག་ཡིན་རུང་བཞག་བཏང་རྒྱུ་ན། ཨ་ཤི་རེ་གོ

B: I guess there aren't any thieving dogs who wear leather boots.

ཁ དཕྱི་རྐུན་གོ་ལྷམ་གོན་ནི་བཞིག་ད་མེད་ལ།

A: [as an old man] "I don't know what method they use. They probably do wear boots, since they don't need any yaks but those with the best skins." He said.

ཀ ཅི་བཞིག་གི་བཀོད་པ་འཐེན་བཏང་ཤེས་ན་མ་ཤེས་ནོ་མིན་ནས། གོ་ལྷམ་ད་གོན་ཡོད་རྒྱུའི་རེད། གཡག་གོ་གཞི་དགའ་བོ་ཚན་གོ་མིན་ནས་མི་དགོ་གི་ར་ཟེར་ཡ།

B: What did he say? The dogs drove the yaks off?

ཁ ཅི་བཟེ། ཁྱིས་གཡག་དེད་འགྲོ་ནི་ཨེ་རེད།

A: [as himself] I didn't understand either. I asked Uncle Village Leader, and...

ཀ ངས་ར་ཏུ་མ་གོ་ཨ་ཁུ་སྦྲེ་དཔོན་ན་དྲིས་ཤེས་ར།

B: What did he say?

ཁ ཅི་ཟེར་གི

A: [as the village leader] "These so-called thieving dogs are human thieves. While they are 'human thieves' they are also 'thieving dogs.' Except that some have tails and some don't, they're all thieves. Now if they're not thieving dogs, then what are they?" [To B] Do you understand now?

ཀ ཁྱི་རྐུན་བཟེ་ནོ་མི་རྐུན་རེད། མི་རྐུན་བཟེ་རུང་ཁྱི་རྐུན་རེད། རྔ་མ་ཡོད་མེད་བཞིག་གི་ཁྱད་པར་མིན་ནས་ཚང་མ་རྐུན་མ་རེད། ད་ཁྱི་རྐུན་མ་ར་ཅི་བཞིག་རེད། ད་གོ་ཐལ།

B: [with a voice of sudden realization] Oh, now I understand. Those so-called thieving dogs are human thieves. The so-called human thieves are thieving dogs. In actuality they are thieves.

ཁ ཨོད་གོ་ཐལ། ཁྱི་རྐུན་བཟེ་ནོ་མི་རྐུན་རེད། མི་རྐུན་བཟེ་ནོ་ཁྱི་རྐུན་རེད། དོ་མ་བཏང་ན་རྐུན་མ་རེད་ལ།

A: [as himself] Exactly!

ག མ་འཁྲུག་ཐལ།

B: So the ones that sleep in Thangkoli are also human thieves.

ཁ དེ་བཟེ་ན་ཐང་ཀོ་ལིའི་ནང་ན་ཉལ་ཡོད་ནོ་ར་མི་རྐུན་རེད་ལ།

A: [matter-of-factly, as himself] Sure are! The ones without tails!

ག མིན་ནས་ད་ང་མ་མེད་ནོ།

B: Even if you reported it to a real *lama*, he wouldn't be able to do anything to the human thieves without tails.

ཁ ང་མ་མེད་ནོ་མི་རྐུན་ད་བླ་མ་དོ་མ་བཞིག་ག་ཞུས་ར་བཀོད་པ་མེད་ལ།

A: There was nothing they could do, so last year they invited this *"Ra dzu na ma."*

ག བཀོད་པ་མེད་ལ་ད་ན་ཞིང་ར་ཙུན་མ་བདག་གོ་ཞུས་ཞིས་ཟེ་ཡ།

B: What did this *"Ra dzu na ma"* say?

ཁ ར་ཙུན་མ་བདག་གོས་ཆེ་ཟེར་གི

A: "Oh! He said, don't look down on him who has come from elsewhere. Build a stupa at the mouth of Thangkoli, and there will be no escape for you thieving dogs.

ག ཨོ། ཧོ་ཐང་ནས་ཡོང་ནི་བཞིག་ག་མཐོང་ཆུང་མ་ཡེད། ཐང་ཀོ་ལིའི་ཁ་ནས་མཆོད་རྟེན་བཞིག་བཞེངས་ད་བཏང་ར། ཁྱོ་ཁྱི་རྐུན་བཞིག་ག་འཚོར་ས་ཆེ་ཡོད་ད།

B: What did he say he would make happen?

ཁ ཆེ་བཞིག་ཡས་འཛོག་ག་ཟེར་གི

A: "Even when those that were human thieves have become thieving dogs, then if they don't grow tails then they can say 'he is not a real *lama*.'" He said.

ག ད་ཁྱི་རྐུན་བཞིག་ཡིན་རུང་ཁྱི་རྐུན་བཅས་བཏང་ཚར་དུས། ང་མ་བཞིག་མ་སྐྱེས་ན་ཧོ་བླ་མ་མ་རེད་བཟེ་ར་ཆོག་ཟེར་གི་ཟེར།

11. Careful Village's Thief

B: *Oya*! How powerful!   ཁ ཨོ་ཡ། ཅི་མོ་གཉན་པོ་བཟིག་ཡིན་ན།

A: From the time they heard this speech until the stupa was built....   ཀ སྐད་ཆ་དེ་གཅིག་གོ་ནེ་ར་མཚོད་རྟེན་དེ་གཅིག་འགྲུབ་རྒས་གོ

B: The thieves got fewer, didn't they?   ཁ རྐུན་མ་རེ་ཉུང་ད་ཕུད་སོང་ནི་མིན་ན།

A: They said that the thieves grew in number!   ཀ རྐུན་མ་རེ་མང་ད་ཕུད་ཐལ་ཟེ།

B: [matter-of-factly] So they are growing tails. And then?   ཁ དྲ་མ་སྨེས་གི་དེ་ནས།

A: So listen to what Uncle Village leader said.   ཀ ད་ཨ་ཁུ་སྦྲེ་དཔོན་གི་སྐད་ཆ་ཉོན་རོ།

B: What did he say?   ཁ ཅི་ཟེར་གི

A: [as the village leader] At that moment, those with tails were nowhere to be found. Really, as soon as we completed the stupa, there was not even a footprint of a thief.   ཀ ད་ཁ་མ་དེ་ནས་ང་མ་སྨེས་རྒྱུའི་བཟོ་གང་ནས་སྣང་ར། ངོ་མ་མཚོད་རྟེན་འགྲུབ་ནེ་ར་རྐུན་མ་བཟིག་གི་ཀྱང་རྗེས་ར་མ་བརྒྱབ་ཐལ།

B: So they must have been afraid of growing a tail.   ཁ ད་རྲ་མ་སྨེས་ཨེ་འཛོག་ག་སྣག་གོ་ནི་མིན་ནས།

A: [as the village leader] But before long, there were also thieves who did not fear tails.   ཀ ཅང་མ་འགོར་ཐལ། རྲ་མ་མི་སྣག་བའི་རྐུན་མ་ར་ཡོད་གི

B: Oh, that's bad.   ཁ ཨོ། ད་མ་བ་ནི་རེད།

A: [as the village leader] First, we lost a strong nanny goat, round and white like a potato. And yet, there was no talk of people having tails.   ཀ སྔོན་མ་ཡས་ར་མ་ཉེད་ཅན་ཡུད་མ་གི་ལོག་གས་བསྲུད་ཡོད་ནི་བཟིག་བོར་ཐལ། ཅང་ད་རྲ་མ་ཡོད་ནིའི་སྐད་ཆ་མ་གོ་ཐལ།

B: Perhaps the thief was clever and hid the tail inside the pouch of his robe.   ཁ རྐུན་མ་སྤྱང་པོ་བཟིག་ཡིན་ནས་རྲ་མ་རུམ་མ་བསྡུས་བསྲུད་ཡོད་ནི་ཡིན་རྒྱུའི་རེད།

A: [as the village leader] "Now, if you're a thief who doesn't fear growing a tail, then I won't begrudge you one doe."

ཀ། དྰོ་ཁྱུན་མ་ངྰ་མ་སྐྱེས་རྒྱུའི་མི་སྐྲག་ན། ང་ར་ར་མ་གཅིག་ག་སེར་སྟུ་མེད།

B: Fair enough.

ཁ། དེ་བཟོ་རེད།

A: [as the village leader] "I thought so at that time, but looking back I was wrong."

ཀ། དེ་དུས་དེ་མོ་འདོད་ལ་ར། དེང་སང་བལྟས་ན་ནོར་སོང་བཞག

B: Ya?

ཁ། ཡ།

A: [as the village leader] Now this tail-less thief, wasn't satisfied with one goat.

ཀ། ད་འདི་རྒྱུན་མ་ངྰ་མ་མེད་ནོ་འདི། ར་མ་གཅིག་གིས་མ་ཚིམས་ཐལ།

B: How many goats did he take?

ཁ། ཡང་ར་མ་དུ་ཁྱེར་སོང་བཞག

A: [as the village leader] Then in addition to the goat, he took a *tulma*.[7] Now I'm certain that they didn't grow tails.

ཀ། ཡང་ར་མ་མ་གཏོགས་ག་ཕུལ་མ་བཞག་མེད། ཐལ། ང་མ་མ་སྐྱེས་ཁོ་ཕག་ཅད་ཐལ།

B: Oh, so they really didn't grow tails.

ཁ། ཨོ་ད་དོ་མ་ངྰ་མ་མ་སྐྱེས་ནི་རེད།

A: [as the village leader] And because they didn't grow tails, it all went wrong again.

ཀ། ངྰ་མ་མ་སྐྱེས་ནོའི་སྟབས་གིས་ཡང་ལམ་མ་མ་སོང་།

B: And they grew braver right?

ཁ། ད་སྟོབས་པ་རྗེ་ཆེར་བུད་སོང་ནི་རེད་མོ།

A: [as the village leader] But why would they stop at the doe and the *tulma*. They've also taken our pregnant mares.

ཀ། ད་ར་མ་ཕུལ་མ་ཆེ་སྐྱར་ར། ཆོད་མ་རྟེའུ་མ་ར་ཁྱེར་འགྲོ་གི

---

7   Tulma, ཕུལ་མ། is a term for young, newly mature and very strong female yaks.

11. Careful Village's Thief

B: Oh, that thief didn't need anything other than female livestock?

ཁ། ཨོ། རྐུན་མ་དེར་མོ་ཕྱུགས་མིན་ནས་མི་དགོ་ས་ཡོད་ག

A: [as the village leader] He's not only satisfied with the females.

ག དེའི་མོ་ཕྱུགས་རྐྱང་རྐྱང་བཞིག་གིས་མི་ཚིག་གི་ཡ།

B: He wouldn't be.

ཁ། ཚིག་རྒྱུ་མ་རེད་མོ།

A: [as the village leader] "So he chooses the strongest of male sheep. He picks the strongest and fattest yak bulls and cows from the flock. He steals everything, from big things like horses, cattle, and sheep to small things like household items such as like nuts and bolts. How can people survive?" he said.

ག དཔ་བཟན་ཤེད་ཅན་བསལ་འཛོག་གི་གཡག་སྤྲམ་འབྲི་སྤྲམ་འཕྲུས་འཛོག་གི་ཚེ་ན་ཏུ་ནོར་ལུག་གསུམ་རྒྱུ་གི་ཆུང་ན་མཛོར་མ་མཛོར་ཏྲེན་འདུ་བརྒྱུ་གི་སེམས་ཅན་དེས་ཁ་སོས་རྒྱུ་ཞི་རེད་ཟེར་ཡ།

B: That's understandable. Dealing with that thief is difficult.

ཁ། དོ་ས་ཁག་མེད་གི་རྐུན་མ་དེ་ཅིག་དག་འ་རྒྱུ་རེད།

A: [as himself] As soon as Uncle Village Leader sat down, someone next to him stood up.

ག ཨ་ཁུ་སྤྱི་དཔོན་མར་ར་བཅོག་མ་བཅོག་ག་ཅིབ་ནས་གཅིག་ཡར་ར་ལངས་བཏང་ཐལ།

B: Who would that be?

ཁ། སུ་ཡིན་ནས་ན།

A: I didn't know who it was, but I clearly saw that his two front teeth were covered with iron.

ག སུ་ཡིན་འདི་ཡིན་བཟོ་མ་ཤེས་ར། མདུན་སོ་གཉིས་ག་ལྕགས་གིས་ཕན་ནོ་ལ་གསལ་པོ་བཞིག་རིག་གི

B: Why are you talking about the teeth in his mouth? Listen to the speech coming from his mouth!

ཁ། ཁྱོ་དེའི་ཁ་ནང་གི་སོ་གི་ཚེ་ཡེད་རྒྱས། ཁ་ནང་གི་ཁ་བརྗོད་ནོ་རོ།

A: [in the slightly higher voice of another man] That thief, by both my parents' flesh, did not grow a tail, but if he grows a tail, I hope he doesn't grow it from the normal place but from his cervical spine.

ག རྐུན་མ་ཡིན་ན། དེ་དུ་མ་གཉིས་གའི་ག དེ་ང་མ་བཟིག་སྐྱེས་རྒྱུ་མེད་ནོ་མིན་ནས། སྐྱེས་རྒྱུ་ཡོད་རྒྱུ་ན། དེ་སྐྱེས་པོ་ནས་མ་སྐྱེས། དེ་སྨེ་ཚིགས་ནང་ནས་གཅིག་སྐྱེས་དགོ

B: If it didn't grow from the normal place, it wouldn't have grown from his cervical spine either.

ཁ། དངོས་པོ་ནས་མ་སྐྱེས་དུས་སྐྱེ་ཚོགས་ནད་ནས་དངོས་ནི་མ་ར།

A: [the man with the iron teeth] By both my parents' flesh, that bastard's misdeed should be exposed but wasn't. It's embarrassing to tell someone about it. He's shameless!

ག དུ་མ་གཉིས་ཀའི་ཤ་གི་ཤུག་ག་སྟོན་རྒྱུའི་ཤུག་ག་སྟོན་རྒྱ་མེད་གི་བཟེ་ན་མིན་ནས་ཅིག་ག་བཤད་སོལ་མེད་ལ། དོ་ཚ་རྒྱ་མེད་ལ།

B: If he had any shame, would he be stealing?

ཁ་ དོ་ཚ་རྒྱ་ཡོད་ན་རྐུས་ཡེད་ནས།

A: [the man with the iron teeth] Old spinster Granny Lugu Jyi's only lamb was taken.[8] It wasn't an eagle. If it had been an eagle, wouldn't it have left the tether behind?

ག ཨ་ཨེ་རྒན་ཆང་ལུ་གུ་སྐྱིད་གི་ལུ་གུ་གཅིག་གོ་ར་ལས་མ་དུད་བཏང་བཞིན་ དེ་ར་བཞིག་སྒྲ་མ་རེད་མོ། སྒྲ་ཡིན་རྒྱུ་ན་རྟོད་ཐག་དཔུལ་ན་བསྐྱུར་མེད་ནས།

B: He also made off with the tether?

ཁ སྤྱི་གིས་རྟོད་ཐག་ར་ཁྱེར་སོང་བཞིག་ག

A: [the man with the iron teeth] "Who knows how many cartons of cigarettes he smoked with that lamb's skin. May he grow wings."[9]

ག ལུ་གུ་དེའི་ཚ་རུ་ཁ་གི་ཡང་དོ་བག་ཆ་དུ་འཐེན་ཡོད་ཉིས་ཆེ་གོ་གཏོག་སྟོ་སྐྱེས་རྒྱ་བདོག་གོ་ཟེར་ཡ།

B: What a nice turn of phrase comes from that pair of silver teeth.[10]

ཁ དེ་དངུལ་སོ་གཉིས་ཀའི་བར་ནས་སྨད་ཆ་ད་བསོ་མོ་ཏག་ཏག་ཡོང་ག

A: Oh! And what Granny Lugu Jyi said was even better, *aro*!

ག ཨོ། ཨ་ཨེ་ལུ་གུ་སྐྱིད་གི་སྨད་ཆ་དེའི་ར་ཧུ་རེད་ཨ་རོ།

B: What did Granny Lugu Jyi say?

ཁ ཨ་ཨེ་ལུ་གུ་སྐྱིད་གིས་ཆི་ཟེར་གི

---

8 ཀུན་ཆང་། translated here as "spinster," is a derogatory term for an unmarried woman, possibly divorced but not widowed, who lives in a separate household, and is old enough to have grown-up children.
9 Here "may he grow wings" is a curse.
10 Note that the speaker has (perhaps kindly) changed Menla Jyab's description of "iron teeth" to "silver teeth."

A: [as Granny Lugu Jyi] If only that lamb hadn't come to me. If only it had been led by a quick ewe instead of being raised by such an old woman, then it certainly wouldn't have fallen into the thief's hands.

ཀ བྱང་ལུ་གུ་དེ་ངའི་ལག་ག་མི་ཡོང་རྒྱུ་ན། དེ་རྒན་མོ་འདི་མོ་བཟིག་གིས་གསོ་རགས་གོ་མ་མོ་མགྱོགས་མོ་བཟིག་གིས་ཁྲིད་ཡོད་རྒྱུ་ན། རྐུན་མ་དེའི་ལག་ག་མ་ཤོར་ཁོ་ཐག་ཡིན།

B: That might be true.

ཁ དེ་བཟོ་བདེན་ན་ཐང༌།

A: [as Lugu Jyi] I am a surrogate mother for that lamb. That thief certainly has a mother too. Ama, ama! While he could carry off that droma-like one, he couldn't kill it, could he?[11]

ཀ ང་ལུ་གུ་དེའི་ཨ་མ་གི་ཁ་མ་རེད། རྐུན་མ་དེ་ར་ཨ་མ་བཟིག་ལོས་ཡོད། ཨ་མ་ཨ་མ། གྲོ་མ་བཟིག་འདི་འདྲོ་དེ་ཅིག་གི་འཁྱེར་ཕུབ་རུང༌། གསོད་ཕུབ་ནས།

B: The old woman thought that someone had killed it.

ཁ རྒན་མོས་ཅིག་གིས་བསད་བཏང་བཟིག་འདོད་གོ་ག

A: [as Granny Lugu Jyi] Not only did they kill it, they butchered it, and having butchered it, made off with its skin.

ཀ བསད་ནི་མི་ཆད་བཤས་བཏང་བཞིབས་བཏང་ནས་ཕྱུན་པགས་ཁྱེར་སོང་བཞིག

B: Oh then...it was really killed![12]

ཁ ཨོད། ཏོ་མ་བསད་བཏང་བཞིག་གོ

A: [as Granny Lugu Jyi] And they left the corpse behind. It would have been better if they had just left the tether.

ཀ ད་ཕ་ཧྲུད་ཕྱུལ་ནས་བསྐུར་བཏང་བཞིག་དེ། བསླུས་གི་ཐོད་ཐག་བསྐུར་བཏང་རྒྱུན་ར་ཚོག་ག

B: That's true.

ཁ བདེན་གི་མོ།

---

11 Droma (གྲོ་མ།), known by the Latin name *potentilla anserina L.*, is valuable for its sweet roots, the lumpy shape which Lugu jyi is evoking with this simile. Menla Jyab also uses it for the "a" vowel sound to create assonance with "ama."

12 This phrase means both that the thief killed the lamb, and that the speaker feels sorry for the pain this caused Lugu Jyi.

A: [as Granny Lugu Jyi] If that damned one had to "end a life," If only he had killed me rather than that lamb. I'm more than ready to die.

B: Slaughtering her only lamb really killed Lugu Jyi.[13]

A: [As Lugu Jyi] No! He needed money, not some old woman, and so the lamb died before Lugu jyi could. The saying "Birth happens in a certain order, but death doesn't follow it," is true!

B: Oh. The old woman is over-thinking things!

A: [as the old woman] I have a lot to think about! I have a lot to think about!

B: So what did she have to think that much about?

A: [as Lugu Jyi] I feel compassion for the lamb. I also feel compassion for the thief.

B: How can that be?

A: [as Lugu Jyi] When I think about that lamb, I close my eyes, and I can still hear it bleating in my ears. *Om mani padme hum.*

B: Fair enough.

---

13 Lugu Jyi's name literally means "happy with lambs"

11. Careful Village's Thief

A: [as Lugu Jyi] And if I think about that thief, I wonder what will happen to him in the afterlife? *Om mani padme hum*

ཀ ངས་རྐུན་མ་དེར་འདད་བཟིག་བཀྱབ་ན། དེ་ཚེ་ཕྱི་མ་སོང་ན་ཆེ་བཟིག་ཡིད་རྒྱུས། ཨོྃ་མ་ཎི་པདྨེ་ཧཱུྃ།

B: She's so kind-hearted that she is even concerned for the thief.

ཁ སེམས་བཟང་ཡིན་བཏང་ན། དུ་རུང་རྐུན་མ་བཟོ་སེམས་ཁུར་ཡིད་གོག

A: Uncle Village Leader stood up again.

ཀ ཡང་ཨ་ཁུ་སྦྲེ་དཔོན་ཡར་ར་ལངས་བཏང་ཐལ།

B: So he will comfort that kind-hearted granny.

ཁ ད་ཨ་ཡེ་སེམས་བཟང་མ་དེར་སེམས་གསོ་བཟིག་ཡིད་རྒྱུ་རེད་མོ།

A: [as the village leader] Old woman, now don't worry about that thief. Thieves these days end the lives of freed livestock,[14] they sure don't give a thought to the afterlife. If they're not afraid, then why should we fear for them?

ཀ རྐུན་མོ། ད་རྐུན་མ་བཟོ་སེམས་ཚོགས་མ་ཡིད། དེང་སང་གི་རྐུན་མས་ད། ཐོག་ཆེ་ཐར་ར་བཏང་ངས་བཞག་ཡིད་ནོའི་ཚེ་སྲོག་བཟོ་བཅད་འཇིག་གི་ར། ཕྱི་མ་བཟོ་བབ་གི་འདད་རྒྱག་ནི་མ་རེད། དེ་ཁོ་ཚོ་མི་སྐྲག་ན་ཨུ་ཚོ་འཛིགས་གས་ཆེ་རྒྱུས།

B: True, true.

ཁ དོ་མ་རེད། དོ་མ་རེད།

A: [as the village leader] Now those things that have fallen into the thieves' hands are lost. The main thing is to be diligent with what we still have.

ཀ ད་རྐུན་མའི་ལག་ག་ཤོར་སོང་ནོ་ཤོར་སོང་ནི་རེད། གཙོ་བོ་ཤུལ་ན་ཡོད་ནོ་ཕུ་རེ་ཡིད་དགོ་ནི་རེད།

B: It can't be that bad.

ཁ དེ་ར་བཟོ་ར་ཆི་གོ་ར།

A: [as the village leader] Truthfully, those tailless thieving dogs won't let the cattle sleep nor will they let the people rest.

ཀ དོ་མ་ཚན་གིས་ཧ་མ་མེད་ནོ་ཁྱི་རྐུན་དེས་ད་ ཐོག་ཤུལ་གི་ཆེ་འཐུག་ར་ཕྱི་ར་འདུག་གི་མི་ འཐུག་གི

---

14 This refers to the practice of life release. Also mentioned above in "The Dream" (Chapter 3, Note 60).

B: So what did he say they do to people?

A: [as himself] He said that they didn't let them sleep.

B: *Ona*, didn't he say that neither dogs nor people could hear the coming of the thieves?

A: That's what I said, but Uncle Village Leader said that he didn't say that.

B: *Ona*?

A: [as the village leader] "If we wait for the thieves to come, we stay up night after night, and they only come on the nights we've fallen asleep" he said.

B: If they come when they're awake, what can they get hold of?

A: [as the village leader] "Sleeplessly we kept our eyes peeled for a long time. *Ah, ah, ah,* how long we waited for those thieves" he said.[15]

B: It's better to come up with a plan than just sit and wait.

A: [as the village leader] We came up with plenty of plans. As a last resort, we tied horses to the stupa at the mouth of Thangkoli with tethers.

---

15 The word རེ་བསྒུས། used by the village leader is usually used to refer to something people look forward to. Here it is used sarcastically.

11. Careful Village's Thief

B: Would that be helpful?

ཁ་ དེ་བཟོ་ཕན་ཐོགས་ཨེ་ཡོད་ལ།

A: [as the village leader] Who knows if they really were afraid of the *lama*, or afraid of growing a tail, but we didn't even see the footprint of a thief.

ག ངོ་མ་བླ་མ་སྐྲག་ནས་ན་ཧ་མ་སྐྲག་ནས་སུས་ཤེས་ར། རྐུན་མ་བཟིག་གི་རྐང་རྗེས་མ་རིག་ཐལ།

B: So it was helpful!

ཁ་ ཕན་ཐོགས་ཡོད་ག

A: [as the village leader] We said it was a blessing! Before long, every one of the horses was handed over to them.

ག ཕྱིན་རླབས་རེད་བཟེ་ཅད་མ་འགོར་ར་ཧ་རྒུན་ ཚོ་ཁ་ཚང་ད་སྤྲེར་ཕྱིན་བཏང་ནི་རེད།

B: The thieves drove them away too!

ཁ་ ཡང་རྒུན་མས་དེད་སོད་བཟིག་ག

A: If they were like bandits of the past who rode horses, the posse could chase them. But thieves these days ride in cars. Who can catch them?

ག སྔོན་ཆད་གི་ཇག་པ་ཏ་ཞོན་འདུ་འདུ་ཡིན་ན་ ར་མདའ་རྒྱགས་མོ། དེང་སང་གི་རྐུན་མ་བྲེ་ ཞོན་བཟོའི་ཐ་སུས་ཚོད་གི

B: Once they reach the road, you won't know which direction they went.

ཁ་ ལམ་མ་གཅིག་ཞུགས་བཏང་ཚར་རས་གང་ས་ བཟིག་ག་སོང་ནས་ར་ཤེས་རྒྱུ་མ་རེད་ཡ།

A: [as the village leader] "We don't know where they went, they're modern thieves. If they went to India or China, where would I, who doesn't know anything but Tibetan, go to look for them?"

ག དེ་གང་ང་བུད་ཐལ་ཟེར་རྒྱུ། དེང་རབས་གི་རྐུན་ མ་རེད་མོ། སྟོད་རྒྱ་གར་ར་སོང་གི་སྲད་རྒྱ་ནག་ ག་སོང་ན། ང་བོད་སྐད་མིན་ནས་མི་ཤེས་ནི་ བཟིག་གང་ང་བཙལ་གི་འགྲོ་རྒྱུ།

B: Fair enough.

ཁ་ ཁག་མེད་གི

A: [as the village leader] "Damn it all. As soon as we began saying that this stupa was not blessed, a vulture-like horse returned home;[16] now how do you explain that?" he said.

ཀ བྱ་འདི་ན་བྱ་འདི། མཆོད་རྟེན་འདིར་བྱིན་རླབས་མེད་ཀྱི་བཞེ་བཞད་མ་བཞད་ལ། རྟ་གོད་བྱ་གོད་འདུ་བཞིག་ཡོད་ནོ་ཕྱིར་ར་ཡུལ་ཐོན་ཐལ་ད་བཞད་ལས་ཇི་ཞེས་ཀྱི་རེད་ཡ།

B: It probably escaped from the thieves.

ཁ དེ་རྐུན་མའི་ལག་ནས་ཐོར་སོང་ནི་ཡིན་རྒྱུ་རེད།

A: At that time, an old man with a number of knots around his neck stood up.[17] [as this old man, addressing the *lama*] "Here in the presence of the Alak, we should speak in truths! We should talk speak in truths!"

ཀ སྐབས་དེ་ད་སྐྱེ་ན་ཕྱུག་མདུད་གང་གང་ཅན་གྱི་རྐེད་པོ་བཞིག་ཧོག་སེ་ཡར་ར་ལངས་བྱུང་ཐལ། ད་ཨ་ལགས་ཡོད་ས་འདི་རེད་གོ་ཨ། ལས་འདན་ཚོ་ལས་རྒྱུ་འབྲས་ཀྱི་སྐད་ཆ་བཤད་དགོ་ཡ། ལས་རྒྱུ་འབྲས་ཀྱི་སྐད་ཆ་བཤད་དགོ།

B: [in agreement] Un, un!

ཁ ཨུན། ཨུན།

A: [as the old man] "There are, in general, many thieving dogs. What special harm could they do? The main thing is that we can't allow a 'conspiracy of dogs and wolves.' If dogs and wolves conspire, it will be difficult for both men and livestock," he said.[18]

ཀ སྤྱང་ཁྱི་རྐུན་ཆེ་ར་མེད་ཀྱི་ནས་ར་ཁེར་རེ་ཆེ་བཞིག་ཡས་བཏང་རྒྱུས། གཙོ་བོ་ཁྱི་སྤྱང་འདྲེས་ཡོད་མི་ཉན་ཡ། ཁྱི་སྤྱང་འདྲེས་ཡས་བཏང་ན་ཁྱི་ཟོག་གཉིས་གས་ཅིག་དཀའ་ནེ་རེད་ཡ་ཞེས་ཡ།

B: It will be difficult.

ཁ ཅིག་ཅིག་འདུག་རྒྱུ་རེད།

---

16 Vulture is a positive metaphor in Tibetan. "Vulture-like horse" then suggests that this is a fast horse that the thieves would probably want to keep. It is not a common expression for horses but is used for the repeated sound of the second syllable in each of the Tibetan words.

17 The "knots" refers to the practice of tying "sacred knots" (ཕྱག་མདུད།), blessed by contact with holy sites and people, around someone's neck. The description suggests the man is very pious.

18 This is phrase from the Cultural Revolution, translating the Chinese phrase *langbei wei jian* (狼狈为奸). Here it suggests that thieves alone aren't the problem, but the people in the village helping them. Thus the metaphor about dogs (the thieves) and wolves (those in the village).

A: So that old man spoke clearly: [as the elder] "Well, the reason I'm using this Cultural Revolution-era proverb, 'the conspiracy of dogs and wolves,' is:

'To stop the thieves from without, you need to defeat the thieves within.

and to defeat the thieves within, then we must unite our strengths.'"

B: That guy has a lot of Cultural Revolution-era language, *aro*!

A: [as the elder] "Ah! I'll say this: In the past,

If you worked a lot, you got a lot,

If you worked a little, you got a little,

Those who didn't work got nothing.[19]

The thieves want to earn capital without working for it. I say that's capitalist thought. And I say we proletarians won't take it."

B: Well put!

A: [as the elder] "Ah! If we were to speak from a Buddhist perspective…"

B: He's going to keep speaking.

---

19 This is a Cultural Revolution era saying, referring to the concept of 'distribution according to work' *anlao fenpei* (按劳分配). The saying translates the Chinese: *duolao duode, shaolao shaode, bulao bude* (多劳多得, 少劳少得, 不劳不得).

A: [as the elder] "I'll say that if you ask whether the causes and consequences of karmic action exist, these days it seems like they don't, but they almost certainly do."[20]

B: That's right!

A: [as the elder] "Ah, I say that if you ate what I had saved would your stomach be comfortable? Oh, and I say that if you impoverish me and it gives you an ulcer then we're both worse off! Instead of that…"

B: What did he say to do?

A: [as the elder] I say it would be better to swear oaths, make *sang* offerings, and give up stealing, and then dismiss the meeting, rather than to block the *lama* in, and regale him about how bad the thieves are.[21] How's that? [without pausing] I'm not saying that you guys are forgetting what today's issues are, but I say my sheep are getting away.

B: That's so.

ཀ ལས་རྒྱུ་འབྲས་ཡོད་ནི་ཨེ་རེད་བཟེ་ན། དེང་སང་མེད་ནི་བཟིག་ག་རེག་གི་ར། ཡོད་རྒྱུའི་ཡོད་ནི་རེད་བཟེ་ནོ།

ཁ དེ་རེད།

ཀ ཨ། ངས་གསོག་ནོ་ཁྱོས་ཟོས་བཏང་ན་ཁྱོའི་ཁོག་ག་ཁམས་རྒྱུ་ཨེ་རེད་བཟེ་ནོ། ཨོ་ནའི་ཕོགས་ག་ཁྱོང་བཟིག་བརྒྱབ་བས་ཁྱོའི་ཁོག་ག་སྐྱུན་བཟིག་བཙོས་བཏང་ན་ཨུ་གཉིས་ཀ་མི་ཏུ་ག་བཟེ་ནོ། དེར་བསླུས་གི་ད།

ཁ ད་ཅི་བཟིག་ཡེད་གོ་གི་བཟེ།

ཀ བླ་མ་བཀག་གས་བཞག་གས་རྒྱུན་མ་བྱུ་སྦྱོལ་བཞད་ལས་འདུག་རགས་གོ་བསང་ཏུད་བཏང་ངས། རྒྱས་བཅད་བཏང་ངས་ད་གྲོལ་སོང་ན། ཅི་མོ་རེད་བཟེ་ནོ། དེ་རིང་གི་དོན་དག་བཟེད་ཐལ་བཟེ་ནི་མིན་ར། ང་རང་གི་ལུག་ཚོ་བཞུར་ཐལ་བཟེ་ནོ།

ཁ དེ་བཟོ་རེད།

---

20 This is a highly popular line, and is often quoted in Amdo Tibetan speech.

21 *Sang* (བསང་།) refers to the practice of making "fumigation offerings": burning juniper and other materials as offerings, an essential part of many religious practices on the Tibetan Plateau.

11. Careful Village's Thief

A: [as the old man] Ah, I say: admit past thievery and take oaths not to steal from now on! For me personally, that in 1958 I stole an omasum for my stomach, and I say it was properly dealt with during the Cultural Revolution: I got in a struggle session [for stealing] and one of my ribs was broken. I'll say that after that, by the three jewels, I haven't stolen even a lamb's rib.

B: He's really clean.

A: [as the old man] Ah, by the grace of good policies, our stomachs are full, our backs are warm and our minds are happy. I say that from now on, I won't steal again, by the three jewels! So that's it!" He said.

B: It seems that we can really trust him.

A: [as himself] After that, everyone, young and old, swore serious oaths in front of the big *sang* offering that they hadn't stolen in the past and wouldn't steal in the future.

B: If a few don't end up eating their words, then that's good.[22]

---

22 The Tibetan phrase for breaking one's oath is to "eat" it. Here we use "eating words" as an easy translation.

A: How could they? Making them talk and be embarrassed is better than them eating their words in secret. For example, one young herder held nothing back:

B: What did he say?

A: [embarrassedly, and haltingly as the young herder] Dear Alak, by my father's flesh! *Ah, ah, ah, Atsi atsi, Ah ah ah!*

B: He hasn't revealed a single secret yet!

A: [as the young herder] *Ah, ah,* I'm not not telling it, but I can't say it. *Ah ah, ashirego,* I wish I had some alcohol.

B: Hypocrite! How can someone who can steal not be able talk about it?

A: [as himself] Ah, after an entire afternoon had passed, he finally spit it out.

B: *Ya?*

A: [as the young herder] *Ah, ah, ah!* By my entire lineage. By my father's flesh if I'm not so embarrassed that I'm all red! By my father's flesh, if I won't say it!

B: It'd be better if he just said it.

A: [as the young herder] By my father's flesh, in truth, I found a rein in the mountains, and even though I knew to which family it belonged, I didn't return it, by my father's flesh! From now on, I won't do this again, by my father's flesh!

ཀ ཨ་རྒྱའི་ཕ་དྲང་མོར་བཤད། སྐྱང་ནས་སྒྲུབ་མདའ་བཟིག་རྙེད་ལས་སུ་ཚང་གི་ཡིན་ནི་ར་ཤེས་ར། ཕྱིར་ར་གཅིག་ཕྱིན་ན་ཨ་རྒྱའི་ཕ། དེང་ཕྱིན་ཆད་ད་དེ་མོ་དེ་ཡིན་ན་ཨ་རྒྱའི་ཟེར་ཡ།

B: And what else?

ཁ དེ་མིན་ནས།

A: [as himself] That was it!

ཀ ད་དེ་རེད།

B: Ah, I thought he'd admit to stealing an entire flock of sheep!

ཁ ཨ། དེ་བཟོས་དེས་ལུག་ཁྱུ་བཟིག་ཁས་ལེན་རྒྱུ་ན་འདོད་ལ།

A: Still some discussed why this is difficult for them to accept.

ཀ ད་རུང་ཁ་ཤེར་གིས་ཁས་ལེན་དཀའ་སྟོལ་གི་སྐད་ཆ་ར་བཤད་ཐལ།

B: Who?

ཁ སུ་རེད།

A: Those like Uncle Gontoe.

ཀ ཨ་ཁུ་མགོན་སྟོ་ཅན་པོ་རེད།

B: What did this Gontoe say?

ཁ མགོན་སྟོ་བདག་གོས་ཅི་ཟེར་གི

A: [as Gontoe] We can't keep it secret from the *lama* or from our next reincarnations. Prosperous Village: if we all had admitted and promised, we could just pull our blankets over our heads and go to sleep. But by Rudo's flesh, our burglars really cannot be trusted.[23]

ཀ ཡ། ཕྱི་མ་གསང་ད་བླ་མ་གསང་། གཡང་སྟེ་བོ། ཁ་བླངས་ནས་ཁག་ཐེག་ཡས་བདང་ན་མགོ་རུམ་མ་བཏང་དས་གཉིད་རྒྱང་རེད་དུ། རུ་རྡོའི་ཕ་ཡུ་གཉིའི་རི་ཁོར་ཚོ་ད་རྫོས་རྒྱུ་ཡོད་ནི་མ་རེད་གོ

B: Who were these burglars?

ཁ རུ་ཁོར་ཚོ་བདག་གོ་སུ་སུ་ཡིན་ནས་ན།

---

23 Rudo is a personal name that is being used to create rhymes with Rishor (translated here as burglars) with the first syllables of each being homonyms in Amdo pronunciation.

A: [as Gontoe] Ah. The first is my son who defrocked and fled to Lhasa. And if you speak of Gontoe family's *gewo*,[24] he's like a mountain deity, when you think of him, he'll appear; and he's gone again before the dust settles, and everyone knows that he never leaves empty handed.

ཀ། ཨ། དེད་ཀྱིའི་སྲས་བབས་བས་ཞྭ་ས་ཕྲོས་སོང་ནོ་དད་པོ་རེད། མགོན་ཏོ་ཚང་གི་དགེ་པོ་བཟེ་བཏང་ན། རང་ང་གཞི་བདག་བཟེག་ག་རིག་ག་ཡིད་ལ་གཅིག་དྲན་དུས་ཐོན་བཏང་ནི་རེད། རྡུལ་ཕར་མི་སོང་དུས་ཕྱིར་སོང་ནི་རེད་ལག་སྟོང་ང་མི་འགྲོ་ནོ་མཁྱེན་རྒྱུའི་རེད།

B: That really is like a mountain deity.

ཁ། དོ་མ་གཞི་བདག་བཟེག་ག་རིག་ས་ཡོད་གི།

A: [as Gontoe] So next. Doedoe from the Dada family is the second. He went wandering for a few years, and when he guides the thieves he looks like he is just looking for stray livestock, and we only realize that he is one of the thieves after several months.

ཀ། ཨ། དེའི་འཕྲོ་ད་ད་ཚང་གི་རྡོ་རྡོ་གཉིས་པ་རེད། ལོ་མས་ལོ་འགའ་འགོར་སོང་། རྐུན་མ་ལམ་ཁྲིད་བཏང་དུས་རང་ད་ཕྱུགས་བཙལ་བཟིག་ག་རིག་ག་ཀྱིའི་ཡིན་ནོ་ར་ཟླ་འགའ་འགོར་རས་མིན་ནས་མི་ཤེས།

B: That's the worst, when one can be both a thief and a collaborator.

ཁ། ཨ་བྱུར་གྱི་ཐུ་མོ་བོ། རྐུན་མ་གི་ཕྱི་མ་ནང་མ་གཉིས་ཀ་ཉན་ནོ་རེད་མོ།

A: [as Gontoe] Ah, the third is the one named Ndregordo [horn-less ghost], he doesn't have a father. It seems as though he was expelled from school, but he keeps going back and takes things when he does. He doesn't take anything big, but he takes small things even from his own home.

ཀ། ཨ། གསུམ་པ་ད་འདི་མགོ་རྟོ་ཟེར་གོ་ནོ། ཕ་ཡོད་ནི་མ་རེད། སློབ་གྲྭ་ནས་བདའ་བཏང་ཁ་ལ་བཟིག་རེད་ད། ཕྱིར་ར་འགྲོ་གི་འདུག། གི་འགྲོ་ཁ་འཕྱིར་གི་འདུག་གི་ཆེ་བཟིག་མི་བཀྱུ་ར། ཆ་རེ་ཆུང་ངེ་བོ་ཡུལ་ནས་ཡིན་རུང་ཁྱེར་འགྲོ།

B: So then he is a child thief.

ཁ། ཡང་དེ་རྐུན་ཕྲུག་བཟིག་ཡིན་རྒྱུ་རེད།

---

24   *Gewo* (དགེ་པོ) is a word used to refer to a defrocked monk.

11. Careful Village's Thief

A: [as himself] He said that if we don't make it clear that these three are part of the village, but not part of the oath swearers, then nobody will be able to accept it.

ཀ འདི་གསུམ་པོ་དྲྭ་སྟེ་བའི་གྱུབ་ན་ཡོད་ནོ། མནའ་གི་གྱུབ་ན་མེད་ནོ་མ་ཡས་ན་ཁས་ལེན་ཐུབ་ནིའི་བུ་བཟིག་ཡོད་ནི་མ་རེད་ཟེར་ཡ།

B: That's understandable for them.

ཁ དེ་བཟོ་ར་ཁེར་ཚོ་ར་ཁག་མེད་གི

A: Finally, Uncle Village Leader summed it all up.

ཀ མཐུག་མཐར་ཨ་ཁུ་སྟེ་དཔོན་གིས་སྟི་བསྡོམས་ཡས་ཐལ།

B: Ya.

ཁ ཡ།

A: [as the village leader] Ya, good people, protected by heaven. You were all honest. By admitting all of our secrets, we have accomplished today's task.

ཀ ཡ། ད་གནམ་གིས་སྱུང་རྒྱུའི་ཚོ། དྲང་ནོ་མི་ཉན་གི ཁ་ཆོག་མེད་ལ་ཁས་ལེན་ཡས་བྱས་ནོའི་སྟེད་ནས་དེ་རིང་གི་དོན་དག་འགྲུབ་སོང་ནི་ཡིན།

B: You couldn't accomplish more than that!

ཁ དེའི་ཡན་གི་འགྲུབ་རྒྱུ་ཡོད་ནི་མ་རེད་གོ

A: [as the village leader] Ah, not only is it difficult to get people to give up stealing, but if you think about it, those thieves are pitiful. Of course they would steal, right? Ah, we are manual labourers, and I say that we have bad karma. In comparison, mental labourers have it better. They need only to move their minds and not their fingers. And look at their light fingers!

ཀ ཨ། རྐུ་གཅོད་རྒྱུའི་དཀའ་ནོ་མིན་ནས། ཞིབ་འདྲད་བཟིག་བརྒྱབ་ན། རྐུན་མ་སྙིང་མ་རྗེ་ལོས་བརྒྱུ་བཟེ་ནོ། ཨ། ལུ་བཟོ་ལུས་ཤུགས་པའ་ཚོལ་པ་རེད། ལས་མི་ཇུ་གི་བཟེ་ནོ། དེ་བསྡུར་ན་བློ་ཤུགས་པའ་ཚོལ་པ་བཟོ་ཚེ་ར་སྟིད་གི ལག་པ་འགུལ་དགོ་ནོ་མིན་ནས་ལག་པ་འགུལ་མི་དགོ་གི་ར། ལག་པ་རིང་ནོའི་ཟུ་ལྟོས་ར་བཟེ་ནོ།

B: What did he say? Mental labourers are light-fingered?

ཁ ཅི་ཟེར། བློ་ཤུགས་པའ་ཚོལ་བ་བཟོའི་ལག་པ་རིང་གི

A: [as the village leader] They are not just light-fingered, but famous for their light fingers as well! They are called scholars, but they discretely steal others' writings.

ཀ རང་ང་རིང་ནི་མ་རེད། སྒྱིང་ང་གྲགས་གས་བསྡུང་ཡོད་གི་མཁས་པ་ཟྲོགས་ནོ་མིན་ནས་གཞན་གིས་བྲིས་ནོ་ཞིབ་གི་བརྐུས་ནི་རེད་བཟེ་ནོ།

B: That's true.

ཁ དེ་བཟོ་བདེན་གི་གོ

A: [as the village leader] Ah, I say "teeth labourers" have it even better.

ཀ ཨ་ད། སོ་ཕྱུགས་ངལ་རྩོལ་པ་བཟོ་དེའི་ར་སྒྱིད་རེད་བཟེ་ནོ།

B: The word "teeth labourers" is a new one.

ཁ སོ་ཕྱུགས་ངལ་རྩོལ་བ་གི་མིང་ཚིག་དེ་བཟོ་སོ་མ་བཞིག་རེད་ལ།

A: [as the village leader] I'd say there are many who were decent, but some who are not.

ཀ ཁ་མ་ཡོད་ནོ་མང་མ་རེད་དུ ལ་ལ་བཞིག་ལམ་མ་འགྲོ་གི་མེད་ཀ་བཟེ་ནོ།

B: Which are they?

ཁ གང་ཙན་གོ་ཡིན་ནས་ན།

A: [as the village leader] I say they're the ones who are driving cars provided by the State, sitting on thrones, and with bellies filled by the government.

ཀ རྒྱལ་ཁབ་གི་དྲིན་ན་རྒྱག་ཁྲི་ཐོག་རེད། བཞུགས་ཁྲི་ཐོག་རེད་དུ པོ་གཞུང་ཐོག་རེད་ལ་བཟེ་ནོ།

B: *Oh*, you're talking about the corrupt!

ཁ ཨོ། ཧམ་ཟ་མཁན་བཟོ་བཤད་གོ་ག

A: [as the village leader] "I say there are people stealing the country's wealth, and they certainly steal the smallest things from our homes. Uh, there's no problem as long as they can stop like we did. It is a difficult thing to talk about.[25] Now come have an audience, offer your scarfs, and we'll go!" he said.

ཀ རྒྱལ་ཁབ་གི་རྒྱུ་ནོར་བརྐུ་ནི་ཡོད་གི་ར། ཁྱིམ་ཚང་གི་ཆ་ངས་ཀྱང་ངས་པོ་ལོས་རྒྱ་བཟེ་ནོ། ཨ། ཨུ་བཟོའི་ལྟ་ཡས་གཅོད་ཐུབ་འགྲོ་རྒྱུན་སྟོན་མེད་གི་བཟེ་ནོ། དགའ་པོ་བཤད་བཏང་ནི་རེད། ད་མཇལ་ལ་ཁ་ལོངས་ད་མཇལ་དར་འབུལ་ར་འགྲོ་ཁ་ཡོད་ཟེར་གི་ཡ།

---

25 This is a phrase that people use to cut a topic short, and change the subject.

11. Careful Village's Thief

B: *Atsi!*[26] You accepted offerings again?

ཁ། ཨ་ཙི། ཡང་འབུལ་བ་བླངས་ནས།

A: [as himself] Ah, after accepting it, I wanted to give it to support the building of the school [that was to be built at the end of "Careful Village's Grassland Dispute"]. But what I had given them before had already been taken a long time ago, *aro*!

ཀ། ཨ། བླངས་བཏང་ནས་སློབ་གྲྭ་འཛུགས་སྐྱོང་གི་ཁ་སྐོན་ན་བྱེར་འདོད་ལ་ར། གནའ་བཞག་ག་ཕྱིན་ནོ་གནའ་བཞག་ག་ཕྱིར་སོང་བཞག་ཨ་རོ།

B: By whom?

ཁ། སུས།

A: "That Ra dzu na ma.... That 'Ra dzu na ma' was a fake *lama*, and now he is a prisoner!" they said.

ཀ། ར་ཛུ་ན་མ་བདོག་གོས། ར་ཛུ་ན་མ་བདོག་གོ་དབླ་མ་རྫུན་མ་རེད། དེང་སང་བཙོན་མ་ཡིན་ཟེར་ཡ།

B: Truly, he seems to have been a thief!

ཁ། ངོ་མ་བཞད་ན། དི་ར་རྐུན་མ་བཞིག་ཡིན་ས་ཡོད་ག

A: I was thinking about that while I was out on the street yesterday. And as I was walking silently, the title of the *khashag* came to me, *aro*!

ཀ། ངས་ར་ཁ་སང་རྒྱ་སྲང་ནས་དེ་མོ་བཞིག་འདོད་ལས། ཁ་རོག་ག་འགྲོ་གོ་དུས་ཁ་ཤགས་གི་ཁ་བྱང་ཁ་ནང་ད་ཐོན་ཐལ། ཨ་རོ།

B: What was it?

ཁ། ཅི་བཞིག་རེད།

A: "Thief!" I said, and my wife looked at me angrily and said, "You don't have a penny to your name, why would a thief target you?"[27]

ཀ། རྐུན་མ་བཟེ་ར། རྐུན་མོས་ཤྲིག་སྲང་གིས་ཅིག་བསླས། ཁྱོ་སྨར་མ་གད་མེད་ནི་བཞིག་ག གང་ད་རྐུན་མ་གིས་བསད་འདོག་རྒྱ་ཟེར་ཡ།

---

26 *Atsi* is a colloquial interjection used to express surprise.
27 The Tibetan word translated here as "target" is literally "to kill."

Index

Amdo ix, x, xi, xii, xiii, xiv, xv, 2–24, 27–30, 32–34, 37–40, 56, 65, 70, 86, 88–89, 93, 98, 103, 112, 114, 120, 123, 138, 146, 155, 157, 170, 177, 179, 181, 194, 196, 200, 208–209, 217, 224, 226–228, 233–235, 245, 248–250, 254, 265, 275, 290, 293
Amdo Oral Dictionary xi
ethnic diversity 4–5, 7
intellectuals xi, 2, 8, 14–15, 20, 32, 38–39
language ix, x, xi, xii, xiv, xv, 4–5, 15–16, 157, 227, 275
oral traditions ix, 1, 6–7, 10–11, 22, 28–29, 39
Sprachbund 5
weddings 10–11, 17–18, 30, 38
"The Artist" (སྒྱུ་རྩལ་པ།) 10, 13, 21–24, 33

Balza Tritsun (བལ་བཟའ་ཁྲི་བཙུན།) 91
"boasting" (ལབ་རྒྱག་པ།) 36

Careful Village 2, 3, 10, 11, 15, 19, 20, 21, 23, 24, 25, 26, 27, 28, 29, 30, 31, 33, 34, 35, 37, 38, 193, 194, 197, 218, 219, 220, 221, 222, 223, 224, 225, 228, 229, 234, 241, 242, 245, 248, 249, 258, 264, 271, 297. *See also* "Careful Village's Bride"; *See also* "Careful Village's Grassland Dispute"; *See also* "Careful Village's Thief"; *See also* "Careful Village's Wedding"
"Careful Village's Bride" 2, 19–21, 24, 26, 28

"Careful Village's Grassland Dispute" 10, 15, 20–21, 24, 297
"Careful Village's Thief" 20–21, 24, 28–29, 33–34, 38
"Careful Village's Wedding" 20, 27, 29
chang 28, 76, 255
Chinese ix, xiii, xiv, xv, 4, 6–7, 9–12, 14, 17, 19, 32–33, 36, 39, 41, 54, 68, 71–72, 74, 76, 86, 167, 183, 199, 204, 227, 249, 253, 260, 273, 288–289
Mandarin xiii, xiv, 19
comedies xi, xv, 1–4, 8–10, 12–15, 30, 33, 35–37, 122
Cultural Revolution 7, 9–10, 13, 33, 208, 288–289, 291

dialect ix, x, xi, xii, xiii, xiv, xv, 3–6, 15–16, 29, 72, 83, 157, 227, 230–231
Dondrup Gyal (དོན་གྲུབ་རྒྱལ།) x, xv, 8, 10
Dranyen (སྒྲ་སྙན།) 98
dunglen 98

"Elders' Conversations" 10, 23, 26, 34
English xi, xiv, 3, 18, 24, 28, 32, 40–41, 68, 119, 147, 155, 183, 188–189, 234

garchung 2, 13–14
Gar Tongtsen (མགར་སྟོང་བཙན།) 36, 91
Gesar 229, 267

Golok Dabhe (མགོ་ལོག་ཟླ་བྱེ།) 12
Gomé Dorje Rinchen (སྒོ་མེ་རྡོ་རྗེ་རིན་ཆེན།) 11
Gyaza Kongcho (རྒྱ་བཟའ་ཀོང་ཇོ།) 91

honorifics ix, 11, 16, 22–23, 29–30, 40, 83, 89, 104, 170, 212
Hou Baolin 10
humilifics 11, 16, 29–30, 36, 83, 100, 226

Jamyang Lodro (འཇམ་དབྱངས་བློ་གྲོས།) 12
Jetsun Drolma (རྗེ་བཙུན་སྒྲོལ་མ།) 147
Jingdezhen 253
Jowo Rinpoche 150

Kangtsa Sherab (ཀང་ཚའི་ཤེས་རབ།) 12
Kanjur 19, 103
"karmic enemy" (འདུལ་སྐལ།) 38
khabde (ཁ་བདེ།) 133
khashag 1–3, 8–14, 19–20, 35, 37, 39, 97, 112–113, 133–136, 153, 175, 177–179, 190, 193, 222, 241, 271, 297
khatak 90, 194, 196, 204, 221, 252–253

labtse (ལབ་ཙེ།) 149, 194
lama 16, 28, 30, 35, 38, 111, 199–206, 209, 212–214, 221, 229, 242, 255, 271, 273–274, 278, 287–288, 290, 293, 297
  fake *lama*s 38, 201, 212, 264, 271, 297
Langdarma (གླང་དར་མ།) 234
Lhalung Hwalkyi Dorje (ལྷ་ལུང་དཔལ་གྱི་རྡོ་རྗེ།) 234
Lhasa xiii, xv, 9, 16, 29, 91, 259, 294

Lobsang Yongdan ("Donkey Herder", བོང་རྫི།) 14

Manikhang 137
Menla Jyab ix, xi, xv, 1, 3, 8, 10, 12–22, 24–26, 29–40, 47, 59, 77, 83–84, 87, 89, 95–96, 98, 100, 109, 118, 133, 135, 153, 170, 173, 177, 186, 193, 196, 212, 214–215, 218–219, 221–223, 226, 233, 239, 241, 249, 258, 271–272, 282–283
Menla Kunzang ("the all-good Menla) 10, 36, 109–110, 113, 131
Milarepa 135
Moton Phakgo 96

Ngawa 4, 6, 259

Om mani padme hum 118, 150, 284–285
"Open the West" campaign 8

Pema Tsedan (པདྨ་ཚེ་བརྟན།) 8
Phagmo Drashi 1, 14, 18, 32, 36–37, 39, 47, 83, 87, 109, 133, 153, 161–162, 177–178, 186, 193, 223, 241, 271
Phuntshogjyal (ཕུན་ཚོགས་རྒྱལ།) 12
Phurwa (ཕུར་བ།) xv, 11, 37, 153, 155, 157
"Please, Dear Leader" 26, 30, 33
prajnaparamita ("perfection of wisdom") 70

Rebgong 6–7, 104
"reform and opening up" (Ch. *gaige kaifang*) 13
renminbi 72–73
romanization 16

Sakya Pandita Kunga Gyeltsen (ས་སྐྱ་པཎྜི་ཏ་ཀུན་དགའ་རྒྱལ་མཚན།) 93
Sengcham Drukmo 267
"Seven Wise Men" (མཛངས་མི་མི་བདུན།) 94
Shar Kalden Gyamtso x
Shinjé Chojya (གཤིན་རྗེ་ཆོས་རྒྱལ།) 27, 37, 123–124, 130
Shokdung (ཞོགས་དུང་།) 8
Songtsen Gampo (སྲོང་བཙན་སྒམ་པོ།) 84, 91, 93, 95
"Studying Tibetan" xi, 10
Suzuki, Hiroyuki x, 4, 11, 16, 30, 32

tamhwé 6, 11, 16, 25–29, 67
taru 262
Tenjur 19, 103
Thangdong Gyalpo (ཐང་སྟོང་རྒྱལ་པོ།) 93
"The Dream" 19–20, 23–24, 30, 34–35, 39, 285
Thonmi Sambhota (ཐོན་མི་སཾ་བྷོ་ཏ།) 93
Tibetan
 dictionary xiii, 162

literature x, 7–8
 oral 28, 86, 88
 plateau ix, 1–2, 5, 7–8, 11, 13, 143, 209, 236, 290
transliteration ix, xiii, xiv, xv
Tri Ralpachen 199, 206
Tri Songdetsen (ཁྲི་སྲོང་ལྡེའུ་བཙན།) 84
Tri Tsukdetsen (ཁྲི་གཙུག་ལྡེ་བཙན།) 84
Tsering Dondrup (ཚེ་རིང་དོན་གྲུབ།) 8
tsétar (ཚེ་ཐར།) 89
Tsongonpo Lake 86–87
tulma 280

xiangsheng 9–12

Yangchenma (དབྱངས་ཅན་མ།) 219
yumdumpa 70. See also *prajnaparamita* ("perfection of wisdom")

Zalejyal 2, 38, 223, 224, 225, 227, 229, 230, 231, 232, 235, 236, 237, 238
Ziling 13, 259
Zonthar Gyal (བོན་ཐར་རྒྱལ།) 8
Zou, Yuxia x

About the team

Alessandra Tosi was the managing editor for this book.

Adèle Kreager proof-read this manuscript. Annie Hine compiled the index.

Jeevanjot Kaur Nagpal designed the cover. The cover was produced in InDesign using the Fontin font.

Annie Hine typeset the book in InDesign. The fonts used in this book are Tex Gyre Pagella, Noto Serif SC and Noto Serif Tibetan.

Jeremy Bowman produced the PDF, paperback, and hardback editions and created the EPUB.

The conversion to the HTML edition was performed with epublius, an open-source software which is freely available on our GitHub page at https://github.com/OpenBookPublishers

Hannah Shakespeare was in charge of marketing.

This book was peer-reviewed by Xénia de Heering, EHESS-Ecole des hautes études en sciences sociales, and an anonymous referee. Experts in their field, these readers give their time freely to help ensure the academic rigour of our books. We are grateful for their generous and invaluable contributions.

This book need not end here…

Share

All our books — including the one you have just read — are free to access online so that students, researchers and members of the public who can't afford a printed edition will have access to the same ideas. This title will be accessed online by hundreds of readers each month across the globe: why not share the link so that someone you know is one of them?

This book and additional content is available at
https://doi.org/10.11647/OBP.0452

Donate

Open Book Publishers is an award-winning, scholar-led, not-for-profit press making knowledge freely available one book at a time. We don't charge authors to publish with us: instead, our work is supported by our library members and by donations from people who believe that research shouldn't be locked behind paywalls.

Join the effort to free knowledge by supporting us at
https://www.openbookpublishers.com/support-us

We invite you to connect with us on our socials!

BLUESKY
@openbookpublish.
bsky.social

MASTODON
@OpenBookPublish@
hcommons.social

LINKEDIN
open-book-publishers

Read more at the Open Book Publishers Blog
https://blogs.openbookpublishers.com

You may also be interested in:

Shépa
The Tibetan Oral Tradition in Choné
Bendi Tso, Marnyi Gyatso, Naljor Tsering, Mark Turin, and members of the Choné Tibetan Community

https://doi.org/10.11647/OBP.0312

Long Narrative Songs from the Mongghul of Northeast Tibet
Texts in Mongghul, Chinese, and English
Translated by Li Dechun and edited by Gerald Roche; Introduction by Mark Turin

https://doi.org/10.11647/OBP.0124

The Politics of Language Contact in the Himalaya
Edited by Selma K. Sonntag and Mark Turin

https://doi.org/10.11647/OBP.0169

www.ingramcontent.com/pod-product-compliance
Lightning Source LLC
Chambersburg PA
CBHW050202240426
43671CB00013B/2221